Best Places to Stay in the Southwest

GW00500517

THE BEST PLACES TO STAY SERIES

Best Places to Stay in America's Cities
Second Edition/Kenneth Hale-Wehmann, Editor

Best Places to Stay in Asia
Jerome E. Klein

Best Places to Stay in California
Second Edition/Marilyn McFarlane

Best Places to Stay in the Caribbean
Second Edition/Bill Jamison and Cheryl Alters Jamison

Best Places to Stay in Florida
Second Edition/Christine Davidson

Best Places to Stay in Hawaii
Second Edition/Bill Jamison and Cheryl Alters Jamison

Best Places to Stay in Mexico
Bill Jamison and Cheryl Alters Jamison

Best Places to Stay in the Mid-Atlantic States
Dana Nadel

Best Places to Stay in the Midwest
John Monaghan

Best Places to Stay in New England
Fourth Edition/Christina Tree and Kimberly Grant

Best Places to Stay in the Pacific Northwest
Second Edition/Marilyn McFarlane

Best Places to Stay in the Rocky Mountain Region
Roger Cox

Best Places to Stay in the South
Carol Timblin

Best Places to Stay in the Southwest
Third Edition/Anne E. Wright

Best Places to Stay in the Southwest

THIRD EDITION

Anne E. Wright

Bruce Shaw, Editorial Director

Houghton Mifflin Company
Boston • New York

Third Edition

ISBN: 0-395-62230-1
ISSN: 1048-549X

Printed in the United States of America

Illustrations by Chris Schuh
Maps by Charles Bahne
Design by Robert Overholtzer

This book was prepared in conjunction
with Harvard Common Press.

VB 10 9 8 7 6 5 4 3 2 1

Contents

Introduction

This isn't another "inn book," nor is it an attempt to judge all of the lodgings in Arizona, New Mexico, Oklahoma, and Texas by one rigid criterion. Instead, we have looked at the full range of places to stay in the Southwest and noted first and foremost their astonishing variety, from Grand Old Mansions to National Park Lodges, and we have picked only the outstanding examples. *Best Places to Stay in the Southwest* describes Romantic Getaways, Family Favorites, and Gourmet Getaways. It includes places to ride horseback, inns catering especially to golfers, tennis players, hikers, and birding enthusiasts, elegant, small urban hotels and working ranches covering tens of thousands of acres, as well as lake resorts, health spas, ski resorts, and throughout, lodgings with the historical mix of Southwest Indian, Hispanic, and Anglo-American cultures for which the Southwest is justly famous.

When we are asked for advice on a place "to get away to," we notice that people usually don't have a specific spot in mind, although sometimes they want to be near the great beaches of the Gulf of Mexico or the incomparable southwestern desert. More often they want outstanding food, a romantic atmosphere, or a special place to go as a family. There are many places that fit these requirements perfectly but are not listed in any guidebooks, hence our unique system of grouping lodgings by type rather than geography. This way we are able to include many wonderful places that do not fit other books' formats. For maximum ease of use, we have included state maps to help you see what is near Houston, or Taos, or the Grand Canyon; thus the book can still be used geographically.

Obviously we judge the best ranches and the best city stops according to different criteria. Our primary standards are cleanliness, palpable presence of a host or, at the larger hotels, a personal style of service, and a conviction that we would like to stay in the place for more than one night. As with all the books in this series, no fees have been collected for inclusion—these are not paid advertisements.

Anne Wright has covered a total of 25,000 miles preparing for this book, and she understands the distinct traditions of lodging and hospitality that make the Southwest different from, say, New England.

Innkeepers tell us these days that travelers want more and are willing to pay for it. Certainly there are many small places with high prices, but there are also many bargains. The key to planning a trip for yourself, we believe, is value—what you get for your money. For example, families can stay comfortably and economically in many of the new condominium resorts, where the rate is per unit rather than per person. On the other hand, a number of fine old resorts, large and small, maintain the same standards and traditions that have attracted generations of devotees, and many hotels with illustrious histories have been brilliantly refurbished to stand as superior alternatives to the standard (that is, dull) motel.

We have done our best to provide you with accurate and up-to-date information. For each accommodation in the book, we've given basic facts that you'll probably want to know before booking a room. In general, lodgings will accept personal checks (with proper identification) except where noted, and those that take major credit cards will accept one of the top three: Visa, MasterCard, and American Express. We suggest that you list the four or five points that most concern you and, when making reservations, ask the clerk or host about them. If money is important, be sure you know what your room rate will be. If noise bothers you, be sure that you ask for a quiet room. We have found over and over that we get what we ask for.

Maps

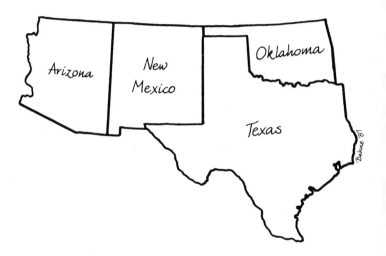

North Rim
Grand Canyon
89
40
Flagstaff
40
Sedona
Prescott
17
Wickenburg
Carefree
Litchfield Park
Scottsdale
10
Phoenix
8
Oracle
10
Tucson
10
19
Price Canyon
Tubac
Patagonia
Sasabe
Bisbee

Arizona

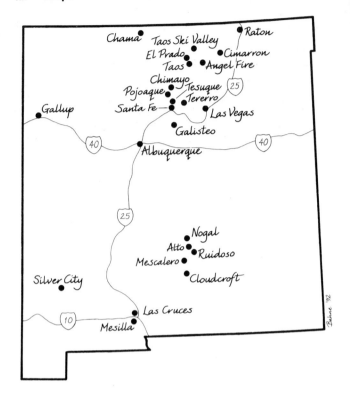

New Mexico

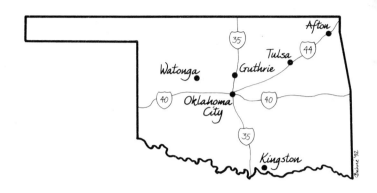

Oklahoma

Texas

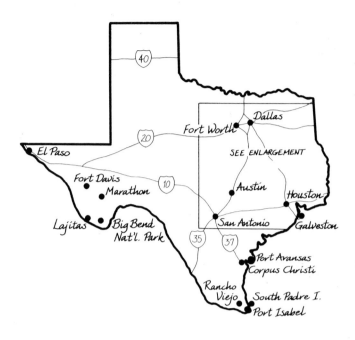

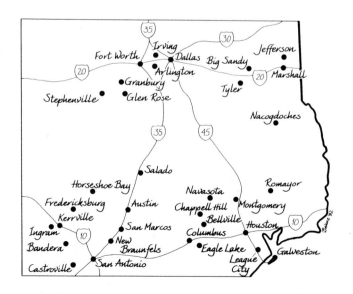

B&B Associations and Reservation Systems

One phone call can put you in touch with as many as 140 B&Bs. Some of these organizations represent guest houses and inns as well as more traditional B&Bs.

Arizona

Arizona Association of Bed & Breakfast Inns
3661 North Campbell Avenue
P.O. Box 237
Tucson, Arizona 85719
602-231-6777

Accommodations: About 25 listings in Ajo, Bisbee, Flagstaff, Oracle, Phoenix, Prescott, Sedona, Tucson, and Williams
Rates: Vary
Included: Usually breakfast
Added: Tax; varies from city to city
Payment: Some take credit cards; many accept checks or cash only
Children: Sometimes permitted
Pets: Sometimes permitted
Smoking: Sometimes permitted
Open: Most open year-round

All the members of this group have been approved by the association's strict code of ethics. In addition to having met high standards of cleanliness and hospitality, these B&Bs offer variety. From a turn-of-the-century home in downtown Tucson to a ranch in the high desert to a small resort in Phoenix, there's an accommodation for just about any traveler. Each B&B has between three and 20 rooms. Some of the inns have extra features such as tennis, swimming, horseback riding, and hot tubs. To receive a complete and current listing of inns, send a self-addressed stamped envelope to the association.

Bed and Breakfast in Arizona
P.O. Box 8628
Scottsdale, Arizona 85252
602-995-2831
800-266-7829
Fax: 602-840-3806

Manager: M. Stephanie Osterlitz
Accommodations: More than 70 listings statewide, in Ajo, Apache Junction, Bisbee, Flagstaff, Globe, Mesa, Oracle, Phoenix, Pinetop, Prescott, Sedona, Tempe, and Tucson
Rates: single or double, $45–$125; suites, $60–$150
Included: Breakfast
Added: 6.5%–10.5%; varies from city to city
Payment: Major credit cards
Children: Often welcome
Pets: Not permitted
Smoking: Sometimes permitted
Open: Year-round

Bed and Breakfast in Arizona is true to its name, with listings throughout the state. It offers traditional B&B homes with resident owners as well as guest houses and ranches—one ranch served as a movie set. Some of the B&Bs are in cities, offering intimacy in a bustling metropolis; others are more remote, with superb mountain or desert views. This service also lists properties with special amenities, such as swimming pools, hot tubs, and fireplaces.

One listing in Phoenix has antique furnishings, a Jacuzzi, a backyard gazebo, and an open-pit fireplace. The hostess is a tour guide at the Phoenix Art Museum and a gourmet cook. The host made the colorful stained glass pieces found throughout the home. In Prescott, you can stay at a Victorian home that is on the National Register of Historic Places.

Bed and Breakfast Scottsdale and the West
P.O. Box 3999
Prescott, Arizona 86302-3999
602-776-1102

Owner: George Thomson
Accommodations: About 45 listings in the Scottsdale area
  and elsewhere
Rates: double, $50–$125
Included: Breakfast in most cases
Added: 10.5%–11.5% tax; varies from city to city
Payment: Cash or traveler's check; personal checks accepted
  as deposit
Children: Over 12 welcome in some homes
Pets: Not permitted
Smoking: Sometimes permitted
Open: Year-round

Bed and Breakfast Scottsdale and The West specializes in small suites, guest cottages, and villas. Many have a private entrance, private bath, wet bar, and a southwestern flavor. All of the hosts live on the grounds. For instance, one home is a luxurious villa in Fountain Hills with a tile roof, walled gardens, a pool, and a tennis court. In the morning you are offered a special breakfast that may include homemade sausage, hot breads, and espresso.

Inns as well as B&Bs are listed with this service. The Marks House Inn in Prescott is an elegant, intimate hostelry dating from 1894. You are treated to breakfast in the parlor, hors d'oeuvres in the afternoon, bed turndown, and fresh fruit and flowers.

Mi Casa Su Casa

P.O. Box 950
Tempe, Arizona 85281
602-990-0682 (8 A.M.–8 P.M.)
800-456-0682 (Reservations only)
Fax: 602-990-3390

Operator: Ruth Young
Accommodations: More than 140 homes, guest houses,
  ranches, and inns in 37 cities and rural areas: Ajo, Apache
  Junction, Bisbee, Cave Creek, Cottonwood, Flagstaff,
  Jerome, Madera Canyon, Mesa, Oracle, Patagonia, Payson,
  Phoenix, Prescott, Scottsdale, Sedona, Sierra Vista, Tempe,
  Tombstone, Tucson, Wickenburg, and Yuma
Rates: single, $35–$150; double, $40–$150; suites, $65–$150
Included: Breakfast
Added: 1.2%–10.5% tax; varies from city to city
Payment: Cash or traveler's checks
Children: Often welcome
Pets: Occasionally permitted

Smoking: Occasionally permitted
Handicapped facilities: Several available
Open: Year-round

Ruth Young runs a very professional service and takes pride in matching guests with the right setting for them. Host families are selected for their warmth and interest in people, and every listing is inspected before it becomes part of the service. The B&Bs include historic homes, ranches, and small inns throughout the state, in cities as well as in the mountain and lake country.

In Tombstone, home of the infamous O.K. Corral, a Victorian B&B with gingerbread trim and family antiques is adjacent to the town's lively historic district. In central Tucson, an adobe mansion listed on the National Register has courtyards, fountains, and lush gardens. In Flagstaff, a three-level home has views of Mount Elden from every level and porches that reach into the pines.

In fact, Mi Casa Su Casa has so many unique and interesting listings that Ruth has published a directory: the comprehensive 100-page book gives descriptions of all of the properties she handles as well as some basic tourist information for each area. The directory is available for $9.50.

New Mexico

Mi Casa Su Casa
P.O. Box 950
Tempe, Arizona 85281
602-990-0682

Operator: Ruth Young
Accommodations: 7 homes, in Albuquerque, Carlsbad, Las Cruces, Ramah, Santa Fe, and Silver City

Please see the preceding entry for a full description of Mi Casa Su Casa.

The Taos Bed & Breakfast Association
P.O. Box 2772
Taos, New Mexico 87571
505-758-4747
800-876-7857

President: Dusty Davis
Accommodations: About 15 listings
Rates: $50–$180
Included: Breakfast
Added: 10.25% tax
Payment: Varies with individual listing
Children: Sometimes permitted
Smoking: Sometimes permitted
Open: Most open year-round

Many of these B&Bs view the spectacular mountains and scenery that surround picturesque Taos, and some are filled with original art, often done by the owners themselves. Breakfast gets special attention, and some properties provide afternoon hors d'oeuvres as well. All feature southwestern-style architecture.

Texas

Bed and Breakfast Hosts of San Antonio
166 Rockhill
San Antonio, Texas 78209
512-824-8036

Operator: Lavern Campbell
Accommodations: About 30 in the San Antonio area
Rates: single, $45–$120; double, $60–$180
Included: Continental breakfast
Added: 13% tax within San Antonio city limits
Payment: Major credit cards
Children: Sometimes permitted
Pets: Sometimes permitted
Smoking: Not permitted
Open: Year-round

Lavern Campbell is known for her hospitable and efficient service, and her B&Bs range from families who welcome guests into their own home to inns run by a full-time staff.

San Antonio is a popular city with lots of hotels, but B&B Hosts offers lodgings with intimacy. Some are near downtown, in the historic King William residential area; others are close to the Riverwalk, Sea World, Fort Sam Houston, and the airport.

In the King William area, a new guest house includes a downstairs bedroom with a double bed, a loft bedroom with twin beds, and a sofa bed in the living room. The adjacent hosts' home dates from 1871. Bikes are available for exploring the area.

Also available are several well-known lodgings. The Norton-Brackenridge House, which has won awards for its restoration, is a Victorian house with four guest rooms. Terrell Castle, near Fort Sam Houston, is fanciful and fun. Built in 1894 to resemble a mix of European castles and French châteaux, it's furnished with antiques. Nine guest rooms, all furnished differently, occupy the second and third floors; a loft-style room is on the fourth floor. The Colonial Room is hexagonal.

Bed and Breakfast Texas Style
4224 West Red Bird Lane
Dallas, Texas 75237
214-298-5433, 214-298-8586 (8 A.M.–5:30 P.M. weekdays)

Owner/Director: Ruth Wilson
Accommodations: About 180 rooms in about 60 cities, towns, lake, and farm areas
Rates: $40–$85; some special listings up to $150
Included: Breakfast
Added: Tax; varies, but averages 13%
Payment: Major credit cards
Children: Often welcome
Pets: Sometimes permitted
Smoking: Sometimes permitted
Open: Year-round

This service's listings are widespread and offer lots of variety —everything from an executive condo in Dallas to a guest ranch on a lake. Some of the inns were built before the turn-of-the-century; others are sparkling new urban homes. Some have hosts in residence; others are guest houses offering complete privacy.

Accommodations range from budget to luxurious. In addition to listings in Houston and other major metropolitan areas, you can find accommodations in Bryan (home of Texas A&M University), Granbury, Midland, Palestine, and Galveston.

The service represents inns with their own identity as well as homes with one or two guest rooms. As a result, Ruth Wilson can help guests choose the lodging that is best for their needs. She asks guests to complete evaluation forms so that she can keep close tabs on the lodgings she represents. A current list of accommodations is available for $5.

Gastehaus Schmidt
231 West Main
Fredericksburg, Texas 78624
512-997-5612 (10:00 A.M.–5:00 P.M. weekdays; 1:00–5:00 P.M.
  Saturdays)
Fax: 512-997-8282

Proprietor: Loretta Schmidt
Accommodations: About 50 listings in the Fredericksburg area
Rates: Start at $50 per night
Included: Continental or full breakfast in many cases
Added: 6%–13% tax
Payment: Major credit cards
Children: Often welcome
Pets: Sometimes permitted
Smoking: Sometimes permitted
Open: Year-round

Gastehaus Schmidt has a rich variety of lodgings, many reflecting the historic character of Fredericksburg. You can choose from farms, "Sunday houses" (built by pioneer farmers as a place to spend the night when they went to town for church), log cabins, and modern homes. Some homes are occupied by their owners; in others, you have the entire lodging to yourself.

For $2, the service will send you a complete description of their listings. Browsing through the choices gives you a well-rounded view of this community settled by German farmers. Some of the more unusual accommodations offered are guest rooms in buildings that were once a one-room schoolhouse, a limestone barn, and a log cabin on a 26-acre Texas historical site. Other historic homes include a log and stone house from the early 1850s, and a Victorian charmer only two blocks from Fredericksburg's historic district.

Sand Dollar Hospitality Bed and Breakfast
3605 Mendenhall
Corpus Christi, Texas 78415
512-853-1222 (8:00 A.M.–9:00 P.M.)

Operator: Pat Hirshbrunner
Accommodations: About 18 rooms in 12 host homes in the
  Corpus Christi area
Rates: single, $51–$72; double, $54–$75; suite, $100
Included: Breakfast in some cases
Payment: Personal checks accepted as deposits

Children: Sometimes permitted
Pets: Sometimes permitted
Smoking: Not permitted
Open: Year-round

Pat Hirshbrunner's goal is to offer guests a "taste of the South" with families who exemplify high standards of hospitality. In a popular coastal region she has a variety of lodgings, including in-town homes and cottages by the sea.

Harbor View Bed and Breakfast in Port Aransas lives up to its name, featuring balconies on each of its three levels that afford excellent views of the harbor. At Sunset Retreat Bed and Breakfast in Ingleside-on-the-Bay, which is also on the water, you can fish right from the inn's own dock.

Beachside

The Texas coast is a 624-mile crescent of shoreline with a ribbon of barrier islands. Galveston, Corpus Christi, and South Padre are the centers of activity.

Texas

Best Western Sandy Shores Beach Hotel
3200 Surfside Boulevard
Corpus Christi Beach
Corpus Christi, Texas 78403
512-883-7456
800-528-1234
Fax: 512-883-1437

Owner: Stern Feinberg
Accommodations: 252 rooms
Rates: single, $45–$85; double, $65–$105; suites, $175
Added: 13% tax
Payment: Major credit cards
Children: Under 12 free in room with parents; over 12 additional $10 per day
Pets: Not permitted
Smoking: Nonsmoking rooms available
Open: Year-round

Corpus Christi Beach is a mile-long stretch of sand on Corpus Christi Bay, about a 5-minute drive across Harbor Bridge from downtown. Best Western Sandy Shores, directly on the beach, is a good choice for those who want an upbeat environment at a moderate price.

When you enter the lobby, chairs shaped like seashells and the bay view beyond are the first things you notice. They suggest the two most prevailing features of the hotel — whimsy and location. There is a spirit of creativity throughout. How many hotels do you know of that have a kite museum? Sure the museum is small, but there's an adjoining kite shop, and the concept is interesting and fun. The museum is free, but you might just be tempted to purchase a colorful flyer and test it out immediately on the beach.

The hotel comprises a motel section, built in the 1960s, and a 1980s five-story building. The guest rooms in the newer building are decorated with beach scenes and wicker chairs, and tend to be larger than those in the rest of the hotel. The rooms are comfortable but not luxurious; some have bay views and most have balconies. Many rooms in the motel section open onto the pool deck and have direct access to the parking lot. Lanai rooms open right onto the beach. Two-room suites are in the corners of the hotel building, overlooking the bay or downtown Corpus Christi. Look for playful rubber duckies in your bathroom. Overall, the feeling here is that someone cares about more than the profit margin.

In the Espresso coffee shop, which offers a variety of coffees, every table has a pair of binoculars for watching beach and bay activities. The Pantry will deliver breakfast, pizza, sandwiches, chili rellenos, or seafood platters right to your room, or you can pick up your order and save the 15% delivery charge. Seafood entrées ($10–$16) dominate the menu at the Calypso Restaurant.

An activities center in the lobby keeps guests informed about such recreations as volleyball, golf, fishing, and bike rental. Joggers will appreciate that the owner, a runner himself, has written a brochure detailing several routes as well as jogging tips. The pool courtyard is pleasant and family-oriented, with palapas, palms, a kiddie pool, and a Jacuzzi and sauna inside a Japanese pagoda. The beach in front of the hotel is wide, but the sand is fairly coarse. Be advised that jellyfish are prevalent during some seasons.

There are many other attractions in the area, such as North Padre Island's beautiful beaches, city museums, and a wildlife refuge. The Texas State Aquarium is just down the street, and the hotel is adjacent to the new Lady Lex Museum on the Bay. Corpus Christi is also a popular area for windsurfing, and many sailboarding tournaments are held in front of or near the hotel.

Hotel Galvez
2024 Seawall Boulevard
Galveston, Texas 77550
409-765-7721
800-392-4285
Fax: 409-765-7721

General manager: George VanEtten
Accommodations: 228 rooms and suites
Rates: single or double, $70–$120; suites, $175–$350
Added: 13% tax
Payment: Major credit cards
Children: Under 18 free in room with parents
Pets: Not permitted
Smoking: Nonsmoking rooms available
Open: Year-round

Galveston has a dual personality, for it is both a beach destination and a historic town. Hotel Galvez, the city's only beachfront lodging listed in the National Register of Historic Places, links the two sides of its character.

In 1911 the Spanish-style stucco hotel rose proudly as the "Queen of the Beach." Eleven years earlier, a devastating storm had permanently altered the city's history, killing 6,000 people and virtually leveling the onetime Wall Street of the Southwest. The hotel, built with funds raised from the community, was the island's first opulent beach attraction and symbolized a city reborn. At that time Galveston was known as a gambling center and attracted top entertainers to its casinos. The Galvez was their hotel, for not only was it the finest lodging around, but one of the two best casinos in town was right across the street.

The Spanish architecture of the hotel reflects the island's heritage. It is named for Bernardo de Galvez, an 18th-century Spanish governor and general. Galvez never saw Galveston, but the island was named for him by the chartmaker he commissioned to explore the Texas coast. As governor of Louisiana and Florida, Galvez fought with the colonials against the British in the American Revolution.

In 1980 the Hotel Galvez was restored, inciting a wave of historic preservation throughout the city. While the guest floors were totally redesigned, the lobby was refurbished to its 1911 charm. Graceful arches, a handsome wood ceiling, and chandeliers create a nostalgic mood. Bernardo's restaurant, just off the lobby, has historic ambience (surf and turf entrées run from $12 to $17). Potted palms and ceiling fans line the hall to the Veranda Bar (light and airy) and the Galvez Lounge (dark and masculine, with live entertainment).

The hotel's main entrance is on the north side, away from the beach. Through the lobby and overlooking the Gulf is an indoor pool and hot tub. Beyond is the outdoor pool, which is on the small side for a beach resort but well landscaped and appealing.

The guest rooms are ordinary and rather small, with tiny bathrooms. The furnishings are tasteful if not distinctive. The views of the ocean are not what you might expect, given a parking lot between the hotel and the water; rooms facing the ocean run about $10 more per night than those overlooking the city.

The hotel staff is friendly and hospitable. Self-parking is free, and valet parking is $5.

The Galvez is convenient to attractions such as the Strand entertainment area, and Sea-Arama, historic homes and buildings, and the beach, just across Seawall Boulevard. After the 1900 storm, a massive seawall was built along shoreline; as a result, all the structures along the 10.4-mile beach are behind the seawall instead of directly on the beach.

Port Royal by the Sea
P.O. Box 336
Port Aransas, Texas 78373
512-749-5011
800-242-1034 in Texas
800-847-5659 in U.S.

General manager: Stephen Sheldon
Accommodations: 210 condos
Rates: 1-bedroom (1–4 persons), $95–$155; 2-bedroom (1–6 persons), $110–$210; 3-bedroom(1–8 persons), $155–$290; special rates available for long stays
Minimum stay: 2 nights on weekends, 3 nights on holidays
Added: 13% tax
Payment: Major credit cards
Children: Welcome
Pets: Not permitted
Smoking: Nonsmoking units available
Open: Year-round

On Mustang Island, on the Gulf of Mexico, Port Royal is a resort apart from the crowd. Beautiful grounds, attractive condos, and a service-oriented staff make it an excellent destination. Port Aransas, also on the island, is seven miles north. Corpus Christi, on the mainland, is a 10-mile drive away.

The condominiums are in four buildings arranged around one of the best water extravaganzas in Texas. A composite of four pools, waterfalls, a swim-up bar, and a water slide, it's the focal point of the resort. Beyond it, boardwalks lead over the dunes onto the wide beach.

Although Port Royal's condos are individually owned, the resort is operated as a hotel, with a full range of services and planned activities during the high seasons. The units are all spacious and nicely appointed; kitchens are fully equipped with dinnerware, a microwave, coffeemaker, and dishwasher. Extra touches include a stereo, whirlpool tub, iron and ironing board, and washer and dryer. Each condo has a private patio or balcony. The three-bedroom units are the most luxurious: they are the only ones that directly face the ocean, and they have extra touches like balcony whirlpools.

The Café Royal Restaurant, decorated in Kon Tiki style, serves all three meals. Seafood gets top attention, but there are also beef and chicken entrées. Smaller portions at much lower prices are offered not only for children but to senior citizens as well.

The San Luis
5222 Seawall Boulevard
Galveston, Texas 77551
409-744-1500
800-392-5937 in Texas
800-445-0090 in U.S.
Fax: 409-744-8452

General manager: Ron Vuy
Accommodations: 244 rooms
Rates: single or double, $84–$139; suites, $104–$300
Added: 13% tax
Payment: Major credit cards
Children: Free in room with parents
Pets: Not permitted
Smoking: Nonsmoking rooms available
Open: Year-round

There's a touch of the Caribbean about the San Luis. Perhaps it's the free-form pool with a palapa swim-up bar, tropical gardens, waterfalls, and bridges. Or maybe it's the breezy lobby with its wicker furniture, brass flamingos, and laid-back atmosphere—even the bellmen are casual in their colorful Hawaiian shirts.

The San Luis is two lodgings in one. The hotel is a 15-story building with restaurants and 244 guest rooms overlooking the Gulf. Next door is a sister building with privately owned condominiums, most of which are available for rent. Opened in 1984, the San Luis set a new standard for Galveston beach resorts. It has two restaurants (Maximillian's and the Spoonbill, which overlooks the pool and gardens), a lounge with live entertainment, two tennis courts, and a beachfront activity center with rental equipment.

The hotel sits on a hill overlooking the ocean, and the beach is across the street, since a seawall extends along most of Galveston's beachfront.

The rooms are large and sunny with tropical print bedspreads, the smell of sea air, and narrow balconies. The bathrooms are small but adequate. The condos range from hotel rooms to large two-bedroom units with kitchens. Access to the condo area is by security key.

Sheraton South Padre Island Beach Resort
310 Padre Boulevard
South Padre Island, Texas 78597
512-761-6551
800-672-4747 in Texas
800-222-4010 in U.S.
Fax: 512-761-6570

General manager: Jason Dixon
Accommodations: 256 rooms and condos
Rates: single or double, $80–$130; condos, $130–$2190
Added: 13% tax
Payment: Major credit cards
Children: Under 17 free in room with parents
Pets: Not permitted
Smoking: Nonsmoking rooms available
Open: Year-round

Opened in 1986, the 12-story Sheraton is right on the beach. Every guest room has a balcony and an angled view of the ocean. Decorated in cool colors and rattan furniture, the accommodations are both attractive and comfortable.

The king parlors are worth the extra charge: the sleeping and sitting areas are separated by a floor-to-ceiling armoire housing a TV that swivels. Both king and king parlor rooms are furnished with sleep sofas. The rooms also have air-conditioning units (king parlors have two).

The beachside pool and deck area is a social center, with a grill, a small outdoor-indoor pool, an outdoor hot tub, and lots of lounge chairs. Tennis courts are also on the grounds.

Brandi Renee's Café, facing the ocean, is a fine restaurant. Pepper's Lounge has dancing and live entertainment, and the High Tide Bar adjoins the indoor pool.

Bed & Breakfasts

These B&Bs, run by gracious families in their homes, have a distinct warmth and personality that set them apart from corporate properties. Some are historic, some are in the city, and some are country retreats—each has its own character.

Arizona

Birch Tree Inn
824 W. Birch
Flagstaff, Arizona 86001
602-774-1042

Innkeepers: Donna and Rodger Pettinger & Sandy and Ed Znetko
Accommodations: 5 rooms
Rates: single or double, $60–$80
Included: Full breakfast and afternoon refreshments
Added: 8.61% tax
Payment: Major credit cards
Children: School age and above preferred
Pets: Not permitted
Smoking: Not permitted
Open: Year-round

On the local chapter of historic sites, the Birch Tree Inn was built in 1917 by a builder from Chicago to resemble a midwestern farmhouse. In keeping with its midwestern roots, the home has an open, welcoming feel, accentuated by the inn's warm and friendly hosts, Donna and Rodger Pettinger and Sandy and Ed Znetko (all childhood friends), and resident dogs Daisy and Muffin.

Downstairs there's a large comfortable living room, a game room outfitted with a pool table and piano, and a breakfast room that has a cheerful country look. Upstairs the five guest rooms are individually furnished, and many reflect the owners' heritage.

The Pella room, named after a Dutch festival in Pella, Iowa, called Tulip Time, has Dutch lace curtains, a painted spool bed, a patchwork quilt with tulip motif, and a mirrored armoire. It shares a hall bath. Carol's room is decorated in hunter greens and Shaker pine furniture and has its own bath. The wicker room, furnished of course with wicker, has mountain views.

The Wagner-Znetko room, referred to by the owners as "Grandma's attic," contains a number of heirloom pieces from Ed's family, including an old-fashioned wooden washstand (the plumbing still works) and a 1913 sewing machine that belonged to his grandmother. The Southwest suite, decorated in cool greens and peaches, is the most modern of the rooms. Its giant bathroom is hard to miss, with aqua and black fixtures.

Breakfasts are not taken lightly at the Birch Tree. Skillet breakfasts of potatoes, eggs, sausage, and vegetables are popular, and Sandy's sinfully delicious raisin bread french toast stuffed with cream cheese and pineapple and topped with a homemade pecan-praline sauce keeps guests coming back for more. No matter what the dish, you won't leave hungry.

If you're looking for a way to burn off breakfast calories, there's a park across the street with four tennis courts, and tennis rackets and bicycles can be borrowed from the inn. Fifteen miles from the inn is the Snowbowl ski area, a Nordic track for cross-country skiing is ten miles away, and the Grand Canyon with its many hiking trails is an hour and a half away. For indoor activities, the Lowell Observatory is just up the street, and the Museum of Northern Arizona is nearby.

Casa Alegre

316 E. Speedway
Tucson, Arizona 85705
602-628-1800

Innkeeper: Phyllis Florek
Accommodations: 4 rooms
Rates: single, $65–$75; double, $70–$80
Included: Full breakfast and afternoon refreshments
Added: 9.5% tax and $1.00 per day
Payment: Major credit cards
Children: Over age 12 preferred
Pets: Not permitted
Smoking: Permitted only outside
Open: Year-round

Casa Alegre means "happy house"—a name well suited to this pleasant B&B. The white stuccoed exterior with bright blue trim is cheerful; inside, from the moment you are greeted by Phyllis Florek, you feel right at home.

The craftsman-style bungalow was built for a pharmacist in 1915 when Speedway was just a dirt road—not the main thoroughfare in the heart of Tucson it is today. The home was later owned by a doctor and his family for fifty years, and the doctor practiced here as well.

Casa Alegre's living room has a distinctive front window, bringing lots of light into the house. A piano invites the musically inclined to sit down and play a tune, while sofas and a stone fireplace entice others to relax. The room is accented with mahogany trim and ivy stenciling. The adjoining dining room has a built-in mahogany cupboard and more stenciling. An unusual chandelier highlighted by porcelain insets is painted with old-fashioned romantic scenes. Full breakfasts are served each morning in the sun room next door, where colorful papier-mâché birds hang from the ceiling.

Each of the four guest rooms has a theme reflecting a different aspect of Tucson's history. The Rose Quartz room is dedicated to mining: there's a small rock collection on the bedside table and a coal miner's hat and lantern on the molding above the window. The morning glory wallpaper in the Amethyst Room is original, and the Victorian theme is complete with a four-poster bed, floral print pillows, a needlepoint footstool, mirrored vanity, potpourri, quilt stand, and a christening gown that belonged to the innkeeper's father. The bath next door has a clawfoot tub and lavender wallpaper reminiscent of a Monet painting.

The high-ceilinged Spanish Room, once the doctor's examining room, has a massive carved bed that was made in Mexico for a priest. The appliquéd quilt is hand-painted and has matching pillows. Chairs are covered in bright Mexican weavings; the coat rack on the wall came from a mission. A tin mirror with a peacock motif is especially appealing, and the pheasant print wallpaper complements it nicely.

And there's the Saguaro Room, in recognition of Tucson's desert surroundings: it is furnished in southwestern pinks, creams, and aqua. The decor includes willow and pigskin chairs, an armoire with saguaro rib doors, a queen-size bed topped with a cozy down comforter, a Mexican dresser, a stone slab table with a petroglyph, a working fireplace, and live cactus plants. The innkeeper has employed a few inventive touches of her own, using saguaro ribs for curtain rods and a small kiva ladder to hold towels and washcloths in the bath. All of the rooms have ceiling fans, private baths, travel toothbrushes, and terrycloth robes.

In the back of the house is a sunny sitting room with a large dollhouse and a television and VCR. Guests may help themselves to cold sodas from a Coca-Cola cart that came from a movie set, lounge on the patio, or take a dip in the swimming pool—a rare amenity at a downtown B&B. There's a carport for parking, and the University of Arizona and downtown Tucson are only minutes from the inn.

El Presidio Bed & Breakfast Inn
297 North Main Avenue
Tucson, Arizona 85701
602-623-6151

Innkeepers: Patti and Jerry Toci
Accommodations: 3 suites
Rates: single or double, $85–$105
Included: Full breakfast
Added: 9.5% tax and $1 per day
Payment: Major credit cards
Children: Over 13 preferred
Pets: Not permitted
Smoking: Permitted only outside
Open: Year-round

El Presidio, in Tucson's historic district, is a charming Victorian adobe with wraparound porches and gingerbread trim. Built in 1886, it is listed on the National Register of Historic Places. The owners, Patti and Jerry Toci, have won awards for their beautiful restoration work. But as lovely as the house is, it's the gardens one notices first—pink oleanders and orange nasturtium spill onto the front sidewalk. The fountain courtyard in the back is ablaze with color, and there's always something blooming: yellow cat's claw, bright red bottlebrush, roses in the Victorian garden, blossoms on the citrus trees. The air smells like a sweet perfume.

The guest rooms are equally enjoyable. The Victorian Suite in the main house is like an indoor garden, with white wicker furniture, floral cushions, plants in the fireplace, and a sideboard painted with a floral motif in the living room. The bedroom is furnished in pinks and light greens, country quilts, and botanical prints. Glass doors lead from the living room out onto the front porch overlooking the South and Victorian gardens. The Gate House Suite has its own entrance, tan wicker furniture, French country fabrics, shuttered windows, a hand-painted blanket chest, and a small galley kitchen.

The Carriage House Suite is in a separate building. The owners' love of gardens is clearly evident here: there's a floral screen in the living room, flower patterns on the china plates, a floral print on the bedspread, and a dried flower wreath hanging on the wall above it. The suite has its own kitchen.

All of the suites have pleasant private baths and top quality mattresses and linens. They have sufficient living space, and guests are welcome to use the formal living room in the main house—this elegant room is appointed with antique furnishings that include a grandfather clock, Oriental rug, one corner cupboard filled with flow blue china, another cabinet displaying Indian artifacts, and more plants and dried floral arrangements. The small sitting room next door has a television and VCR for entertainment.

Since Patti is a caterer (she caters luncheons for resort guests who come into town for historic tours, gives classes on the use of Victorian herbs, and is writing a cookbook), breakfasts, served in the Veranda Room overlooking the garden courtyard, are a treat. She describes her breakfasts as "southwestern," as opposed to Mexican, using ingredients from her own gardens whenever possible. You may sit down to eggs Benedict southwestern style, chile rellenos, vegetable frittatas, or stuffed french toast. Her specialty is muffins, such as strudel-topped lemon-pecan (with lemons from her own trees), spiced orange-pineapple bran, and corn topped with homemade marmalade.

For guests on business, El Presidio has a fax machine and can provide other business services when needed. Guests may use the facilities at a nearby YMCA free of charge.

Graham's Bed & Breakfast Inn

150 Canyon Circle Drive
Village of Oak Creek
Mailing address: P.O. Box 912
Sedona, Arizona 86336
602-284-1425

Innkeepers: Bill, Marni, and Nancy Graham
Accommodations: 5 rooms (all with private bath)
Rates: single, $85–$130; double, $95–$180
Included: Full breakfast and afternoon refreshments
Added: 5.5% tax
Payment: Major credit cards; personal checks must be
   received 10 days before arrival

Children: Over 12 preferred
Pets: Not permitted
Smoking: Permitted only on balconies and patio
Open: February to the first week of January

This two-story western contemporary house sits at the base of Bell Rock in the Village of Oak Creek, about six miles south of Sedona. Graham's is a pleasant lodging, professionally run by resident owners who enjoy getting to know their guests.

Bill and Marni Graham, former Californians, built their house as a B&B in 1985. Designed to take full advantage of its setting in Red Rock country, the house has lots of glass in the living areas and balconies off each guest room. The decor brings the outdoors in. For example, the downstairs terra cotta rug reflects the red of the mountains visible through the windows.

Since the house itself is new, the Grahams have imbued the guest rooms with their personal history. Heritage Suite is done up in red, white, and blue to honor Marni's father and his lifetime in the service. The Southern Suite—a collage of soft blues and greens furnished with an antique love seat, four-poster twin beds, and a marble washstand—is a tribute to Bill's mother, who was raised in the South.

Every room has a marble bath and shower, a balcony, air conditioning, and an assortment of books. The San Francisco Suite is the prettiest. Furnished with a custom-made California king-size bed, peach lacquered bureau and desk, and a chaise lounge, it is the Grahams' salute to their years in the Bay Area. It also has a double whirlpool tub and views of the countryside.

The breakfast menu changes daily, and guests eat together in the dining room. In the backyard there's a nice pool and spa. Other activities are shopping at the nearby boutiques and art galleries, playing golf at one of two excellent courses a half mile away, jeep rides through the countryside, and day trips to the Grand Canyon, which is 2½ hours away.

The Inn at Four Ten

410 N. Leroux Street
Flagstaff, Arizona 86001
602-774-0088 or 602-774-1424

Innkeepers: Carol and Mike Householder
Accommodations: 6 rooms
Rates: $55–$89
Included: Full breakfast
Added: 8.61% tax

Payment: Personal checks; no credit cards
Children: Welcome
Pets: Not permitted
Smoking: Not permitted
Open: Year-round

About four blocks from the center of downtown Flagstaff, the Inn at Four Ten offers guests fine accommodations in a pleasant environment. The swing and wicker set on the front porch are inviting, and once inside the home—built in 1907—you'll see plenty of evidence of the superior craftsmanship of the day. The staircase and moldings, made from golden oak, and the polished hardwood floors are a few examples of quality that one doesn't see in houses built today. Carol Householder has retained the attention to detail and decorated the inn with charm and style.

What was once an entrance hallway has been converted to a living and breakfast room. On one side of the room are comfortable sofas and an Oriental rug; on the other, wicker-backed chairs pull up to tables covered in red and white checked cloths. Lace curtains drape the many windows; old bird cages hang from above. A floral wreath tops the fireplace and a model of a town stretches along the deep mantel. In the morning, a full, home-cooked breakfast is served in this room.

Separated from the breakfast room by lace-covered French doors is Kristine's suite. Once the dining room, it has a beautiful built-in buffet made from Philippine mahogany. The high-ceilinged room is feminine, its white iron bed topped with a pretty yellow floral spread. There's a white sofa at the end of the bed, a walnut armoire, and a wicker rocking chair. The suite has its own kitchenette and breakfast nook.

Kathleen's suite is probably the most "southwestern" of all the rooms: it has an exposed brick wall, lodgepole pine furniture, a fireplace, tile bath, kiva ladder, turquoise armoire, and its own kitchenette. Upstairs, Jean's suite, with its slanted ceilings, is the smallest guest room. Decorated in sunny yellows and blues, the room is cheerful and cozy. Next door, Vera's suite is similar in design and decor, but is larger and has a washbasin. The two suites share a bath.

Carolyn's suite, in a separate building that the owners built, has a handicapped accessible bath—rare for a bed-and-breakfast. The room is attractively furnished in plums, ivories, and greens, with bunnies on the molding and atop the armoire, and an antique children's toy—a wooden bunny on wheels. The room opens onto the inn's backyard, complete with covered gazebo.

At press time, work was underway on two additional guest rooms. One was to have pendleton blankets and Shaker furniture, the other a nautical theme; you may want to inquire about these rooms when making your reservation.

La Posada del Valle
1640 North Campbell Avenue
Tucson, Arizona 85719
602-795-3840

Innkeepers: Debbi and Charles Bryant
Accommodations: 5 rooms
Rates: single or double, $90–$115
Included: Full breakfast on weekends, Continental on
   weekdays
Added: 9.5% tax plus $1.00 city room tax
Payment: Major credit cards
Children: Over age 12 preferred
Pets: Not permitted
Smoking: Not permitted
Open: Year-round

In a fine residential section of Tucson, behind a gray stucco wall, stands this pristine gray adobe with a red tile roof. A fountain adds grace to its courtyard, and orange trees, palms, and colorful container plants are scattered about the manicured grounds. Designed in 1929 by a renowned Tucson architect, Josias T. Joesler, the home exemplifies the early Santa Fe style of architecture. Inside, it sparkles with art deco furnishings.

La Posada del Valle opened as a B&B in 1986, one of the city's first, setting a high standard for other B&Bs to come. The extra touches make this place special, from stained glass art to peach potpourris. The living room is large and inviting, with a Japanese screen, satin couches, an old-fashioned radio, and a good selection of books and magazines.

Each room honors an illustrious woman of the 1920s. Zelda's room is a tribute to Zelda Fitzgerald—there's a biography of Zelda by Nancy Mitford on the dresser, along with several of F. Scott Fitzgerald's works, and a photo of husband and wife rests on the vanity. The dresser, vanity, bed, and bedside table are a lovely matching set with the same inlaid patterns. If the literary surroundings spark a creative urge, the interesting armoire in the corner has a pullout writing desk, or you can step out onto the adjoining patio and dream of a more glamorous era. Isadora's room is decorated in pale green with geometric designs. Claudette's is mauve, featuring a maple king-size bed. Sophie's, done in peach, has a Victorian bedroom set, fainting couch, and an 1818 king-size bed. (The bedroom suite once belonged to a fan dancer at the notorious Crystal Palace in Tombstone.) In keeping with the mood, a feather boa is draped over the dresser mirror, and a fancy lace hat rests on the vanity. Every room has a private bath (Zelda's is especially attractive, with an embroidered shower curtain and floral tiles) and entrance. There are no TVs in the rooms, but guests are welcome to use the set on the sun porch while lounging in cushioned wicker sofas and chairs. TVs can be supplied upon advance request.

Breakfast, served in the dining room or on the patio, features fresh fruit, fresh bread, bagels, and cereals during the week. On weekends, guests feast on entrées such as vegetable strudel with Parmesan, gingerbread pancakes with lemon curd, or cream cheese blintzes topped with fresh raspberry sauce. In the afternoon, apricot and raspberry teas are served with homemade scones, shortbread, and cheesecakes. Turndown service, complete with a mint on the pillow, is provided in the evening.

The University of Arizona and University Medical Center are an easy walk from La Posada.

Lynx Creek Farm
P.O. Box 4301
Prescott, Arizona 86302
602-778-9573

Innkeepers: Greg and Wendy Temple
Accommodations: 6 rooms
Rates: single, $90–$100; double, $95–$105; suites, $125
Included: Full breakfast and afternoon refreshments
Added: 5.5% tax
Payment: Major credit cards
Children: Age 2–12, $10 extra
Pets: Permitted
Smoking: Not permitted in guest rooms
Open: Year-round

One of the most delightful B&Bs in all of the Southwest is seven miles east of Prescott. A sign points to Lynx Creek Farm, Orchards and Bed and Breakfast, and you drive down a farm road through the orchards to the home of Greg and Wendy Temple. In the mid-1980s this energetic young couple from Phoenix bought the 20-acre hillside orchards on Lynx Creek, intending to run a B&B. It opened in 1987, offering a country getaway in beautiful surroundings.

Two guest rooms are in a wood building about 50 feet from the family's home. A wonderful cedar deck with a large hot tub and chaise lounges looks down on the creek below. The rooms themselves are like a fairy tale come true. Victorian antiques, country crafts, and imaginative decorating create romantic, enchanting interiors. Everywhere you look there's something special—an old-fashioned school desk, antique quilts, old Farmer's Almanacs, and framed pages from old Prescott newspapers. More like small apartments than bedrooms, the units are spacious and comfortable. The Sharlot Hall Suite (named for Arizona's first state historian) has two king-size beds, one in a cozy loft. The White Wicker Suite has a queen-size bed with a canopy and down comforter as well as a day bed.

Molly's and Mac's rooms, decorated for "little girls and boys of all ages," are in the main house. Molly's Room has an old vanity and queen-size bed; Mac's has a private entrance and two twin beds that can be pushed together upon request.

Breakfast is geared to suit the tastes of the guests, whether it's fresh fruit (from the orchards, of course) and homemade granola or heartier fare such as huevos rancheros and homemade tortillas.

After breakfast you can hike by the creek, pick fruit in the orchard, and enjoy the seclusion. The Temples can arrange for horseback rides or mountain bike rental. Nearby Prescott is a historic town with museums, antiques shops, and many festivals. Catering to families, this B&B has a playground and sandbox—part of an attitude that truly means "Children welcome." Babysitters are arranged upon request.

At press time, construction was under way on a log cabin that will add additional guest rooms to the farm. Two of the rooms will have their own private decks, hot tubs, and wood-burning stoves, so you may want to inquire about the availability of these rooms when making reservations.

Maricopa Manor

P.O. Box 7186
15 West Pasadena Avenue
Phoenix, Arizona 85011
602-274-6302

Innkeepers: Mary Ellen and Paul Kelley
Accommodations: 6 suites

Rates: single or double, $79–$99
Included: Breakfast
Added: 10.25% tax
Payment: Personal checks
Children: Over 6, $15 additional
Pets: Not permitted
Smoking: In designated areas only
Open: Year-round

On a quiet residential street, one block from bustling Camelback Road and not far from downtown Phoenix, Maricopa Manor offers comfortable accommodations to a variety of tastes. The manor is a member of the American Association of Historic Inns—a fact that owner Paul Kelley says foreigners and travelers from the East get a real chuckle over since the inn was only built in 1928. However, in Phoenix, a relatively modern city, almost anything dating to the 1920s is considered historic.

The red-roofed Spanish-style house is surrounded by towering palms, giving it a Floridian feel. The old-fashioned pull doorbell with musical chimes adds a nostalgic air. Inside the entryway, silk flowers surround a statue that was once an operating fountain. Beyond, the formal parlor is decorated with antique furniture and inlaid end tables. The dining room next door has an Oriental rug and crystal chandelier.

The back living room, called the "gathering place," is very casual. Two stories high, it has a double-sided fireplace, a sunken TV viewing area, and a basketball hoop. (The Kelleys raised twelve children in the house, three of their own and the rest foster children or exchange students, so the basketball hoop is not just for show.)

Although its bathroom is across the hall, the Victorian suite is one of the prettiest rooms at the inn. The bed is covered in an embroidered satin spread, and the bedside tables are topped in marble. A charming sitting room is set off in an alcove. The Library suite is popular with honeymooners and business travelers. A white comforter with lace trim and matching pillow shams make the four-poster bed inviting. The bedroom opens onto a backyard deck. The separate library has a desk fit for any busy executive, fully stocked bookshelves, a sofa bed, and a TV.

The remaining guest suites are in an adjacent building that was once a separate residence. The Palo Verde is a two-bedroom suite with an adjoining sun room. The larger bedroom is decorated in pinks and mint greens. It has a wicker settee with matching chairs, a Franklin stove, and two twin four-poster beds. The small bedroom is delightfully cozy with a three-quarter spool bed draped by a lacy canopy, a country print quilt, and matching curtains and pillow shams. Mirrors line one wall of the living room in the masculine Reflections Past suite. There's a gas fireplace in the living room, a king-size bed in the bedroom, a spacious bath, and a large closet. Reflections Future is ultramodern, with black and brass furniture and a mirrored coffee table, a full kitchen, and a breakfast nook. All suites have ironing boards, irons, TVs, phones, and off-street parking.

A breakfast of fresh juice, fruit, homemade breads, jams, and quiches arrives at your door in a basket each morning. The china is unique and changes daily. In the backyard, bordered by oleander, there's a gazebo with a hot tub for guests' use. The Kelleys, who have long been welcoming foreigners into their home, know how to make their guests feel welcome.

The Marks House
203 E. Union Street
Prescott, Arizona 86303
602-778-4632

Innkeepers: Dottie and Harold Viehweg
Accommodations: 4 rooms
Rates: single or double, $75–$110; $105 for 2 in suite; $130 for 4 in suite
Included: Full breakfast and afternoon refreshments
Added: 8% tax
Payment: Major credit cards
Children: Older children preferred
Pets: Not permitted
Smoking: Not permitted
Open: Year-round

The Marks House perches on a hill in downtown Prescott, a maize-colored Queen Anne house with turrets, gables, and a pleasant front porch. Built in 1894, the Marks House is on the National Register of Historic Places, and rightly so. During the Depression the house was divided into five apartments, and it's been converted into a charming bed-and-breakfast with four guest suites.

Guests are welcomed in a parlor furnished with Victorian pieces, including a display case that came from an old Prescott drug store and a fainting bed. The patterned trim around the ceilings is hand-painted, and portraits of the Viehwegs' grand-parents adorn the walls. A full breakfast and afternoon hors d'oeuvres are served in the adjoining dining room.

The guest suites are upstairs; the Ivy suite is the largest, with two bedrooms. The larger bedroom has a feather mattress draped with an ivy print spread. The inner bedroom is quite sweet—lace curtains give it a comforting feel. The Princess Victoria suite has a copper-lined bathtub that dates to 1892; its wooden exterior is painted with roses. A family christening gown hangs on the wall, and the walk-in closet has ample room to accommodate extended visits. The Tea Rose suite, in rose tones, is the only room with a hall bath, which is not shared.

The Queen Anne suite was originally the home's master bedroom. Now a favorite with honeymooning couples, the room is decorated in cool mint greens with white wicker furniture and lace pillows. Bow windows create a sunny sitting area and offer a view of Prescott's natural rock formation called Thumb Butte.

In the upstairs hallway there's a piece said to have come from FDR's White House. Throughout, attractive floral wallpaper and dried flower arrangements add a country touch to this urban home. The Marks House is just a block from Prescott's main square—the site of numerous arts and crafts and antique shows, as well as other civic events throughout the year.

The Peppertrees

724 East University
Tucson, Arizona 85719
602-622-7167

Innkeeper: Marjorie Martin
Accommodations: 6 rooms with shared baths
Rates: single, $78; double, $90; $160 per guest house
Included: Breakfast and afternoon tea
Minimum stay: 2 nights
Added: 9.5% tax and $1 per day
Payment: Major credit cards
Children: Welcome
Pets: Not permitted
Smoking: Permitted only outside
Open: Year-round

This pleasant brick Territorial house built in 1905 is named for the two large California peppertrees that dominate the front yard. Marjorie Martin can show you an old photograph of the house in which it looks like a lone homestead in the desert. Today it is just a couple of blocks from the University of Arizona and convenient to the downtown sights.

Inside, guests are welcomed by refreshments, sunny rooms, Oriental rugs on hardwood floors, lace curtains, and Victorian family furnishings from Marjorie's native England. The main guest room is romantic, with lots of windows, French doors that open to the outside, and an inviting white wrought-iron bed covered by a flowered spread and extra pillows. Across the hall, the main bathroom is finished in green Italian marble, brass fixtures, and wooden cupboards. The bathroom is shared by the cavelike but cozy guest room downstairs, once the coal cellar (the old stove is still there). Some guests prefer this room's special ambience, and its sitting room is a bonus.

In the back, which is filled with plants, there's also a central fountain, a flagstone terrace, and two guest houses. Each house has two bedrooms, a living room, a full kitchen with washer and dryer, a bathroom, and a private patio.

The guest houses have small kitchen tables, though breakfast is usually served on the porch near the fountain in nice weather. Breakfasts are memorable since Marjorie is an excellent cook (her recipes have appeared in a number of cookbooks), but the shortbread served at afternoon tea is the house specialty.

Marjorie once owned a travel agency, and she is more than happy (and able) to give you sightseeing tips. The Peppertrees is right on the main trolley route, which covers such places as the Arizona State Museum, Flandrau Planetarium, and Children's Museum.

Villa Cardinale
P.O. Box 649
Oracle, AZ 85623
602-896-2516
800-266-2660

Proprietors: Judy and Ron Shritt
Accommodations: 4 rooms
Rates: $40–$55
Included: Breakfast and tax
Payment: Personal checks or money orders
Children: $5 additional per child per night
Pets: By prior arrangement
Smoking: In one room only
Open: Year-round

Just off Highway 77 in Oracle, Villa Cardinale is far enough out of Tucson to have a country feel, yet close enough to make the city and its sights easily accessible. The house was built in 1987, and the Shritts opened it as a bed-and-breakfast in 1988.

Since this is an area known for bird-watching, the guest rooms are named for birds. The rooms surround an outdoor courtyard highlighted by a central copper fountain. The Hummingbird room has two twin half-canopy beds from the '20s; the Cactus Wren has a double bed and antique dresser. The Quail room features antique peacock chairs, a parquet end table, lace curtains, Wedgwood plates, and a queen-size bed. The Roadrunner (the only room for smokers) has pigskin tables and chairs, a queen bed, and an antique oak dresser. All rooms have little Mexican fireplaces, tile floors, and private baths. Some have TVs, others have stereos. Since business travelers make up a percentage of regular guests, there are telephone outlets in the rooms and a fax that guests can use.

Breakfast, which changes daily, is served in the dining room in the main house. A typical meal might include apricot frittata, fresh fruit, bran muffins, and kielbasa. After breakfast, guests may entertain themselves with the collection of games and puzzles in the living room or browse through Judy's collection of antiques, many of which are for sale. Ron repairs old clocks, and sometimes has unusual ones for sale. The Shritts are members of the Antiques and Collectibles Guild of Tucson, and they are happy to point antiquing guests in the appropriate direction for further treasure hunting.

New Mexico

Adobe Abode
202 Chapelle
Santa Fe, New Mexico
505-983-3133

Innkeeper: Pat Harbour
Accommodations: 2 rooms, 1 casita
Rates: single, $85–$95; double, $90–$110
Included: Full breakfast
Added: 10.125% tax
Payment: Major credit cards
Children: 6 and older preferred
Pets: Not permitted
Smoking: Permitted
Open: Year-round

Adobe Abode, on a residential street several blocks from Santa Fe's plaza, was built in 1904 by the army to house officers from nearby Fort Marcy. The only aspect of its exterior that makes Adobe Abode stand out from its neighbors is a purplish-blue door — it's a dead giveaway to the creativity and whimsy that await inside.

The sunny living room, a gathering spot, is an eclectic mix of styles. Philippine planters, a needlepoint chair, a comfortable easy chair with matching ottoman, Indian pottery, folk art animals, and a bright painting by the owner that hangs over the fireplace add color and visual interest to the room. Here guests are welcome to help themselves to cookies and sherry and watch cable TV.

Two of the guest rooms have British themes, and one is uniquely southwestern. The art nouveau bed in the English Garden room is topped with a pretty floral spread and antique quilt. Attractive artwork adorns the walls, and there's a marble-topped writing table for jotting down inspirational thoughts. The Bloomsbury room has a four-poster bed draped in fabric patterned after that made popular by the famous artistic and literary Bloomsbury group of London. The tiles in the bath were painted in Madrid, New Mexico, especially for the inn to match the Bloomsbury print fabric. The cheerful bedside table was a piece that innkeeper Pat Harbour picked up at a flea market and brought back to life with her own paintbrush.

The Casita de Corazon, in a separate building that was once a garage, is the most secluded of the guest rooms. It has extras such as a small refrigerator, coffeemaker, cable TV, and its own private entrance off of a pleasant patio. Twin aspen-pole beds made by innkeeper Pat Harbour double as sofas during the day. Cowhide print pillows and spreads add a sense of fun. There's a table lamp made from a pre-Columbian ceramic figure thought to be the rendering of a Mayan god. Weathered old Mexican doors covered in lace stand between the bedroom and the bath, and the bath is equipped with a telephone and towel warmer. All of the baths are tiled, have custom toiletries, and soft terry robes. All the rooms have clock radios, private phones, and an information book put together by the innkeeper to help guide her guests to local sights and restaurants.

Full breakfasts are served in the kitchen on different china each day. Fresh juice, fruit, and homemade muffins or scones are staples, but entrées vary. Crustless quiches are a specialty, and some of Pat's recipes are going to be published in an upcoming cookbook. Overall, it's Pat's ingenuity and attention to detail that set Adobe Abode apart from other inns.

Adobe and Roses
1011 Ortega NW
Albuquerque, New Mexico 87114
505-898-0654

Innkeeper: Dorothy Morse
Accommodations: 3 rooms
Rates: single or double, $50–$75; $105 for entire guest house
  accommodating up to 5; $10 surcharge for single-night stays
Included: Full breakfast
Added: 5.5% tax
Payment: Personal checks; no credit cards
Children: $5 additional per day if more than two people in
  room
Pets: Allowed
Smoking: Permitted only outside
Open: Year-round

Adobe and Roses is the type of bed-and-breakfast that lets you
truly be yourself. There are no rigid check-in or breakfast hours
here. If you want a full hot breakfast, one will be cooked for
you. If you prefer a Continental breakfast, you will awake to
fresh fruit and muffins instead. If you like privacy, you can
come and go as you please — each unit has its own entrance. If
you enjoy socializing, innkeeper Dorothy Morse is an affable
host, and it is easy to get lost in conversation with her. No matter
what your taste, you're likely to feel right at home here.

Two of the rooms are in a new adobe guest house at the back
of the property. The larger of the two accommodations has a
kitchenette, separate living room and bedroom, skylights, a
nice Mexican tile bath, and a TV, stereo system, and clock radio
in the bedroom. The smaller unit includes a beautifully carved
wooden bench in the shape of a swan and has a microwave and
toaster oven rather than a kitchenette. The two rooms share a
porch overlooking a lovely Japanese lily pond, and can be
rented as one unit.

The remaining suite is connected to the main house. With an
entrance hallway, separate living room, large kitchenette, bedroom, and spacious bath, the suite feels more like a private
home. Horses munch on the lawn just on the other side of the
living room's picture windows, and musically inclined guests
will enjoy the suite's own piano. All of the guest rooms have kiva
fireplaces, Oriental rugs, brick floors, ceiling fans, plants,
stocked bookshelves, and reading lamps above each bed. In
appropriate seasons, vases with fresh flowers from Dorothy's
handsome gardens are placed in the guest rooms.

Sometimes the Adobe and Roses sponsors musical evenings.
Dorothy is associated with the local symphony and occasionally puts up visiting musicians — on such occasions, she puts
together an impromptu evening of music, company, and food,
and any guest staying at the inn is welcome to join in the

festivities. Since these events can't be planned ahead of time, you just have to hope there's an out-of-town musician needing a room during your stay.

About 20 minutes from downtown Albuquerque, Adobe and Roses feels secluded, yet with most of the area's attractions only a short drive away, the inn is conveniently located for sight-seeing.

Alexander's Inn

529 East Palace Avenue
Santa Fe, New Mexico 87501
505-986-1431

Innkeeper: Carolyn Lee
Accommodations: 5 rooms (3 with private bath)
Rates: $70–$120 double
Included: Continental breakfast and afternoon refreshments
Added: 10.125% tax
Payment: Major credit cards
Children: Over 6 welcome; additional $15 if more than 2
    people in room
Pets: Not permitted
Smoking: Not permitted
Open: Year-round

Alexander's Inn is a cozy 1903 cottage facing an open field of wildflowers. With its traditional brick face and shingled roof, it's is a departure from the dominant adobe construction in Santa Fe. Throughout the house, stenciled patterns, hardwood floors, and beautiful furnishings (many of them antiques) add to the country flavor.

The array of old family photographs that greets you in the entrance hall suggests that you are being welcomed as one of the family. Similarly, the guest rooms are warm and inviting. Wide dormer windows attractively draped with floral print curtains fill the upstairs rooms with sunshine. Room 4 has a four-poster brass bed and a private deck. Room 1, which shares a large, sunny bathroom with Room 2, has sloping ceilings with gingerbread trim and is decorated in pastel pinks, making it the most feminine of the rooms. Room 5, on the ground floor, has a king-size four-poster bed, a colorful stained glass window, and a working fireplace.

Continental breakfasts—homemade breads, muffins, granola, cereal, fresh fruit, juice, tea, and coffee—are served on the backyard deck in the summer or inside by the fire during the winter. In the afternoon there are salsa and chips or homemade cookies and other goodies and a wide selection of teas. Guests are welcome to help themselves to cold drinks in the fridge.

Casa Benavides
137 Kit Carson Road
Taos, New Mexico 87571
505-758-1772
800-554-9552

Innkeepers: Tom and Barbara McCarthy
Accommodations: 21 rooms
Rates: single or double, $80–$175; $15 extra per day for each additional person
Included: Full breakfast and afternoon tea
Added: 10.25% tax
Payment: Major credit cards
Children: Welcome
Pets: Not permitted
Smoking: Not permitted in guest rooms
Open: Year-round

With twenty-one guest rooms, Casa Benavides is the largest bed-and-breakfast in Taos. Yet each room is so individually decorated, and the hosts go to such great lengths to welcome every guest, that visitors feel like they're staying in a private home.

The guest rooms are spread among a group of closely knit buildings about a block from the Plaza. The main building has five guest suites, including La Victoriana, Dona Tules, and the Flagstone. La Victoriana lives up to its name with Victorian furnishings, lace curtains, and a Tiffany lamp. The masculine Flagstone suite, decorated in grays, blacks, and whites, has Native American art, a leather couch, a fireplace, and a flagstone floor. The Dona Tules is a pretty, feminine room with a chintz day bed and matching pillows, chintz curtains with flouncy valances, a white brass bed, a beautiful dresser with curly maple trim, old photographs, and a Tiffany lamp with beaded fringe.

The Artist's Studio now houses two guest suites. El Mirador upstairs is quite large and is attractively furnished in a southwestern style. It has an efficiency kitchen, a view of Taos Mountain, and a kiva fireplace. La Fuente, downstairs, is also southwestern in theme and has a full kitchen. The rest of the guest rooms are in the Benavides house (the childhood home of innkeeper Barbara McCarthy—her maiden name was Benavides) and an old trading post. The staff will patiently describe each room for you when you make your reservation, or they can send you information with brief descriptions of all of the rooms.

Breakfasts, on Mexican china atop pink and purple table-cloths, are served in the pleasant breakfast room in the main building. The meal includes granola, fresh fruit, yogurt, home-made tortillas, muffins, Mexican eggs, and either pancakes, waffles, or french toast. Afternoon tea is served with a different homemade treat each day (the brownies made with homemade raspberry jam are especially tasty), and guests are welcome to use the outdoor hot tub at their leisure.

Casas de Sueños

310 Rio Grande SW
Albuquerque, New Mexico 87104
505-247-4560

Owner: Robert C. Hanna
Accommodations: 12 rooms and suites
Rates: double, $85–$175; quadruple, $165–$200
Included: Full breakfast
Added: 10.75% tax
Payment: Major credit cards
Children: Over 12 welcome; $10 additional
Pets: Not permitted
Smoking: Not permitted
Open: Year-round

Casas de Sueños, which means houses of dreams, is named for the various casitas that were built here as artists' residences and studios in the 1930s by J. R. Willis, an artist himself. Over the years noted artists have lived and worked on the property. Robert Hanna has tried to retain the communal feel of the compound while affording guests plenty of privacy for relaxation and contemplation. The inn's staff goes out of its way to ensure every comfort is extended to guests.

The most obvious reminder of the inn's early roots as an artists' colony stands at the entrance: a unique, futuristic cylindrical structure made from brick, glass, and wood. Created by architect Bart Prince, who recently designed the Los Angeles County Museum, the structure is functional as well as intriguing. Inside, lounges and terraces on several levels offer views of the mountains, city, and golf course; there are also comfortable spaces for relaxing, reading, socializing, or watching television (the TV set is hidden when not in use behind sliding wooden doors). Sofas are built into the semicircular walls, and the unusual mix of glass, brick, and carpeting gives the interior a distinctive Japanese, if thoroughly modern, look.

The common dining room, where breakfast is served, was once a writer's and artist's studio. Vibrant stained glass now graces the sunny room, and changing exhibits from local artists adorn the walls. Breakfasts such as asparagus soufflé with green chiles served with English scones, homemade tomato jam, fresh pumpkin or sweet potato empañadas (a local treat), bizcochos, coffee cakes, and granola are works of art in their own right. The inn has its own blend of coffee, and meals are served outside on the patio in the summer.

Rooms vary greatly in size and decor. Some are tucked away in quiet corners, others overlook courtyard gardens. The Taos and Zuni casitas are furnished with southwestern and Indian pieces, while the Rose room has a more romantic air. The Elliot Porter suite is a tribute to the famed photographer, and some of his fine pictures hang on the walls. La Miradora suite, meaning "the vision," is located in J. R. Willis's original residence and is the most elegant of all of the guest suites. A beautifully intricate Oriental table is the centerpiece of the large living room, and the two bedrooms (one with a four-poster pine bed) are tastefully appointed.

Casas de Sueños is adjacent to the Albuquerque Country Club Golf Course, which hosts an enchanting hot air balloon glow every Christmas Eve. The Albuquerque Museum, the New Mexico Museum of Natural History, and the historic old town with its many shops, restaurants, and galleries are all within walking distance. The Rio Grande Zoo is also nearby.

Dancing Ground of the Sun

711 Paseo de Peralta
Santa Fe, New Mexico 87501
505-986-9797
800-645-5673

Innkeepers: David and Donna McClure
Accommodations: 4 suites
Rates: single or double, $115–$150
Included: Continental breakfast and afternoon refreshments
Added: 10.125% tax
Payment: Major credit cards
Children: Over 12 welcome
Pets: Not permitted
Smoking: Not permitted
Open: Year-round

If you are looking for private and spacious accommodations in a convenient downtown location, Dancing Ground of the Sun more than fits the bill. Only a few blocks from Santa Fe's plaza, the inn has four casitas, each with a private entrance, full kitchen, fireplace, living room, cable TV, telephone, and parking space. Two casitas, Buffalo Dancer and Rainbow Dancer, have washers and dryers, and Kokopelli Casita, the largest, comes with a garage.

Throughout the inn, great care has gone into decorating, and only the finest furnishings have been used. Each casita has a hand-painted mural reflecting its name (corn dancers in the Corn Dancer casita, buffaloes in the Buffalo Dancer casita) and individual terra cotta light fixtures outside the entrance. Wherever possible, local artisans were used to contribute to the southwestern decor. Taos artist Katherine Henry painted the murals, Santa Fe artist Rebecca Parson created the light fixtures, and the high-quality living room sofas were made by the Taos Furniture Company. Color schemes in all the casitas, right down to the table linens and china, complement the colors used in the wall murals.

Needless to say, each casita has a personality all its own. The Buffalo Dancer, furnished in earth tones, has lots of willow furniture and Taos drums. The Rainbow Dancer, in maroons and blues, has a unique aspen headboard with matching dresser in the bedroom. Although the Corn Dancer is the smallest casita, it is a cheerful space in teal, sage, and burgundy, and has an especially nice bath. In the living room there's a nicho painted with a lovely mural of a Santa Fe mountain landscape in addition to the corn dancers that surround the walls. The Kokopelli casita (named for a figure in Anasazi legend) is the most elegant, with a remarkable sinewy driftwood table at its entrance, a stone coffee table, aspen and willow chair with ottoman in the living room, and a king-size willow bed (all other rooms have queens) with a matching willow fainting couch in the bedroom. The Kokopelli also has a small balcony.

Each casita has its own breakfast nook, and freshly-squeezed orange juice, muesli, fruit, and homemade goods are served in the casitas each morning. In the afternoon guests can snack on cheese and crackers or chips and salsa.

Although the casitas do afford lots of privacy, the McClures are gracious hosts and are always willing to help their guests in any way they can. Overall, Dancing Ground of the Sun offers the best of both worlds—solitude when you want it and attention when you need it.

El Rincón Bed and Breakfast
114 Kit Carson Street
Taos, New Mexico 87571
505-758-4874

Innkeepers: Nina Meyers and Paul "Paco" Castillo
Accommodations: 12 rooms (all with private bath)
Rates: $45–$125
Included: Continental breakfast
Added: 10.25% tax
Payment: Major credit cards
Children: Welcome
Pets: With approval
Smoking: Permitted
Open: Year-round

Only half a block from the Taos Plaza, El Rincón is a charming and unusual B&B. With a compact design, the inn has rooms tucked away on several levels, some opening onto a courtyard.

The owners take great pride in seeing that their guests enjoy a pleasant stay that is visually memorable. Each guest room offers a different mood. The work of local artists abounds, from santos in wall niches to hand-carved doors to intricately crafted furniture. Flowers spill out everywhere, adding color and gaiety.

Most of the building is one hundred years old; the "newer" section has been around for ninety years, although some rooms were added to the second floor in 1990. Next door is the Original Trading Post of Taos, founded years ago by the Indian trader Ralph Meyers, the father of today's innkeeper, Nina.

La Doña Luz Room is the most private, since it stands alone in a separate building in front of the Trading Post. It is named for Doña Luz, a well-known Taos hostess who entertained Kit Carson, Governor Charles Bent, and other generals of the day. In the 1800s the building was a popular bar that D. H. Lawrence later frequented. Decorated with sheepskin rugs, a handsome batik print, Spanish colonial furniture, and retablos painted by Anne Forbes, a Taos artist, La Doña Luz Room also has a skylit hot tub, a full kitchen, and a washer and dryer.

The other rooms are equally engaging. The Yellow Bird Deer Room is filled with Indian paintings, pottery, Hopi kachina dolls, Navajo rugs, Taos drums, and Sioux beaded moccasins. Los Angelitos is adorned with angels from all over the world. The Santiago Room is luxuriously furnished in a European-Spanish style. The blanket chest at the end of the black and brass king bed is topped with kilim pillows. There's a fireplace to take off the winter chill, and most of the dark, carved, wooden furniture is from Spain. The colorful tile bath is partially lit by a skylight, and the room also has air conditioning and mountain views.

Los Flores is popular with honeymooners because of its two-person Jacuzzi surrounded by a tile mural depicting the Garden of Eden. Each room has a television with a VCR (guests can borrow movies from the inn's extensive collection) and refrigerators. Most rooms also have fireplaces.

The dining room is charming, with an old hand-dug well, though breakfast is served on the cheerful patio (weather permitting). Guests can choose the time that best fits their schedule. The menu usually includes fruit, muffins, yogurt, cereal, and fresh orange juice.

Galisteo Inn
HC 75, Box 4
Galisteo, New Mexico 87540
505-982-1506

Innkeepers: Joanna Kaufman and Wayne Aarniokoski
Accommodations: 12 rooms (8 with private bath)
Rates: single, $60–$70; double, $90–$170
Included: Breakfast
Added: 8.75% tax
Payment: Major credit cards
Children: Over 12 welcome; additional $15 per day if more than 2 people in room
Pets: Not permitted; though horses can be boarded
Smoking: Not permitted
Open: Year-round except for last 3 weeks in January and early February

A sleepy cat curls up on a Mexican bench. Visitors sit on willow furniture on the front porch and talk about their day while they watch a croquet match on the lush green lawn. Out back, the athletic types are swimming in the pool or going for a horseback ride. Others are stealing a quiet moment with a book in the library.

About 250 years ago, what is now the Galisteo Inn was built as a Spanish homestead. Today, ancient trees shade its grounds, and a picturesque stone wall surrounds the property. The road out front is dirt. Santa Fe is a comfortable 23 miles away.

Here is a historic hacienda-style inn offering tranquillity yet decorated with a modern eye. The living room has a big fireplace, a piano, and an extensive library. The guest rooms—all named for trees (the inn even smells like freshly chopped wood)—are airy and fairly spacious, with Mexican furniture. Several have kiva fireplaces. Eight rooms have private baths; the others share two baths that are especially attractive, with viga ceilings and lots of Mexican tile.

Breakfast features homemade pastries such as blue corn muffins and scones, fresh fruit, juice, granola, and coffee. Special southwestern dinners are served Wednesday through Sunday evenings ($25 additional). The menu changes weekly, but you can expect inventive entrées such as a crab and chèvre burrito with a spicy red bell pepper sauce served with black beans and sautéed spinach.

The inn has its own horses, and guided rides can be arranged upon request (a fee is charged). Mountain bikes for touring the surrounding desert are available, and guests can rest their tired bones in the inn's hot tub or sauna.

Grant Corner Inn
122 Grant Avenue
Santa Fe, New Mexico 87501
505-983-6678

Innkeepers: Louise Stewart and Pat Walter
Accommodations: 13 rooms (9 with private bath)
Rates: single, $55–$65; double, $55–$135
Included: Full breakfast
Added: 4% room tax
Payment: Major credit cards
Children: Over 8 welcome
Pets: Not permitted
Smoking: Not permitted
Open: Year-round

Walk through the latticed archway of the Grant Corner Inn to a nostalgic world of pinafores and quilts, warmth and hospitality. Whether your childhood included visits to Grandma's house or not, you'll feel as if it did when you visit this inn.

The Colonial manor home was built in 1905 by a wealthy ranching family, and was opened as an inn in 1982 by Louise Stewart (daughter of Jack Stewart, the founder of the Camelback Inn in Scottsdale) and her husband Pat Walter. Past the white picket fence and softly swaying weeping willows, through the etched glass front door, you walk into a living room furnished in antiques. From the Wedgwood blue ceiling and walls to the gleaming wood floors and the Oriental carpets, the house exudes warmth. The adjoining dining room gets lots of use, for the inn serves breakfast to the public as well as its guests. It only takes a moment to start noticing the rabbits—

calico rabbits, wooden rabbits, furry rabbits, porcelain rabbits, even rabbit napkin holders on the dining room table.

Throughout the house, there are other touches that give the inn its special charm. Hanging on the door of each guest room is a stuffed heart saying "Welcome." Arriving guests find a small fruit basket, a carafe of wine, fresh flowers in a demivase, chocolates on monogrammed pillowcases, and a welcoming note from their hosts in their room.

Eleven guest rooms are on the first three floors. Each has its own decor, with brass and four-poster beds, quilts and tieback curtains. Some rooms have small refrigerators, covered in frills. Every room has a private phone, TV, air conditioning, and a ceiling fan. The rooms aren't large, but the overall ambience makes up for any loss of space. Adjoining rooms with a shared bath are a good choice for families. The bedrooms range from one twin bed to one king-size and have enough space for a roll-away. Room 11 is perfect for a child, for it has a single brass bed and is filled with stuffed toys.

Five blocks away is Grant Corner Inn Hacienda, an adobe-style condominium with two guest rooms upstairs and a living room, dining room, and kitchen downstairs. Its modern decor includes cathedral ceilings and skylights. The entire unit can accommodate up to eight; each guest room can be rented individually. Both have queen-size beds; one has a beehive fireplace. Rates range from $90 for one room to $250 for eight people renting the entire unit.

Guests in both the main house and the condominium eat a breakfast feast in the inn's dining room or on the front porch, draped with hanging plants. There are two entrées—perhaps pumpkin raisin pancakes or artichoke mushroom crêpes with sour cream sauce—along with homemade jellies and breads, fruit frappes, a selection of fine teas, and fresh coffee. The breakfasts are so special that even fried eggs, bacon, and home fries taste like elegant treats. Brunch is served on Saturdays (7:30 A.M. to noon) and Sundays (8 A.M. to 1 P.M.). These meals are so popular that the inn sells its own cookbook, along with jellies and country crafts. (If you're in the area and want to eat at the inn, be sure to make reservations.)

Guests at Grant Corner Inn can use a nearby sports club (a 10-minute drive), which offers tennis, racquetball, indoor and outdoor pools, a whirlpool, sauna, and massage.

La Posada de Chimayo
P.O. Box 463
Chimayo, New Mexico 87522
505-351-4605

Innkeeper: Sue Farrington
Accommodations: 2 suites and 2 rooms (each with private bath)
Rates: single, $75–$95; double, $85–$125; $25 additional for a
   third person in room (reduced weekly rates in winter)
Included: Breakfast
Added: 5.375% tax
Payment: Personal checks; no credit cards
Children: Over 12 welcome
Pets: With approval
Smoking: Permitted only outside
Open: Year-round

The tiny village of Chimayo, renowned for its weavers and their masterful creations, is not exactly on the beaten path. From Santa Fe, 25 miles to the south, you wind through wide-open countryside after leaving the main highway. Taos via the High Road, which passes through the craft villages of Cordova and Truchas, is 45 minutes north.

But even more remote is La Posada de Chimayo, a B&B with southwestern charm. You turn off Highway 76 onto a narrow dirt road that ambles by such landmarks as "Moose," "a building with a fan-shaped roof," and "a house with blue trim." Just when you think you must have missed it—or that you're on the wrong road altogether—there it is, with a sign in front to prove it. Sue Farrington will send you a map when you make your reservation.

Rooms are in two separate buildings—two in a guest house adjacent to Sue's own home and two in a restored farmhouse down the road. Built in 1981, the guest house blends beautifully into the surroundings—quite a trick considering that the ancient settlement of Chimayo dates from 1598. Sue calls it a "new old adobe."

A traditional adobe structure, the guest house has viga ceilings, brick floors, and corner fireplaces. The furniture is comfortable and the decorations are pure Southwest, with Mexican rugs and handwoven bedspreads as accents. The house has two separate apartments. Each has a sitting room with a "Taos bed" (sleeps one), a small bedroom with a double bed, and a bath. There's a hanging porch swing on the shared front porch.

The farmhouse is just around the bend. It was built in stages beginning in 1891, and Sue completely renovated it in 1992. The two guest rooms are spacious, with Mexican furnishings and their own fireplaces. Guests staying in these rooms are free to use the adjoining common living area, where breakfast is served family-style for all guests.

Breakfast is not for the fainthearted, the innkeeper warns. Sue's specialties include Spanish tortillas made with green chile, cornmeal pancakes topped with honey-lemon syrup, bread pudding, and French toast stuffed with cream cheese, chopped nuts, and vanilla topped with apricot-orange sauce. Bring a big appetite, because portions are generous.

In addition to visiting the local sights — notably the weavers' shops and a historic church where miraculous cures are said to have taken place — you can take day trips to several Indian pueblos, Bandelier National Monument, Santa Fe, and Taos. Skiers wanting to avoid the crowds can head to Sipapu Ski Area. There are also hiking trails in the nearby desert country and alpine forests.

Lundeen Inn of the Arts Bed and Breakfast

618 South Alameda
Las Cruces, New Mexico 88005
505-526-3327
Fax: 505-526-3355

Innkeepers: Linda and Gerald Lundeen
Accommodations: 15 rooms
Rates: single or double, $53–$58; suites, $85
Included: Continental breakfast, afternoon hors d'oeuvres and cider
Added: 11% tax
Payment: Major credit cards
Children: Discouraged
Pets: Discouraged
Smoking: On balconies and in courtyard only
Open: Year-round

You don't have to be an art expert to stay here, but if you are, you won't be disappointed. Either way, you will enjoy being surrounded by the work of numerous contemporary artists. Linda Lundeen runs an art gallery in the same adobe building with the B&B and the Lundeens' home. Art is everywhere, creating a lively look.

The living room is fresh and modern, setting just the right tone for your visit. Each guest room is named for an artist, with furnishings designed to reflect that artist's style. The Georgia O'Keeffe Room, decorated in blacks, grays, and whites, has an antique bed and a private balcony. The Olag Wieghorst Room, with blue quilts and red accents, has two double beds and a red clawfoot tub.

In the afternoon, guests gather for hors d'oeuvres and apple cider. At breakfast, the Lundeens serve perhaps blueberry muffins or cinnamon swirls accompanied by fruit, herb tea, and coffee.

Catering to groups as well as individuals, the hosts can coordinate such special functions as theater nights. They also schedule such events as art seminars, watercolor workshops, mystery weekends, archaeological digs, and even trips to the nearby Deming Duck Races.

Monjeau Shadows
Bonito Route
Highway 37 (3 miles north of Highway 48 junction)
Nogal, New Mexico 88341
505-336-4191

Innkeeper: Brenda Brittain
Accommodations: 5 rooms
Rates: single, $50; double, $60; suite, $90
Added: 7.125% tax
Included: Breakfast
Payment: Major credit cards
Children: Over 12 welcome; younger children not encouraged
Pets: Permitted
Smoking: Permitted only in certain areas
Open: Year-round

The highway leading to Ruidoso is only a few hundred feet below. But at this hillside guest home you feel removed from the crowds. From any of the three porches you look out at miles of wooded terrain. To the northeast is Capitan Mountain, where a frightened bear cub was found after a devastating forest fire in 1950, inspiring a national awareness of forest conservation under the name Smokey the Bear.

Monjeau Shadows, built as a home on 10 acres in 1980 and transformed into a B&B four years later, is an excellent hub for a New Mexico mountain vacation any time of the year. Ski Apache, with eight lifts including a four-passenger gondola, is 18 miles away. Hiking and fishing enthusiasts can find plenty to do. One of the most popular attractions is Ruidoso Downs, where horse racing is held from May to September.

Bird-watching is a special activity here. Blacktail and Rufous hummingbirds are constant visitors to the feeders on the second-floor balcony. Brenda Brittain claims that when the feed runs low, the birds let her know by flying around the kitchen windows.

Breakfast is included in the room rate, and generally Brenda will fix whatever you'd like. If you want a high-energy breakfast because you're going skiing, she'll oblige; if you want something light, she'll do that too. The breakfast hour is flexible, catering to guests' individual needs. It can be served in your room, in the dining room, or outside. For an extra charge, and with advance notice, other meals can be arranged.

The guest rooms are on four levels, from the basement to the loft. Bryan's room is red, white, and blue, and has a nautical theme. The adjoining bath has several surprises—wallpaper that you can read (advertisements from a Victorian-era catalog) and a red, white, and blue clawfoot tub. Elaina's room is the nicest, with lace curtains, a chenille bedspread, a straw heart wreath over the bed, and a marbletop bedside table. It can be rented alone or with Lisa's room to form a suite. Every bedroom has a TV, a digital clock, and well-matched furnishings.

A look of orderliness and comfort prevails throughout. In the living room, distinctive with its apricot carpet and yellow walls, a stained glass skylight is the focal point.

There's lots of space available for guests. Especially popular in winter is the basement game room, with a tournament-size pool table, a dart board, a jukebox, and a sitting area beside the fireplace. For games like badminton, croquet, and horseshoes, you don't have to go any farther than the front lawn.

Brenda is flexible and creative. Ask about the inn's Murder Mystery weekends and tennis packages. For groups (the inn can accommodate up to 16), special arrangements can be made upon request, including meals and entertainment.

Water Street Inn
427 West Water Street
Santa Fe, New Mexico 87501
505-984-1193

Innkeepers: Dolores and Al Deitz
Accommodations: 7 rooms
Rates: single or double, $75–$130; $15 additional person
Included: Breakfast and afternoon hors d'oeuvres
Added: 10.125% tax
Payment: Major credit cards
Children: $15 per day if eating breakfast
Pets: With prior approval only
Smoking: Not permitted
Open: Year-round

Tucked away next to a popular Santa Fe restaurant, the Water Street Inn is one of the classiest bed-and-breakfasts in town. Run by a pleasant couple from Louisiana, the inn offers guests a combination of southern hospitality and Santa Fe charm.

It's hard to believe that the attractive, 70-year-old adobe once housed apartments, but the advantages today are private baths for each room and no noise from other rooms. They are tastefully furnished and immaculate.

Sunny Room 1, in light blues and creams, is a favorite, with a four-poster bed, brick floor, ceiling fan, Mexican chairs, and a private patio. Room 2 has a fireplace and nice sitting area. Room 3 has a cypress four-poster bed from Louisiana, invitingly topped with a pink floral spread and down comforter. Afghan rugs accent the sitting-room floor and walls. Room 4 is the largest and Room 2, with pine twin beds, is the smallest, though it has the use of a balcony across the hall with fine sunset views. All rooms have cable TV, telephones, and air conditioning.

Breakfast, nicely laid out on a tray, arrives at your door in the morning. Hot entrées such as eggs Benedict, eggs Mornay, huevos rancheros, or quiches are served in ramekins, and there is always a pot of hot coffee. In the evenings hors d'oeuvres are served with wine — sometimes in the upstairs sitting room (an appealing room with family photos and portraits) to take advantage of the beautiful New Mexico sunsets. Complimentary soft drinks, tea and coffee are available at all times in the downstairs common room.

William E. Mauger Estate

701 Roma Avenue NW
Albuquerque, New Mexico 87102
505-242-8755

Owners: Chuck Silver and Brian Miller
Accommodations: 8 rooms (all with private bath)
Rates: single, $49–$79; double, $59–$99; suite, $89
Included: Breakfast
Added: 10.75% tax
Payment: Major credit cards
Children: Additional $1 per year of age
Pets: Permitted
Smoking: Permitted only outside
Open: Year-round

Just where downtown Albuquerque gives way to a residential section stands a charming brick three-story inn. Built in 1897 for $1,600, it's a stately Queen Anne, ideal for putting you in touch with history yet filled with modern comforts.

The William E. Mauger opened for guests in late 1987, its beautiful restoration the work of Richard Carleno. Great effort was taken to preserve as much of the original home as possible. In the entrance sitting room, the light fixture still has its original Edison bulbs. The current owners have a fully documented history of each and every owner of the home (the only turn-of-the-century building in Albuquerque to have such a record), and old photos of previous occupants are on display on the second-floor foyer.

Decorated with period furnishings, the guest rooms have an air of elegance. The pleasant Tuers room is the smallest. The Boston Sleeper suite accommodates up to five. Hardwood floors are covered with Oriental rugs, stuffed animals sit on the brass beds, and lace-covered satin hangers are found in the closet. The suite has a split bath, and the sofa on the sun porch opens into a twin bed. The Britannia room is spacious with a brass king bed, a small sitting area with a table and easy chairs, and a large closet. The Wool room was Mr. Mauger's (the original owner) office and has its own balcony. Greystone B, on the third floor, has a slanted roof and two queen beds draped with lace. Greystone A, decorated in blacks and fuchsias, is the most modern.

Two new rooms have recently been added on the ground floor. The Williams room has a queen bed, and the Garden room (originally a conservatory and sun porch), has two twins. All rooms have a surprising number of amenities, including small refrigerators, coffeemakers, hair dryers, ironing boards and irons, clock radios, curling irons, air conditioning, ceiling fans, and individual heat controls.

The parlor, with its pretty floral wallpaper, player organ, and old-fashioned phonograph, looks at first glance as if it belongs to another age — yet it too is filled with modern conveniences. There's a laser disc player and VCR with a vast disc and video-cassette library for guests. The refrigerator is always stocked with refreshments. At five o'clock hors d'oeuvres are served, and freshly-baked goods are available all day long. On one table, the hosts have compiled a directory of local restaurants and travel brochures, and they've even put together their own guidebook of photographs they've taken at local tourist sights.

Southwestern breakfasts, served outdoors on the deck in nice weather, vary daily. A typical breakfast might be burritos served with refries and a yogurt and granola fruit cup. Or you might rise to a green chile and bacon soufflé accompanied by pan-fried potatoes and zucchini bread.

The owners' commitment to hospitality makes a visit to this inn so pleasant; they really enjoy their guests and go out of their way to make everyone's stay as comfortable as possible. They keep a scrapbook of visitors' photos and letters, and many guests return again and again.

Because it's adjacent to downtown, the Mauger Estate is close to the Sunshine Opera House and the Kimo and El Rey theaters. All in all, the inn is an excellent alternative to the city's traditional lodgings.

Oklahoma

Harrison House
124 West Harrison
P.O. Box 1555
Guthrie, Oklahoma 73044
405-282-1000
800-375-1001

Owners: Claude and Jane Thomas
Accommodations: 35 rooms
Rates: single or double, $65–$110
Included: Continental breakfast
Added: 7.5% tax
Payment: Major credit cards
Children: Welcome

Pets: Accepted with approval
Smoking: Nonsmoking rooms available
Open: Year-round

Guthrie, once the capital of the Oklahoma Territory, celebrates its history every day of the year. Boasting a wealth of Victorian buildings with spindle tops and Romanesque arches, the town is distinctive with its antiques shops, turn-of-the-century restaurants, and historic celebrations. One of the best reasons to visit Guthrie is to stay at Harrison House, one of the most charming inns in the Southwest. A collage of quilts and lace, Victorian furniture and colorful accents, it invites you to come in and stay awhile.

Each guest room, clever and inventive in its decor, is named for someone who played a part in the town's history. Carrie Nation's room (she lived in Guthrie for a few months) has a simulated hatchet on the wall. Tom Mix's room (he once tended bar at a nearby saloon) is decorated with blue bandannas and has a fainting couch. The lobby, originally built as a bank, is grand, with its tin ceiling and wall vault. The carved wood check-in desk once stood in the Guthrie Post Office.

Harrison House's history is a story of civic pride in action. In the mid-1980s a group of residents decided that the town needed a historic hotel, so they set out to open one. Three downtown buildings dating from 1890 were combined (now five buildings make up Harrison House), and all sorts of people got involved. One artisan reproduced all of the light fixtures. Another designed the window coverings. Local women made the quilts (each with a different design) and the pillow shams. Phyllis Murray, a previous owner, oversaw the entire development, injecting her creativity at every turn. She bought American Victorian antiques (most found within 100 miles of Guthrie), converting some to meet her needs. Wherever you look, you'll see evidence of her imaginative touch. For example, one lavatory was made from an old chicken incubator. The towel racks were once wagon wheels or even streetcar steps.

Every room has a bath and telephone. The only television is in the upstairs parlor, a popular gathering place for afternoon refreshments. Breakfast is served on china and silver plates.

The Pollard Theatre, built in 1910 and restored in 1987, adjoins the inn. Live productions are presented throughout the year.

Texas

Annie's Bed and Breakfast
Highway 155 North
P.O. Box 928
Big Sandy, Texas 75755
903-636-4355

Innkeeper: Les Lane
Accommodations: 13 rooms (some with shared bath)
Rates: $38–$115
Included: Full breakfast
Added: Tax
Payment: Major credit cards
Children: Additional charge if older than 7
Pets: Not permitted
Smoking: Not permitted
Open: Year-round

Folks driving through the East Texas countryside do a double-take when they get to the little town of Big Sandy and come upon three brightly painted houses clearly kin to Victorian days.

Anita Potter is the creator of this tranquil destination. It all started with the headquarters for Annie's Attic—Anita's mail order needlecraft business. Very quickly the operation grew to include a group of businesses that now includes Annie's Tea Room, Needlecraft Gallery, and Gift Shop.

When customers repeatedly asked for a place to spend the night, Anita decided to open Annie's Bed and Breakfast across the street, enlarging a turn-of-the-century home into an inn. A house with seven gables, the lodging has definite charm.

The parlor, with Empire furniture and lace curtains, is the place to meet fellow guests. A wide staircase, excellent for making dramatic entrances, leads to most of the guest rooms. But two of the most elegant rooms are on the first floor. The Queen Victoria is truly romantic—all burgundy and pink, with a bed sized for a queen and a private bath. The Prince Albert with its masculine air adjoins.

The upstairs rooms are smaller, ranging from the Garden View, which has twin beds and a shared bath, to the Garret, which has a double bed, private bath with clawfoot tub, and private balcony. Some rooms have lofts, making them excellent for families. Every room has a telephone and a small refrigerator disguised as an old-fashioned safe. Quilts, needlework, and subdued wallpaper add to the cozy feeling. All the bathrooms are well decorated and modern. The third-floor Queen Anne, by far the most elegant room, has a queen-size bed and private balcony. A spiral staircase leads to its loft, which has twin beds.

On weekdays and Sundays, guests eat a bountiful breakfast across the street at Annie's Tea Room, with waitresses in period costume. On Saturdays, a Continental breakfast is served.

Cotten's Patch Bed and Breakfast Inn

703 East Rusk
Marshall, Texas 75670
903-938-8756

Innkeeper: Jo Ann Cotten
Accommodations: 3 rooms (1 private bath)
Rates: single or double, $65–$75; suite, $95
Included: Continental breakfast
Added: 13% tax
Payment: Personal checks
Children: Discouraged
Pets: Not permitted
Smoking: On porches only
Open: Year-round

Cotten's Patch could well qualify for the definition of "a doll-house lodging." Every furnishing, every decorating detail, has been chosen with care, creating a romantic spot in a slow-paced East Texas town. Built in 1894, the house has been exquisitely restored. Comfort and coziness are the keynote, though the decor is eclectic. Trompe l'oeil touches add to the visual appeal, from hand-painting on the pantry door to a stenciled rug and tree on the back porch. Quilts, lace, handmade wares, and country bonnets proliferate alongside antiques and wicker furniture. A collection of dolls spills from the landing.

The screened-in front porch is a good place to watch the world go by, small-town style. A hot tub offers extra relaxation on the back porch. Continental breakfast includes coffee and juice, fruit, and fresh coffee cake.

Crystal River Inn

326 West Hopkins
San Marcos, Texas 78666
512-396-3739

Innkeepers: Mike and Cathy Dillon
Accommodations: 10 rooms (some with shared bath)

Rates: double, $45–$65 weekdays; $65–$80 weekends; suite,
   $80–$100
Included: Full breakfast
Added: 13% tax
Payment: Major credit cards
Children: Allowed with prior arrangement; $7.50 additional
   per day if there are three or more people in the room
Pets: Not permitted
Smoking: In public areas only
Open: Year-round

The Texas Hill Country is made for vacationing. Scenic beauty,
outdoor recreation, historic sites — it has them all. San Marcos,
midway between Austin and San Antonio, is a good place to
experience this part of Texas.

   The picture-perfect Crystal River Inn has a convivial atmosphere, excellent food, and rooms with exquisite decor. While
the four Corinthian columns across the front of the house signal
grandeur, the mood of the interior is warm and friendly. The
front porch and the second-story verandah are especially good
places to relax.

   The bedrooms' charming decor seems to spring straight
from the pages of a home and garden magazine. Each is named
for a Texas river, bearing testimony to the Dillons' affinity for
canoeing. The Frio Room, with a queen-size bed and wicker
furniture, is in a cool blue. The Medina is especially romantic,
with a queen-size four-poster bed, rosy tones, and white shutters. The Colorado is a good choice if you aren't partial to
ruffles and lace; here symbols of the rugged Southwest predominate. Five guest rooms are in the main house, three are in
the adjacent Young House, and two are in Rock Cottage.

   Breakfast is a main event. The constantly changing menu
includes such treats as banana crêpes, stuffed French toast,
quiche, and hot breads. Guests may enjoy breakfast in the dining room, on the patio, or in bed.

   Seasonal events range from historical tours to river trips,
murder mystery weekends to spa weeks.

The Gilded Thistle
1805 Broadway
Galveston, Texas 77550
409-763-0194
800-654-9380

Innkeeper: Helen Hanemann
Accommodations: 3 rooms (1 with private bath)

Rates: double, $135–$145
Included: Full breakfast and evening refreshments
Added: 17.89% tax on $135, 19.21% tax on $145
Payment: Major credit cards
Children: Welcome (preferably during the week)
Pets: Not permitted
Smoking: Not permitted
Open: Year-round

In all the world, there's only one Helen Hanemann. The best reason to stay at the Gilded Thistle is to hear her stories and join in her laughter. Of grandmotherly age, Helen has more energy than most people half her years, and her wit acts as a catalyst for her guests to enjoy themselves.

One of the first B&Bs in Galveston, the Gilded Thistle opened in 1982. The house itself, a Queen Anne, dates from 1892. It has an inherent charm, with its curly pine and cypress trim, oak fireplaces, and wraparound verandahs. This is a home of warmth as well as character. Teddy bears with names like Ms. Pernella and Chocolate Drop fill the couches, spill from the shelves, and sit coyly on the beds. Helen may try to introduce you to all of them, pointing to the latest additions— presents from her guests. Helen also has a wonderful collection of seashells that figure in her overall decorating scheme. Many of the furnishings are family heirlooms. Decorative touches came from friends, each connoting the friendship that Helen engenders.

Considering the numerous collections, the house is remarkably tidy. The guest rooms, all with double beds, are on the second floor. The master bedroom, the only one with its own bath, has a couch and fireplace. The Umbrella Room has an Oriental theme, with Chinese umbrellas. The Treetop Room, which used to be a nursery, looks straight into the uppermost branches of the trees outside. Two rooms have full-length windows that open, so one can walk out onto the romantic wraparound porch set with chairs and lots of plants.

Helen believes in ironing pillowcases, dressing the beds with decorative sheets, and polishing the silver. Her breakfasts will probably keep you going until midafternoon, for she serves homemade breads, eggs, several breakfast meats, and fresh fruit.

If you want to talk history, Helen is willing and able. A descendant of early West Texas settlers, she can tell you stories of the Texas Rangers. It is said that one of her ancestors, a captain with the Rangers, discovered Carlsbad Caverns while on patrol with his troop.

The Gilded Thistle, in the East End Historical District, is seven blocks from the beach and near many of the area's attractions. Helen has put together a package of tourist information on these local sights for interested guests.

High Cotton Inn Bed and Breakfast
214 South Live Oak
Bellville, Texas 77418
409-865-9796

Innkeepers: George and Anna Horton
Accommodations: 5 rooms (shared baths)
Rates: single, $40; double, $50
Included: Full breakfast
Added: 13.75% tax
Payment: No credit cards
Children: Infants not encouraged; older children additional
   $5 per day
Pets: Not permitted; boarding available nearby
Smoking: Not permitted
Open: Year-round

What better place to escape the humdrum than at High Cotton? Anna Horton always wanted to live in the country, so today she and her husband operate a country B&B in a two-story Victorian with wraparound porches and period furnishings.

The mood is informal at High Cotton, making it a great place to relax. Much of its charm is tied to the Hortons, genuinely nice people whose natural enthusiasm and zest for living can't help but spill over to their guests. They revel in serving bounteous breakfasts, with a repertoire too lengthy to list (locally cured bacon, yard eggs, yeast biscuits, grits, rum cake — you get the idea). When the Hortons aren't welcoming guests, they're apt to be out in their cookie kitchen baking goodies marketed under the name High Cotton Country Cookie and Candy Company. Be sure to try the caramel crisps and the oatmeal raisin spice cookies from their "bottomless cookie jar."

The Hortons like to cook, so they're always looking for an excuse. Thanksgiving dinner at High Cotton may well be the definition of "feast" (make reservations well in advance). But you don't have to wait till Thanksgiving. Call ahead, and the Hortons will cook a dinner just for you, priced at $10 per person. The menu is cook's choice.

Excellent for small groups as well as couples, High Cotton's guest rooms are all on the second floor. No decorating detail has escaped the hosts' notice, and family antiques and memorabilia are the focal point. Uncle Buster's Room has a beautifully carved bed. A beaded gown worn by George's grandmother is displayed in the upstairs parlor. Even the medicine cabinet has a story to tell, with antique gloves and spats on display.

For recreation, there's a pool out back. There are also two porches to rock on and a dozen or so antiques shops nearby. The hosts can arrange golf (a 9-hole course) and horseback riding excursions upon request.

Inn on the River

209 Barnard Street
P.O. Box 1417
Glen Rose, Texas 76043
817-897-2101
Fax: 817-897-7729

Innkeepers: Paul Merritt
Accommodations: 22 units (all with private bath)
Rates: single, $80; double, $90; suite, $125
Included: Full breakfast
Added: 6% tax
Payment: Major credit cards
Children: Discouraged
Pets: Not permitted
Smoking: Not permitted
Open: Year-round

The Inn on the River serves up big healthy doses of R&R. Yes, there are some things to see—Dinosaur State Park, Fossil Rim Wildlife Ranch, and the nearby village of Granbury, with its famed opera house—but just outside the lodging is the gentle Paluxy River, and the inn's design takes full advantage of this setting. Its shady grounds slope down to the river, with several sitting areas sprinkled over the lawn, and there's a swimming pool beneath the centuries-old live oaks.

In 1919 the inn was built as a health resort, using the region's natural mineral waters. In 1984 it was converted into an inn with high visual appeal. Guest rooms were refurbished with a sense of history coupled with comfort. Overall, the inn has a crisp, clean look—airy and welcoming.

Each room is different, right down to its wallpaper. Many of the beds have upholstered headboards with spreads to match. Ceiling fans and individual heating and air conditioning units are in every room. But don't look for TVs or phones, for the inn is truly intended as an escape.

Landhaus Bed and Breakfast

P.O. Drawer E
Fredericksburg, Texas 78624
512-997-4916

Owner: Maria McDonald
Accommodations: 4 rooms (rented as a whole; sleeps up to 8)
Rates: $90 for 2, $20 for each extra person
Included: Cook-your-own breakfast
Added: 6% tax
Payment: No credit cards
Children: Older children only
Pets: Not permitted
Smoking: Not permitted
Open: Year-round

If you yearn for your own place in the country, you can have it at Landhaus. A small one-story house built circa 1880, it sits on a 170-acre ranch about ten miles northeast of Fredericksburg. The owner, who lives in a separate house almost out of sight, allows guests to hunt wild turkey, quail, dove, and deer. Fishing in the creek is another favored pursuit.

Unimposing on the outside, the Landhaus is a glistening treasure inside—charm with a country flair. There's warmth and softness in this house—a composite of quilts, soft cushions, lush carpeting, and two wood-burning stoves. With four bedrooms and one large bath, the house is leased to one group at a time. There are six beds: two doubles, one three-quarter size, and three singles. One bedroom, below the main level, is excellent for children.

The country kitchen, next to an especially comfortable den, is the focal point of the house. The refrigerator is stocked with breakfast food, including locally made sausage and jams.

Guests can cook other meals if they wish; the kitchen is fully modernized, with a microwave oven and dishwasher.

There's a living room at Landhaus and a TV and telephone. If you have requests such as flowers or a cake for a special occasion, Maria will be happy to serve your needs.

Nearby Fredericksburg, settled by Germans in the mid-1800s, has lots of historic sites and country shops to explore. The LBJ Ranch is only six miles away, and Enchanted Rock State Park is also worth a side trip.

Llano Grande Plantation Bed and Breakfast

Route 4, Box 9400
Nacogdoches, Texas 75961
409-569-1249

Hosts: Charles and Ann Phillips
Accommodations: In 3 houses
Rates: $65–$75 for 1 person, $70–$80 for 2 people, $7.50–$10 each additional person (reduced rates for stays of more than one night)
Included: Cook-your-own breakfast
Added: 6% tax
Payment: No credit cards
Children: Accepted only at Gatehouse
Pets: Not permitted
Smoking: Nonsmoking rooms available
Open: Year-round

Hidden away in the pine forests of east Texas, there is an 1840 pioneer-style farmhouse ready to welcome guests, especially those with a bent toward history. The house was once occupied by Taliaferro "Tol" Barret, the man credited with drilling the first producing oil well west of the Mississippi. Today the house is part of Llano Grande Plantation Bed & Breakfast, a group of three homes open to guests run by Charles and Ann Phillips.

The front yard of the Tol Barret House is swept clean of grasses, and early Texas flowers such as widow's tear and lantana still bloom. Listed on the National Register of Historic Places, the house has been beautifully restored by the Phillips, both knowledgeable preservationists. They have rebuilt, re-stenciled, and redecorated the house and its period furnishings. Mrs. Barret's "sittin'" room, furnished with American Empire pieces, looks much as the lady of the house might have left it.

The kitchen and loft, constructed from wood of the same vintage as the house, are connected to the house by a covered walkway. This is the structure that the Phillipses have turned into a B&B, one of the most distinctive in the Southwest. Downstairs in the country kitchen guests cook their own breakfast. The larder is stocked with such specialties as venison sausage and homemade bread, along with standard fare such as eggs and cereal.

The bedroom upstairs is straight out of a history book. Four rope beds (with feather mattresses) under the eaves, handmade quilts and furniture, braided rugs, and wooden floors make for a cozy and comfortable retreat.

The Phillipses' own home, a restored 1840s pioneer house, is about a quarter of a mile down the road. Like the Tol Barret house, it's surrounded by trees, seemingly remote from neighbors. Guests stay on the second floor, ascending from the back porch via a private stairway to two bedrooms, a central sitting area, and a bath. The furnishings are charmingly romantic, circa pioneer days. The original pole rafters still arch overhead.

Also on the property is the Gate House, a small, 20th-century farmhouse with two bedrooms. While it cannot compete with the other two houses for charm, the Gate House is good for families with children.

The Oxford House
563 North Graham
Stephenville, Texas 76401
817-965-6885
Fax: 817-965-7555

Innkeepers: Bill and Paula Oxford
Accommodations: 4 rooms (all with private bath)
Rates: single, $58; double, $75
Included: Country breakfast
Added: 13% tax
Payment: Major credit cards
Children: Over age 6 welcome; additional $10 charge per day
Pets: Not permitted
Smoking: In designated areas only
Open: Year-round

In 1898 Judge William J. Oxford built a fine Victorian home in Stephenville. In 1986 his grandson Bill opened it as a B&B—a gem of a house steeped in local as well as family history. Bill's wife, Paula, has an obvious love of history, and throughout the house she has woven memorabilia into the design. As you sip afternoon refreshments, ask her about the home's history and you'll probably get a grand tour. The pump organ is a family heirloom brought to Texas by wagon. The violins belonged to the good judge himself, as did the law books. The hats and gloves belonged to his third wife.

The guest room at the top of the stairs has interior columns and gingerbread trim, plus a stained glass window. There's a clawfoot tub in the bath along with a big basket of towels. Another room is decorated in peach, featuring a Victorian bed made in Texas. A third room has a sleigh bed and a fainting couch that converts into a single bed.

The Oxfords and their children live elsewhere, but they go out of their way to make you feel welcome. Homemade breads and fruit are served at breakfast with omelettes, quiche, or French toast.

In Stephenville you can visit the Historical House Museum Complex. Other nearby sites include Dinosaur Valley State Park, Fossil Rim Wildlife Ranch, and the historic village of Granbury.

Pride House
409 East Broadway
Jefferson, Texas 75657
903-665-2675

Innkeeper: Ruthmary Jordan
Accommodations: 10 rooms (private baths)
Rates: $65–$100 single or double
Included: Full breakfast
Added: 13% tax
Payment: Major credit cards
Children: In the Dependency only (see below)
Pets: Not permitted
Smoking: Permitted
Open: Year-round

Once guests check into the Pride House, they have trouble leaving. Here is the place for a romantic holiday, a true escape from a hurried pace of life. The house itself—a two-story Victorian trimmed in gingerbread—exudes charm. Of course there's a wraparound porch, set with white wicker rockers and a porch swing for daydreaming on lazy afternoons. And throughout the house there are antique furnishings, swirls of lace, and stained glass windows.

Pride House also has something that no other lodging can boast—Ruthmary Jordan, a delightful lady with a zest for living. She makes the house come alive, creating a sense of warmth and cheer. In a history-filled East Texas town, Pride House was reportedly the first B&B in Texas, and it sets a high standard. Ruthmary believes in letting guests eat in the privacy of their

rooms. Culinary delights appear on the downstairs sideboard
at about 8:30 A.M. (look for coffee earlier if you wish). A restaur-
ateur before she became an innkeeper, Ruthmary is renowned
for her cooking. Favorite dishes include poached pears with
crème fraîche served with a praline sauce and "Not Eggactly
Benedict," Ruthmary's version of eggs Benedict. You serve yourself on a tray set with fine china, crystal, and sterling silver.

The six most elegant guest rooms are in the main house; four
with a country feeling are in a detached building called the
Dependency (the same vintage as the 1888 main house, but
originally the servants' quarters). The beautiful Blue Room is
especially comfortable, with a king-size bed and several easy
chairs. The Bay Room is spectacular: its wallpapered ceiling is
ablaze with stars. The Golden Era is hard to beat for romance
—a half-tester king-size iron bed is set beneath stained glass
bay windows and draped in lace. Most of the bathrooms have
showers, but the West Room boasts a clawfoot tub, perfectly
situated to watch the sunset during a luxurious soak.

Out in the Dependency, the Suite is a top choice, with a
wood-burning fireplace, a queen-size bed, country furnishings,
and a compartmented bath. All rooms have good lighting, soft
sun-dried sheets, and super-fluffy towels.

Prince Solms Inn

295 East San Antonio Street
New Braunfels, Texas 78130
512-625-9169

Owners: Bob and Pat Brent
Accommodations: 10 rooms (all with private bath)
Rates: double, $50–$100; suites, $75–$110
Added: 13% tax
Included: Continental breakfast
Minimum stay: 2 nights on weekends May through
    September and holidays
Payment: Major credit cards
Children: Over 12 welcome
Pets: Not permitted
Smoking: Nonsmoking rooms available
Open: Year-round

Prince Solms Inn is really special. With a historic character, it's
pleasing to the eye, furnished for comfort, and professionally
operated. In the cellar is one of the best restaurants in the Hill
Country, both in cuisine and atmosphere.

Built in 1898, the inn is in a community settled in 1845 by
Germans who were led to the new land by Prince Carl of

Solms-Braunfels. Among the original settlers was the family of the man who built the hotel. Today, the trim two-story building, constructed of locally made brick and native timber, is one of New Braunfels's most visible links to its heritage.

The interior, furnished to reflect the inn's history, has a delicate charm. On one side of the central hall is a parlor furnished with antiques, setting the mood for the entire inn. The Princess Sophie Suite, across the hall, has swags and shutters at the windows, German portraits on the walls, a large sitting room with period furnishings, and a separate bedroom with a king-size bed. The bath is small and modern, and there's also a tiny kitchen. Down the hall is the Prince Carl Suite, similarly furnished but with a more masculine decor.

The rest of the bedrooms are upstairs. The furnishings are not luxurious, just tasteful and appropriate to the setting: cloth-covered tables set with fruit, armoires (without TVs inside), wooden beds, and clawfoot tubs. The names of the rooms suggest their decor — Peony, Magnolia, Rose, and Songbird. Each bath is small but well-designed. In addition to central air conditioning, there's a ceiling fan in each room.

A breakfast of fresh pastries and a choice of coffee and hot tea is laid out on the hall sideboard. Its style, professional and tastefully elegant, typifies the inn's operation.

Whether you're a guest at the Prince Solms or not, Wolfgang's Keller restaurant is worth a special trip. For guests, it's a real luxury to have such a fine establishment only a few steps away. The restaurant is named in honor of Wolfgang Mozart, and a specially commissioned portrait of the composer hangs on the landing. Specialties include chicken piccata, veal Marsala, and linguine with shrimp and clam sauce. Reservations are recommended.

Behind the inn there's a shaded courtyard and an 1850s house which, like the inn, is a registered historic building. The Prince Solms is an ideal place to begin exploring New Braunfels — the main plaza is just down the street. The innkeepers are adept at helping visitors plan their stay.

Rosevine Inn
415 South Vine Avenue
Tyler, Texas 75702
903-592-2221

Innkeepers: Bert and Rebecca Powell
Accommodations: 5 rooms (all with private bath)
Rates: single, $65; double, $75
Added: 13% tax
Included: Full breakfast
Payment: Major credit cards
Children: Over 12 welcome; additional $10 per day
Pets: Not permitted
Smoking: Not permitted
Open: Year-round

Rosevine Inn combines the best qualities of a B&B, offering hospitality, comfort, convenience, and a sense of history. On a hill overlooking a brick street, Tyler's first B&B has a residential feeling, with a white picket fence and a small, tasteful sign. The Vine Avenue area is an emerging visitor attraction, with specialty shops and restored homes. Nearby is the Azalea District, notable for its variety of architectural styles representing many periods in Tyler's history.

On this site once stood the home of Dr. Irwin Pope, the son of one of Tyler's first doctors. Although the original house burned down, the Powells have replicated its 1930s style, placing the present structure over the earlier foundation. Unlike most B&Bs, the Rosevine Inn was designed to accommodate guests, and Bert and Becca Powell chose its site because of the beautiful, spacious grounds as well as its convenience to the city's attractions.

Don't expect a grand old mansion; instead, enjoy the comfort of a well-planned new home. The living areas are cozy and intimate. The guest rooms are cheerful. Three rooms have double beds; one has twin beds. Furnishings range from antiques to country collectibles.

Breakfast—a grand affair with quiches, hot breads, and fresh fruit—is served in the dining room. For socializing, guests can gather in the living room, the denlike setting at the top of the stairs, which has couches and a TV, or on the outside patio. Guests may also relax in the Rosevine's hot tub.

The Powells are a bright, energetic couple, convivial and eager to please. They'll happily direct you to interesting sights, suggest day trips, and even cook your favorite breakfast. In the evenings they serve wine and cheese or, if you prefer, a cup of hot chocolate by the fire.

Sara's Bed & Breakfast Inn

941 Heights Boulevard
Houston, Texas 77008
713-868-1130
800-593-1130
Fax: 713-868-1160

Innkeeper: Donna J. Arledge
Accommodations: 11 rooms (3 with private bath)
Rates: double, $50–$75; suite, $120
Added: 15% tax
Included: Breakfast
Payment: Major credit cards
Children: Accepted in only 1 unit; additional $10 per day, per child
Pets: Not permitted
Smoking: In designated areas only
Open: Year-round

Downtown Houston is four miles away—you can see the skyscrapers on the horizon. But here in the Heights, developed in the 1890s as one of Texas's first planned suburbs, you can relive the days of lemonade and cookies, almost forgetting that the glistening modern city exists. Here Victorian structures dominate; ninety of them are on the National Register. There's a central boulevard set with trees, a park with a lacy gazebo, and a public library that makes you want to curl up for hours.

Right on Heights Boulevard is Sara's, a wonderful two-story Victorian confection of gingerbread with a wraparound porch, a turret, and a widow's walk. In truth, the entire structure is not as old as its architecture suggests: the core of the house, a one-story cottage, was indeed built in 1898, but the flourishes were added in 1980.

In 1983 the Arledges bought the house, and they spent three years renovating it. Now the inn is fanciful and fun, offering lots of diversity. Sara's is a good place to start a visit to Texas, for each room in the main house is decorated to reflect one of its towns or cities. Get a quick tour of the state while choosing a room for the night. Dallas is sophisticated; Galveston has a nautical theme. Fredericksburg has Germanic hand-stenciling; Paris, French furniture. Tyler, named for a city famed for its roses, is decorated in a rose motif. Austin, with its white iron and brass bed and bay window, is the prettiest.

Jefferson, on the first floor, has a queen-size bed and is the only room in the main house with its own bath. The other baths have showers instead of tubs. On the second floor of a separate building, a balcony suite has two bedrooms, two baths, a kitchen (only light cooking allowed), and living area. Good for families, it is the only unit accommodating children, and a two-night stay is required.

Adjoining the main house is a large deck with a hot tub. Since most of the inn's interior is devoted to bedrooms, the deck is the primary gathering spot.

Breakfast is served in a small dining room. Donna's specialties are hot breads and creamy scrambled eggs with cheese.

Southard House
908 Blanco
Austin, Texas 78703
512-474-4731

Innkeepers: Jerry and Regina Southard
Accommodations: 5 rooms (all with private bath)
Rates: single, $49–$79; double, $59–$89; suite, $119–$129 suite
Included: Continental breakfast on weekdays, full breakfast on weekends; beverages available
Minimum stay: 2 nights on special Austin weekends
Added: 13% tax
Payment: Major credit cards
Children: Over 12 welcome
Pets: Not permitted
Smoking: Not permitted
Open: Year-round

On a quiet, tree-lined street just minutes from downtown Austin, Southard House is an attractive hundred-year-old Greek

Revival and Victorian structure with large, inviting front porches. Inside, it is warmly furnished with antiques and original artwork by one of the owners.

The guest rooms have white wrought-iron beds with brass accents and are covered with elegant lace bedspreads and a profusion of pillows trimmed in lace. Antique washbasins, mirrored wardrobes, clawfoot tubs, wicker chairs, ceiling fans, sheer lace curtains, and flowered wallpaper give the rooms a Victorian flavor. The Treaty Oak Room Suite has a sitting room with a sleeper sofa, a TV, refrigerator, telephone, and fireplace.

On weekends, guests can expect breakfast dishes such as Belgian waffles with raspberry sauce, eggs Benedict with chile-hollandaise sauce, and a crustless quiche. During the week Continental breakfasts consist of cereal, fresh fruit, and home-made cinnamon rolls and breads. Although generally served in the dining room (notice the dragon chandelier), the morning meal moves to the pleasant outdoor gazebo in nice weather.

Off-street parking is available free of charge, and complimentary wines, juices, and soft drinks are also served. Southard House offers Honeymoon Delight packages.

The Stagecoach Inn
Main at Chestnut
P.O. Box 339
Chappell Hill, Texas 77426
409-836-9515

Owners: Elizabeth and Harvin Moore
Accommodations: 6 rooms (shared baths), one 2-bedroom
  cottage
Rates: $90 per room
Included: Breakfast
Added: 6.25% tax
Payment: Personal check in advance
Children: Over age 5 welcome; additional charge for children
  over 12
Pets: Not permitted
Smoking: Not permitted
Open: Year-round

With fewer than 400 residents, the town of Chappell Hill, Texas, may not be large, but it is filled with history: more than twenty-five buildings wear historical markers. The most renowned is the Greek Revival stone and cedar Stagecoach Inn. Built in 1850 by Jacob and Mary Haller, the founders of Chappell Hill, it is listed on the National Register of Historic Places. The inn was maintained as a residence until 1989 and now welcomes overnight guests. It was beautifully restored and is furnished with fine antiques as well as braided rugs made by Elizabeth Moore. Guest rooms have been added to the Coach House and Weems House, which also stand on the nicely landscaped three-acre property.

Right across the street is Lottie's, a more casual B&B in a small Greek Revival house. Named for Charlotte Hargrove (Lottie was her nickname), Mary Haller's mother and owner of the Stagecoach Inn from 1851 to 1858, this cozy five-room cottage is furnished in Texas antiques and heirlooms. One bedroom has a double and a youth bed; the other has two twins. There's also a sofa bed in the living room.

Informality reigns at Lottie's. It's a good place for a vacationing family or a group of friends. The house is rented as a whole, so you can use both bedrooms as well as a living room, dining room, kitchen, and one and a half baths.

Wise Manor
312 Houston Street
Jefferson, Texas 75657
214-665-2386

Owner: Katherine R. Wise
Accommodations: 4 rooms (1 with private bath)
Rates: single or double, $55; suites, $70
Included: Breakfast

Added: 13% tax
Payment: Major credit cards
Children: Free in room with parents
Pets: Not permitted
Smoking: In designated areas only
Open: Year-round

To learn about the history of East Texas, especially the charming town of Jefferson, check into Wise Manor and settle down for a talk with the town historian, Katherine Wise. She is proud of the Texas historical marker on her Victorian peach-colored cottage, where she has lived since 1929. In the interim, she has been a significant force in the restoration effort that has transformed this tiny town into a top visitor attraction.

The entire two-story house is decorated with antiques and family memorabilia, giving it an atmosphere of charm and comfort. Guests can choose from a downstairs bedroom, whose bath has a clawfoot tub, or several upstairs rooms. Double beds are in each room; the larger room upstairs has an additional single bed and a TV.

Breakfast, featuring croissants and a fruit compote, is served family-style.

Cabins

Cabins can add a sense of adventure to a vacation. With more space than the average hotel room, they are popular with families. Most have kitchenettes or provide meals, making them even more of a bargain.

New Mexico

Los Pinos Guest Ranch
Route 3, Box 8
Tererro, New Mexico 87573
505-757-6213
505-757-6679 in off-season

Hosts: Bill and Alice McSweeney
Accommodations: 4 cabins
Rates: $80 daily or $525 weekly (individuals 14 years and older), $60 daily or $390 weekly (children ages 6–13)
Added: 6% tax
Included: All meals
Minimum stay: 2 nights
Payment: Personal checks; no credit cards
Children: No children under 6 unless with group using all cabins
Pets: Not permitted
Smoking: Outdoors only
Open: June 1 through Labor Day

If you truly want to get away, Los Pinos may suit your fancy. From Santa Fe, head east on U.S. 85 to Glorietta. Then take the road to Pecos and turn north on SR 63 to Tererro—and you're not even close. The road is dirt from here on. It follows the Pecos River (here a mountain stream) up the canyon, through forests of aspen, spruce, and fir. At Cowles (a sign tells you it's a town), go past two ponds and turn left toward Panchuella

Campground. Los Pinos is about a quarter mile up the narrow dirt trail.

Here in the Pecos Wilderness Area, you're in camping country. Los Pinos lets you enjoy the surroundings in comfort, with hearty meals and hosts who can arrange anything from fishing to exploring. This is indeed the place for seeing the country on horseback. Guided trail rides are scheduled according to the demand, with up to eight riders in a group ($25–$35 for a half day and $35–$55 for a full day).

Los Pinos is surrounded by a national forest, with mountain lakes and peaks as high as 13,000 feet. On a ride to Grass Mountain, the trail leads through aspen forests, ending at the top of the mountain with a panoramic view of the Pecos Wilderness.

Make no mistake about it—the accommodations are rustic, and therein lies the charm. Four clean and cozy log cabins, sleeping up to six, are scattered among the trees. Sit on the front porch or look out the bedroom windows to watch nature's showcase.

Meals are served in the McSweeneys' rambling old lodge. Usually guests show up ahead of time just to visit on the screened-in porch, then go inside to feast on Irish pork chops, sauerbraten, turkey, or salmon.

Other favorite pursuits are trout fishing, hiking, and just plain relaxing. The McSweeneys enjoy taking guests to nearby historic areas upon request.

Story Book Cabins
P.O. Box 472
Ruidoso, New Mexico 88345
505-257-2115

Owner: Joan Bailey
Accommodations: 10 cabins

Rates: $72–$130 depending on size (cabins sleep 2–6); reduced in some seasons
Added: 11% tax
Payment: Major credit cards
Children: Welcome
Pets: Not permitted
Smoking: Permitted
Open: Year-round

Story Book Cabins are certainly not hidden in the woods. Indeed, they are one of the many groups of cabins that line Upper Canyon Road just off Highway 70, which runs through the center of Ruidoso. But if you want a pleasant place to stay in the area, Story Book is a good choice.

The cabins have from one to three bedrooms. The interiors are cozy, with large stone fireplaces and comfortable country furnishings. The kitchens have gas ranges and full-size refrigerators. The bathrooms, while not large, are nicely decorated. There's cable TV in the sitting room, a swing or rocker on the porch, and an outdoor grill.

Only a few steps away is the Rio Ruidoso, popular for trout fishing. Ruidoso Downs is a major attraction, with thoroughbred and quarter horse racing from May through early September. During the winter, Ski Apache, 16 miles to the northwest, draws skiers of all abilities. (The ski basin has no lodgings.)

Texas

Chain-O-Lakes
P.O. Box 218
Romayor, Texas 77368
713-592-2150
713-592-7705

Owners: Jim and Beverly Smith
Accommodations: 30 cabins
Rates: $100–$130 double, each extra person $10 per night (depending upon cabin)
Added: 6% tax
Included: Breakfast and horsedrawn carriage ride
Payment: Major credit cards
Children: Under 5 free
Pets: Not permitted

Smoking: Permitted
Open: Year-round

There's a little bit of everything at Chain-O-Lakes. Campsites and a fine restaurant, pedal boats and horse-drawn carriages, a rollicking water slide and quiet nature trails—all are part of the mix.

It's the cozy log cabins, smelling of cedar and scattered among the trees, that make Chain-O-Lakes special. There's a wood-burning fireplace, antique furnishings, and maybe a loft bedroom to add to the charm. Central heating and air conditioning enhance the comfort, but the best is yet to come: in the morning, just as the mist is rising from the trees, a horse-drawn carriage arrives at your door to take you to an inn nestled in the woods where a superb breakfast awaits, prepared just for you.

Chain-O-Lakes is a series of thirteen small lakes, most connecting, set in the pine-scented woods of East Texas, 18 miles east of Cleveland. It has been a campground since the 1930s. On weekends and during the summer it is popular with campers and day visitors, who frolic on the swimming beach, go boating and fishing, and ride horses. In the mid-1980s the Smiths revitalized the campground, adding romantic cabins in the woods. Older cabins, more rustic and less atmospheric, are also part of the resort.

The Hilltop Herb Farm Restaurant and Gift Shop opened in 1987. The restaurant serves only the freshest ingredients, many of which are grown right on the farm. Sunday lunch buffets and the five-course Saturday night dinners are so popular that reservations are required.

Chain-O-Lakes' huge party barn, with food service sections, entertainment areas, and an upstairs dormitory, is excellent for groups. Conference facilities including a Challenge Course are also available for corporate retreats, seminars, and workshops.

City Stops

City hotels tend to be large, and their wide range of services and their convenience to downtown sights make them a popular choice. Many hotels offer weekday corporate rates for business travelers, and weekend packages are often the best buy in town.

Albuquerque

Barcelona Court All Suite Hotel
900 Louisiana Boulevard NE
Albuquerque, New Mexico 87110
505-255-5566
800-222-1122
Fax: 505-255-5566, ext. 6116

General manager: J.A. Rogers
Accommodations: 164 suites
Rates: single, $75; double, $85; $10 each additional person
Included: Full breakfast, afternoon cocktails
Added: 10.75% tax
Payment: Major credit cards
Children: Up to two children free in room with parents
Pets: Not permitted
Smoking: Nonsmoking rooms available
Open: Year-round

Forget all the other all-suite hotels you've seen. This one is different in both layout and atmosphere. From the outside, it's not particularly impressive, but the front doors open to a gracious lobby with Mexican tile floors, Oriental rugs, and curved staircases trimmed in wrought iron.

Once the hotel was a cluster of apartments. In 1984, the open areas were enclosed and the complex converted into a hotel, hence its sprawling nature and unusual spaces. The suites, which are larger than those in most all-suite hotels, are on the first two floors. With a southwestern decor, they're inviting and comfortable. The living rooms have a sofa bed, an easy chair with an ottoman, and a game table. The bedrooms have two queen-size or one king-size bed and a marble vanity alcove. The well-equipped kitchenette includes a microwave oven and is geared to light meals. Three telephones and two TVs add to the convenience. Four "special occasion" suites include fireplaces and whirlpools.

At the center of activity is Fountain Court, a huge, enclosed atrium. A complimentary breakfast, cooked to order, is served here, as are the free afternoon cocktails; you can invite guests to join you (no tipping is allowed). Although there is no restaurant on the premises, room service is offered through a nearby restaurant. There is also a supermarket across the street where you can shop for your own meals.

There's an indoor pool with a whirlpool and sauna, a small outdoor pool, and laundry facilities. Also available are free underground parking, free airport transportation (also to malls and restaurants Mondays through Thursdays), and valet service.

On the edge of a residential area in uptown Albuquerque, the Barcelona Court is convenient to the Coronado and Winrock shopping malls and next to the New Mexico State Fairgrounds, which has thoroughbred racing from January through May, arts and craft shows all year, and a state fair each September. The University of New Mexico is about 10 minutes away.

The Holiday Inn Pyramid
I-25 North at Paseo del Norte
5151 San Francisco Road NE
Albuquerque, New Mexico 87109-4641
505-821-3333
800-544-0623
Fax: 505-828-0230

General manager: John E. Green
Accommodations: 311 rooms
Rates: single, $86–$98; double, $86–$108; suites, $125–$275
Added: 10.75% tax
Payment: Major credit cards
Children: Under 18 free in room with parents
Pets: Permitted
Smoking: Nonsmoking floors available
Open: Year-round

Opened in 1987, the Pyramid is in the Journal Center business complex, about seven miles north of downtown. True to its name, it is a modern version of Mexico's pyramids, reflecting Albuquerque's heritage. Inside, the hotel is built around a 10-story atrium and a tiered 50-foot waterfall. The lobby is decorated with plants (unfortunately not live) and in green and rose colors, creating an outdoor feeling.

Glass elevators lead to rooms traditionally furnished in upbeat tones, such as peach and blue. The rooms range from standard to queen suites. King rooms have a king-size bed, living area, and desk; king executive rooms have larger living areas than kings; king suites have a large living-dining room, wet bar, and a separate bedroom. Deluxe suites are upgraded kings. The Presidential Suite has a large living room, a dining room, and a whirlpool. One floor has been designated as a concierge floor.

The Gallery serves American and regional cuisine ($10.95–$15.95), while the Terrace Café in the atrium offers casual dining (sandwiches and southwestern fare; $4.75–$7.50). The Pyramid Club is a contemporary dance lounge.

In addition to the small indoor-outdoor pool, there are two indoor hot tubs, a sauna, and an exercise room. Jogging trails wind through the 313-acre Journal Center. Attractive shops are off the lobby, a concierge is on duty, and parking is free. Best of all, the staff is cordial and eager to please. The hotel is owned and operated by John Q. Hammons Hotels, based locally.

The Pyramid is one of the closest hotels to the spectacular Albuquerque International Balloon Fiesta, which takes place every October. It is also a good jumping-off point for Santa Fe and points north.

Hyatt Regency Albuquerque

330 Tijeras NW
Albuquerque, New Mexico 87102
505-842-1234
800-233-1234
Fax: 505-766-6710

General manager: Ken Pilgrim
Accommodations: 396 rooms
Rates: single, $89–$135; double, $109–$155; suites, $325–$725
Added: 10.75% tax
Payment: Major credit cards
Children: Under 18 free in room with parents
Pets: Not permitted
Smoking: Nonsmoking rooms available
Open: Year-round

The 20-story Hyatt Regency opened in 1990 as part of the expansion of the Albuquerque Convention Center. The Egyptian-style hotel, topped by a pyramid, was designed as the premier luxury hotel in the downtown area. The exterior is Texas red granite, while the interior has a neoclassical flavor with geometric stained glass decorations, black Andes marble, and fanciful light fixtures. Close to half a million dollars' worth of contemporary art is displayed throughout the hotel.

The guest rooms are plush. Modern dark wood furniture and marble-topped tables make an appealing contrast to the overall lavender and silver color scheme. Clock radios, full-length mirrors, and video check-out are standard features. The rooms on the two Regency floors, with keyed access, include a Continental breakfast served in the exquisite Regency Club Lounge. The Lounge, which has a wonderful view of the city and the mountains beyond, serves evening hors d'oeuvres and cocktails to Regency floor guests.

There are two bars in the lobby, but McGrath's is the hotel's only restaurant. Although it is named for Lizzie McGrath, a well-known turn-of-the century madam whose "parlor house" stood nearby, McGrath's is strictly above board. Steak and seafood dominate the dinner menu; prices range from $11 to $19. Breakfast and lunch entrées cost $4.25–$8.95.

The Hyatt has more extensive exercise facilities than other hotels in the area; the large workout room has state-of-the-art equipment. The locker rooms have hair dryers and toiletries. There is a dry sauna and an outdoor heated swimming pool, and massages are available for $40–$53.

A concierge is on duty until 10:30 P.M., room service operates from 6 A.M. to midnight, and airport shuttle service is free. The shops adjacent to the Hyatt's lobby include a Native American art gallery and a boutique dedicated to New Mexico's favorite food—the chile pepper.

La Posada de Albuquerque
125 Second Street NW at Copper
Albuquerque, New Mexico 87102
505-242-9090
800-777-5732
Fax: 505-242-8664

General manager: Tilden L. Drinkard
Accommodations: 114 rooms
Rates: single, $75–$95; double, $85–$105; suites, $175–$250
Added: 10.75% tax

Payment: Major credit cards
Children: Under 19 free in room with parents
Pets: Not permitted
Smoking: Nonsmoking rooms available
Open: Year-round

In 1939 Conrad Hilton built his first hotel in his native New Mexico. Now restored and renamed (and no longer a Hilton), La Posada de Albuquerque is the only downtown hotel that really captures the spirit of the old Southwest. It is listed on the National Register of Historic Places. The lobby recalls colonial Mexico, with its muted lighting, arched doorways, Mexican tile floors, tin chandeliers, and tile fountain. The lobby bar is popular with residents and guests alike.

Upstairs, the guest rooms reflect their southwestern heritage with furnishings that are beautiful in their simplicity. Wooden shutters cover the windows, regional art accents the walls, and carved Mexican furniture and hammered tin light-switch covers add interest. Standard, mini-suite, and deluxe units differ primarily in size. Because of the hotel's age, the standard rooms tend to be a little smaller than the more modern ones, but all the rooms have small refrigerators.

Eulalia's has earned a reputation as one of the finest places to dine in Albuquerque, and a talented staff performs Broadway show tunes every evening. Dinner entrées ($12–$20) include roast duckling and a mixed grill of pork medallions, lamb chop, tournedo, and shrimp, each with its own sauce. The restaurant also serves breakfast and lunch, and an all-you-can-eat lunch buffet ($7.95) is served in the lobby on weekdays.

For a small daily fee, guests can visit the Executive Sports Club across the street: it has an indoor pool, racquetball courts and exercise equipment. Room service, free airport transportation, and free parking are nice extras.

Across the street from Albuquerque's convention center, La Posada is about 5 minutes from Old Town (a historic plaza now surrounded by gift shops and galleries) and 10 minutes from the University of New Mexico.

Ramada Hotel Classic
6815 Menaul NE
Albuquerque, New Mexico 87110
505-881-0000
800-2-RAMADA
Fax: 505-881-3736

General manager: Bill Caskey
Accommodations: 272 rooms and 24 suites

Rates: single, $76–$105; double, $93–$115; suites, $125–$250
Added: 10.75% tax
Payment: Major credit cards
Children: Under 18 free in room with parents; $10 additional
  if there are more than three people in the room
Pets: Permitted with approval
Smoking: Nonsmoking rooms available
Open: Year-round

From the public areas to the guest rooms, the Ramada Hotel Classic is visually pleasing. The lobby and adjoining areas— done in peach, mauve, and green—have skylights and lots of plants, creating a cool, soothing environment in Albuquerque's uptown business district. Built in the mid-1980s, this hostelry was the dream of George Maloof, an Albuquerque business- man who died soon after it opened. His portrait hangs in the entranceway.

Take time to see the ornate white pipe organ with five key- boards and twenty-seven sets of pipes. A true showpiece, it originally entertained audiences at the Roxy Theater in New York. Now it is played on Sunday mornings during brunch.

Outside, the hotel is surrounded by activity. The city's largest mall, Coronado, is across the street. Winrock Shopping Center is a half mile away, and numerous corporate addresses are within a few miles. Guests have easy access to the city yet can relax in calming surroundings.

The guest rooms have a sophisticated air. Their colors are soft and warm and their design emphasizes comfort. Extras in- clude small refrigerators, double vanities, and shower massages in the baths. The suites have deluxe whirlpools, and some king rooms have large wet bars complete with bar stools.

The Café Fennel serves all three meals. The menu runs the gamut from southwestern dishes to burgers and pasta ($3.50– $10.50 lunch or dinner), but the desserts get the most attention. The delicious pastries, pies, and cakes are so popular that the restaurant sells them to go. Try to sit in the "train" section: the cozy booths are lined up as if they're in a train, and photo- graphs of an older America pass by slowly like a passing land- scape on a moving train.

Chardonnay's is the hotel's fine restaurant, serving Conti- nental cuisine in an elegant setting of rich woods. Entrées in- clude prawns Chardonnay, lamb chops Madagascar, and Mediterranean saffron scallops ($5.95–$10.95 for lunch, $11.95– $20.50 for dinner). The hotel's nightclub, Quest Lounge, serves early evening drink specials and hors d'oeuvres and has a dance floor and live entertainment. The Lobby Bar also serves com- plimentary hors d'oeuvres during the week.

The Ramada has a small indoor heated swimming pool with an adjacent hot tub. There are dry saunas in the men's and women's locker rooms and a coed fitness room.

The Albuquerque Visitors Bureau has an office on the second floor of the hotel. Parking in the hotel lot is free, as is airport transportation.

Austin

Doubletree Hotel
6505 I-35 North
Austin, Texas 78752
512-454-3737
800-528-0444
Fax: 512-454-6915

General manager: Carl McKee
Accommodations: 335 rooms and 15 suites
Rates: single, $125; double, $145; suites, $350
Added: 13% tax
Payment: Major credit cards
Children: Free in room with parents
Pets: Not permitted
Smoking: Nonsmoking rooms available
Open: Year-round

The Doubletree, built in 1984 on the northern edge of Austin, is a charming Spanish colonial–style lodging. Its focal point is a peaceful inner courtyard with waterfalls, fountains, and a swimming pool shaped like a shell. Nearly half of its guest rooms open onto galleries overlooking the courtyard — sanctuary from the bustling city beyond.

The rooms are spacious and comfortably furnished; some have French doors opening onto small balconies. All have dressing areas next to the bathroom and bath telephones. Two styles of suites are on the Premier Floor, where guests are pampered with Continental breakfast and afternoon cocktails. All guests are treated to fresh chocolate chip cookies the night they arrive.

The second-floor fitness room has a sauna and exercise equipment, and there's an outdoor pool and whirlpool spa.

The hotel's restaurant is the plant-filled Courtyard Café, which looks out onto the garden. The menu runs from seafood to steak, and dinner entrées range from $8 to $20. Dover's

Lounge is a cozy bar with overstuffed chairs and a large stone fireplace.

Guest parking in the hotel's garage is free. Complimentary transportation is offered to both the airport and downtown Austin. And on top of the hotel is a heliport for quick arrivals and departures.

The Driskill Hotel
604 Brazos
Austin, Texas 78701
512-474-5911
800-223-0888
Fax: 512-474-2188

General manager: Mike Kolanek
Accommodations: 177 rooms and suites
Rates: single, $109–$119; double, $119–$129; suites, $200–$500
Added: 13% tax
Payment: Major credit cards
Children: Under 18 free in room with parents
Pets: Not permitted
Smoking: Nonsmoking rooms available
Open: Year-round

Built in 1886 by a Texas cattle baron, the Driskill is an architectural treasure, with an immense arched entrance and ornamented balconies. Its history is intertwined with that of the Lone Star State.

Walk through its doors and you know you're in Texas. Above the registration desk hangs a portrait of Colonel Jesse L. Driskill, watching over his creation. Behind it is an expansive painting of the Texas range. Overlooking the lobby is a massive bronze sculpture depicting a dramatic moment in the lives of two cowboys. Portraits of the state's governors line the walls of the handsome lobby bar, and LBJ often made the hotel his campaign headquarters.

Throughout the hotel there's a feeling of openness and space, a fitting style for a hostelry that is Texas to the core. The guest rooms occupy two connecting buildings: the 1880s hotel, with high ceilings and several room configurations, and the 1930s tower, with lower ceilings and a more uniform room design.

All the rooms are spacious and tastefully decorated, with touches of grandeur such as wall border designs and crystal drawer pulls on the period furniture. The baths in the tower rooms have an adjacent dressing area.

One of the hotel's banquet rooms is designed around eight mirrors framed in gold leaf—the wedding gift of Mexico's Maximilian to his bride, the Empress Carlotta of Belgium. At the top of each mirror is a gilt medallion likeness of the empress, said to be the most beautiful woman in Europe.

Guests may use a health club across the street whose facilities include a workout area with Universal and Nautilus equipment, racquetball courts, a lap pool, a whirlpool, and a sauna.

The Driskill Dining Room, romantically decorated with mirrors and a carved white ceiling, serves nouvelle American cuisine with a southwestern bent.

In the heart of downtown Austin, the Driskill opens onto Sixth Street, a lively entertainment area with restaurants, bars, and specialty shops. Sightseeing trolleys stop right in front of the hotel. The Driskill is also just a few blocks from the capitol and the University of Texas.

Four Seasons Hotel Austin

99 San Jacinto Boulevard
Austin, Texas 78701
512-478-4500
800-332-3442
Fax: 512-477-0704

General manager: Tom Kelly
Accommodations: 292 units
Rates: single, $148–$168; double, $168–$190; suites start at $200
Added: 13% tax
Payment: Major credit cards
Children: Free in room with parents
Pets: Small ones on leash permitted
Smoking: Nonsmoking rooms available
Open: Year-round

On the shores of Town Lake, ten blocks south of the capitol, the Four Seasons Austin is a first-class hotel with a southwestern flair. It opened in 1987, setting a new standard for downtown lodgings.

Outside the entrance, lifelike statues of a gardener bending over a flowerbed, a fresh pot of flowers in his hand, and a businessman absorbed by the daily newspaper (and it will be that day's paper) warrant a second look. The lobby, with a stone fireplace and leather chairs, suggests the home of a wealthy Hill Country rancher instead of a city hotel. Southwestern art, tastefully arranged, adds to the residential feeling.

Luxury is the tone here—extra touches include terrycloth robes and hair dryers, pressing within the hour, and twice-daily maid service. More important, the staff is genuinely friendly and eager to please. The guest rooms are attractive, decorated in soft earth tones. Although not especially large, they bespeak comfort with such conveniences as three phones and digital clocks. Four Seasons rooms are more like suites than standard hotel rooms.

The hotel's lakeside setting is used to full advantage; it's so serene, it's like being in a private park. Whether you're eating in the café, lounging by the pool, or working out in the health club, the lake is the focal point. Jogging trails line its banks. The health club is far above average, with good exercise equipment, nicely appointed locker rooms, saunas, and a whirlpool.

The Riverside Café, at lake level, serves new American cuisine with southwestern and Cajun influences. There's an emphasis on robust sauces, freshness, and innovative combinations. Dinner entrées range from $15.50 to $22.50. Lunch buffets are served upstairs in the Lobby Lounge.

Self-service parking is free; valet parking is also available at $8 per day.

Stouffer Austin Hotel
9721 Arboretum Boulevard
Austin, Texas 78759
512-343-2626
800-HOTELS-1
Fax: 512-346-7953

General manager: Jacques Van Seters
Accommodations: 478 units
Rates: single, $99–$169; double, $99–$189; suites start at $195
Added: 13% tax
Payment: Major credit cards
Children: Free in room with parents
Pets: Not permitted
Smoking: Nonsmoking rooms available
Open: Year-round

In the rolling countryside north of downtown, 15 minutes from the capitol, the Stouffer Austin is a retreat from the city yet near many business addresses, notably the high-tech companies for which Austin is now known. The hotel is part of the Arboretum, a 95-acre development with fancy shops and restaurants as well as sleek office towers. The entire complex sits on a hillside overlooking the Texas Hill Country, with its cedar forests and limestone cliffs.

An atrium-style hotel, the Stouffer has a distinctive look. At its center is an expansive marble plaza with sculptures, dining kiosks, and sitting areas. Large teak bells hang from above while bronze birds, remarkably lifelike, appear to soar overhead. Natural plants surround the atrium on every level.

The Pavilion, in the center of the atrium, serves deli sandwiches, salads, fruit, pastries, and beverages around the clock. The Garden Café serves breakfast and lunch, with a pianist to entertain at noontime. On one side is the Trattoria Grande, a northern Italian bistro with excellent food and service with a flair. Arched windows offer unobstructed views of the scenic terrain. The lobby bar has live entertainment in the evenings.

The guest rooms, decorated in subtle greens and beiges with Queen Anne furniture and Oriental art, are luxurious and large (some of the largest in the city). Many of the rooms have pastoral valley views. Atrium suites have small balconies opening onto the atrium, mini-bars, and separate sitting areas. Conference suites have beds that fold out of sight so that meetings can be held at the suite's own boardroom table. Guests on the private access Club Floor enjoy concierge services from 6:30 A.M. to 10:00 P.M., complimentary breakfast, evening hors d'oeuvres, a lounge bar, and bathrobes and shoe polishers in their rooms.

For luxury, the Presidential Suite is truly royal. Chinese palace lions guard the entrance. Inside, giant Oriental vases hold citrus and palm trees, original oils line the walls, and expansive windows provide a fine view. There's a full kitchen and a separate dining room seating ten, but perhaps the most sumptuous room of all is the bath. A small Sony complete with microcassette recorder lets you watch your favorite program or dictate notes from the double Jacuzzi tub set in marble. The fixtures are all brass, and the antique satin-lined wooden vanity case, fully stocked, adds a special touch.

All guests are treated to complimentary coffee, a newspaper, and the daily weather report with their wake-up call. Other amenities include 24-hour room service, free parking, and free transportation to the airport, about 20 minutes away. Valet parking is available at the cost of $7 per day.

For relaxation, there's an especially wide range of choices for a city hotel—an oval outdoor pool (with an appealing hillside setting), an indoor pool, a sauna, hot tub, game room, well-equipped exercise room, jogging path, short nature trail, and picnic tables tucked among the trees. A separate elevator takes guests to the pool area; both pools are heated.

Next door are the Arboretum shops (several cuts above average, from Banana Republic to fancy boutiques), a four-screen movie theater, and the hotel's club, Tangerines.

Wyndham Austin Hotel at Southpark
4140 Governor's Row
(I-35 and Ben White Boulevard)
Austin, Texas 78744
512-448-2222
800-433-2241
Fax: 512-448-4744

General manager: Dave Hansen
Accommodations: 313 rooms and suites
Rates: single, $119; double, $129; suites start at $350
Added: 13% tax
Payment: Major credit cards
Children: Under 18 free in room with parents
Pets: Permitted with deposit
Smoking: 66 nonsmoking rooms
Open: Year-round

South of downtown Austin, the Wyndham Austin Hotel has a relaxing atmosphere, outstanding recreational features, and a hospitable staff.

The 14-story hotel, opened in 1983, has a contemporary design. Just outside the lobby is a Texas-size indoor-outdoor pool (shaped like a horseshoe) and recreation area. A bridge leads across the pool into the fitness center, with its attractive deck area, whirlpool, sauna, and weight and exercise room. Nearby is the hotel's sports court (basketball or volleyball), jogging track, and shuffleboard.

The rooms have luxurious, modern furnishings—rich fabrics, plush carpeting, and colorful artwork. Comfortable seating, TVs with in-house movies, and digital clock radios add to the pleasure. Some of the ground-floor rooms open out onto the pool. The Executive suites have a parlor with a conference table, a sitting area with a foldout bed, and one or two connecting bedrooms. Both the Presidential and the Governor's suites have a large parlor and two bedrooms; the former has a whirlpool tub.

Onion Creek Grill, a casual dining room, has all-day service. Pasta and pizza are featured, as well as steak and seafood. Sweetwaters Lounge is the hotel's friendly bar.

Airport transportation and hotel parking are free.

Corpus Christi

Corpus Christi Marriott Bayfront
900 North Shoreline
Corpus Christi, Texas 78401
512-887-1600
800-874-4585 in Texas
800-228-9290 in U.S.
Fax: 512-883-8084

General manager: Todd Scartozzi
Accommodations: 474 rooms
Rates: single, $90–$120; double, $90–$140; suites, $140–$320
Added: 13% tax
Payment: Major credit cards
Children: Under 17 free in room with parents
Pets: Not permitted
Smoking: Nonsmoking rooms available
Open: Year-round

There's nothing remarkable about the Marriott from the outside—it's sleek and modern, a white 19-story rectangle juxtaposed against the blue bay beyond. But inside it's a beehive of activity. Catering to both business travelers and family groups, there always seems to be something happening here.

Opened in 1985, the hotel was originally a Hershey Hotel and is now part of the Marriott hotel chain. The new management has retained some of its predecessor's traditions, for example, the Marriott holds a Chocolate Festival in December, with chocolate buffets, demonstrations, and exhibitions.

The hotel recognizes the bayside setting, and the colors and designs tend to bring the outdoors in. The newly renovated guest rooms are angled to have a glimpse of Corpus Christi Bay, and are furnished in teal green with traditional furniture, two queen beds (some have a king-size bed), cable TV, and clock radios.

Reflections Restaurant, on the hotel's top floor, has several levels, so each table has an unobstructed view of the bay. Naturally, seafood dishes dominate the menu, and dinner entrées range from $13 to $18. The High Tide is the Marriott's own comedy club; it has two shows on Friday and Saturday nights and one show on Tuesday, Wednesday, and Thursday nights.

In the second-floor recreational area there's a large whirlpool, Ping-Pong table, weight room, racquetball courts, a sunbathing deck, and indoor and outdoor pools. You can rent bikes, jet skis, Sunfish, and fishing equipment at the marina, three blocks away.

Self-parking in the hotel's covered garage is free; valet parking is $7. Trolleys connect the hotel to shopping centers and area tourist attractions. Downtown Corpus Christi and the exclusive homes along Ocean Drive are just a few minutes away.

Dallas

The Adolphus
1321 Commerce
Dallas, Texas 75202
214-742-8200
800-441-0574 in Texas
800-221-9083 in U.S.
Fax: 214-747-3532

Managing director: Garvin O'Neil
Accommodations: 431 rooms and suites
Rates: single, $156–$220; double, $176–$240; suites, $350–$1,150; weekend packages
Added: 13% tax
Payment: Major credit cards
Children: Welcome
Pets: Not permitted
Smoking: Nonsmoking rooms available
Open: Year-round

Built in 1912 by the beer baron Adolphus Busch, Dallas's grand and glorious landmark hotel was totally renovated in 1981, combining the grandeur of an earlier era with the comforts of a modern luxury hotel.

The exterior is an extravagance of ornamentation—sculptures, bas-relief figures, gargoyles, heraldic characters, even a corner turret shaped like a beer stein. The interior is opulent, with a wealth of antiques from Europe and Asia as well as the United States. The public areas are like a museum and include two huge 1660s Flemish tapestries, a six-foot-tall portrait of Napoleon in coronation robes, and carved English Regency oak furniture.

The centerpiece of the Adolphus is the French Room, a dining room with a vaulted ceiling, columned walls, and rococo murals. On the ceiling, cherubs holding floral garlands fly beneath a pale blue sky.

Unlike those in new hotels, the guest rooms here come in more than thirty configurations. Retaining their original high ceilings, they are warm yet elegant, decorated in reproduction antique furniture, matching draperies and bedspreads, and touches of lace. All the rooms have refrigerators, multiple phones, and TVs in armoires. Down comforters and terrycloth robes add an extra touch of luxury.

Terrace suites have an expansive sitting area, two baths, and a large terrace. Skylight suites, on the nineteenth floor, have slanting glass exterior walls, a large wet bar, and Asian accents mingled with reproduction period furniture. Club Adolphus rooms, on the top three floors of the hotel, are geared towards the corporate traveler. Guests staying in Club Adolphus rooms have exclusive access to the hotel's penthouse suite, once Mr. Busch's own private residence, now staffed with its own concierge and outfitted with business machines such as a fax, credit card phone, typewriter, and personal computer.

Oriented to service, the Adolphus has a concierge, multilingual staff, 24-hour room service, and valet parking ($10). Dining choices include the French Room, which serves dinner only (entrées start at $22; prix fixe dinners, $48.50), the Bistro, which serves Continental fare in a country French decor (all three meals and a late evening supper), the Lobby Living Room, serving afternoon tea and cocktails and offering evening entertainment, and the Walt Garrison Rodeo Bar, serving lunch and cocktails.

For light workouts the Adolphus has a fitness room with treadmills, stair machines, a stationary bicycle, rowing machine and free weights. Guests in need of more extensive athletic facilities can use the Texas Club a block away. The Club has an indoor lap pool, racquetball, squash, an indoor track, a gym, Nautilus equipment, and a steam room. The guest use fee at the Club is $10 per day.

The Aristocrat
1933 Main Street
Dallas, Texas 75201
214-741-7700
800-231-4235
Fax: 214-939-3639

General manager: Chuck Church
Accommodations: 173 units
Rates: single, $95–$150; double, $105–$160
Included: Continental breakfast

Added: 13.25% tax
Payment: Major credit cards
Children: Under 18 free in room with parents
Pets: Small pets only
Smoking: Nonsmoking rooms available
Open: Year-round

A chic downtown hotel, the Aristocrat is personable, cozy, smartly decorated, and convenient, designed especially for the corporate traveler. Through an extensive skywalk and tunnel system, it's linked to ten or so office buildings. The historic Majestic Theater, home of the Dallas Ballet and Opera, is around the corner, and the Dallas Museum of Art is within walking distance.

Built in 1925 by Conrad Hilton, it was the first hotel to bear his name. Since the nearby Adolphus was already the recognized luxury hotel in town, Hilton designed a no-frills property for traveling salesmen. In 1938 Hilton sold the hotel, and over the years it declined. In late 1985, under the guidance of the Texas Historical Commission, it was restored and emerged as the Aristocrat, a gem well worth discovering. Most of its accommodations are luxurious suites, formed by combining pairs of the original rooms. Architectural features such as ornate trim and ceiling plaster were preserved, as were the public areas, decorated with wood paneling, etched glass, and period furnishings.

The intimate suites have cherry furniture, sophisticated colors and fabrics, and lots of amenities, creating a feeling of warmth. Each one has queen-size beds, a small refrigerator, remote control TV, three phones (one in the bath), and a separate vanity area.

The Aristocrat Bar and Grill is the hotel's pleasant dining spot, serving full breakfasts, lunch, dinner, and late evening snacks. It features dishes cooked over a mesquite grill and fresh pastas (dinner entrées range from $9.95–$21.95), and varietal wine by the glass, espresso, cappuccino, and premium liquors. Room service is also available. Complimentary Continental breakfast is served in the cozy Club Room downstairs.

Parking in a covered garage across the street is free—a real advantage in downtown Dallas. Valet parking is not offered.

Fairmont Hotel
1717 North Akard Street
Dallas, Texas 75201
214-720-2020
800-527-4727
Fax: 214-720-5282

General manager: Ray Tackaberry
Accommodations: 551 rooms including 51 suites
Rates: single, $125–$215; double, $150–$240; suites,
   $325–$1,000
Added: 13% tax
Payment: Major credit cards
Children: Welcome
Pets: Seeing eye and hearing dogs only
Smoking: Nonsmoking rooms available
Open: Year-round

The Fairmont is a sophisticated downtown hotel next to the Dallas Arts District. A new Texas marble exterior is just one of the changes made in the 1989 multimillion-dollar renovation. With sweeping public areas and one of the best-known restaurants in town, it is an excellent base when visiting the city of Dallas.

The lobby lounge is dominated by stunning floral arrangements and an eye-catching contemporary work of art celebrating Cabeza de Vaca, the first European to see the interior of Texas, New Mexico, and Arizona. The Pyramid Lounge, also distinctive, has a bright mural depicting events and figures of the 1960s. The Venetian Room is especially dramatic, with slate-colored walls, red chairs, wall sconces, and Spanish arches. Once a supper club, the room now serves an abundant Sunday brunch in a gondola buffet. Pancakes Oscar, its hallmark dish — buckwheat pancakes sprinkled with brown sugar, covered in meringue, and topped with a strawberry sauce — will satisfy the sweetest of sweet tooths.

But it's the Pyramid restaurant, with its intimate settings and award-winning cuisine, that draws the most attention. Entrées, from $19 to $27, include grilled rack of lamb with crab flan and curry Sabayon; roast maple leaf duck with essensia wine, orange peel, and black beans; and grilled Dover sole with citrus compote and black chanterelle mushrooms. A harpist adds to the ambience, and a Spanish guitarist entertains in the late evenings.

The guest rooms are in two towers. The furnishings are attractive, with such luxuries as down pillows and Irish linens. Amenities include round-the-clock room service, nightly turndown, and twice-daily housekeeping.

The sunny Brasserie restaurant is open 24 hours a day. There is also a sports bar that serves deli lunches on weekdays and is decorated with sports paraphernalia lent by hotel employees. The Olympic-size pool and surrounding patio is big enough to satisfy the needs of such a large hotel, and the views of downtown Dallas from the pool deck are terrific. Guests can also use the facilities at the YMCA, next door.

Valet parking is $12 per day.

The Grand Kempinski Dallas

15201 Dallas Parkway
Dallas, Texas 75248
214-386-6000
800-426-3135
Telex: 795515
Fax: 214-386-6937

Managing director: Michael Spamer
Accommodations: 529 rooms and suites
Rooms: single or double, $125–$145; suites, $250–$1,200
Added: 13% tax
Payment: Major credit cards
Children: Free in room with parents
Pets: Not permitted
Smoking: Nonsmoking rooms available
Open: Year-round

In 1987 Kempinski Hotels, a West German luxury hotel chain, took over this modern property, its first venture in North America. Actually in Addison, about 15 minutes north of central Dallas, the Grand Kempinski has a spacious feeling that most downtown hotels can't achieve. A glass atrium adds to the lofty quality, while Italian marble throughout provides elegance.

With 37 suites (18 on two levels) and a concierge floor in addition to the standard rooms, there are plenty of choices. The rooms, with French provincial, English country, or Oriental furnishings, all have a decidedly masculine air. Special touches include turndown service, fresh flowers, and telephones in the bathrooms.

Not to be missed on a Sunday morning is the champagne brunch in the Malachite Showroom. The vibrant green and black surroundings are striking and sumptuous. The brunch runs about $21 for adults, $13 for children under 12.

Monte Carlo is the hotel's fine restaurant. With silk bougainvillea vines overhead and mosaic floors, it has a Mediterranean bistro flavor. Crab and spinach lasagna with crustacean sauce and boneless quails stuffed with spinach and mushrooms in a pastry are examples of the creative fare. Dinner entrées range from $20 to $25, while the restaurant's brasserie serves lighter meals at lighter prices.

Le Café also offers a pleasant atmosphere and inventive menu. A rose on every table compliments the rose and green decor. The dinner menu includes pecan smoked shrimp salad ($12.50) and sirloin chablisienne with white wine mirepoix and shallot sauce ($14.50). English teas are served in the Bristol Lounge, and the Atrium Bar has a piano player and complimentary hors d'oeuvres in the evening.

After dinner you can dance the night away in Kempi's, the hotel's nightclub, complete with neon lights and a fog system. If the dancing doesn't burn off enough calories, there are four lighted tennis courts, two racquetball courts, two heated pools with adjoining hot tubs—one inside, one outside—and a fitness club.

Concierge, laundry, dry cleaning, telex, and fax and room services are available 24 hours a day. The hotel also offers an executive business center—secretarial support, complimentary limousine service within three miles of the hotel, and free transportation to the nearby Galleria mall. Valet parking is $7; self-parking in a covered lot is free.

Hotel Crescent Court

400 Crescent Court
Dallas, Texas 75201
214-871-3200
800-654-6541
Fax: 214-871-3272

Managing director: Seamus McManus
Accommodations: 188 rooms and 28 suites
Rates: single, $220–$310; double, $250–$340; suites,
    $425–$1,250
Added: 13% tax
Payment: Major credit cards
Children: Free in room with parents
Pets: With approval
Smoking: Nonsmoking rooms available
Open: Year-round

Opened in late 1985, the Crescent Court is a Rosewood Hotel, a sister property to the Mansion on Turtle Creek, a mile up the road, and the Bel Air in California. Unlike the other Rosewoods, however, this hotel is designed for the business traveler. But even if you're in Dallas just for pleasure, it is a hotel well worth discovering.

Although its architect, Philip Johnson, was inspired by the Royal Crescent in Bath, England, the Crescent Court, with its light gray exterior and mansard roof, bears a more remarkable resemblance to a Loire Valley château. Inside you are treated like the château's lord; the ever-dutiful staff seem to appear magically just when you need them, then discreetly fade and let you have the run of the manor in peace.

Staying here is an immersion in beauty. Every sense is stimulated from the time you enter the lobby, which is adorned with arched windows, Spanish and Italian marble floors, Louis XV furnishings and European art, massive floral arrangements and airy palms. In the background is classical music. The bellman, the desk clerk, and the concierge are more than attentive. Soon you've forgotten the traffic and daily hassle. You can relax. Somebody else will take care of everything.

Make no mistake, however; this is not a retreat. Indeed, there's a vibrancy about the place, a mood that flows from the lobby to the restaurant to the courtyard beyond. The Beau Nash restaurant and bar, named for the arbiter of taste in 18th-century England, is done in hunter green marble with floral motifs. It has a lively bistro atmosphere and excellent food—southwestern and California cuisine dominate—and is popular with residents as well as guests. Prices run about $6.50 for breakfast, $9–$12 for lunch, and $12–$16 for dinner.

In 1990 the hotel opened the Conservatory, an elegant dining room. Entrées include grilled sea bass with sorrel sea urchin sauce, roast Peking duck with sun-dried cherries, and grilled shrimp with lobster sauce and lemon fettuccine. For special occasions, the hotel's wine cellar can be rented by parties of up to sixteen people. Seated under arched brick ceilings and surrounded by hundreds of vintage wines, a candlelit dinner here can be memorable.

The guest rooms are just as beautiful as the public areas. With a residential feeling, they're spacious and aesthetically pleasing in subtle pastels and rich earth tones. French windows open to a view of the courtyard below. The furnishings are comfortably elegant—easy chairs and sofas with down cushions, armoire desks, and original works of art.

Above all, it is attention to detail that sets this hotel apart. In your room, expect fresh flowers, three phones, the newspaper daily, hooded terrycloth robes, and brass and marble fixtures in the bathroom. Some suites have wet bars and refrigerators. If you want to be truly pampered, a maid will unpack your luggage. When you need a hem repaired, a seamstress will help. Laundry comes back in a lined wicker basket. Turndown service includes a fresh orchid on your pillow and the weather report for the following day.

The hotel is part of a mixed-use project called the Crescent. Off the lobby, a courtyard leads to a three-level marketplace of chic shops and galleries. On the other side of the hotel are three 18-story office towers.

The Spa at the Crescent, a luxurious private health and fitness club, is also part of the complex. Rose marble floors surround the whirlpools, and there are plush sofas in the locker room. The wooden lockers are so well equipped—including designer workout clothes—that guests need only bring their athletic shoes. European treatments are combined with America's zest for fitness. Beauty treatments, water therapy and massage, exercise facilities, and nutrition are all included. The Spa also has a Food and Juice Bar, with naturally healthy lunches and snacks.

Hotel guests can use the workout area for $20 per day and, for an additional $20, can work with a private trainer. Wet area usage is $25. A one-hour European facial is $60. Packages for several days' stay are also available. The hotel's outdoor swimming pool is separate from the spa, and is free to all guests.

The Crescent Court complex stands on a hilltop on the north side of the city. Between the hotel and Dallas's almost futuristic downtown skyline lies the West End Historical District. The hotel is also near the Arts District and Dallas Market Center. D/FW International Airport is a 20-minute drive, while Love Field is only 10 minutes away. There is free transportation to the downtown business district aboard the Crescent Trolley on weekdays.

Loews Anatole Hotel

2201 Stemmons Freeway
Dallas, Texas 75207
214-748-1200
800-23-LOEWS
Fax: 214-761-7520

Managing director: John Thacker
Accommodations: 1,620 units
Rates: single, $135–$145; double, $160–170; suites, $250–$1,150
Added: 13% tax
Payment: Major credit cards
Children: Under 18 free in room with parents
Pets: Not permitted
Smoking: Nonsmoking rooms available
Open: Year-round

Loews Anatole is the kind of hotel in which you need a map to get around. Spread over 45 acres, it's a city unto itself, with nine restaurants, eight lounges, more than a dozen shops, and a huge health spa. Downtown Dallas is about a 5-minute drive away.

The largest hotel in the Southwest, the Anatole is primarily geared to conventions. But groups of all sizes as well as individuals can enjoy its many services. It's worth a stop just to see the public areas. Parking is free, so at least pull off Stemmons Freeway and take a look. Two enormous elephants, carved from monkey pod wood by entire villages in Thailand, stand guard inside the tower section. Behind them is an 18th-century white marble Hindustani pavilion, originally from a royal palace in India. Inside Atrium II hang five fantastic batik banners, created in Ceylon especially for the hotel. The Jade Room, used for receptions, has a magnificent collection of jade artistry. Outside the Wedgwood Ballroom, with its collection of pieces dating from the 18th century, is a rare Wedgwood vase nearly five feet tall. And so the collection continues — much of it inspired by Trammell Crow, who developed the hotel as well as the innovative Infomart across the freeway.

Behind the hotel in a southern mansion–style building is the Verandah Club, a health spa with indoor and outdoor jogging tracks; indoor and outdoor pools; tennis, racquetball, and squash courts; a full-size basketball court; exercise rooms; and a sauna, steam room, and whirlpool section. A private club, Verandah, is available to guests for about $12 a day. Extra fees are charged for racquetball. Outdoor swimming is free.

The guest rooms are in two atrium high-rises and a 27-story tower. The traditional furnishings are comfortable if not distinctive. The 70 tower suites have small parlors and elegant baths (marble vanities, phones, extra amenities). A variety of other suites are also available. Two concierge floors provide Continental breakfast, afternoon wine and cheese, and a full-time concierge.

One can dine at the Anatole at any hour of the day. There are eight restaurants on the premises; several are open 24 hours. Room service is also available around the clock.

The Mansion on Turtle Creek
2821 Turtle Creek Boulevard
Dallas, Texas 75219
214-559-2100
800-527-5432
Fax: 214-528-4187

Managing director: Jeff Trigger
Accommodations: 142 rooms and suites
Rates: single; $215–$305; double, $255–$345; suites, $685–$1,200
Added: 13% tax
Payment: Major credit cards
Children: $40 extra in room with parents
Pets: Not permitted
Smoking: Permitted
Open: Year-round

The only problem with staying at the Mansion is that it spoils you for staying anywhere else. It's a world of quiet opulence—a combination of aesthetic beauty and attentive service. Beginning at registration, guests' preferences for everything from newspapers to wine are noted and attended to, with records filed for future visits. Best of all, the staff's hospitality seems genuine.

The hotel is indeed a mansion, once the home of the millionaire Sheppard King, set on a terraced hillside in one of Dallas's most prestigious residential areas. Built in 1925, it has a 16th-century Italianate design with imaginative spires and turrets. In 1981 Rosewood Hotels restored the original building, converting it into a fine restaurant and building a complementary hotel tower next door.

At this hotel the concierge wears a suit, not a uniform. There are no shops off the lobby, no hints of the commercial world. Instead, there's soft music, handsomely arranged fresh flowers, and a bevy of employees (more than two staff members for every guest) to satisfy every whim. The lobby resembles a fine living room, accented with antique mirrors and a Chippendale breakfront.

The guest rooms are exquisite. Decorated in peach, gold, or beige, they have four-poster beds, overstuffed chairs with ottomans, love seats, armoires with TVs, and French doors opening onto small balconies. (Although the rooms are all the same size, they cost more on the upper floors because of the view.) The bathrooms are not only luxurious but pleasing to the eye, decorated in marble and brass. Terry robes, bathroom telephones, and turndown service add to the feeling of luxury. In the evening, a special treat is delivered, perhaps spice tea or cookies and milk. Other courtesies include overnight shoeshine and 24-hour pressing and room service.

Three guest rooms open onto the hotel's attractive pool, which is heated in cooler weather. Guests also have complimentary use of a nearby health club, with transportation provided.

One of the highlights of staying at the Mansion is dining at its restaurant, an architectural treasure as well as a culinary delight. Much of the grandeur of the original home, such as carved fireplaces and imported marble floors, has been retained in its restoration. A dramatic wrought-iron staircase spirals up from the foyer. The ceiling of the main dining room is a composite of 2,400 pieces of enameled and inlaid wood. A set of stained glass windows depicts British barons signing the Magna Carta, and two pairs of early 19th-century Spanish cathedral doors lead to one of the dining areas.

The cuisine does justice to its surroundings. Nouvelle American dishes with a southwestern flair are well-prepared and attractively presented. Rack of lamb roasted with rosemary and mustard sauce, Louisiana crabcakes, and lobster tacos are popular favorites. The service is polished but unpretentious. Elaborate weekend brunches are popular with residents as well as hotel guests.

Like its sister hotel, the Crescent Court, the Mansion has a wine cellar, stocked with over 28,000 bottles of vintage wine, that seats up to twelve for guests' private dinner parties. Breakfast and lunch are served in the cheerful Promenade.

About 5 minutes from downtown Dallas, the Mansion is near many business, cultural, and shopping areas. D/FW International Airport is a 30-minute drive. Valet parking costs $10.85; there is no self-parking.

Omni Melrose Hotel

3015 Oak Lawn
Dallas, Texas 75219
214-521-5151
800-843-6664
Fax: 214-521-5151

General manager: H. L. Yates
Accommodations: 184 rooms
Rates: single, $120; double, $135; suites, $135–$250
Added: 13% tax
Payment: Major credit cards
Children: Free in room with parents
Pets: Not permitted
Smoking: Nonsmoking rooms available
Open: Year-round

The Melrose opened in 1924 as an apartment hotel. Restored in 1982, it is now a small luxury hotel with real warmth. Recalling another era, it has tall arched windows and stately white columns.

Since the guest rooms were once apartments, they are more spacious than usual, and each room is different, both in size and decor. All are truly charming, furnished with antique reproductions. Four-poster beds, overstuffed chairs, and dressing tables with stools set the tone. The beds have comforters and ruffles. The concierge level provides Continental breakfast as well as turndown service with milk and cookies.

The Landmark Café has a splendid art deco setting. Its enticing menu features such dishes as roast breast of duck with pecan truffle stuffing, served with scallions and plum wine sauce, and Cajun seasoned trout blackened and served with lime and fresh chive butter and New Orleans crawfish cream sauce. Entrées run from $15 to $24. The elegant but cozy Library Bar, doubling as a piano bar, serves lunch and late evening fare.

In the Oak Lawn area north of downtown, the hotel is near the West End Marketplace, the Arts District, Dallas Market Center, and the central business district. Hotel parking is free. Complimentary transportation is available to Love Field.

The Stoneleigh
2927 Maple Avenue
Dallas, Texas 75201
214-871-7111
800-336-4242 in Texas
800-255-9299 in U.S.
Fax: 214-871-9379

General manager: Gary Bruton
Accommodations: 158 rooms
Rates: single, $130–$165; double, $145–$180; suites, $195–$395
Added: 13% tax
Payment: Major credit cards
Children: Free in room with parents
Pets: Permitted with deposit
Smoking: Nonsmoking rooms available
Open: Year-round

This hotel is a gem, hidden in a residential neighborhood on the edge of the prestigious Turtle Creek area. In 1923, the 11-story Stoneleigh opened as a hostelry of distinction. While its doors never closed in the following decades, it definitely declined. Then, in the late 1980s, the Stoneleigh was gloriously reborn, with refurbished interiors, an exterior facelift, and a renewed emphasis on service. Now classical music plays in the background, and antique furniture, marble columns, and fresh flowers grace the lobby.

The beautiful, individually decorated guest rooms, in different shapes and sizes, have armoires, chintz-covered overstuffed chairs, matching drapes and bedspreads, and brass light fixtures. Some suites have kitchens.

In the morning there's a paper at the door. Maid service is twice a day, and the nightly turndown service includes fancy chocolates. Room service is available around the clock, and a concierge meets special requests.

Ewald's serves all three meals, with seafood and Continental dishes the dinner highlights; prices run from $13 to $22. The cozy Lion's Den Lounge serves cocktails, lunch, and appetizers.

The Stoneleigh has excellent recreational facilities. The apartment building next door, also restored, is owned by the same family, and on its grounds a beautiful shaded pool and tennis courts are hidden in a gardenlike setting. There's also a wonderful rock garden and lily pond—a tranquil spot seemingly far from the city beyond.

Stouffer Dallas Hotel
2222 Stemmons Freeway
Dallas, Texas 75207
214-631-2222
800-HOTELS-1
Fax: 214-634-9319

General manager: John R. Fleming
Accommodations: 540 rooms
Rates: single, $134–$179; double, $154–$199
Added: 13% tax
Payment: Major credit cards
Children: Free in room with parents
Pets: With approval
Smoking: Nonsmoking rooms available
Open: Year-round

The Stouffer Dallas is a sleek, 30-story pink ellipse, distinctive in its architecture and its service. A wide spiral staircase winds from the center of the lobby to the mezzanine, flanked by a spectacular curved chandelier that is reputedly the longest in the world (140 feet long, with 7,500 Italian crystals). Works of art from the Orient add aesthetic interest.

But distinctive architecture and art alone do not make a hotel great. Indeed, it's the people at Stouffer Dallas that make it special. Throughout the hotel, the staff members are hospitable and attentive, making you feel that they're glad you're here. Despite its size, the hotel feels intimate. The public areas are small—almost residential in style. The Bay Tree Restaurant is cozy and elegant. The Charisma Café is casual, serving all three meals.

The guests are primarily business travelers, for Dallas Market Center, the largest wholesale merchandise market in the world, is next door. Infomart, the country's first information processing mart, is also part of the complex. Downtown Dallas is about a 5-minute drive.

The guest rooms are refreshingly different, with an Oriental theme. For example, one king-size room is decorated in jade green, Oriental prints, and an apricot-colored lamp. The compartmental bathrooms are also well decorated.

On top of the hotel there's an outdoor pool and a health club with exercise equipment, a whirlpool, sauna, and steam room. With a wake-up call you get coffee and a morning paper brought to your door. Self-parking is free—an important extra in this metropolitan area. Valet parking is $8.

The Westin Hotel Galleria Dallas
13340 Dallas Parkway at LBJ Freeway
Dallas, Texas 75240
214-934-9494
800-228-3000
Fax: 214-851-2869

General manager: Steve Bullock
Accommodations: 431 rooms and suites
Rates: single, $175–$195; double, $200–$220; Executive Club
  level, $230–$250; suites, $375–$1,275
Added: 13% tax
Payment: Major credit cards
Children: Welcome
Pets: With approval
Smoking: Permitted
Open: Year-round

The 21-story Westin Dallas is sparkling and lively. In north
Dallas, it adjoins the Galleria, a sophisticated shopping and
entertainment mall with Macy's, Saks Fifth Avenue, Marshall
Field's, Tiffany's, and many other specialty shops, restaurants,
and cinemas. At the center of activity, an ice skating rink adds to
the festive atmosphere.

Zucchini's Café, next to the Galleria and overlooking the
skating rink, is informal. Huntington's features fine Continental cuisine. Lighter fare is served in Options, and the Lobby
Court serves cocktails daily.

There is a half mile rooftop jogging track and a small outdoor pool at the hotel. Guests can use the University Health
Club, in the Galleria complex, for a small fee.

The guest rooms are appointed with traditional furnishings.
The Executive Club level offers special features in the rooms,
such as hair dryers, makeup mirrors, and valet steamers. Other
services include a concierge and valet parking ($10). Self-
parking is free and ample.

El Paso

El Paso Airport Hilton
2027 Airway Boulevard
El Paso, Texas 79925
915-778-4241
800-284-4837
Fax: 915-772-6871

General manager: Rich Cane
Accommodations: 272 rooms
Rates: single, $83–$85; double, $93–$95; suites, $95–$107
Added: 14% tax
Payment: Major credit card
Children: Free in room with parents
Pets: With approval
Smoking: Yes; nonsmoking rooms available
Open: Year-round

Soothing colors and contemporary design greet you at the El Paso Airport Hilton. Incorporating five buildings, most of which face the pool, it is an attractive, low-key place to stay. The airport itself is only 200 yards from the lobby, making this hotel very convenient when traveling by air.

The guest rooms are especially comfortable. Southwestern prints create a friendly atmosphere, and the beds have mirrored armoire units attached for convenience. More than half of the rooms are suites, with a small parlor with a refrigerator, sofa bed, bedroom, two TVs, and two phones. A few suites have whirlpool tubs; others have wide-screen TVs and whirlpool baths. Two Jacuzzi suites have enclosed double Jacuzzis surrounded by stained glass windows. Rooms on the executive keyed-access level have extras such as fully stocked bars, hair dryers, and robes. There's a small exercise room on the floor, and breakfast is included with the executive level rate.

Magnim's Restaurant, fresh and airy, is delightfully arranged, with lots of intimate dining rooms. Steak, veal, pasta, chicken, and seafood dishes are priced from $13 to $18 on the dinner menu. If you would rather eat by the pool (El Paso is dubbed Sun City, for it boasts sunshine almost every day of the year), you can pick up a poolside phone and order lunch. If you're not sure what you're craving, the bar section of Magnim's has an all-you-can-eat buffet during happy hour for only $3.50. The hotel also boasts the Comic Strip Comedy Club which has shows Tuesday through Saturday nights.

The staff is hospitable and helpful. Extra touches include complimentary shuttle service to the airport, a hot tub, sauna, an exercise room, and guest rooms especially designed for the handicapped.

El Paso Marriott

1600 Airway Boulevard
El Paso, Texas 79925
915-779-3300
800-228-9290
Fax: 915-772-0915

General manager: Scott Ringer
Accommodations: 296 rooms
Rates: single, $99–$124; double, $99–$139 (Monday–
   Thursday); single or double including breakfast, $69
   (Friday–Sunday); suites, $225–$425
Added: 14% tax
Payment: Major credit cards
Children: Free in room with parents
Pets: Small ones permitted
Smoking: Nonsmoking rooms available
Open: Year-round

At the entrance to the El Paso International Airport, the Marriott exudes Texas friendliness. From the outside, the six-story rectangular building is not distinctive, but its service and hospitality are.

The lobby, with a fountain in the center, is fairly small. Off to one side, La Cascada, which also has a fountain at its entrance, serves meals all day, and specializes in South of the Border dishes. Three fresh fish specials each day add depth to the menu. Dinner entrées run from $5 to $9. Chatfield's, behind beveled glass doors, is more intimate. Entrées range from chicken boursin to salmon to prime rib and are priced from $16 to $30. The restaurant, whose theme is "bigger is better," specializes in chocolate soufflés for dessert. The hotel also offers McGinty's Lounge, a popular El Paso night spot.

The guest rooms are fresh and inviting, with matching drapes and bedspreads and plush carpeting. On the concierge level, complimentary Continental breakfast, evening hors d'oeuvres, and dessert are served in a private lounge. There's an office with computer hook-ups and other business equipment for traveling executives. Executive rooms are larger than standard and have a desk, coffeemakers, bottled mineral water, and two phones.

The swim-through indoor-outdoor pool is attractive, and nearby are a Ping-Pong table, exercise room, whirlpool and sauna. A putting green and volleyball court are just beyond the pool.

The hotel has video check-out and handicapped facilities, including Braille menus and rooms designed for the hearing impaired. Parking is free.

The Westin Paso del Norte

101 South El Paso Street
El Paso, Texas 79901
915-534-3000
800-228-3000
Fax: 915-534-3024

General manager: Scott Pickert
Accommodations: 375 rooms
Rates: single, $93–$148; double, $113–$168; suites, $210–$950
Added: 14% tax
Payment: Major credit cards
Children: Under 18 free in room with parents
Pets: Small pets only; additional $15 per day
Smoking: Nonsmoking rooms available
Open: Year-round

Staying at the Westin Paso del Norte puts you in touch with El Paso's history and at the same time immerses you in beauty and elegance. Built in 1912, the hotel was restored completely and reopened with a new 17-story tower in 1986. The environment is refined, the staff is Texas-friendly, and the combination makes for a top-quality hotel—the finest in the area.

Tradition has it that Pancho Villa wined and dined here between his skirmishes across the border. During the Mexican Revolution, guests were said to have requested rooms on the south side of the hotel so that they could watch the conflict from their windows. In what is now the hotel's nightclub, Uptown's, local cattlemen had their offices. Gunfights to settle disputes were not uncommon here, and bullet holes were still visible in the walls until the renovation in 1986. Today only the glory of Paso del Norte's past is evident.

There is no question that the exquisite Tiffany stained glass dome at the center of the aptly named Dome Bar, off the lobby, takes center stage. Apricot-colored scagliola columns and walls, crystal chandeliers, and tall, arched windows surrounding the dome combine for a true aesthetic delight. (Notice the unusually large light bulbs on the chandeliers. They were selected purposely as a status symbol because the owner, Zach T. White, wanted to play up the fact that the Paso del Norte was the first building in El Paso to have electricity.) The massive marble and mahogany bar beneath the famed dome matches it in circumference. It's a great place to soak up the hotel's ambience.

The Dome Grill next door, decorated in soft yellows, is elegant with its high ceiling, octagonal columns, and mirrored walls. Dinner entrées feature fresh seafood as well as beef. Dishes such as blue corn crêpes filled with smoked chicken, wild mushrooms, avocado and a creamy mirasol sauce, salmon with shiitake mushrooms wrapped in phyllo dough topped with a champagne butter sauce, and lobster and steak fajitas are imaginative, and range from $16–$19.50. Appetizers are also special.

Café Rio, which serves all three meals, has a Mexican theme and regional dishes. It opens onto a courtyard that antedates the original hotel. A plaque commemorates the spot where "four men were shot dead in about five seconds" in 1881, when El Paso was "the wildest 24-hour town in the Old West."

The rooms have Queen Anne–style furniture, with two-poster beds and mirrored armoires that replace closets. The baths have telephones and Caswell-Massey toiletries. Suites have hair dryers and coffeemakers. Rooms on the executive floors have fully stocked refrigerators and include breakfast in the morning and hors d'oeuvres and cocktails in the evening. If you prefer a lot of space when you travel, you might choose the Presidential suite, which has two bedrooms, a living room (complete with baby grand piano), full kitchen, dining room, and two baths (more than 2,400 square feet in all).

The hotel has a swimming pool, a whirlpool tub, a steam bath, and an exercise complex. Guests requiring a more comprehensive workout can use the facility across the street for $8 per day. Mexico is a mere seven blocks away. The city's civic center is next door. Parking at the hotel is free.

Fort Worth

Radisson Plaza Hotel Fort Worth
815 Main Street
Fort Worth, Texas 76102
817-870-2100
Fax: 817-870-2100, ext. 1555

General manager: Armel Santens
Accommodations: 517 rooms

Rates: single, $128–$140; double, $143–$160; suites, $225–$1,000; weekend rates available
Added: 13% tax
Payment: Major credit cards
Children: Free in room with parents
Pets: Permitted with deposit
Smoking: Nonsmoking rooms available
Open: Year-round

The Radisson Plaza Hotel opened in 1921 as the Hotel Texas. At one end of downtown Fort Worth, it reigned for years as the city's social center. Big bands played in its ballroom, and the rich and famous stayed in its guest rooms. One of its most noteworthy guests was President John F. Kennedy, who spent his last night in the hotel before going to Dallas. The hotel closed in 1979, reopening in 1981. By then it had been named to the National Register of Historic Places.

The 14-story hotel is a rectangle of red brick and terra cotta. While its exterior was virtually unchanged in the renovation, the interior was gutted and is now totally modern. The lobby is soothing, with waterfalls, lush plants, exotic cockatoo, and reflecting fish ponds.

There are two restaurants. The Café Centennial is casual and relaxed. The Crystal Cactus serves southwestern cuisine. In the evenings, a piano player entertains in the lobby bar beneath a glass atrium.

The guest rooms, traditionally furnished in blues, burgundies, and beiges, are masculine and spacious, but not particularly distinctive. The plaza level has such extras as Continental breakfast and afternoon hors d'oeuvres. The health club in an adjacent office tower has a heated pool, sauna, and exercise room.

The concierge and staff make every effort to attend to guests' needs. Room service operates from 6:00 A.M. to midnight. Self-parking in an underground garage costs $6 per day; valet parking ($9) is also available. Since the hotel is within a few blocks of the Tarrant County Convention Center and I-30, it is easy to reach all the area's sights.

Stockyards Hotel
109 East Exchange
Fort Worth, Texas 76164
817-625-6427
800-423-8471
Fax: 817-624-2571

General manager: W. Mike Davis
Accommodations: 52 rooms
Rates: single, $95; double, $105; suites, $125–$350
Added: 13% tax
Payment: Major credit cards
Children: Welcome
Pets: Not permitted
Smoking: Permitted
Open: Year-round

In many ways the Stockyards lives up to the expectations of first-time visitors to Texas, for they find here what they imagine the whole Lone Star State to be. The hotel, in the Stockyards National Historic District in a city affectionately called Cow Town, is a slice of history, reflecting the world of the affluent cattlemen of the early 1900s who dealt at the livestock markets just down the street.

Dating from 1907, the hotel building was transformed in 1983 into a gem of a luxury hotel. Not intended as a historical reproduction, it is inventive and vivacious, capturing the spirit of the era it portrays; outside, western-style shops, restaurants, and saloons line the streets in the area that was once the cattle center of the Southwest. Today it supports thriving tourist businesses and cattle auctions.

The lobby is decorated with leather sofas, carved wooden chairs covered with animal hides with the fur still on them, bronze sculptures, and western art. One of the most dramatic pieces is a mirror framed in doeskin and topped with antlers.

The guest rooms offer Indian, western, mountain man, and Victorian decor—each beautifully executed. The decorating touches are indeed unique, such as deerskin headboards and ram's skull chandeliers. The Victorian rooms are soft and feminine, with white wicker furniture, lace curtains, and fringed lamps. There are also king-size beds, baths with chain-pull water closets, and wardrobes that conceal TVs.

The Bonnie and Clyde Suite, reportedly frequented by the infamous twosome, has appropriate memorabilia: Bonnie Parker's gun, newspaper clippings of their escapades, and vintage photographs. The Celebrity Suite (with a celebrity price of $350) has a living area with a fireplace, a private deck with a hot tub, and a private entrance.

In Booger Red's Saloon, downstairs, you can order a drink while sitting on a saddle that's mounted on a bar stool. The adjacent restaurant serves home-style cooking with a southwestern flavor. Valet parking is $5.

Just one word of caution: the hotel does fall short in the area of service. The staff is uninterested at best and rude at worst. If service is important, you may prefer one of the other downtown Fort Worth hotels. However, to add a little "wild West" flavor to your trip, the Stockyards is your best bet.

The Worthington Hotel

200 Main Street
Fort Worth, Texas 76102
817-870-1000
800-772-5977 in Texas
800-433-5677 in U.S.
Fax: 817-332-5679

General manager: Robert L. Jameson
Accommodations: 507 rooms and suites
Rates: single, $129–$169; double, $139–$179; suites, $300–$400
Added: 13% tax
Payment: Major credit cards
Children: Under 18 free in room with parents
Pets: Not permitted
Smoking: Nonsmoking rooms available
Open: Year-round

A hospitable staff, a good location, and an excellent fitness club make the Worthington a topnotch hotel. Built in 1981, it occupies three city blocks at one end of downtown Fort Worth. Its ultramodern exterior makes an interesting contrast to Sundance Square, a turn-of-the-century shopping and entertainment area just across the street with fancy boutiques and restaurants. For a romantic tour of the city, you can climb into a horse-drawn carriage right at the hotel's doors. The city's attractions as well as many business addresses are a short drive away.

The Worthington's fitness club has an indoor pool, outdoor tennis courts, a sundeck, sauna, whirlpool, and exercise room with free weights, Lifecycles, and treadmills. The club is welcoming, from a sociable staff to such extras as a comfortable sitting area with magazines and newspapers, baskets of fruit, and a big-screen TV. The pool and whirlpool are free for hotel guests; the other facilities can be used for a daily fee.

Dining gets lots of attention at this hotel. In addition to elegant Reflections and the casual Brasserie LaSalle, it operates Winfield's '08 family restaurant and the Houston Street Bakery, both across the street, and Firehall Marketplace Deli, in Sundance Square. The room service menu is several cuts above the average, featuring treats from the bakery as well as the hotel's own kitchen. Afternoon tea and lavish Sunday brunches are Worthington traditions.

The hotel has a distinctively contemporary design. Its marble lobby is softened by gentle waterfalls and lots of greenery. Redecorated in 1990 with contemporary furniture, rich mahogany, art deco lamps, and deep mauves and grays, the guest rooms are modern and sleek, with especially comfortable sitting areas. The prints in the rooms are from originals in Fort Worth museums. Terrace suites have expansive balconies overlooking the city, separate living rooms and bedrooms, and lots of extra features.

Throughout the hotel, the staff is Texas-friendly, and a concierge is on duty for special requests. Valet parking costs $9; self-parking is $6.

Houston

Four Seasons Hotel Houston
1300 Lamar Street
Houston, Texas 77010
713-650-1300
800-332-3442
Fax: 713-650-8169

General manager: Francisco Gomez
Accommodations: 399 rooms and suites
Rates: single, $180; double, $205; suites, $435
Added: 15% tax
Payment: Major credit cards
Children: Under 12 free in room with parents; ages 12 to 18 half price
Pets: Permitted with leash
Smoking: Nonsmoking rooms available
Open: Year-round

For the traveler who values quality and aesthetics, the 30-story Four Seasons Houston is worth a special trip. Opened in 1982, it is truly grand—a combination of classic European style and Texas hospitality. The hotel occupies a city block in the downtown business district and is connected by a skywalk to the Park, a three-tier mall with boutiques and restaurants. The George R. Brown Convention Center, a state-of-the-art facility that opened in 1987, is two blocks away.

A grand staircase spirals up from the hotel's lobby, joining three floors of public space. On the fourth floor is a garden with one of the most attractive swimming pools in the city. A whirlpool, sauna, and game room are adjacent. Guests can also use the Houston Center Athletic Club (accessible by indoor walkway), which has racquet sports, jogging, and exercise equipment.

The guest rooms, decorated with custom furniture, have a residential feeling, and the bathrooms are stylish. All of the rooms are spacious and luxurious, especially the Four Seasons rooms, which feature a sleeping area in an alcove and a separate sitting area.

Service is cheerful and professional at the Four Seasons. Bed turndown, 24-hour room service, complimentary shoeshines, and 1-hour pressing service are all standard. There's also free limousine service to downtown restaurants, businesses, and entertainment (even on weekends).

De Ville is an outstanding restaurant, headed by a bright young chef bursting with creativity. Dinner entrée choices, ranging from $13 to $18, may include smoked lamb nachos or sautéed Big Spring rattlesnake with anco linguine on lime cream and hickory crisp duck with black bean salad. The Terrace Café serves lighter fare. The Lobby Lounge has buffet lunches and evening cocktails.

Valet parking costs $12 per day.

J. W. Marriott Hotel

5150 Westheimer Road
Houston, Texas 77056
713-961-1500
800-228-9290
Fax: 713-961-5045

General manager: Bob Pittenger
Accommodations: 494
Rates: single, $139–$159; double, $149–$169; suites, $500–$600; weekend rates available
Added: 15% tax
Payment: Major credit cards
Children: Free in room with parents
Pets: Small pets accepted with deposit
Smoking: Nonsmoking rooms available
Open: Year-round

Just across from the Galleria shopping mall, the 23-story J. W. Marriott is a sophisticated hotel. The lobby gleams with marble, polished paneling, brass, and crystal. A gift shop, hair salon, clothing boutique, and airline reservation desks are off the lobby. The Brasserie, with rare pre-Columbian artifacts, is the hotel's restaurant. The Lobby Lounge fills the air with the sound of live piano music.

The guest rooms are among the most tastefully decorated and comfortably appointed in the Southwest. The art was especially commissioned from Houston artists, and the furniture is refined. There's a sitting area with a small couch, an armoire with a TV, and a convenient desk. The bathrooms have phones, small TVs, terrycloth robes, and built-in hair dryers.

The hotel's health club has good workout equipment and a coed sauna and steam room. The fifth-floor indoor-outdoor pool, although small, is a convivial gathering spot; a food service bar is by the indoor portion. The health club has racquetball at $3 per hour.

The Lancaster Hotel

701 Texas Avenue
Houston, Texas 77002
713-228-9500
800-231-0336
Fax: 713-223-4528

Managing director: Kim Nugent
Accommodations: 93 rooms
Rates: single, $145–$165; double, $170–$190; suites, $300–$800
Added: 15% tax
Payment: Major credit cards
Children: Under 16 free in room with parents
Pets: Small pets permitted with a $50 deposit
Smoking: Nonsmoking rooms available
Open: Year-round

In the midst of the downtown cultural district, the Lancaster is a small, elegant hotel with European style à la Texas and service spelled with a capital S. Its look is polished and refined. The lobby, like the rest of the hotel, is intimate, more like a parlor than a standard hotel lobby. Handsome elevators with mirrors and polished wood take guests to their rooms. No more than nine rooms are on each floor, adding to the sense of intimacy.

In truth, the hotel hasn't always been so fine. Built in 1926 as the Auditorium Hotel, it has a colorful history. Gene Autry once rode his horse into the Stage Canteen in the basement. Symphony musicians and circus performers, wrestlers and ice skaters, stayed here. So did the young Clark Gable, and rumor has it that he left his trunk as ransom until he could pay his bill.

In 1982 the building was transformed into a luxury hotel. The guest rooms, intimate in size as well as styling, have a British theme, with imported English tartan and chintz fabrics and wallpapers, prints of the English countryside, overstuffed chairs with stools, and carved two-poster beds. The bathrooms are sleek, in white marble and brass. Multiple two-line speaker phones, fully stocked refreshment centers, remote control TVs in armoires, terry robes, and such unexpected extras as umbrellas enhance the feeling of luxury. Expect a newspaper at your door in the morning and bed turndown at night.

The clublike Lancaster Grille, whose walls are covered with equestrian and hunt scenes, also has a British tone. The Grille, which serves all three meals and late night fare, is a popular dinner spot for theatergoers. For recreation and fitness, guests can use the Texas Club, a block and a half away. Facilities include a rooftop pool, Nautilus equipment, squash and racquetball courts, and a gym.

If you enjoy the performing arts, there's hardly a better place to stay in Houston. The Lancaster is next door to the Alley Theater, across the street from Jones Hall, a block from Wortham Center, and within a few blocks of the Music Hall.

The hotel has a concierge, complimentary downtown limousine service, and 24-hour room service. Parking is $10 per day.

Omni Houston Hotel

Four Riverway
Houston, Texas 77056
713-871-8181
800-332-3442
Fax: 713-871-8116

General manager: Louis Martinelli
Accommodations: 381 rooms and suites
Rates: single, $190; double, $215; suites start at $300
Added: 15% tax
Payment: Major credit cards
Children: Under 17 free in room with parents
Pets: Not permitted
Smoking: Nonsmoking floors
Open: Year-round

A tranquil oasis in the bustling city, the Omni Houston hotel is only a few minutes' drive from the Galleria and many business addresses. Its parklike setting, among gleaming office towers, is unexpected. The wooded banks of Buffalo Bayou are on the eastern perimeter, and there's a reflection pond, the home of a family of swans, surrounded by weeping willows to the west.

Just inside, the Palm Court Lounge sets the tone. A lush tropical garden, it has a gentle waterfall, soft piano music, and views of the hotel's pools and fountains. The colors of the garden are repeated throughout, with a profusion of green marble in the lobby accented with Asian screens and modern paintings.

The guest rooms, with luxurious modern furnishings, look out on the grounds or the bayou. All the rooms have overstuffed chairs, remote control TVs, stocked mini-bars, hair dryers, and bath telephones. Terry robes add to the feeling of luxury.

A good choice for a weekend retreat or a business stop, Inn on the Park is geared to recreation. It has two pools—one heated and with underwater music, four tennis courts, and bikes to rent, with trails in nearby Memorial Park. The health club has extensive exercise equipment and a whirlpool.

The dining choices are all good. Café on the Green, open from 6:30 A.M. to midnight, has a sumptuous Sunday brunch. La Réserve, a fine restaurant, serves French, American, and regional dishes. Entrées such as smoked chicken and eggplant salad served with a warm goat cheese torta range from $13 to $20. Afternoon tea, evening hors d'oeuvres, and Viennese desserts are all part of the Palm Court Lounge's bill of fare. Downstairs is the Black Swan, a pub named for the hotel's mascots. Offering more than one hundred brands of beer, it serves light evening fare and has live entertainment, board games, darts, and dancing.

The hotel's mascots are two beautiful black swans that glide tranquilly across the reflecting pond. If you get too close, their docile nature disappears, and you may find yourself running from an irate swan. Apparently the prolific birds are suspicious of intruders, since fledgling swans are often given up for adoption.

The service is attentive, if somewhat slick. Self-parking is free, valet service costs from $10 to $15. Free limousine service is available to the Galleria and to a shuttle terminal, where you can catch a bus to either Intercontinental or Hobby Airport. Downtown Houston is about 10 miles east of the hotel.

The Ritz-Carlton
1919 Briar Oaks Lane
Houston, Texas 77027
713-840-7600
800-241-3333
Fax: 713-840-0616

General manager: Luis Argoteg
Accommodations: 232 rooms and suites
Rates: single, $170–$285; double, $190–$295; suites, $450–$1,900
Added: 15% tax
Payment: Major credit cards
Children: Under 18 free in room with parents
Pets: With approval
Smoking: Nonsmoking rooms available
Open: Year-round

The Ritz-Carlton is a gleaming palace that combines sophistication with hospitality. Despite its size, it has a residential feeling. No large lobby looms at its front door; instead, guests sign in at an unimposing hall desk. The public spaces are pretty, featuring rotundas with skylights, alcoves with comfortable chairs, and arched corridors with greenery.

Best of all, the hotel treats its guests as honored visitors. Personal preferences are noted and attended to, and staff members call guests by name. Valet parking ($12.50), 24-hour room service, and complimentary transportation to nearby shopping areas are available.

To the strains of harp music, the Lobby Lounge serves high tea as well as light desserts, cordials, chocolate fondues, and champagne in the evenings. Nearby is the handsome bar, resembling an English men's club, with couches and a fireplace.

The guest rooms are comfortable and pleasing to the eye. The deluxe rooms are especially large, with bay windows and separate sitting areas. The baths are warmly decorated, with colored marble vanity tops. Suites have canopy beds, expansive wet bars with refrigerators, and large bathtubs with Jacuzzi jets. Extras include terrycloth robes, a choice of down or synthetic pillows, three phones, and remote control TVs. When you walk into your room you feel expected: the thermostat is set, the lights are on, and soft music is playing.

The second-floor pool is a tranquil hideaway. Though the pool is small, the setting is like a garden, far removed from the city streets.

Dining is a stellar event. Choose from the formal Restaurant or the Bar and Grill. The Restaurant's cuisine is new American, and the service is impeccable. Of special note on the menu are entrées designated as Fitness Cuisine. Lunch items such as grilled chicken with papaya al pesto ($12.50) and dinners such as venison medallions with crushed peppercorns in a lingon-berry sauce ($26) and steamed salmon filet served in a dill vermouth sauce ($21) are very satisfying whether or not you're watching what you eat.

In Post Oak Park off Loop 610 West, the Ritz is a few blocks from the Galleria. It is easy to get to most business addresses, including those downtown.

The Westin Galleria and Westin Oaks

Westin Galleria: 5060 West Alabama
713-960-8100
Westin Oaks: 5011 Westheimer
Houston, Texas 77056
713-623-4300
800-228-3000
Telex: 4990983
Fax: 713-960-6553

Managing director: Raymond Sylvester
Accommodations: Galleria, 489 rooms; Oaks, 406 rooms
Rates: single, $160–$190; double, $190–$220; suites, $300–
$1,200
Added: 15% tax
Payment: Major credit cards
Children: Under 18 free in room with parents
Pets: Small ones permitted on leash
Smoking: Nonsmoking rooms available
Open: Year-round

Houston has two Westins, each offering luxury coupled with vivacity. Both are part of a "city under glass," the Galleria Mall, which was inspired by the Galleria Vittorio Emanuele in Milan, Italy. Houston's version has more than 300 shops and restaurants, an Olympic-size skating rink, and several cinemas, as well as these two excellent hotels.

The 21-story Oaks, the first of the two, opened with the en-closed mall in 1971. The 24-story Galleria opened in 1977. About a 5-minute walk apart, the two complement each other in style and mood.

The guest rooms, furnished in contemporary decor, are large and well appointed. Each has a stocked bar and refrigerator, multiple phones, and balconies. Rooms have either one king- or two queen-size beds. Cable TV and movies are complimentary.

For dining and entertainment, there are six choices. (Guests at either hotel can charge services to their room at the other.) Delmonico's, at the Galleria, offers fine dining. Shucker's Sports Bar, at the Oaks, serves seafood and casual fare. Both hotels have an informal restaurant. Annabelle's, at the top of the Galleria, is the spot for dancing, and the Roof nightclub, at the Oaks, has live entertainment and happy-hour buffets.

For recreation, you can swim at either hotel, play tennis at the Galleria, and jog at the Oaks. The Galleria also has a putting green. Guests can also use the University Club, in the mall, which has 10 indoor tennis courts, a ball machine, whirlpools and saunas, and massage.

Hotel courtesies include a concierge, 24-hour room service, express check-in and check-out, and valet parking ($11.75). Self-parking is free.

The Wyndham Warwick

5701 Main Street
Houston, Texas 77005
713-526-1991
800-822-4200
Fax: 713-639-4545

General manager: Patrick Lupsha
Accommodations: 308 rooms and suites
Rates: single, $149–$169; double, $169–$209; $20 each
   additional person in room; suites start at $175
Added: 15% tax
Payment: Major credit cards
Children: Under 17 free in room with parents
Pets: Not permitted
Smoking: 3 nonsmoking floors
Open: Year-round

In a fast-paced city where change is the norm, the Warwick is a welcome link to the past. The hotel itself is not particularly old, though. The original structure was built in 1926, but its opulence only dates from 1964, when the hotel was completely renovated by the oilman John Mecom, Sr.

The furnishings in the public areas are far from ordinary. A virtual museum of European treasures, they include ornate pilasters and exquisite paneling from the Murat palace in France, 18th-century statues from Italy, Baccarat crystal chandeliers (with over 5,000 pieces each), a 275-year-old Aubusson tapestry, and a profusion of art—all collected by the Mecoms.

John Mecom was a visionary, striking oil where others swore there could be none. He also had an eye for beauty. His business took him around the world, and wherever he went he added to his collection. While overseeing the renovation of the hotel (its purchase was sentimental as well as an investment, for Mecom had stayed in the hotel with his mother as a youth, and she had later taken an apartment there when he was a student at nearby Rice University), Mecom instructed his wife to use any color she wanted—as long as it was blue. Why blue? "Green is beautiful, too," he said. "But you look down at the grass to see green. You look up to see blue."

In Houston's museum district—a few blocks from the Museum of Fine Arts, the Cullen Sculpture Garden, the Contemporary Arts Museum, and the Museum of Natural Science— the Warwick is surrounded by beauty. Just outside its doors is one of Houston's favorite landmarks, the Mecom Fountains.

In recent years the hotel became a little worn around the edges, in contrast with the sparkling luxury hotels that opened in Houston in the early 1980s. So the Trammell Crow Company purchased the hotel, renovated it, and reopened the property as the Wyndham Warwick in 1989, maintaining its status as an elegant hotel. The list of notable people who have stayed at the hotel, which includes royalty, heads of state, and entertainers, is truly impressive.

The guest rooms at the Warwick vary in size and decor. Most are furnished in the style of Louis XV, with custom furniture, marble-topped dressing tables, botanical prints, flowered bedspreads, and a choice of king-size or twin beds. The bathrooms have phones and hair dryers. Lanai rooms, in a separate wing, face the swimming pool. All rooms have two baths and a balcony or patio, with easy access to the men's and women's saunas. One of the best room choices is a junior suite; some of them have refrigerators and microwave ovens. Most of the suites are one of a kind, and some have outstanding views of the city to the south (Bob Hope once labeled this view as the prettiest sight in the world).

The Warwick's dining rooms are the Hunt Room and Café Vienna. The Hunt Room, the more formal of the two, is decorated in rich woods and has a fireside setting. The menu is good, and entrées, such as capon breasts with artichokes and rack of lamb, range from $17 to $25. The paneling in Café Vienna came from the Château la Motte au Bots in northern France. There's a pasta bar at lunch, and dinner entrées range from $7 to $15.

Hotel services include valet parking and room service.

Oklahoma City

Oklahoma City Marriott
3233 Northwest Expressway
Oklahoma City, Oklahoma 73112
405-842-6633
800-228-9290
Fax: 405-842-3152

General manager: Jim Olsovsky
Accommodations: 354 rooms
Rates: single, $99; double, $111; suites, $175–$350
Added: 9.375% tax
Payment: Major credit cards
Children: Welcome
Pets: Small pets permitted
Smoking: Permitted
Open: Year-round

The Marriott has attractive guest rooms and offers good recreational facilities. Conveniently located northwest of downtown Oklahoma City off Northwest Freeway, it's across the street from the Baptist Medical Center. The city's attractions and business centers are easily accessible.

The traditional guest rooms are comfortably furnished and well decorated. The executive suites are especially nice, with large sitting areas, private balconies, and bedrooms sectioned off with curtains. A concierge floor offers special services, Continental breakfast, and afternoon hors d'oeuvres.

The indoor-outdoor pool is larger and more appealing than most, and the inside portion functions as a social center. Board games and FM cassette headsets are available for the asking. There's also an exercise room, sauna, and locker rooms.

Beechwood's is a popular restaurant, especially for families. Russell's Lounge is light and airy—a pleasant, convivial spot. Hotel parking is free.

The Waterford Hotel
6300 Waterford Boulevard
Oklahoma City, Oklahoma 73118
405-848-4782
800-522-9440 in Oklahoma
800-992-2009 in U.S.
Fax: 405-843-9161

General manager: Buddy E. Chick
Accommodations: 197 rooms
Rates: single, $110; double, $120; suites, $138
Added: 9.375% tax
Payment: Major credit cards; no personal checks
Children: Welcome
Pets: Not permitted
Smoking: Permitted
Open: Year-round

The Waterford is a class act—an elegant hotel with all the attributes that term connotes. Guests sit at a desk to check in. A concierge is ready to meet special requests. There's a fine restaurant down the hall, plus dining in a verandah café. In one of the best residential neighborhoods in the city, the hotel is eight miles northwest of downtown.

The rooms are appointed with a sofa, writing desk, and a TV concealed in an armoire. It feels like a fine home rather than a hotel. The Italian marble baths have separate dressing areas. In the suites, the sleeping and parlor areas are completely separate, creating a sense of spaciousness. A concierge floor has such extras as morning coffee or tea delivered to the room along with a newspaper.

Some rooms overlook the landscaped pool (unusually attractive for a city hotel). The fitness center has a great whirlpool, locker rooms with saunas, and excellent exercise equipment. There are also two hard-surface tennis courts and two squash courts. All of the recreational facilities are used by members of an associated athletic club as well as hotel guests.

The Waterford Restaurant, with entrées from $13 to $24, serves such dishes as grilled salmon with ginger cream sauce and filet of sautéed veal loin in a white wine cream sauce with golden chanterelles and angel hair pasta.

Phoenix

The Ritz-Carlton
2401 East Camelback Road
Phoenix, Arizona 85016
602-468-0700
800-241-3333
Telex: 543299
Fax: 602-468-0793

General manager: John Rolfs
Accommodations: 281 rooms
Rates: single, $90–$320; double, $90–$340; $50 each
  additional person, suites, $270–$695
Added: 10.25% tax
Payment: Major credit cards
Children: Under 18 free in room with parents; roll-aways $20
  extra per day
Pets: Not permitted, but concierge can make boarding
  arrangements
Smoking: Nonsmoking rooms available
Open: Year-round

The modern pink exterior of the Ritz-Carlton is deceptive.
When you walk into the lobby expecting contemporary decor,
you're greeted by gleaming Italian marble, Oriental rugs, and
priceless antiques. The feeling of Old World elegance is remarkable for a new hotel.

Off to the side is the Lobby Lounge, the site of high tea every
day from 2:00 to 4:30 P.M. The scones with Devonshire cream
are a real treat. During the Christmas season "Teddy Bear Tea"
is served for children. The lounge is filled with Teddy bears, hot
chocolate is served, and stories are read to eager ears. On Friday
and Saturday nights, couples dance to live entertainment.

Next door, the Grill has a men's club atmosphere. Original
paintings of sporting and equestrian scenes, all predating the
1890s, hang on the paneled walls. The fireplace came from a
castle in Germany. The Grill's specialties are prime aged meats,
fresh fish, and pheasant, but if you don't see what you want, just
ask—the chef will whip up something special for you. The
Restaurant is formal and features beautifully presented Continental cuisine. The menu changes weekly to take advantage of
whatever ingredients are in season.

The guest rooms are plush and attractive in gray and salmon
tones. Marble baths, two telephones, hair dryers, robes, honor

bars, safes, twice-daily maid service, and nightly turndown with chocolates are just a few of the many extras the Ritz offers. Guests on the keyed-access club level can take advantage of complimentary meals throughout the day, including Continental breakfast, midmorning snacks, evening hors d'oeuvres and cocktails, and late cordials and sweets.

Recreation has not been overlooked at this city hotel. In addition to the requisite pool, there's a fitness center, sundeck, and two tennis courts. Massages are available for $25 a half hour, $40 per hour. Tee times on the nearby Biltmore golf course can be arranged; transportation is free.

More than anything, attention to detail stands out at the Ritz. Even the public restrooms are marble, with fresh flowers and a supply of washcloths. The paneled elevators have marble floors covered with Persian rugs. The devoted staff is unequaled. The front desk keeps a record of guests' special requests for their next visit. The hotel also offers concierge, valet, and 24-hour room service. Shoeshines are complimentary; valet parking is $7 per day.

The Ritz has a convenient central location; it's about 15 minutes from the airport and near downtown Phoenix and Scottsdale's many golf courses. It is directly across the street from the Biltmore Fashion Park, which houses such fine stores as Saks Fifth Avenue and I. Magnin.

San Antonio

The Crockett Hotel
320 Bonham
San Antonio, Texas 78205
512-225-6500
800-292-1050 in Texas
800-531-5537 in U.S.
Fax: 512-225-7418

General manager: Kenny Gibson
Accommodations: 202 rooms and suites
Rates: single or double, $80–$160; suites, $125–$400
Added: 13% tax
Payment: Major credit cards
Children: Under 18 free in room with parents
Pets: Not permitted
Smoking: Nonsmoking rooms available
Open: Year-round

Built in 1909, the Crockett Hotel is on the National Register of Historic Places. Although it was completely refurbished in 1985, much care was taken to see that its original character was maintained. You are always aware of the building's age, and the Alamo's presence just across the street only adds to the ambience.

In keeping with the sense of the building, the hotel is simply decorated. The most striking elements in the lobby and adjoining enclosed atrium (once an outdoor courtyard) are the polished slate floors and mellowed brick walls—exposed in the lobby, softly painted in the atrium.

The guest rooms in the main building, called the Tower, are unpretentious yet comfortable and spacious. Large windows keep them sunny and afford fine views of the city. The Courtyard rooms are in a separate annex, added to the hotel in 1978. These rooms may lack the charm of the older building, but they are popular with families because they have more sleeping space and surround the hotel's tropical garden and swimming pool. Be sure to visit the Tower's rooftop hot tub and sundeck for a bird's-eye view of San Antonio.

The Crockett has two restaurants, Ernie's Bar & Grill and the Landmark Café. The Landmark's menu leans toward seafood and Texas steaks, and on weekend nights the waiters sing show tunes. Ernie's is more casual, serving burgers and other typical bar fare. Room service is also available.

Valet parking costs $7; self-parking in nearby lots is $4 per day. However, once the car is parked you probably won't have much need for it because the Riverwalk and most city sites are a short walk from the hotel.

The Emily Morgan Hotel

705 East Houston
San Antonio, Texas 78205
512-225-8486
800-824-6674
Fax: 512-225-7227

General manager: Sandy Harper
Accommodations: 177 rooms
Rates: single, $80; double, $90; suites, $100–$175
Added: 13% tax
Payment: Major credit cards
Children: Under 12 free in room with parents
Pets: Under 20 pounds permitted with deposit

Smoking: Nonsmoking rooms available
Open: Year-round

The Emily Morgan's neo-Gothic tower with a flag on top catches the eye from almost every street corner in downtown San Antonio. This graceful hotel was built in 1926 as the Medical Arts Building, and you can still see medical symbols above some of the windows. Turned into a hotel in 1985, it is across the street from the Alamo.

Inside, the look is contemporary. Attractive modern art hangs in the halls and guest rooms. The guest rooms are spare but have fine furnishings such as curly maple dressers and wardrobes and wooden blinds. Large windows give the rooms an airy feeling. The bathrooms have scales, which may not be a positive attribute in a city with so many fine restaurants. Many of the rooms have Jacuzzis and mini-refrigerators.

The hotel has one restaurant, open for breakfast only. It's named the Yellow Rose Café after Emily Morgan, the Yellow Rose of Texas, who is said to have helped Sam Houston bring down Santa Ana. Each table is set with fresh roses. Guests may also wish to spend some time in the Emily Morgan Bar, the small pool, whirlpool, exercise room, or sauna.

Parking in nearby city lots is $6.50 per day.

The Fairmount Hotel

401 South Alamo Street
San Antonio, Texas 78205
512-224-8800
800-642-3363
Fax: 512-224-2767

Managing director: Linda Finger
Accommodations: 36 rooms and suites
Rates: single, $145–$185; double, $155–$195; suites, $225–$375
Added: 13% tax
Payment: Major credit cards
Children: Free in room with parents
Pets: Not permitted
Smoking: Nonsmoking rooms available
Open: Year-round

If you like class, pack your bags and head for the Fairmount. To call this wonderful hotel "service-oriented" is an understatement. From the moment you drive up until the moment you leave, you are pampered by a warm, friendly staff. The only bad thing about staying here, in fact, is leaving.

Built in 1906 in Italianate Victorian style, the hotel operated until the 1960s, when it was boarded up. In 1985 it made head-lines when it was moved six blocks, becoming the largest build-ing ever moved in one piece. The new owners transformed the structure into a luxury hotel, building an addition that comple-ments the original structure.

The Fairmount is next to San Antonio's La Villita Historic District, a picturesque assortment of shops and restaurants within a few steps of the famed Riverwalk. Across the street from the hotel are HemisFair Plaza and the city's convention center.

Each room has a different decor. Common to all are high ceilings, reproduction antiques, bleached wood floors, and muted colors. The bathrooms have Italian marble and solid brass appointments. Luxury abounds: terry robes, bath tele-phones, makeup mirrors, oversize towels, remote control TVs with VCRs and a complimentary film library to select from (including a tape of the Fairmount's move), twice-daily maid service, bed turndown, and complimentary shoeshine.

Some rooms are designed for families, with two queen-size beds. (Children get milk and cookies.) The Veranda suites have separate living and sleeping areas, canopy beds, and stereos. The Master Suite is the largest, with all of the features of Ve-randa suites plus a whirlpool tub, wet bar, and separate dressing area.

Polo's is the Fairmount's restaurant; it serves all three meals. Dinner entrées include beef tenderloin stuffed with chorizo, spinach and mushrooms and roasted Szechwan duck in a hoi-sin pear sauce and range from $17.95 to $22.95. The appetizers are exotic and desserts are memorable. Breakfasts and lunches are sometimes served on the patio, and Polo's bar has live enter-tainment in the evening.

Hotel Menger

204 Alamo Plaza
San Antonio, Texas 78205
512-223-4361
800-345-9285
Fax: 512-228-0022

General manager: J. W. McMillin
Accommodations: 320 rooms

Rates: single, $78–$98; double, $98–$122; $10 each additional person in room; suites, $152–$456; weekend packages available
Added: 13% tax
Payment: Major credit cards
Children: Under 18 free in room with parents
Pets: Not permitted
Smoking: Nonsmoking rooms available
Open: Year-round

The Menger claims to be the oldest continuously operating hotel west of the Mississippi. When William Menger, a German brewer, built it in 1859, he had a practical reason: the patrons of his brewery frequently needed a place to spend the night, and he was tired of converting bar tables into beds. San Antonio was still a frontier town (the Battle of the Alamo had taken place only twenty-three years earlier), and Menger added a strong dose of refinement, building a fine lodging with beautiful furnishings.

Over the years the Menger has played a part in Texas history. During the Spanish-American War, Teddy Roosevelt recruited his Rough Riders in the hotel's bar. The lodging was long popular with visiting cattlemen. Today, with its central location and moderate prices, it attracts families and other vacationers as well as business travelers.

The Menger continues to grow, sprawling from its original design to include a motor inn. In early 1988, thirty-three rooms were added as part of a major refurbishment undertaken in conjunction with the creation of a new section of the city's Riverwalk. Care was taken to blend the additions as naturally as possible with the old hotel to keep the strong sense of history about the Menger. The Victorian rotunda in the original section is spectacular, with a stained glass ceiling and two oval mezzanine floors, which are filled with antiques, overlooking the lobby.

To savor the history of the hotel, choose a one-of-a-kind suite such as the Devon Cattle or the King Suite. Each has a large carved bed with a canopy and a parlor with antique furnishings. The Roy Rogers Room was decorated to accommodate Roy and Dale when they visited HemisFair in 1968. All of the suites open onto the mezzanines. Other choices include the new guest rooms (they are top of the line, especially the palatial Presidential Suite), standard rooms (completely refurbished in 1987), and motel rooms (fairly ordinary). Rich greens, flowered drapes and spreads, and botanical prints dominate the courtyard rooms, reflecting the garden below. The rooms facing the Alamo have beige tones, mirroring the Alamo's honey-colored brick.

The hotel's pool, surrounded by lush landscaping, is especially attractive, as is the courtyard, which has a fountain and is used for dining in nice weather. The Colonial Room serves southwestern specialties for breakfast, lunch, dinner, and Sunday brunch. The Menger Bar, decorated with photos of Teddy Roosevelt and the hotel's early years, is well worth a visit.

Self-parking in a nearby lot is $3.95 per day. Valet parking is $7.95

La Mansion del Rio
112 College Street
San Antonio, Texas 78205
512-225-2581
800-292-7300 in Texas
800-531-7208 in U.S.
Fax: 512-226-0389

General manager: Jan Leenders
Accommodations: 337 rooms
Rates: single, $130–$220; double, $150–$240; suites, $360–$1,500
Added: 13% tax
Payment: Major credit cards; no personal checks
Children: Under 18 free in room with parents
Pets: Not permitted
Smoking: Nonsmoking rooms available
Open: Year-round

At the heart of this popular tourist city is the Riverwalk, a gentle canallike river flanked by shops and restaurants. The most charming hotel near the water is La Mansion del Rio, a quiet retreat within a few steps of the Riverwalk's energy.

The Spanish colonial building dates from 1852, when it opened as St. Mary's Institute, a Catholic school that became a distinguished law school. A hotel since 1968, it is a composite of classical arches, wrought iron, and red tile. At its cedar-shaded Riverwalk entrance, a profusion of greenery cascades from stone walls, and an arched bridge spans the waterway. A rambling structure, due to sections being added during its years as a school, La Mansion has guest rooms spread over seven floors.

Perhaps the most requested rooms are those overlooking the river, which have balconies ideal for watching the stream of people flow by on the Riverwalk below. Other rooms open onto two inner courtyards, one with an attractive swimming pool.

Spanish in decor, the rooms have beamed ceilings, luxuriant bedspreads, and plush carpets. While some rooms are rather small, all are attractive and comfortable. Every room has a dry bar with a refrigerator and a remote control TV in an armoire.

Restaurante Capistrano serves southwestern cuisine, with an emphasis on authentic Mexican dishes. The romantic Las Canarias restaurant overlooks the river and is known for its fine cuisine. Paella, grilled swordfish, blackened snapper, and veal scallopini are typical entrées, ranging from $19 to $25. Las Canarias also holds a champagne brunch on Sundays for $19.95.

Hotel guests can use the facilities at two nearby health clubs. One has tennis courts, an indoor-outdoor pool, and exercise equipment (no fees); the second has racquetball, squash, handball, Nautilus equipment, and an indoor pool ($10 fee). Hotel services include a concierge, 24-hour room service, and valet parking ($7).

San Antonio is a romantic city with a Spanish heritage. La Mansion del Rio is the essence of the city, enveloping you in its charm.

Plaza San Antonio

555 South Alamo
San Antonio, Texas 78205
512-229-1000
800-421-1172
Fax: 512-223-6650

General manager: Rod Siler
Accommodations: 252 rooms and suites
Rates: single, $150–$190; double, $170–$210; suites, $250–$700
Added: 13% tax
Payment: Major credit cards
Children: Free in room with parents
Pets: Small pets permitted
Smoking: Permitted
Open: Year-round

The six-story Plaza San Antonio is a hacienda hideaway only a few blocks from the Riverwalk, yet far removed in its tranquillity. Here you can get to a multitude of attractions within minutes, but retreat to the hotel's grounds in between sightseeing jaunts. A swimming pool surrounded by gardens, two tennis courts, a croquet lawn, and a health club are all on the premises.

The mood is Old Mexico — perfect for enjoying San Antonio and its missions, Mexican markets, and nearby La Villita Historic District. The entrance to the lobby is through a small Mexican-tiled courtyard with a fountain. Also on the grounds are remnants of early Texas. Three historic cottages, each representing a different style of architecture, serve a practical purpose as well as add character. Both the Alsace-Lorraine bungalow and the Victorian cottage are used for private groups. The restored Germanic house holds the health club, with a sauna and exercise facilities, and a front porch swing for lazy summer evenings. Next door to the main hotel is the 19th-century school built for the children of the German settlers. Today it's the hotel's conference center.

The guest rooms, in two connecting wings of the hotel, are spacious and attractively furnished in soft pastels and flowered fabrics. Extra pillows on the beds make them especially inviting. Many rooms have balconies overlooking the lush gardens. Junior suites have sitting areas with TVs and another TV in the bedroom. Bathrobes, bottled water, hair dryers, and cable TV with a movie channel are in every room.

Staffed by a concierge, the hotel has 24-hour room service and lots of special touches, from complimentary shoeshines, morning coffee and newspapers, and twice-daily housekeeping service to nightly turndown. Bicycles are available free of charge. There is a poolside bar and a small children's pool. Parking is $5 per day.

The Anaqua Restaurant, named for the stately trees that generously shade the grounds, has one of the most unique menus in town. A chef's station, featuring "hot rock" cooking where food is slow-cooked on granite slabs that come from the German Alps, opens right out into the restaurant. "Bamboo Blue Plate" specials are Oriental dishes cooked in bamboo steamers, while Tex-Mex entrées are cooked on a wood-burning grill. Eurasian satays, Spanish Tapas, homemade vinegars and breads, and exotic drinks such as kiwi margaritas and "Banana Boat Blues" (vanilla bean ice cream with blackberry brandy, fresh bananas, blue curaçao, vodka, and cranberry juice) add to the restaurant's international flavor. For more informal dining and lighter fare, meals are served by the pool or in the Palm Terrace Restaurant and lobby bar.

San Antonio Marriott Rivercenter
101 Bowie Street
San Antonio, Texas 78205
512-223-1000
800-648-4462
Fax: 512-223-4092

General manager: Ed Paradine
Accommodations: 1000 rooms and suites
Rates: single, $165; double, $185; suites, $250–$850
Added: 13% tax
Payment: Major credit cards
Children: Under 12 free in room with parents
Pets: Permitted
Smoking: Nonsmoking rooms available
Open: Year-round

The Rivercenter, with its many shops, restaurants, and theaters, has become the hub of activity for San Antonio's celebrated Riverwalk. The 38-story Marriott Rivercenter opened in 1988 to take full advantage of a prime location. Its busy glass-covered atrium lobby mirrors both the hustle and bustle and the glass architecture of the Rivercenter just outside.

The hotel has come up with just about every possible type of room a traveler could want. In the junior-king suites the bedroom is separated from the sitting area by French doors. Bed-sitting suites are two and a half times larger than a standard room. Two concierge floors serve complimentary breakfast in the morning, hors d'oeuvres in the evening, and late night desserts in the floors' private lounge. The rooms on the ladies' executive floor have special features such as razors, hair dryers, and satin hangers. The marquis floor has somewhat nicer furnishings than the traditional decor of the standard rooms, and includes extras such as shoe polishers and hot taps and instant coffee for making coffee in the room. Concert pianists won't have to miss a day's practice if they stay in one of the two presidential suites, equipped with baby grand pianos. Some rooms have Riverwalk views, and of course connecting rooms are available for families.

The Garden Café has a good salad bar and serves breakfast, lunch, and dinner buffets. Occasionally it runs special events, such as strawberry and seafood festivals, where the food of honor is spotlighted in a variety of dishes. The River Grill, featuring southwestern cuisine, offers elegant dining, with entrées ranging from $17 to $22. After dinner, guests can sample a wide range of liqueurs from the apéritif cart or move over to the

Atrium Lounge, where a huge stuffed armadillo is perched at the keys of a player piano.

The hotel has a heated indoor-outdoor pool—the outdoor portion surrounded by an attractive sundeck. Guests without a bathing suit can purchase disposable ones at the pool office. A workout room, hot tub, and saunas are all next to the pool area.

The hotel maintains a business center for executives and a laundry room where guests can wash and dry clothes free of charge; a concierge is on duty in the lobby for 12 hours a day. Room service is available around the clock. Parking is $7 per night.

Sheraton Gunter Hotel

205 East Houston Street
San Antonio, Texas 78205
512-227-3241
800-222-4276
Fax: 512-227-9305

General manager: Lester Jonas
Accommodations: 325 rooms and suites
Rates: single, $89–$121; double, $99–$134; suites, $195–$490
Added: 13% tax
Payment: Major credit cards
Children: Under 18 free in room with parents
Pets: Small ones permitted with a $20 deposit
Smoking: Nonsmoking rooms available
Open: Year-round

The Gunter, built in 1909, is a classic, mirroring an earlier, grander era. Its expansive lobby is graced by columns, sparkling crystal chandeliers, and a molded ceiling. Throughout the twelve-story hotel, marble floors and walnut paneling date from the time that the Gunter was the largest building in San Antonio. A montage of the hotel's history is displayed near the main elevators.

Newly decorated in 1990, the spacious yet intimate rooms have Queen Anne furniture and matching drapes and bedspreads. Four different color schemes have been used, so the rooms aren't carbon copies. There's a look of subdued plushness here accented with tradition, from high ceilings to heavy wooden doors.

Unlike some historic hotels, the Gunter is well aware of the modern bent toward recreation and fitness. There is a heated swimming pool on the second floor and an exercise room with

Nautilus equipment. For kids, there's a small video arcade in the hotel basement.

Just off the lobby and popular with theatergoers is Café Suisse, which serves European fare in a convivial setting of rich wood and soft lighting. Before your meal comes, one of the waiters keeps you entertained with his repertoire of magic tricks. Entrées such as lamb, duck, and prime rib range from $16 to $21. The dessert tray is tempting even after a filling meal. The pastries are prepared by the Swiss chef, who's also responsible for the luscious creations in the hotel's Pâtisserie Suisse Bake Shop. Café Suisse also serves a champagne brunch on Sundays.

Muldoon's, named for Padre Muldoon—an Irish priest who converted early Texans—is a bar on several levels next to an enclosed glass terrace. Lunch buffets are served upstairs during the week, and singalong happy hours usher in weekday evenings.

Service is important at the Gunter. A friendly staff, valet parking ($6), 24-hour room service, and bed turndown are all part of your stay. Two floors function as concierge levels. In addition to the not-to-be-missed pâtisserie, shops in the hotel include a barber shop and a fancy gift shop. Discount tickets to places such as Sea World are often available at the front desk.

The Gunter is in the heart of downtown, one block from the Riverwalk and five blocks from the Alamo. The Majestic Theater, which attracts top performers, is just across the street. Its ornate Moorish interior is so extraordinary, it's worth the price of a concert ticket just to see it. Special machines produce actual clouds that move across its seemingly starlit ceiling—making for a most memorable atmosphere and evening.

St. Anthony

300 East Travis
San Antonio, Texas 78205
512-227-4392
800-338-1338
Fax: 512-227-0915

General manager: Nick Ghawi
Accommodations: 362 rooms and suites
Rates: single, $85–$109; double, $85–$129; suites, $135–$500
Added: 13% tax
Payment: Major credit cards, no personal checks
Children: Under 19 free in room with parents

Pets: With approval
Smoking: Nonsmoking rooms available
Open: Year-round

Designated a Texas and National Historic Landmark, the St. Anthony grandly reflects the sumptuous grace of an earlier age. Built in 1909 by a prominent cattleman, B. L. Taylor, and a former San Antonio mayor, A. H. Jones, the hotel is European in design and decoration and pure Texan in tradition and hospitality.

Now a Park Lane Hotel, the St. Anthony was for many years owned by a wealthy railroad builder and rancher, R. W. Morrison, who turned it into a showcase for the art he collected in his travels. Today it's a treasure house of fine furnishings and paintings.

Venetian mosaic tile floors, Oriental rugs, leather sofas, bronze statues, 19th-century Chinese urns, and Empire chandeliers dripping with crystal grace the ornate lobby and public areas. Particularly beautiful is a rosewood and gold leaf grand piano from the czarist embassy in Paris.

A quiet retreat from the flurry is Peacock Alley, which runs parallel to the main lounge and overlooks Travis Park — a spot of green in the midst of downtown. The Alley is actually a long hall with high ceilings interrupted by tall, arched windows, furnished with large bamboo chairs for intimate conversation; it has been a favorite San Antonio meeting place since the 1930s.

Do stop by the Anacacho Ballroom, where Prince Rainier and Princess Grace were once entertained. The Travis Room has a huge painting of cowboys on the range, again reflecting the St. Anthony's Texas soul.

The guest rooms have a sense of refinement with their traditional furniture, matching drapes and bedspreads, and brass accessories. No two are alike, and many have antiques and art objects. Doorbells add a nice touch.

Guests may dine all day at the informal Café, specializing in southwestern and Continental cuisine. For evening and live entertainment, Pete's Pub is the place to go. With its deep green interior and marble tables, it is remarkably elegant for a saloon. Pete's also serves lunch, snacks, and cocktails, and is open until 1:00 A.M.

Unusual for a hotel of its vintage, the St. Anthony has a heated rooftop pool and a large redwood sundeck with a view of downtown, as well as a small fitness room. Other features include room service (6:30 A.M.–11 P.M.) and valet parking ($8). Self-parking in an outdoor lot is also available ($5).

Santa Fe

Hotel Plaza Real
125 Washington Avenue
Santa Fe, New Mexico 87501
505-988-4900
Fax: 505-984-8786

General manager: Rand Levitt
Accommodations: 12 rooms and 44 suites
Rates: $95–$115; suites, $120–$425
Included: Continental breakfast
Added: 10.125% tax
Payment: Major credit cards
Children: Under 12 free in room with parents
Pets: Not permitted
Smoking: Nonsmoking rooms available
Open: Year-round

One of the newer hotels in Santa Fe, the Plaza Real is just a few steps from the historic plaza. Completed in 1990, it was built in a traditional Territorial style to complement the architecture of the neighborhood.

The lobby is tasteful, with wrought-iron chandeliers, Native American sculptures, sofas, and an unusual painted chest with a matching sideboard. The bar just off the lobby is even more intimate. Most of the guest rooms are in two-story town houses on either side of an open walkway that begins just outside the lobby. The suites, which make up the better part of the hotel, are comfortably appointed with commodious southwestern furniture made from fine woods. Most of the rooms have fireplaces, king-size beds (traditional rooms have two double beds), small refrigerators (guests can ask to have them stocked with specific items), wet bars, tile baths, ceiling fans, and balconies.

A self-service Continental breakfast (included in the room rate) of home-baked muffins, pastries, granola, and fresh fruit is served in the upstairs common room of the main building. Or for a $3 service charge, you can have it delivered to your room. Also convenient is the hotel's underground parking garage with 24-hour security ($5 per day).

Inn of the Anasazi
113 Washington Avenue
Santa Fe, New Mexico 87501
505-988-3030
800-688-8100
Fax: 505-986-9005

General manager: Robert D. Zimmer
Accommodations: 59 rooms
Rates: single, $150–$200; double, $175–$275; suites, $275–$400
Added: 10.125% tax
Payment: Major credit cards
Children: Under 12 free in room with parents; $10 additional
  for roll-aways
Pets: Not permitted
Smoking: In bar only
Open: Year-round

The Inn of the Anasazi was developed by Robert Zimmer, a
well-known hotelier who also had a hand in creating the first-
class Bel-Air, Mansion on Turtle Creek, and Hana Maui hotels.
With the Inn of the Anasazi, Zimmer wanted to build a luxury
hotel, but one that was in keeping with the values of the American Indian Anasazi it was named for.

As you walk past the large terra cotta pots filled with native
and flowering plants at the inn's entrance, the smell of cedar
incense greets you in the lobby. The lobby, whose fireplace is
ablaze with a warming fire in winter, sets the tone for the rest
of the inn. The flagstone floor, potted cacti, and overstuffed
leather chairs have a down-to-earth feel—you'll find no pre-
tentious or overtly ornate objects here.

The guest rooms are furnished in the same vein. Decorated
in beiges and earthy colors with pine four-poster beds, soft
down comforters, easy chairs, basket lamps, hand-woven rugs,
and folk art made by local artisans, the rooms seem pristine
and natural. The unusual Do Not Disturb signs—Anasazi
motifs painted on blocks and strung on bolo tie cords—have
confused more than one guest. And although a great effort has
been made to create an age-old flavor throughout the hotel,
modern comforts have not been forgotten. All rooms have coffeemakers, gaslit fireplaces, safes, televisions, and VCRs. Suites
come with a stereo and CD player. There's a video library available through room service, and if the hotel does not have a film
you want, they'll send someone out to rent one for you.

A stone water wall runs between the second and third floors.
On the ground floor, guests are welcome to use the library

(where the bookshelves interestingly enough are filled with artifacts rather than books), and the living room. There's a wine cellar in the basement that can be rented out for private parties. The inn's restaurant, serving all three meals, puts an inventive southwestern and Native American spin on such dishes as chile glazed duck with mango cilantro vinaigrette ($16.75), and grilled lamb loin with tomatilla-serrano vinaigrette and a spring squash tart ($19). For a truly unique dining experience, the inn's concierge, who is herself a Navajo, can arrange special meals at local pueblos for guests. In-room massages are available, as is aromatherapy. Valet parking is $10 per day.

La Fonda

100 East San Francisco Street
Santa Fe, New Mexico 87501
505-982-5511
800-523-5002
Fax: 505-982-6367

General manager: James Bradbury
Accommodations: 160 rooms
Rates: single, $125–$155; double, $135–$165; suites, $225–$365
Added: 10.125% tax
Payment: Major credit cards
Children: Under 12 free in room with parents
Pets: Not permitted
Smoking: Nonsmoking rooms available
Open: Year-round

If you like to be at the center of activity, La Fonda is the place. Its motto, The world walks through our lobby, has more than a ring of truth to it during busy periods. Right on the Plaza, it's a nucleus for tourists. Step outside to an ongoing Indian market. Walk a half block to St. Francis Cathedral. Cross the Plaza to the Palace of the Governors and the Museum of Fine Arts.

At the hotel you can sign up for sightseeing tours, river rafting, the Cumbres and Toltec Scenic Railway, even trips to the Grand Canyon. You can also start your Santa Fe shopping; there's an art gallery and many fine shops right in the hotel.

While town records show that Santa Fe has had a fonda, or inn, since it was founded in 1610, the present La Fonda was built in 1920 on the site of an earlier hotel. Today's version is a rambling adobe filled with local flavor and a festive spirit.

The guest rooms come in standard, deluxe, mini-suites, and suites. Color spills from the rooms in the form of gaily painted headboards, rich teal or rose carpeting, bright white old-fashioned bedspreads, and hand-decorated Spanish colonial furniture. Sofas and small refrigerators add to your comfort, and carved wood molding adds to each room's individuality.

Standing in the halls, you'll swear that a band of elves had a marvelous time decorating everything in sight. Look in one direction to see a flock of birds in midflight; in the other, the air-conditioning vents are trimmed in bright designs. Even the elevator entrance didn't escape.

La Plazuela, the hotel's main restaurant, is in a festive court-yard, where brightly painted windows screen diners from the busy lobby. You'll feel as though you're in Mexico as you eat New Mexican specialties under a skylit viga roof. La Plazuela serves all three meals. Lunch entrées range from $5.95 to $7.95; dinner entrées start at $7.95.

La Terraza, overlooking St. Francis Cathedral, offers rooftop dining during the summer. Weather permitting, lunch is served from 11:30 A.M. to 5:00 P.M. and cocktails from 5:00 P.M. until closing, occasionally with entertainment. The Belltower, with magnificent city and mountain views, serves cocktails season-ally. There's also a French pastry shop and crêperie at La Fonda, and La Fiesta lounge offers nightly entertainment just off the lobby.

An outdoor pool, two indoor hot tubs, and a cold plunge pool are on the first floor. Massages are available by appointment. Covered garage parking is available for guests at $2 per night.

If you're interested in the history of Santa Fe and the area, be sure to stop by La Fonda's newsstand. From outside, it looks like any hotel gift shop, but inside is one of the best selections of regional guides around.

Tulsa

Doubletree Hotel at Warren Place
6100 South Yale
Tulsa, Oklahoma 74136
918-495-1000
800-528-0444
Fax: 918-495-1944

Resident manager: Will Temby
Accommodations: 371 rooms
Rates: single, $99–$109; double, $109–$119; junior suites, $150; deluxe suites start at $325
Added: 12.5% tax

Payment: Major credit cards
Children: Under 18 free in room with parents
Pets: Permitted with deposit
Smoking: Nonsmoking rooms available
Open: Year-round

One of the most outstanding hotels in Oklahoma, the Doubletree is beautiful and gracious. It caters to the corporate traveler, but whatever your reason for being in Tulsa, this hotel is an excellent choice.

Built in 1985, the ten-story Doubletree is part of the Warren Place office park in southeast Tulsa, a 20-minute drive from downtown. St. Francis Hospital is across the street. Despite the surrounding development, there's almost a pastoral feel to the hotel, and some rooms and public areas overlook rolling, well-landscaped grounds. Covered parking is free.

A 1½-mile jogging track threads through the property. The indoor pool, several cuts above average, is next to a whirlpool, steam room and sauna. This is a good place to relax, with views of the grounds adding to the mood. Guests can also use the Physical Performance Center across the street. Part of the hospital, it has an indoor jogging track, aerobic classes, and weight equipment. Nearby LaFortune Park has tennis and golf.

The guest rooms are well appointed. The Executive Level offers such extras as robes, Continental breakfast, evening cocktails, newspapers, and free local phone calls.

Greenleaf's on the Park is an airy café, and Encounters lounge has dancing. Whether you stay at the hotel or not, try the Warren Duck Club restaurant, known for its duck dishes as well as meats grilled on a rotisserie. Sophisticated and club-like, it has an appetizer bar and a dessert buffet (open for lunch and dinner daily except Sundays).

Tulsa Marriott

10918 East 41st Street
Tulsa, Oklahoma 74146
918-627-5000
800-228-9290
Fax: 918-627-4003

General manager: Tony Swainey
Accommodations: 336 rooms
Rates: single or double, $108; corporate and weekend rates available
Added: 12% tax
Payment: Major credit cards

Children: Under 18 free in room with parents
Pets: Small pets permitted
Smoking: Nonsmoking rooms available
Open: Year-round

The 11-story Marriott, on the outskirts of Tulsa about eight miles southeast of downtown, is a pleasant, low-key place to stop and relax. Many business addresses and several shopping malls are within a few miles. (Business travelers account for nearly eighty percent of the hotel's guests.) The lobby is welcoming, like a bouquet of fresh flowers.

There's an outdoor pool, an adjoining indoor pool with a nearby hot tub, and a health club with exercise equipment. There's also table tennis, volleyball, basketball, and board games.

The guest rooms have contemporary furnishings. The top-floor concierge rooms are worth the difference in price, with such extras as Continental breakfast, evening hors d'oeuvres, newspapers, and bathrobes.

Beechwoods restaurant has a wide variety of choices and offers a waffle dessert bar for Sunday brunch. Bronson's lounge is lively, with dancing, a wide-screen TV, and Las Vegas–style blackjack ("no gambling: for amusement, entertainment, practice, and instruction").

To arrange a candlelit dinner in your room, call the hotel direct (ext. 6619) before checking in. The restaurant staff will be happy to accommodate you.

The Westin Hotel, Williams Center
10 East Second Street
Tulsa, Oklahoma 74103
918-582-9000
800-228-3000
Fax: 918-582-0012

General manager: Peter N. Quattrone
Accommodations: 450 rooms
Rates: single or double, $120–$170; suites, $275–$975
Added: 12.5% tax
Payment: Major credit cards
Children: Under 18 free in room with parents
Pets: Permitted with approval
Smoking: One nonsmoking floor
Open: Year-round

Not only is the Westin a luxurious hotel with top service and extra flourishes, but it's part of a shopping mall with an ice skating rink in the center and it's next door to Tulsa's Performing Arts Center. In short, it's the place to be.

The guest rooms, decorated in rich colors, have a classic look and are furnished for comfort. All have cable TV in an armoire, stocked mini-bars, and large desks. Premier rooms have two TVs (one in the bath), three phones, a mini-bar, terrycloth robes, and extras such as fresh fruit and flowers.

Tucked away on the third floor is an outdoor pool overlooking the city and an adjoining indoor pool with a nearby hot tub. Happily, guests can get to the pool without going through the lobby or other public areas. Indoor tennis courts and exercise equipment are available at a health club next door.

There are many dining choices. The hotel's fine establishment is Montagues; Glass on the Green is informal, with all-day service and special Sunday brunches; and Le Bistro serves northern Italian fare, with an antipasto bar and make-your-own sundaes. Barristers lounge has live entertainment. Just through the glass skywalk and into Williams Center are many small places that add still more options.

Outside, across the square designed with gardens and pools, is the Performing Arts Center, the home of the Tulsa Ballet Theatre, Tulsa Opera, and Tulsa Philharmonic. It also has several small stages used by theater companies and performing artists.

Hotel parking, both valet ($8.75 per day) and self-service ($6.25), is in a covered garage.

Condominiums

Not only do condominiums offer space and privacy, they can be the most economical lodging for a family or a group of friends.

Arizona

Junipine Resort Condo Hotel
8351 North Highway 89A
Sedona, Arizona 86336
602-282-3375
800-742-7463
Fax: 602-282-7402

General manager: Jolynn Greenfield
Accommodations: 23 units
Rates: suites, $106–$260
Added: 5.61% tax
Payment: Major credit cards
Children: Under 12 free in condo with parents
Pets: Not permitted
Smoking: Nonsmoking condos available
Open: Year-round

Oak Creek Canyon, north of Sedona, is one of the area's top scenic attractions—a combination of evergreen forests and rugged mountain vistas. Junipine Resort, nestled among huge ponderosa pines on the banks of Oak Creek, provides spaciousness and comfort in a beautiful wooded setting.

Families will appreciate all the outdoor activities such as volleyball, horseshoes, hiking, and swimming in Oak Creek, which runs behind the property. Those seeking seclusion will also find what they're looking for here, since condo units are well designed for privacy.

All privately owned, the condos—called "creekhouses" by management—were built in 1985. Attractive natural wood structures, they blend well with the surrounding forests. The modern interiors are comfortable, accented with southwestern decor, but the outdoor setting is the prime focus, so each unit has a large deck, accessible from both the living and sleeping areas through sliding glass doors.

Each creekhouse has a small but very functional kitchen, complete with all you need, including full table settings. All units have fireplaces, and baths have separate vanities. Some units have lofts.

New Mexico

Fort Marcy Compound Condominiums
320 Artist Road
Santa Fe, New Mexico 87501
505-98-CONDO
800-745-9910
Fax: 505-984-8682

Owner: John Smallwood
Accommodations: 100 units
Rates: Start at $80 for 1-bedroom condo, $125 for 2 bedrooms, $175 for 3 bedrooms
Minimum stay: 2 nights; 4 nights in August and Christmas holidays
Added: 10.125% tax
Payment: Major credit cards
Children: Welcome
Pets: Not permitted
Smoking: Permitted
Open: Year-round

Just a short drive from Santa Fe's Plaza is Fort Marcy Compound, a 100-unit complex of one-, two-, and three-bedroom adobe condos in a residential neighborhood, offering vacationers a spacious accommodation close to the sights in the area.

These condos are the closest commercial lodging facilities to the Santa Fe Ski Basin, 15 miles away, which boasts a 12,000-foot summit and a 1,650-foot vertical descent. There are 7 lifts and 32 runs at the mountain as well as a certified ski school.

The condos, built in 1973, are on land that was once the Fort Marcy Military Reservation. According to some archaeologists, an Indian pueblo may have been on this site as early as A.D. 1000, thus predating Santa Fe by more than 500 years.

The complex spreads over 10 acres dotted with cedars and piñon. An indoor lap pool and hot tub as well as a full laundry are pluses. The units, some on hillsides with mountain views, include one- and two-bedroom flats and two- and three-bedroom town houses. The interiors reflect Santa Fe style, with kiva fireplaces and Mexican tile. Because the units are privately owned, they have more personality than a standard hotel room. Brightly colored folk art animals, dried flowers, and handwoven baskets filled with magazines give the condos a homey atmosphere. The kitchens are well equipped, with microwave ovens, toasters, and coffeemakers. In addition to the expected cable TV, the condos also have stereo-cassette systems.

Daily maid service is provided. And the Fort Marcy personnel respond happily to personal requests, from stocking refrigerators to making dinner reservations.

Otra Vez
Galisteo at Water
P.O. Box 2927
Santa Fe, New Mexico 87504
505-988-2244

Property manager: Patsy Block
Accommodations: 18 units
Rates: 1 bedroom, $110–$135; 2 bedrooms, $135–$160
Added: 10.125% tax
Payment: Major credit cards
Children: Under 12 free in room with parents
Pets: Not permitted
Smoking: Discouraged
Open: Year-round

For small groups or families, either for skiing or visiting Santa Fe, Otra Vez condominiums offer an excellent downtown location and spacious living quarters. One- and two-bedroom units are available in a three-story building about three blocks from the Plaza.

The emphasis is on comfort and convenience, yet framed folk art quilts, Taos drums, baskets, live plants, and earth-tone pastel fabrics add to the visual appeal of each unit. The living rooms have fireplaces (firewood is supplied) and TVs, and the kitchens are thoughtfully equipped with dishwashers, coffee-makers, and blenders—even cheese graters and extra spatulas. The dining areas can seat six people.

The units are arranged around a second-floor outside area with a hot tub. Each floor has a washer and dryer; daily maid service is included in the rates, and parking is free. Guests check in between 8:00 A.M. and 5:00 P.M. daily. Later arrivals can be arranged with the security guard. No weekly rates are available, but when you consider that the two-bedroom units can sleep up to five and you can make your own meals, Otra Vez is a truly affordable possibility.

Texas

Bridgepoint
334 Padre Boulevard
South Padre Island, Texas 78597
512-761-7969
800-221-1402
Fax: 512-761-2844

Property manager: Richard Brandel
Accommodations: About 35 units
Rates: 1 bedroom, $150–$250; 2 bedrooms, $175–$300; 3 bedrooms, $225–$350; 4 bedrooms, $275–$400; penthouse, $275–$425
Payment: Major credit cards
Children: Welcome
Pets: In some units
Smoking: Nonsmoking units available
Open: Year-round

For luxurious vacationing high above the crowds, Bridgepoint is the place. The sleek 28-story beachfront condominium tower opened in 1984, and about a quarter of its 114 privately owned units are available for rent. While each is individually deco-rated, they are all super luxurious.

Differing from standard condos in their floor plans, the units are especially spacious, airy, and inviting. (One-bedroom units have 1,400 square feet; 2-bedrooms have 1,800 square feet, 3-bedrooms have 2,000 square feet.) Most of the rooms have ocean views. The penthouses (three bedrooms) are truly exquisite, with sweeping panoramas. The kitchens are well equipped, and each unit has a washer and dryer.

There is an attractive outdoor area with a children's pool, a sunken whirlpool tub, an adult pool, and a palapa snack bar. There is also a well-equipped exercise room and two lighted tennis courts. Of course, the beach itself is right outside the front door. Beach umbrellas and chairs are free.

Not only is the property itself topnotch, but the condo manager runs the rental units like a hotel. In short, you're treated like a valued guest. There is a security gate (be sure you're expected) and covered garage parking.

Although South Padre Island is a popular destination for spring break, the condos are not rented to students. A telephone deposit is required of all guests.

Seascape
10811 San Luis Pass Road
Galveston, Texas 77554
409-740-1245

Rental manager: Helen Z. Bateman
Accommodations: 75 condominiums
Rates: 1 bedroom (accommodates six), $69–$135; 2 bedrooms (accommodates eight), $99–$200
Added: 13% tax
Payment: Major credit cards
Children: Welcome
Pets: Not permitted
Smoking: 1 nonsmoking unit available
Open: Year-round

On Galveston Island's West Beach, just past the seawall, Seascape condominiums are directly on the beach. (Most of the condos in the area are behind the 10.4-mile-long seawall.) The units are attractive and well furnished, with a pool, kiddie pool, Jacuzzi, and tennis court on the grounds, and the management is efficient and accommodating.

The units come in a choice of six designs. All have well-equipped kitchens, including a full-size refrigerator (one of the six floor plans has an under-the-counter refrigerator only), dishwasher, two-burner cooktop, microwave oven, cookware, and tableware. Since these are privately owned condos, all are individually decorated. In addition to the usual sleeping accommodations, the living rooms have sofa beds and the entry halls have two built-in bunk beds. The bathrooms are divided into three compartments, with a total of two toilets, two lavatories, and one tub-shower. (One floor plan has two full bathtubs with showers.) There is a private telephone line in each unit.

If you like privacy, for an extra charge you can get one of the beachfront units. While all of the condos have a gulf-view balcony, they also look onto their neighbors. In contrast, the beachfront units look straight out to sea, offering a definite sense of isolation.

Boardwalks lead over the dunes and onto the beach. Parking is free. There are coin operated washer and dryers on two floors of each building, although some units have their own laundry facilities. Housekeeping service is available for an additional charge.

Family Favorites

Some of these accommodations have a wealth of recreational facilities that appeal to visitors of all ages, some are economical, and some have programs, such as a day camp, especially designed for children.

Arizona

The Bisbee Inn
45 OK Street
P.O. Box 1855
Bisbee, Arizona 85603
602-432-5131

Owners: John and Joy Timbers
Accommodations: 18 rooms (shared baths)
Rates: single, $29; double, $34–$39; credit card rates slightly higher; $5 each additional person
Included: Full breakfast
Added: 10.55% tax
Payment: Major credit cards
Children: Welcome
Pets: Permitted
Smoking: Outside only
Open: Year-round

On one of the steepest streets in a town known for steep streets is the Bisbee Inn, with very affordable prices. When it opened as the LaMore Hotel in 1917, across the street was Brewery Gulch, lined with bars.

A certified historic restoration, the inn reflects its past yet also has a fresh appeal. Many of the furnishings have a history of their own. The iron beds, recently sandblasted and repainted, date from the original hotel. The oak tables and chairs came from the old Brooks Apartments next door.

Each guest room is different, both in decor and configuration. All have period wallpaper, perhaps deep blue with flowers or another dainty design. Quilted spreads and antique dressers complete the look. Bed arrangements include one double, two doubles, or one double and one twin. Central air conditioning and heating have been added. There are no TVs in the guest rooms, but there is a TV room on the main floor. Each room has a washbasin, but bathrooms are down the hall. Also available are a coin operated washer and dryer.

In the morning, guests gather around oak tables for a generous breakfast of fresh fruit, French toast, cereal, hash browns, honey wheat pancakes, bacon and eggs, and homemade bread. Then it's time to explore Bisbee. Tours of the Queen Mine, narrated by former miners, lead through an old copper mine with turn-of-the-century mining demonstrations. Also nearby are Chiricahua National Monument, Fort Huachuca, and the western town of Tombstone.

Marriott's Camelback Inn
5402 East Lincoln Drive
Scottsdale, Arizona 85253
602-948-1700
800-228-9290 or 800-24-CAMEL
Fax: 602-951-2152

General manager: Wynn Tyner
Accommodations: 423 units
Rates: single or double, $95–$290; suites (up to 5 people per unit), $160–$1,600
Added: 9.05% tax
Payment: Major credit cards
Children: Under 18 free in room with parents
Pets: Permitted
Smoking: Nonsmoking units available
Open: Year-round

The Camelback Inn dates from 1936, when it was built by Jack and Louise Stewart. With their hospitality and dedication, they wrote a romantic chapter in the story of American resorts. Their inn attracted noted guests from around the world, many of whom returned year after year to the popular desert resort. "In all the world, only one," was the Stewarts' guiding principle as they molded a lodging of rare charm, emphasizing attention to detail and personal service.

In 1967 the Stewarts sold the resort to the Marriotts, a family that had been visiting Camelback for 14 years. Today's resort is much larger than the one the Marriotts bought. But you don't have to look far to sense the tradition—a real plus in an area now crowded with posh new playgrounds.

"Where time stands still" is emblazoned on the inn's clock tower and at the entrance to the lobby. The message to guests is clear: forget about time and the outside world—just relax and enjoy. Spread over 125 acres of desert terrain, numerous recreational facilities help "real world" cares slip away quickly. Camelback has two highly acclaimed 18-hole championship golf courses (greens fees, including golf cart rental, range from $25 to $70, depending on the season), a driving range, putting green, 10 tennis courts ($10 per hour), 3 pools, and 5 restaurants and lounges. The front lawn is an 825-yard executive golf course. Stables with horseback riding are nearby (free transportation is provided). Hiking trails lead up Mummy Mountain, at the resort's back door. There's a playground for kids, bikes to rent, shuffleboard, and lots of space to roam. Social programs during holiday seasons reflect the spirit of the Stewarts' resort.

Guests stay in low rooms scattered over the rolling grounds, which are studded with citrus, olive, and mesquite trees and more than 40 varieties of cactus. Lodgings include single rooms, sun deck rooms (decks adjoin the rooms), and a variety of suites. There is a 4-bedroom manor house with a full kitchen, washer-dryer and private pool. All the rooms have refrigerators and small cooktops. Even the standard rooms are spacious, with such extras as two phones, built-in hair dryers, coffeemakers, ironing boards, safes, stocked mini-bars, and remote control TV. The decor is southwestern in style.

The main lodge, small for a resort of this size, looks like a real lodge. Decorated with an Indian theme, it has wonderful painted beams, Navajo rugs, and light fixtures made from arrows. The lobby is listed on the National Register of Historic Places.

Dining offers lots of choices, both in cuisine and price, and everyone (even finicky children) should be able to find something to suit their taste and mood. MAP, FAP, and CAP (Camelback American Plan, with breakfast and lunch) are available. Popular with both guests and residents, Chaparral specializes in classic Continental cuisine. Entrées such as beef Wellington, steak Diane, rack of lamb, scampi flambé, and Dover sole range from $18 to $26.

The Camelback also has its own spa, with state-of-the-art exercise equipment, a wellness center, revitalizing skin and body treatments, and a highly trained staff. Guests can use the facility for $18 per day ($10 after 5:00 P.M.). The outdoor massage rooms are especially pleasant, as is the spa's own outdoor 25-meter lap pool, surrounded by terraced cacti with a glorious view of both the city and the mountains. Sprouts, the spa's attractive café, has a tempting menu even if you're not keeping track of calories, fat, and cholesterol.

Above the spa, there's a mock Old West town where popular steakfrys and cookouts are held. The inn also has its own hiking trail up Mummy Mountain.

Red Lion's La Posada
4949 East Lincoln Drive
Scottsdale, Arizona 85253
602-952-0420
800-547-8010
Fax: 602-840-8576

General manager: Derick MacDonald
Accommodations: 264 rooms
Rates: single or double, $65–$205; suites, $400–$1,050
Added: 9.05% tax
Payment: Major credit cards
Children: Under 18 free in room with parents
Pets: Permitted
Smoking: Nonsmoking rooms available
Open: Year-round

Red Lion's La Posada brings water to the desert and adds an extra dollop of glitz to Scottsdale's hotel row. In a lobby more like Las Vegas than the Southwest, with a profusion of fuchsia, gold, and sparkle, you can tell this is no ordinary resort. It's a lively place, where the tone is definitely upbeat and the staff greets you with a smile.

Out back there's a half-acre swimming pool, actually more of a lagoon, with a manmade boulder mountain, splashing waterfalls, and a partly hidden grotto bar. Directly behind the hotel is the area's most distinctive landmark—Camelback Mountain. The Garden Terrace Restaurant is a great place to eat while overlooking the pool and the mountain (the Sunday champagne brunch is a popular event, at $17.95). Like the lobby below, it has a refreshingly energetic decor. The adjoining Terrace Lounge has live entertainment.

The guest rooms are in long stucco buildings with red tile roofs arranged over the resort's 32 acres. Inside brocades, formal furniture, and mirrors prevail. The smallest room is large by hotel standards—450 square feet. The cabanas are 759 square feet, the casitas, 950 square feet. All the rooms have small refrigerators, honor bars, TVs in armoires, and patios or balconies.

La Posada has 6 tennis courts, 2 racquetball courts, a volleyball court, fitness center, massage services, a putting green, table tennis, horseshoes, basketball, a sauna, and hot tubs. There's also a camp for children, concierge service, car rental, and airport transportation. A shopping plaza on the grounds has an Italian restaurant.

Sheraton El Conquistador Resort and Country Club

10,000 North Oracle Road
Tucson, Arizona 85737
602-544-5000
800-325-STEC
Fax: 602-544-1222

General manager: Alan Fuerstman
Accommodations: 434 rooms
Rates: single or double, $85–$275; $15 each extra person
Suites: $215–$225
Added: 8.5% tax
Payment: Major credit cards
Children: Under 17 free in room with parents
Pets: Permitted
Smoking: Permitted
Open: Year-round

Spread over 150 acres of high rolling desert about 10 miles north of Tucson, the Sheraton El Conquistador looks up at the 2,000-foot Pusch Ridge cliffs directly beyond. A resort with a colonial Mexican theme, it's a composite of one- to three-story buildings. The lobby itself is expansive, with many sitting areas and a desert scene above the front desk that is said to be the largest copper mural in the country.

The guest rooms have traditional furniture and southwestern decor in attractive cool colors. All the rooms have private patios or balconies. Junior suites are spacious, with writing desks, cushioned bancos and sofas for extra seating, tie racks and wooden valets in the closet, makeup mirrors, coffeemakers, and telephones in the bath. The most luxurious accommodations are the Casita suites which have their own fireplaces.

A variety of recreational facilities are available, highlighted by El Conquistador's 45 holes of championship golf. Its 30 tennis courts are excellent. There's a stadium court, pro shop, and tennis instructors. About forty horses are stabled on the grounds for trail rides into Coronado National Forest. Cookout and sunset champagne rides can be scheduled upon request. For groups, hayrides, barbecues, and square dances can also be arranged. Of course, there's a large central swimming pool and a smaller one in the midst of the casitas, along with such extras as 10 racquetball courts, jogging paths, and fitness centers.

The summer is an excellent time to get top value for your dollar, with prices for both rooms and recreation at the low end of the rate schedule. There is a Kid's Club during the summer, with supervised activities such as tennis, arts and crafts, swimming, and movies.

El Conquistador's five restaurants and poolside snack bar (the Desert Spring) give dimension and variety to dining choices. The casual Sundance Café serves breakfast and lunch; it has a children's menu, and kids under six eat for free. The Last Territory is a rustic steakhouse with entertainment and dancing. Dos Locos, fashioned after a Baja beachside cantina, serves Mexican food and turns into a lively disco after 9:00 P.M. The White Dove is El Conquistador's newest restaurant. Gourmet pizzas, grilled meats, and seafood are prepared with Southwestern flair and spice. La Vista atop the clubhouse at El Conquistador's country club offers panoramic views while dining.

Other services such as a concierge, 24-hour room service, a morning newspaper at your door, free self-parking, a weekly newsletter of events at the resort and in Tucson, and a friendly staff contribute to El Conquistador's appeal.

Sky Ranch Lodge
Airport Road
P.O. Box 2579
Sedona, Arizona 86336
602-282-6400

Owner: Sheri Graham
Accommodations: 94 rooms
Rates: single, $50; double, $55–$100; double cottages, $125
Added: 10.5% tax
Payment: Major credit cards and personal checks from
  Arizona only
Children: Under 12 free in room with parents; over 12 an
  additional $5 per day
Pets: Permitted; $5 fee
Open: Year-round

On Table Mountain about two miles from downtown Sedona is a family-run motel offering comfort and serenity at a good value. Highway 89A, into Sedona, is a mile below. Tiny Sedona Airport (one 5,100-foot runway) is a few hundred feet up the road, at the top of the mesalike mountain.

Built in 1982, the motel is spread over six acres, with units in wooden buildings. Most are one-story. The prime location is on the mountain rim, with views of the Red Rock country for which Sedona is famed. The Rim Rooms open onto wooden decks, where nothing other than an occasional cedar tree comes between you and the valley below. Garden rooms open out onto the pool but don't have views.

The rooms are not fancy but are thoughtfully decorated with nice touches such as dried floral wreaths and Mexican tiling in the vanity area. Some have fireplaces and small kitchenettes. Sleeping accommodations include a choice of one king-size, two queen-size, or two double beds. Air conditioning, electric heat, a TV, and phones are in every unit. The two rim cottages, for two people, have a kitchenette, fireplace, and deck.

The grounds are attractive and well tended. Obviously, this place has a sense of pride. The pool and separate spa are inviting. There's no restaurant, but hot coffee is always brewing in the lobby, and there's a family-style restaurant at the airport, within walking distance.

Westward Look Resort

245 East Ina Road
Tucson, Arizona 85704
602-297-1151
800-722-2500
Fax: 602-297-9023

General manager: John Dailey
Accommodations: 244 rooms
Rates: single or double, $80–$200

Suites: Start at $145
Added: 6.5% tax
Payment: Major credit cards
Children: Welcome
Pets: Permitted
Smoking: Nonsmoking rooms available
Open: Year-round

Westward Look, about eight miles north of Tucson, glistens on the high desert landscape. It has a wide assortment of sports, a highly rated restaurant, and well-designed lodging, plus a friendly atmosphere conducive to family vacations. Westward Look is the type of place guests return to year after year.

Spread over 84 acres, the resort has 3 swimming pools and hot tubs, 8 Laykold tennis courts, basketball and volleyball courts, a fitness center, and a fitness trail with desert plants identified, plus such extras as horseshoes and shuffleboard. Tennis gets lots of attention at Westward Look. There's a pro shop, a clubhouse, and viewing deck. An hourly fee is charged for court time, but tennis packages are frequently offered. There is no golf course, but the staff can arrange for you to play at one of seven courses in the area.

The Gold Room restaurant has an inventive and inviting menu, plus beautiful views of Tucson and the mountains to the west—hence the resort's name. Loin of lamb served with spinach and chicken mousse and rosemary Bordelaise, grilled tenderloin of pork with black figs and Bermuda onions, and sautéed shrimp topped with a julienne of celery and leek in a Chardonnay beurre blanc sauce are a few of the dinner entrées; papaya and prosciutto, and confit of duck in wonton served over avocado beurre blanc are just two of the tempting appetizers. Entrées range between $5.25 and $9.50 for lunch, $16.50 and $22 for dinner. A twilight menu, offered from 5:30 to 6:30 P.M., offers smaller portions and smaller prices, and the Sunday brunch is always a popular event. For light meals, there's the Lookout Lounge and Cafe. The Lounge frequently has live entertainment, and guests can enjoy Sunday afternoon tea dances to the music of a swing band.

The lodgings are sprinkled over the beautifully landscaped grounds, with nearby parking for each unit. Units themselves have different configurations, but all are comfortable and well designed for privacy. The decor is pure Southwest, with light wood furnishings, attractive fabrics, terracotta lamps, beamed ceilings and desert art. Each unit has a private balcony or patio, small refrigerator, stocked servi-bar, coffeemaker, wet bar, cable TV, and a choice of one king-size or two double beds. The baths are large, decorated in yellow or terra cotta and accented with painted tiles. Extra towels, hair dryers, and night lights are thoughtful touches.

Wickenburg Inn

P.O. Box P
Highway 89
North Wickenburg, Arizona 85358
602-684-7811
800-528-4227
Fax: 602-684-2981

General manager: Roger E. Wilcox
Accommodations: 47 rooms
Rates: single, $95–$240; double, $165–$310; additional
    persons aged 7 and up, $50 extra per day
Included: All meals, ranch activities, horseback riding, and
    tennis
Added: 5.5% state tax; 15% service charge
Payment: Major credit cards
Children: Welcome
Pets: Not permitted
Smoking: Permitted
Open: Year-round

Wickenburg Inn offers an innovative mix of attractions in an informal atmosphere that's especially suited for families. Tennis, horseback riding, nature observation, and arts and crafts are popular events. Spread over gently rolling desert landscape studded with saguaro cactus, the inn consists of a ranch-style lodge, luxurious adobe casitas, and a host of recreational activities. The 11 acrylic tennis courts are among the best in the state. Its instruction center has automatic ball machines, strategy boards, fixed targets, and practice walls. Clinics and individual lessons are easy to arrange.

The stables house about 100 horses during the winter months, 40 or so in the summer. Rides go out daily, with special cookout, breakfast, and moonlight rides according to the season. Private lessons and horsemanship clinics are also offered.

The arts and crafts center, unusual at a resort, has excellent programs for all ages, including leatherwork, stained glass, pottery, and weaving. Sometimes local artisans are on hand to demonstrate their craft.

One of the inn's most imaginative offerings is its nature program. A resident naturalist introduces guests to the Sonoran Desert through interpretive walks, slide presentations, and stargazing seminars, as well as exhibits and a natural history library in the nature center. Surrounding the resort is a 47,000-acre wildlife preserve, the home of more than 200 species of animals and 300 kinds of plants. Special desert ecology programs and desert study weekends are scheduled during the year. Day-long guided excursions to the Grand Canyon, Oak Creek, Sedona, and Prescott are also offered (check with the inn before you arrive).

Of course, the resort has a pool, as well as a hilltop outdoor spa, archery, a children's playground, and a jogging trail. The main lodge's dining room serves all three meals—buffet style when the inn is full—but there is usually a choice of entrées such as prime rib, crab cakes, or chicken alfredo. The menu changes daily. Saturday nights are special, with western cookouts and maybe a hay ride. For parents, there's a bar in the main lodge with a stone fireplace and big-screen television.

Most accommodations are in the casita complexes scattered over the grounds. (A few rooms are in the main lodge.) There's nothing rustic about this lodging, even though Wickenburg Inn is often referred to as a ranch. Well decorated and spacious, the casitas have modern southwestern furnishings and such amenities as fireplaces, TVs, and wet bars with a two-burner cooktop and refrigerator. The deluxe suites are definitely deluxe, with their own rooftop decks.

Best of all for a family resort is the attention staff gives to its younger guests. Not only are there plenty of activities for children, but the staff really enjoys "working" with them, and goes out of their way to make their stay special. One guest said a staff member helped her son catch a gecko. Another said prized stuffed animals that were accidently left behind at the inn were promptly returned by mail. On one visit, the front desk clerk cheerfully tried to locate the room number of a newfound friend with only the first name to go on. There must have been over 50 children staying at the resort at the time, but through process of elimination she was able to track down the little girl's playmate and the two girls went off happily to dinner together.

New Mexico

El Rey Inn
1862 Cerrillos Road
P.O. Box 130
Santa Fe, New Mexico 87504-0130
505-982-1931

Owner/manager: Terrell White
Accommodations: 56 rooms
Rates: single or double, $54–$98; suites, $92–$130
Included: Continental breakfast
Added: 10.125% tax
Payment: Major credit cards; no personal checks
Children: Free in room with parents
Pets: Not permitted
Open: Year-round

El Rey may look like just another motel, as it is on Santa Fe's strip of fast-food restaurants and motels. But when you check in, you'll find it's far from ordinary: in fact, it's unlike other motels. The grounds, dotted with spruce and elm trees and fountains, are well groomed. Special touches are everywhere, from porch swings to painted murals on Mexican tile to colorful potted plants. The swimming pool is set in the trees, and the playground looks as if it were designed for beloved grandchildren.

Owned by the same family since 1973, El Rey gives you high value. When you leave, you feel that you have gotten more than your money's worth. Surprisingly for a motel, the rooms have lots of variety. They all have air conditioning, TV, radios, and phones. The interiors are definitely southwestern, with foot-thick adobe walls and either viga and latilla or ceilings. Such features as brass or wooden carved beds, kiva fireplaces, tile murals, skylights, and bathrooms with colored tile add individuality. Apartments accommodating up to six people have kitchenettes or kitchens; some have fireplaces.

The lobby, with a fireplace and game tables, is unusually attractive and spacious and is a good gathering place for groups. A hot tub and greenhouse add to the fun, while a laundry adds to convenience.

Although El Rey does not have a restaurant, there are plenty of choices nearby, on Cerrillos Road. (Children will no doubt spy the Baskin-Robbins just across the street.) In the morning, Continental breakfast is served in the skylit breakfast room or on the sunny terrace in the main lodge.

Inn of the Mountain Gods

P.O. Box 269
Carriz Canyon Road
Mescalero, New Mexico 88340
505-257-5141
800-545-9011
Fax: 505-257-6173

General Manager: Fredda Draper
Accommodations: 250 rooms
Rates: single or double, $115–$125; suites, $125–$135
Added: 9.5% tax
Payment: Major credit cards
Children: Under 12 free in room with parents if no crib or
  roll-away required; over 12, additional $12 per day
Pets: Not permitted
Smoking: Nonsmoking rooms available
Open: Year-round

High in the Sacramento Mountains, the Inn of the Mountain
Gods sprawls along the shore of Lake Mescalero below the
spectacular snow-capped Sierra Blanca peak. Although the
tourist center of Ruidoso is only 3½ miles north, this resort is a
world of its own, beautiful in its seclusion. Owned and run by
the Mescalero Apache Indian Reservation, it sits at the heart of
its forested land. The inn, built in 1975, is made up of a series of
rambling buildings connected by long enclosed walkways. (Be
sure to drive as close as possible to your room with your luggage
after check-in, because unless your room is in one of the hall-
ways closest to the lobby, you'll have to carry your bag quite
some distance.) There's no pretension about the place, just informality and relaxed fun.

Every room has a balcony or patio and overlooks the lake or
the mountains. The decor is modern, with some Indian art
accents. These accommodations rank high in spaciousness and
convenience; in the bathrooms, the vanities and mirrors are
separate from the rest of the bath. Suites have a Murphy bed,
sitting area, and wet bar.

The inn has three restaurants, five lounges, and a hot dog
stand by the pool specializing in international versions of the
snack food. The Apache Tee serves breakfast and lunch. The
finest restaurant, Dan Li Ka Room (Mescalero Apache for
"good food"), has excellent fare and an attractive environment.
Entrées such as mountain trout and a southwestern sauté made
with venison, chicken breast, and beef medallions in a marsala
cilantro sauce range from $14 to $18. The Top of the Inn coffee
shop is open in summer only.

Golfing, boating, tennis, fishing, horseback riding, archery,
and trap and skeet shooting are enough to keep most vacationers happy. The inn's 18-hole championship golf course is
one of the finest in the Southwest. Scenic, challenging, and well
maintained, it's a prime drawing card for the resort. The greens
fee for guests is $32; cart rental is $20.

Tennis is also important, with six outdoor courts, a pro shop, and viewing deck. (Court time is $14–$32 per hour.) Boaters can rent canoes, rowboats, and pedal boats; no motor boats are permitted. For anglers, the lake is stocked with rainbow and cutthroat trout, and there's a bait and tackle shop by the pier. The stables, about 1½ miles from the inn, offer 1-hour to all-day rides.

For hunters, the inn operates a hunting program from mid-September through December. The reservation abounds with trophy-size elk, white-tailed deer, and pronghorn antelope herds. Black and brown bear, turkey, and mountain lions are also featured game.

The inn runs a bus service to Ski Apache (also owned by the tribe) during ski season and to Ruidoso Downs Race Track on race days. For guests with a yen for gambling, the inn runs bingo, poker, lotto, and video games.

Oklahoma

Roman Nose Resort
Route 1
Watonga, Oklahoma 73772
405-623-7281
800-654-8240
Fax: 405-623-2538

General manager: Pam Rickey
Accommodations: 56 rooms
Rates: single, $50; double, $68; suites, $150
Added: 4.5% tax
Payment: Major credit cards
Children: Free in room with parents
Pets: Permitted in cottages only
Smoking: Nonsmoking rooms available
Open: Year-round

The southern Cheyenne chief Henry Roman Nose once settled his tribe in the canyon where the state park named for him now stands. At Roman Nose Resort, the waiters wear buckskin, Indians perform native dances, and folk legends come alive around the campfire.

There's a comfortable air about Roman Nose Lodge. It's never crowded, and it's well managed and maintained. Recreational facilities—a swimming pool, 9-hole golf course, mini-golf, horses, paddleboats, and canoes—are used by lodge guests and park campers alike. The lodge has its own small pool as well as a recreation staff that plans such activities as tram tours, games, arts and crafts, nature hikes, and trips to nearby sites. Trout fishing is popular from November through March. Overall, the mood is very relaxed.

From April through November, the lodge presents Indian Adventure packages that celebrate the area's heritage. Included are an Indian cookout, native arts and crafts workshops, Indian cooking lessons, and an outdoor interpretive program, plus two nights' lodging. You can even spend the night in a tepee (accommodating up to eight) if you wish.

The rooms in the main lodge have pleasant furnishings. Some have two queen-size beds, others have one king. Many have private balconies overlooking the cedar-studded hills.

High season is from mid-May to mid-September. Senior citizen rates are available Sundays through Thursdays.

Texas

Indian Lodge
P.O. Box 786
Fort Davis, Texas 79734
915-426-3254

General manager: Michael L. Crevier
Accommodations: 39 rooms
Rates: single, $40–$50; double, $50–$55; suites, $50–$65
Added: 10% tax
Payment: Personal check written on a Texas bank
Children: Under 6 free in room with parents; children aged 6 to 13, additional $2 per day per child
Pets: Not permitted
Smoking: Not permitted in restaurant
Open: Year-round except 2 weeks in mid-January

Indian Lodge is nestled in a valley in the Davis Mountains. The mountains themselves are rugged and distinctive, their rock outcroppings tempered by lush green foliage. The air is fresh with cedar at this tranquil retreat; the elevation is 5,000 feet.

The white adobe lodge, built on multiple levels, is a visual treat. All of its rooms open to the outdoors, some onto verandas with excellent views of the canyon. Part of Davis Mountain State Park, the lodge is run by Texas Parks and Wildlife. But make no mistake—this is not an ordinary state park accommodation. There are no luxuries such as room service, but the overall atmosphere is polished. The rooms all have carpeting, a TV, a phone, and central air conditioning. The beds are stenciled in an Indian theme.

The 15 rooms in the original building (with numbers in the 100s) are the most desirable, varying in size and design. Built by the Civilian Conservation Corps in the 1930s, the building's adobe walls are 18 inches thick. Room 121 is the largest, more like a suite than a standard hotel room. The newer rooms, built in 1967, are of average size and have cinder block interior walls.

The lodge's restaurant serves three meals a day. Dinner entrées range from $5 to $7, but buffets are the restaurant's specialty. Holidays such as Thanksgiving, Mardi Gras, and Oktoberfest are celebrated with equal revelry—each with a theme buffet, entertainment, and decor. In December, Santa Claus pays a breakfast visit to the lodge for guests' and area children.

The lodge has a heated pool below the lobby, but the top attractions are in the scenic countryside. In Davis Mountain State Park there are miles of hiking trails. Campfire programs are presented during the summer. Old Fort Davis is 4 miles away; McDonald Observatory (with the twelfth-largest telescope in the world, visitors center, tours) is 13 miles from the lodge.

Inn of the Hills River Resort

1001 Junction Highway
Kerrville, Texas 78028
512-895-5000
800-292-5690
Fax: 512-895-1277

General manager: Charlotte Thompson
Accommodations: 150 rooms, 68 condos
Rates: single, $50–$60; double, $65–$85; condos, $110–$175; additional adults, $6
Added: 12% tax
Payment: Major credit cards
Children: Under 12 free in room with parents
Pets: Small ones permitted
Smoking: Nonsmoking rooms available
Open: Year-round

In the Texas Hill Country, this resort has a wide range of offerings, both in style of accommodations and in recreation. Inn of the Hills began welcoming guests in the early 1960s, and in the mid-1980s it added a luxurious condominium complex on the banks of the Guadalupe River, greatly enhancing its appeal.

Guests now have a choice of motel rooms, cabanas, junior suites, and executive suites—all in the older section—and of condos with or without kitchenettes.

The motel centers around a pleasant swimming pool and playground; the new complex provides a river view for every unit. While the original motel reflects its age, there's a look of TLC about it. The rooms are pleasantly decorated, and the grounds are well maintained. The elegant, high-rise condos, ranging from 700 to 1,500 square feet, are a decided contrast to the older lodgings.

Guests have full use of all the resort's facilities. That translates to two outdoor pools, lighted tennis courts, and a 9-hole putting green; a marina on the riverbank with canoes and paddleboats; a fishing pier; rental bikes; and the sports center next door with racquetball, handball, an exercise room, indoor pool, and bowling. The inn also runs a family summer camp and frequently holds music and art festivals.

Two casual restaurants are on the grounds. One of the dining rooms has an outdoor terrace shaded by an ivy trellis.

The Nutt House Hotel and Inn

Town Square
Granbury, Texas 76048
817-573-5612

Manager: Sam Overpeck
Accommodations: 15 units (6 with private bath) in the hotel, 2 rooms in the inn
Rates: single or double, $39–$85; $75 per room at the inn
Added: 13% tax
Payment: Major credit cards
Children: Welcome; infants not encouraged
Pets: Not permitted
Smoking: Nonsmoking rooms available
Open: Year-round

Granbury calls itself "a door to yesterday"; its town square was the first in Texas to be listed on the National Register of Historic Places. Lining its streets are a bevy of antiques stores, gift shops, and restaurants. The restored Granbury Opera House, one of the region's most popular attractions, overlooks the square. So does the Nutt House hotel and restaurant, a two-story stone building dating from 1893.

Downstairs is an old-fashioned restaurant serving dinner at midday, Tuesdays through Sundays, and supper on weekends. An all-you-can-eat buffet, the country food is quite good (hot water cornbread and buttermilk pie are two specialties), and the price is a real bargain ($5 during the week, $7 on weekends).

Upstairs is a hotel straight out of 1919. At the top of the stairs there's a gathering spot with a coffeepot. It's a Nutt House tradition that the first guest up in the morning makes coffee.

The rooms themselves have screen doors (there's a curtain behind the screen), iron beds, simple furnishings, and lavatories. The bathrooms are down the hall; and nine rooms share three baths. The apartment unit is perfect for a family, with one double and two twin beds, a full kitchen, sitting area, and private bath. Don't expect phones or TVs, but the hotel is centrally air-conditioned and heated.

About a block away is the Nutt House Bed & Breakfast in a log cabin right on the water. There are two rooms, each with their own bath and cable TV; and unlike the hotel, Continental breakfast is included with the room rate.

Radisson Suite Hotel

700 Avenue H East
Arlington, Texas 76011
817-640-0440
800-333-3333
Fax: 817-649-2480

General manager: Audrey Waldrop
Accommodations: 202 suites
Rates: single, $104; double, $124; $10 each additional person
Included: Full breakfast and happy hour
Added: 13% tax
Payment: Major credit cards
Children: Under 18 free in room with parents
Pets: Not permitted
Smoking: Nonsmoking rooms available
Open: Year-round

Six Flags Over Texas, Wet 'n Wild waterpark, and Arlington Stadium (home of the Texas Rangers baseball team) are only a shuttle bus ride away from this all-suite Radisson, which opened in 1986. Its exterior arches, lit at night, have a high-energy look. Inside, the lobby is airy and refreshing. Next door is a seven-story atrium—not massive and overpowering, but almost intimate. The suites all open onto the atrium. Their sitting areas are fairly small but well equipped, with a sofa bed, TV, phone, and wet bar with refrigerator. The bedrooms, decorated in soothing colors, have two double beds or one king-size and a remote-control TV. The baths are larger than average but do not have separate vanities. Downstairs there's a heated oval swimming pool, hot tub, and sauna.

Mandolins Restaurant is elegant, with etched glass at the entrance, soft music in the background, and a menu with such dishes as veal Marsala, shrimp scampi, and grilled lamb. Prices for adults range from $12 to $15; children's are from $4 to $5. Sunday brunch is a champagne-style affair, with a buffet featuring everything from fresh fish to eggs Benedict. A special selection is available for children. Mandolins Lounge has live entertainment three nights a week.

Gourmet Getaways

All of these lodgings are known for their fine cuisine as well as their comfortable accommodations.

Arizona

Garland's Oak Creek Lodge
P.O. Box 152
Sedona, Arizona 86336
602-282-3343

Innkeepers: Mary and Gary Garland
Accommodations: 15 units
Rates: single, $112–$132; double, $148–$168
Included: Breakfast and dinner
Minimum stay: 2 nights
Added: 5% tax
Payment: Major credit cards
Children: Welcome
Pets: Not permitted
Smoking: Not permitted
Open: Mid-March to mid-November (closed on Sundays)

To get to Garland's, turn off Highway 89A at the Banjo Bill Campground about eight miles north of Sedona. Then drive through the campground, over the creek, and onto the property. All of a sudden you're in a private world—peaceful, serene, and far removed from the tourists in Sedona. Garland's Lodge is right on Oak Creek, the same creek that created the surrounding canyon renowned for its beautiful views. The family's orchards surround the lodge with a total of about two hundred fruit trees, including apples, pears, peaches, and cherries.

The main lodge is a rambling log building that serves as office, dining room, and social center. With rustic wood furniture, a piano, and a stone fireplace, it has a casual, inviting atmosphere.

Fifteen log cabins are scattered over the grounds, each with a porch overlooking the creek, orchards or the gardens abloom with luminous sunflowers or purple cosmos. Some cabins have views of the red cliffs that close in the canyon. Large cabins have a combination bedroom–sitting room and a fireplace with either one king or two double beds. Small cabins have one queen-size bed. Truly, this is a retreat, for the cabins have no TVs, radios, or phones.

Run by the Garlands since 1972, the lodge is so popular that guests make reservations a year in advance. Note that it is unusual in two ways: there's a two-day minimum stay and the lodge is closed on Sundays. This means that guests can stay Monday and Tuesday, Wednesday and Thursday, or Friday and Saturday. Of course you can stay longer, but not on a Sunday.

Breakfast features homemade breads, hot entrées such as griddle cakes or a smoked trout and leek frittata made with eggs from the farm's chickens, and fruit from the orchard. Dinner is a fancy affair; you don't have to dress, but you dine rather than simply eat. Even though the lodge itself is rustic, tables are set with crisp linens. The menu changes daily, but there is always an emphasis on using fresh ingredients from the Lodge's own gardens. A typical meal starts with French onion soup, followed by Caesar salad, shrimp with a red garlic sauce, linguine with creamy basil sauce, carrots and cauliflower (from the garden), and Kahlua cheesecake. Another night you may dine on sesame oat bread, minestrone soup, warm cabbage salad with walnuts and gorgonzola cheese, breast of chicken al Limone, carrots and broccoli, and orange and black currant sorbet. The wine list, featuring California wines, has about thirty choices by the bottle, as well as a number of selections by the glass. In the afternoons, an informal, or "low," tea is served.

When guests aren't enjoying the seclusion amid the forest, they can fish in Oak Creek, hike, browse in Sedona's shops and galleries, and take day trips to numerous sights, especially the Grand Canyon (100 miles to the north).

L'Auberge de Sedona

301 Little Lane
Sedona, Arizona 86336
602-282-7131
800-272-6777

General manager: Dirk Oldenburg
Accommodations: 95 units
Rates: European Plan (room only): $200–$365 cottages,
    $130–$170 lodge rooms, $100–$160 Orchards rooms;
    Modified American Plan (includes room, six course
    gourmet dinner and gourmet breakfast): $250–$425 for
    guests in cottages only
Added: 10.6% tax
Payment: Major credit cards
Children: Welcome
Pets: Not permitted
Smoking: Not permitted
Open: Year-round

In a town where run-of-the-mill Mexican and American restaurants dominate the dining scene, there is one bright spot — L'Auberge de Sedona. Featuring gourmet French cuisine, a visit to L'Auberge is a gastronomic delight. Situated beside babbling Oak Creek, tables on the restaurant's porch have a view of a small waterfall. Inside L'Auberge, pink table linens and fresh flowers complement Pierre Deux French country print wallpaper and upholstery. But of course it's the food that takes center stage. The menu changes daily, but you can expect delicacies such as sautéed rib eye of veal served with a saffron rice timbale and Spanish hollandaise, or grilled salmon served in an onion butter sauce with California citrus. Prix fixe meals run about $45 per person.

Rooms at the inn are equally enchanting. The most luxurious accommodations are in the creekside cottages. With distinctive combinations of French country fabrics, canopied beds, cushiony sofas, stone fireplaces, and dried floral wreaths, the rooms are a visual delight, and highly romantic. Outside your door you can hear the soothing sound of Oak Creek as it flows by, and the surrounding grounds are beautifully landscaped. It is easy to imagine that you have somehow been transported to Provence.

Lodge rooms are similar in decor to the cottages, but without the space or privacy. Rooms at the Orchards atop the hill resemble more traditional motel rooms, but retain a few country touches that are distinctly L'Auberge. There's a restaurant at the Orchards, and an outdoor pool. A "hilavator" connects the Orchards with the lower portion of the inn so that guests can travel between the two with ease.

The Armoire Boutique is L'Auberge's charming gift shop. If you like French country (if you like the inn, you'll like the shop), a visit to the boutique is a must.

Since L'Auberge is right in the center of Sedona, it makes an ideal jumping off point for area sightseeing. The inn's staff is happy to arrange Jeep tours and golf and horseback riding excursions for guests.

New Mexico

Hacienda Rancho de Chimayo
P.O. Box 11
State Road 520
Chimayo, New Mexico 87522
505-351-2222
800-477-1441

Owners: The Jaramillo Family
Accommodations: 7 rooms (all with private bath)
Rates: single, $49–$65; double, $82–$95
Included: Continental breakfast
Added: 9% tax
Payment: Major credit cards
Children: Over age 3 welcome; over age 9 additional $10 per night
Pets: Not permitted
Smoking: Not permitted
Open: Year-round

Heading north from Santa Fe, the road to Chimayo turns east at Pojoaque. Once you leave U.S. 285, between Santa Fe and Taos, you're definitely on "the road less taken." Highways 503 and 520 are beautiful stretches of road, rising and falling over the wide-open countryside, with expansive views of the Sangre de Cristo Mountains in the distance.

Chimayo, with a population of about 3,500, is an old Spanish settlement dating from 1598. Today known for its weavers, it is one of New Mexico's most famous craft villages, continuing a tradition begun by the Ortega family eight generations ago. Shops in the area include Ortega's Weavers and Art Gallery, Trujillo's Weavers, and El Chimayo Weavers. Visitors come from all parts of the country to buy their work, especially blankets, rugs, curtains, and placemats.

The Jaramillos, another old Chimayo family, trace their roots to the area's first Spanish settlers, and they have created their own tradition in recent years. Today they have two operations—a large restaurant serving native cuisine and an inn across the street. In the 1880s, two Jaramillo brothers helped each other build family homes, now separated by the little road leading into town. In 1965 their descendants restored one of the homes and converted it into a hacienda-style restaurant.

Highly popular despite its remote location, Restaurante Rancho de Chimayo is a festive spot. The dining areas are authentic Southwest, with hand-stripped vigas and whitewashed walls. Terraced patios spill down the hillside. Everybody has a great time developing a sense of camaraderie in this place that is well off the beaten track.

Comidas nativas (native dishes) are all tempting: chicken breasts topped with red chili and melted cheese; sopaipillas stuffed with beef, beans, Spanish rice, carne adovada (pork marinated and cooked in a red chili sauce); and more than a dozen other choices. For those who yearn for more ordinary fare, such dishes as hamburgers and trout almandine are on the menu as well.

So popular is Rancho de Chimayo's cuisine that a cookbook has recently been published featuring the restaurant's most loved recipes. Usually open from noon until 9:00 P.M., the restaurant closes on Mondays during part of the year. Whatever the season, be sure to make reservations (505-351-4444).

Since the restaurant was so successful, the Jaramillos restored the second home, across the road, opening it as an inn in 1984. Now travelers can dine at the restaurant and spend the night at Hacienda Rancho de Chimayo. (Again, with only seven rooms, reservations are strongly recommended.)

The hundred-year-old brown adobe home, trimmed in white, has a wreath of dried peppers on the front door. The atmosphere is casual with a country flavor. All of the guest rooms open onto a sunny courtyard with a central fountain. Stepping into any of them is a beautiful surprise; not reminiscent of Santa Fe or Taos decor, they are country Victorian. Antique mahogany beds, Queen Anne chairs, and touches of lace all combine for a look of casual elegance.

Uno, which can adjoin Dos, is the largest room, with high ceilings, two twin pine beds that can be pushed together to form a king, a sofa, an easy chair with ottoman to stretch out in front of the fire, and double doors that open out onto a private balcony. The antique dresser, mirrored wardrobe, and writing desk make a nice matching set. Even the bath is appealing, with a wooden vanity and a water closet. Siete is exquisite, with a king-size four-poster bed, fireplace, and a Queen Anne chair and antique mirror.

Most rooms can be joined with at least one other for families or couples traveling together. Cuatro can adjoin Tres to form a two-bedroom–living room suite. Guests have a choice of twin, double, queen-size, and king-size beds.

Continental breakfast — served either in your room, the lobby, or the courtyard — is likely to be croissants and fresh fruit. You can spend the morning visiting the weavers' shops and El Santuario, a church where miraculous cures are said to have taken place since it was built in the early 1800s. Every Easter thousands of faithful New Mexicans make a pilgrimage on foot to visit the sacred Santuario.

At lunch and dinnertime you can head over to Restaurante Rancho de Chimayo.

Meson de Mesilla

1803 Avenida de Mesilla
P.O. Box 1212
Mesilla, New Mexico 88046
505-525-9212
800-732-6025

Innkeeper: Chuck Walker
Accommodations: 13 rooms (all with private bath)
Rates: single, $45; double, $52; suite, $72–$82
Included: Full breakfast
Added: 6.3125% tax
Payment: Major credit cards
Children: Additional $10 for roll-away
Pets: Permitted with approval
Smoking: Permitted
Open: Year-round

Mesilla was once the largest town in the southern New Mexico territory. During the Civil War, it was declared the Confederate capital of a territory that extended to California. Billy the Kid stood trial in Mesilla, and the Gadsden Treaty, transferring 45,000 square miles of land that is now southern Arizona and New Mexico, was signed on Mesilla's plaza. Old Mesilla, now a village of about 2,000, is known for its galleries, shops, and restaurants, while neighboring Las Cruces (population 45,000) is the economic leader of the region.

About six blocks from Mesilla's plaza is an adobe inn, vintage 1985. From the outset Meson de Mesilla was designed as an inn, hence the large, airy rooms and the spacious restaurant.

The guest rooms, all on the second floor, open onto a porch that leads down to the pool and covered patio. Honeysuckle twines down the wrought-iron stairway. Beyond the pool, past the yard, stretch miles of cotton fields. Every room at Meson de Mesilla is different and some have views of the distant mountains. With names like Yucca and Roadrunner, their decor reflects the surrounding locale. Brass beds, southwestern art, and ceiling fans provide comfort while handsome vertical window blinds provide seclusion. The three suites have kiva fireplaces and a sitting area. There are no phones in the rooms, but all have TVs and clock radios.

Breakfast is beautifully served in the restaurant downstairs. Through the windows you look out on a landscaped cactus garden. Inside you enjoy such dishes as eggs Créole and orange yogurt pancakes, served with panache. And as good as breakfast is, dinner is the meal to savor.

The evening menu includes seven or eight choices, such as sea scallops with curried apples, veal roulade Florentine, quail sauté à la messine, and king salmon piccata. You might begin with escargots followed by soup, salad, and then the main course, served with wild rice pilaf. The price of the entire meal, including dessert, ranges from $14 to $25. A wine connoisseur, Chuck Walker offers a wide selection of California, Spanish, Italian, German, and New Mexican wines.

Although the cuisine is Continental, the restaurant's decor has a Mexican feel, with tiled fountains and carved wooden columns. It is open for dinner Tuesdays through Saturdays and for lunch Wednesdays through Fridays. Sunday brunch is a highlight. Reservations are recommended at any time.

Texas

La Colombe D'Or
3410 Montrose Boulevard
Houston, Texas 77006
713-524-7999
Fax: 713-524-8923

Owner: Stephen N. Zimmerman
Accommodations: 6 suites
Rates: single or double, $175–$600
Included: Continental breakfast
Added: 15% tax
Payment: Major credit cards
Children: Free in room with parents
Pets: Not permitted
Smoking: Permitted
Open: Year-round

La Colombe d'Or combines the style of a country manor with the convenience of a city hotel. Small and intimate, it's also elegant and grand. Once it was the home of a wealthy family; today it welcomes guests from around the world.

Here you are treated as a valued house guest, with an abundance of personal service. Expect a basket of fruit when you arrive. Enjoy a breakfast of fresh orange juice, croissants, and fruit served in your own dining room each morning.

The three-story yellow brick inn, built in 1923, has an attractively landscaped front yard with plants and sculptures, a welcoming front porch, a residential lobby decorated in treasures from Europe, a cozy bar named for the hedonistic wine god Bacchus, and a library where you can sip cognac. While some of the architectural elements have been added, the mahogany staircase and the decorated ceilings are original to the home. The second-floor hallway is lined with paintings, among them a work by Calder and watercolors of Houston landmarks.

Five guest suites, named after famous artists, are on the second floor. Each one is different—artfully decorated and unusual in its use of space. All have a king-size bed, sitting area, separate dining room, silk floral arrangements, telephone, clock-radio, and bathrobes. Some have ceiling fans.

The Renoir Suite, although the smallest, is a favorite. Its dining area is separated from the bedroom by interior columns and draped fabric, yet the theme is Oriental, with Japanese prints, a carved screen for a headboard, Oriental rugs and a chest, and a glass-topped dining table. Its sunny dining room opens out onto a terrace. The Cézanne, once the master bedroom, is boldly decorated in green, rust, and blue. Playful paintings hang on the walls, while the floor is covered by a rich Oriental rug. The Degas suite, in rose pastel florals, looks like an Impressionist painting. Ivy vines grow along the ceiling of its airy dining room. Mauve and burgundy are the dominant colors in the Monet Suite, and there's a Bartlett print in the bath. Reminiscent of the artist's work, the Van Gogh Suite is more flamboyant, in ruddy browns and rusts.

The third-floor penthouse is even larger than the suites. Its antique furnishings are no surprise; the luxurious bathroom with an elevated whirlpool tub is.

The tempting aromas that waft upstairs are a constant reminder that there is a fine restaurant below. Always popular with residents, it gained national attention during the Texas oil crash of the 1980s, when the owner charged businessmen for lunch whatever the going rate was for a barrel of crude so as not to deplete their almost empty wallets. His plan worked, and he's done a brisk business ever since.

Decorated in soft pinks and mauves, the restaurant is sophisticated and grand on a small scale. With an emphasis on regional products and fresh herbs, the cuisine is French Provençal. Entrées such as seafood Monaco, lamb lyonnaise, and pasta portofino keep guests from straying too far. The restaurant is open for lunch on weekdays and dinner every day but Sundays.

There is 24-hour concierge service; valet parking is free for guests.

La Colombe d'Or is about a 5-minute drive from downtown and within easy access of the Galleria, Texas Medical Center, Alley Theater, Wortham Center, and Jones Hall. The University of St. Thomas is a block away. Plans are under way to add about twenty more suites on an adjoining lot.

Grand New Resorts

Although these resorts are relatively new, they have quickly established fine reputations by offering superb recreational facilities and excellent service.

Arizona

The Boulders
34631 North Tom Darlington
P.O. Box 2090
Carefree, Arizona 85377
602-488-9009
800-553-1717
Fax: 602-488-4118

General manager & vice president: William J. Nassikas
Accommodations: 136 casitas
Rates: single, $195–$370; double, $250–$495
Included: Breakfast and dinner
Added: 10.25% room, 6.7% meal tax
Payment: Major credit cards and personal checks
Children: Welcome
Pets: Permitted
Smoking: Nonsmoking rooms available
Open: Early September to mid-June

The Boulders is an exclusive resort hidden away in the foothills of Scottsdale on the first plateau out of the desert. Huge boulders dominate the landscape, like the toys of a wayward giant haphazardly discarded as he ambled through the countryside. At first glance, you have to look twice to distinguish the casitas from the surrounding rock formations. A wonderful free-form pool set amid the rocks looks almost natural.

There's plenty to do at the Boulders, but not so much that you have to schedule your day frantically to get it all in. A residential community as well as a resort, it has 36 holes of golf and six Plexi-cushioned tennis courts, all set against spectacular desert scenery. Through the concierge you can arrange such things as horseback riding, Jeep tours, hot air ballooning, and flights to the Grand Canyon.

The main lodge is a stone extravaganza, and entering it is like stepping into a science fiction movie. A circular structure, it has boulderlike doors and polished stone floors. The architecture reflects the physical setting, and the interior reflects the area's Indian heritage. For instance, the latilla dining room represents the inside of a Hopi kiva.

The casitas are large and luxurious, with beamed ceilings, adobe walls, and fireplaces (in the winter, temperatures drop into the forties at night). The baths have step-in showers as well as large tubs.

There's a choice of five dining areas. The evening meal is formal, with jackets required for men in two of the restaurants.

Transportation can be arranged between the resort and Sky Harbor Airport in Phoenix. The resort is about 30 minutes north of Scottsdale, and rental cars are available on the property.

Hyatt Regency Scottsdale at Gainey Ranch
7500 East Doubletree Ranch Road
Scottsdale, Arizona 85258
602-991-3388
800-233-1234
Fax: 602-483-5550

Manager: Bill Edier Orley
Accommodations: 493 rooms

Rates: single or double, $115–$335; suites, $225–$2,200
Added: 10.25% tax
Payment: Major credit cards
Children: Welcome
Pets: Not permitted
Smoking: Permitted
Open: Year-round

The Hyatt Regency Scottsdale is a true oasis in the midst of the desert, with a water playground and beautiful setting that surpass just about anything else in the Southwest. There are 27 holes of golf, a health and fitness center, eight tennis courts, lawn croquet, and jogging and cycling trails. The hotel opened in late 1986 as part of the Gainey Ranch complex, which includes residential and retail development. With hundreds of palm trees and other lush foliage, it's an elegant resort. So special is the landscaping outside and the artwork inside that art and flora and fauna tours are given once a week.

The water playground is truly dazzling. Built on several levels, it has 28 fountains, 10 pools, and a 3-story waterslide—but statistics don't tell the story. It's a water fantasy, a quasi-Roman-Grecian creation with a pure American sandy beach. There's also Fort Kachina playground and Camp Hyatt Kachina for kids, making it especially appealing for families.

The lobby, decorated with international art, leads down to three dining rooms. The Squash Blossom, offering southwestern cuisine, has all-day service with both indoor and outdoor dining. It is tastefully decorated, particularly for an informal restaurant, with nice touches such as hand-blown Mexican glassware. The more formal Golden Swan overlooks Koi Pond. Sandolo offers the most intimate dining experience. The waiters sing as you enjoy Italian specialties, and the meal is followed by a romantic gondola ride on the pond, complete with a complimentary glass of wine. Sandolo's dinner entrées range from $8 to $12. Reservations are necessary.

The guest rooms are decorated in plums, mauves, and grays and have private balconies and stocked mini-bars. Cactus print robes are a refreshing change from the standard terrycloth. Regency Club rooms on the third floor have complimentary breakfast, afternoon hors d'oeuvres, and upgraded amenities. Several deluxe casitas (with a living room, two to four bedrooms, and stereo systems) are on the lake.

The resort's Regency Spa surpasses fitness centers in typical hotels. In addition to sunny workout rooms, excellent exercise equipment, saunas, massage rooms, and herbal wraps, it has the Mollen Clinic, a physical fitness and medical facility that offers personal health evaluations and health programs.

Sample fees for the recreational facilities are $15 per court hour for tennis; exercise classes, $7 (spa use is complimentary); 18 holes of golf, including cart rental, is $56 in the summer, $100 in winter.

Loews Ventana Canyon Resort
7000 North Resort Drive
Tucson, Arizona 85715
602-299-2020
800-234-5117
Fax: 602-299-6832

Managing director: Johnny So
Accommodations: 398 units
Rates: single, $95–$305; double, $105–$325; suites,
    $135–$1,400; golf, tennis, spa, and holiday packages available
Added: 6.5% tax
Payment: Major credit cards
Children: Welcome
Pets: Not permitted
Smoking: Not permitted
Open: Year-round

Ventana Canyon, with an 80-foot waterfall in the center, is the tranquil backdrop for Loews Ventana Canyon Resort, which is built of deep taupe cement to blend with the mountains behind. The natural landscape has been kept very much intact around this new resort, and the setting could hardly be more dramatic.

Loews, with 94 acres of facilities, is part of a 1,000-plus-acre planned community. Next to the hotel is the Lakeside Spa and Tennis Club, with ten championship tennis courts, a lap pool, fitness trail, exercise center, and a spa. Also nearby is Ventana Canyon Golf and Racquet Club, with a 27-hole Tom Fazio PGA golf course. Loews guests have privileges at both clubs.

Behind the hotel itself there's a large, attractive pool (luncheon buffets are served there), a croquet lawn, and a shallow lake at the base of the mountain. Best of all, a path leads to the waterfall—an invitation to explore the mystical desert landscape. Desert lizards scurry in front of you, stately saguaros cover the hillside above, and within minutes you've forgotten there's a world somewhere with traffic jams and deadlines.

The guest rooms, with views of either the mountains or the city, have private balconies or terraces, mini-bars, and armoires with concealed TVs. The bathrooms, accented in marble, feature double whirlpool tubs.

Art is integral to the hotel's decor, from Arizona landscapes in the foyer to original lithographs in the guest rooms. The Ventana Restaurant, serving dinner only, specializes in new American cuisine. Entrées such as range-fed hen with a pecan crust in a honey-mustard sauce and grilled quail with roasted garlic sauce and foie gras range from $17 to $26. Canyon Café has all-day service. The Flying V Bar and Grill serves lunch and dinner overlooking the golf course. After 9:00 P.M. it's transformed into a video disco.

The Phoenician
6000 East Camelback Road
Scottsdale, Arizona 85251
602-941-8200
800-888-8234
Fax: 602-947-4311

General manager: Hans Turnovszky
Accommodations: 442 rooms, 107 casitas, 31 luxury suites
Rates: single or double, $270–$405; casitas for 2, $270–$405; each additional person $50 per night; 1-bedroom suites, $750–$950; 2-bedroom suites, $1077–$1,275
Added: 10.25% tax
Payment: Major credit cards
Children: Under 12 free in room with parents
Pets: Permitted in the casitas only
Smoking: Nonsmoking rooms available
Open: Year-round

The Phoenician plays on its desert location in the Valley of the Sun with a sun motif in the marble floor of the lobby and with the name of its lobby bar, the Thirsty Camel. The resort really does feel like an opulent oasis. Developed by Charles Keating, the Phoenician opened in late 1988 as the newest and perhaps the most opulent resort in the area ($6.5 million was spent on art alone). Spread over 130 acres, the lushly landscaped property is dotted with lagoons and streams. The semicircular hotel has Camelback Mountain as a backdrop. Casitas, a spa, a clubhouse, and an 18-hole golf course complete the lower half of the circle with multilevel pools (one with mother-of-pearl tile) and fountains in between.

The guest rooms are light, airy, and spacious. Furnished with painted rattan furniture and soft pastel fabrics, they are some of the largest around. The bathrooms are luxurious as well, with commodious oval tubs, separate showers, and marble floors and washbasins. Robes are provided: terrycloth in the winter, cotton in summer. All the rooms have closet safes, hair dryers, ironing boards, scales, and telephones in the baths. The televisions are bigger than average, and VCRs are available upon request. Most rooms have balconies. Governors suites have two terraces, two rooms (the sitting room has a day bed), and two baths—one with a huge walk-in shower. The casitas have a more residential feeling; some have fireplaces and kitchenettes. For those who require even more space, the two elaborate Presidential suites offer 3,300 square feet of pure luxury.

The Phoenician has a number of restaurants. The Terrace Restaurant serves Italian-American cuisine (entrées range from $15 to $25) and an elaborate Sunday brunch. For southwestern cuisine, try Windows on the Green, overlooking the golf course. The Thirsty Camel serves a fancy afternoon tea, the Oasis serves meals by the pool, and Mary Elaine's specializes in Mediterranean delicacies.

In addition to swimming and golf, there are 11 lighted tennis courts (one has an automated practice court) and a full-service health and fitness center. Guests can use the center for $10 daily. Treatments such as massage and aromatherapy are charged at an hourly rate. Bicycles can be rented for $5 per hour or $20 for the day. Supervised programs for children are also available. Interestingly enough for an active desert resort, there are no drinking fountains in the public areas, although the bartender will happily provide an ice-cold glass of water in the Thirsty Camel.

The Pointe at Tapatio Cliffs
11111 North Seventh Street
Phoenix, Arizona 85020
602-997-6000
800-934-1000
Fax: 602-993-0276

General manager: Bob Brooks
Accommodations: 591 suites
Rates: $75–$260
Added: 10.25% tax
Payment: Major credit cards,
Children: Welcome
Pets: Not permitted
Smoking: Nonsmoking suites available
Open: Year-round

The mood is festive at the Pointe. With pool parties and a host of special activities, it's like a giant cruise ship moored at an inland shore. The lobby, three stories high, has a central fountain, and large windows overlook the resort's main pool, which always seems to be surrounded by happy guests. (Cocktails are served poolside in the evenings.) To one side of the glass elevators is a plaque listing famous Pointe guests, such as Robert Redford, Julius Irving, Liza Minelli, Walter Mondale, and many others, from rock stars to professional athletes.

Spread over 400 cliffside acres, the Pointe is a sprawling Mediterranean-style resort village. It's a complete vacationland with seven pools, 16 lighted tennis courts, four racquetball courts, horseback riding, hiking, mountain biking, three major restaurants, and an 18-hole golf course. The tennis courts are excellent—the court quality is good and extensive landscaping between the courts adds to their appeal (there is an extra fee for tennis). There's a pro shop for both golf and tennis, and there are four golf pros on the Pointe's staff. Horseback rides are available by the hour or half-day; special rides include breakfast, lunch, and pony rides for children under seven.

The guest suites are in the main building or are arranged in buildings throughout the resort which have arches, courtyards, and fountains. Standard are separate sitting rooms with wet bars and refrigerators, bedrooms with armoires, baths divided into sections, and balconies. Other features include room safes, two TVs (one in the living room and one in the bedroom), coffeemakers, tile baths, and rich marble vanities. Twenty-eight "presidential suites" up on the hill have views and are especially roomy with large living rooms, bedrooms, and baths. They each have 1½ baths, a kiva fireplace (firewood is supplied), and stained glass windows above the baths. They can connect with a standard suite.

Pointe In Tyme restaurant has Mexican marble at its entrance, crystal chandeliers, and Honduran mahogany paneled ceilings and walls decorated with old photos of famous restaurants taken in their heyday. There's a huge oval bar in the center, a large fireplace on one side, and comfortable booths all around. The restaurant serves all three meals, and the full breakfast buffet is especially popular.

The crème de la crème is Étienne's Different Pointe of View, on top of the mountain. Étienne's has innovative architecture, a sleek modern decor, and an unequaled setting. In the highest building in Phoenix, it has windows all around and impressive views. Guests may enjoy cocktails overlooking the city on the multileveled terrace and then dine on roast chicken with périgourdine sauce or baked salmon filet with green peppercorn butter (entrées range from $22 to $27). The restaurant boasts a long list of awards and has one of the most impressive wine lists in the country—more than twenty pages of unusual bottles, including an extensive selection of California Cabernets. (Be sure to stop down and see the glass-encased wine cellar while you're there.) After dinner the adjacent lounge is a popular night spot, with two shows a night featuring Al Raitano, Phoenix's "entertainer of the year."

More casual dining is available at La Cabana, a snack bar between the resort's two main pools, and the Watering Hole Chuckwagon and Saloon. A shuttle service runs throughout the resort, which with the resort being set on a hill can be a real plus —especially if you're dining at Étienne's. The Pointe publishes a monthly newsletter called Pointes of Interest to inform guests of current happenings at the resort, and there's a children's day camp called Coyote Camp. A 2,700-acre preserve adjoins the resort.

The Registry Resort
7171 North Scottsdale Road
Scottsdale, Arizona 85253
602-991-3800
800-247-9810
Fax: 602-948-9843

General manager: Manfred Braig
Accommodations: 318 rooms
Rates: single or double, $80–$210; suites, $285–$2,050
Added: 10.25% tax
Payment: Major credit cards
Children: Under 17 free in room with parents
Pets: Not permitted
Smoking: Nonsmoking rooms available
Open: Year-round

One of the resorts along Scottsdale Road, the Registry stands apart from its neighbors with its abundant tennis and golf and its varied dining. It is part of the McCormick Ranch development, comprising residential, office, and recreational facilities. The two golf courses, one next to the hotel, are 18-hole, par 72 championship courses. The 21 lighted tennis courts are exceptionally fine and are set next to a small grandstand. (Court time is $15 per hour.) The main swimming pool is one of the best in the area; not only is it large, it also has a three-meter and one-meter diving board (rare for hotels these days) and a lifeguard on duty. Several smaller pools are also on the grounds.

The lobby, with fine furnishings, has an elegant tone. The Café Brioche features southwestern cuisine and has outdoor seating by the pool. The Kachina Lounge has live entertainment nightly during the winter season. The Phoenician Room, used for special functions, is opulent—a step back into supper club days, with a stage for live entertainment.

About a third of the guest rooms are attached to the main building. Casitas are spread over the grounds, interspersed with courtyards and flowering shrubs. Modern in decor, they have all the expected amenities and are by far the most appealing accommodations.

The resort also has room service, a health spa ($5 per day), and a putting green.

Scottsdale Princess

7575 East Princess Drive
Scottsdale, Arizona 85255
602-585-4848
800-223-1818
Fax: 602-585-0086

General manager: Stephen J. Ast
Accommodations: 600 rooms
Rates: single or double, $100–$300; suites for two, $225–
 $2,200; each additional person $20 in summer, $30 in winter
Added: 10.25% tax
Payment: Major credit cards
Children: Under 16 free in room with parents
Pets: Not permitted
Smoking: Nonsmoking rooms available
Open: Year-round

Opened in 1987, the first Princess hotel in the U.S. is an estate-like resort covering 450 acres several miles north of the other Scottsdale resorts. Hand your car keys to a parking attendant when you arrive—with all that this resort has to offer, and a capable staff to attend to your every need, there's really no reason to leave.

Built in a Mexican colonial style, the main building is truly grand. There are majestic palms, fountain courts, and intimate nooks and crannies with wicker sofas. Two thirds of the guest rooms are in the sprawling main building; the casitas are clustered near the tennis courts, and the villas are next to the golf course.

Recreational choices cover the grounds. There are two 18-hole TPC (Tournament Players Club) golf courses designed by Jay Morrish and Tom Weiskopf (the Phoenix Open is held here), nine tennis courts which include a 10,000-seat stadium court that witnesses the WCT Eagle Classic in late February, three swimming pools (one is especially large and has an interesting shape), and a health club and spa with racquetball and squash courts, state-of-the-art exercise equipment, saunas, whirlpools, and health and beauty treatments. (Club usage is $10 per day, which includes squash and racquetball court time.) Next to the hotel, the city of Scottsdale has built a 400-acre horse park with nine equestrian arenas, two stadium arenas, a polo field, a grand prix field for jumping, and 500 stables.

The guest rooms are large and have interesting configurations, setting them apart from standard hotel rooms. They are attractively furnished in southwestern peaches, creams, and earth tones, and they have big terraces and wet bars. The extra-large bathrooms are luxurious, with separate tubs and showers, a telephone, robes, loofah sponges, and other top-of-the-line amenities. The casitas come in two styles: bed-sitting and casita suites. The casita suites have separate sitting rooms. All have balconies and fireplaces and share a common swimming pool. The villas are similar to the casitas but do not have fireplaces.

The Marquesa is the resort's fine restaurant, specializing in Catalan cuisine. For Mexican food, try La Hacienda. The casual Las Ventanas serves all three meals, and the Cabana Café serves food and frosty drinks by the pool. At the end of the day, you can head to Club Caballo Bayo for a night of dancing. The Grill at the TPC clubhouse is popular with the golfing set.

Tucson National Golf and Conference Resort

2727 West Club Drive
Tucson, Arizona 85741
602-297-2271
800-528-4856
Fax: 602-297-7544

General manager: Charles V. Dyke
Accommodations: 167 units
Rates: single or double, $75–$195; spa and golf packages
   available
Added: 6.5% tax
Payment: Major credit cards
Children: Under 18 free in room with parents
Pets: Not permitted
Smoking: Permitted
Open: Year-round

About 15 miles north of downtown Tucson, the Tucson National resort is surrounded by 650 acres of saguaro-studded desert. It is a resort that wears many faces. Designed as a private golf club, its 27-hole USGA championship golf course has featured such tournaments as the Tucson and Northern Telecom Opens. (The 18th hole is known for being one of the most challenging finishing holes on the PGA tour.) As a family resort, it has a large attractive pool, tennis courts, two restaurants, several lounges, and beautifully designed rooms and suites. As a spa, it has few equals, offering a variety of services, professional attention, and flexibility in its program.

The club opened to the public in 1986. The spa, downstairs in the main building, is one of the highlights of the resort (when you're not out on the golf course). It offers herbal wraps and massages, loofah rubs and body facials, hydrotherapy pools and tanning beds. Special services on the women's side include Swiss showers (water ranging in temperature from 60 to 105 degrees comes from 14 shower heads and sprays from all directions, activating the capillary nerve endings in the skin and stimulating circulation) and steam cabinets. There's also a panthermal (one of the few in the United States) that is designed to break down cellulite, along with a Finnish sauna. The locker room is equipped with robes, spa shoes, high-quality toiletries, and hair dryers; and there's a full-service beauty salon for those who don't want to bother doing their own hair.

The men's spa features a Scottish water massage (16 needle-spray shower heads and two high-pressure hoses controlled by an attendant, with varying pressure and temperature) and a Russian bath (a special steam room that opens pores and reduces toxicity, hence reducing tension).

Both men and women have inhalation rooms (eucalyptus and other herbs that help open sinuses and allow freer breathing). The lounges are plush, quiet, and relaxing. Exercise classes include aerobics, water exercise, stress management, and creative movement. The machines in the exercise room are designed primarily for lower body workouts. Spa programs are extremely flexible: you can enjoy just one of its services or buy a two- to seven-day package that includes room, meals, and an abundance of spa services.

The rooms are designated as villas (hotel size), poolside, casitas (ranging from hotel size to near-suites), and executive suites. All have a patio or balcony with views of the golf course, swimming pool, or the Catalina mountains. Some have fireplaces. The rooms are spacious with sitting areas, refrigerators, and a separate tub and shower in the bath. While the rooms differ in decor, each has special touches such as beamed ceilings, copper light fixtures, and matched southwestern fabrics.

The Fiesta Room, the resort's main restaurant, serves all three meals. Dinners include steak and seafood choices, and diners with smaller appetites will find a number of light entrées and sandwiches on the menu as well. In pleasant weather there is outdoor dining, and Sunday brunch is always a popular event.

Westin La Paloma
3800 East Sunrise Drive
Tucson, Arizona 85718
602-742-6000
800-876-DOVE
Fax: 602-577-5878

General manager: Tom Cortabitarte
Accommodations: 487 rooms
Rates: single, $120; double, $140; suites, $175
Added: 6.5% tax
Payment: Major credit cards
Children: Under 18 free in room with parents
Pets: Not permitted
Smoking: Nonsmoking rooms available
Open: Year-round

The Westin La Paloma is a pink palace in the desert. It has first-class facilities—some of the best in the Southwest. The arched entryway is dramatic, as are the massive arched windows in the lobby that frame the distant mountain view. Just beyond the lobby, a small waterfall cascades over rocks into a lily pond.

The resort's 27-hole championship Jack Nicklaus golf course is challenging—its unusual layout takes advantage of its Sonoran Desert setting while making a minimal impact on it. (Indeed, the developers were so sensitive to the landscape that with careful planning they were able to save more than 7,000 of the 8,000 saguaro cacti on the site of the resort.)

The tennis courts (eight hard surface, four clay) are top quality, in a scenic setting, and next to a good pro shop. La Paloma's free-form pool has bridges, waterfalls, and lagoons, like pools at Caribbean resorts. Hot tubs are tucked away invitingly among the shrubs. There's also a health club with racquetball, Nautilus equipment, and aerobics, a spa with massage, facials, waxing, and body wraps, and a game area with croquet, volleyball, and bike rentals.

At mealtime, choose from the gracious and elegant La Paloma Dining Room (part of the private La Paloma Country Club), La Villa (in a charming hacienda), and Desert Garden (in the main building). Entrées at La Paloma ($17–$21) feature escalope of duck breast with apples, Dover sole with avocado and crayfish, and grenadins of lamb with asparagus and morels.

Throughout the resort, the look is refined Southwest with a modern flair. Accommodations are in two- and three-story buildings arranged in a semicircle facing the mountains. All are painted La Paloma rose, a color that suggests the sunset. The interior colors reflect the desert—sage green, cobalt blue, mauve, and gray.

While the rooms tend to be small, they are cleverly decorated and arranged with angled beds and interesting layouts. Each has a patio or balcony, a refrigerator, and a remote control TV in an armoire. The bathrooms are also on the small side but have a separate tub and shower, phone, and robes.

Day-care is available for children from 6 months to 12 years old.

Wyndham Paradise Valley Resort

5401 North Scottsdale Road
Scottsdale, Arizona 85253
602-947-5400
800-822-4200
Fax: 602-946-1524

General manager: Randy Kwasnieski
Accommodations: 387 rooms and suites
Rates: Start at $69 in the off-season and $175 in high season
  for single or double; suites start at $400

Added: 9.05% tax
Payment: Major credit cards
Children: Under 18 free in room with parents
Pets: Not permitted
Smoking: Nonsmoking rooms available
Open: Year-round

The Wyndham Paradise Valley Resort has an unusual facade: it is built of angular cement blocks that have the effect of mirroring the bark patterns of the surrounding palm trees. At the entrance, there's a striking brass fountain of horses rising from the water.

The guest rooms surround attractively landscaped courtyards, and colorful desert flora seem to be in bloom everywhere. The rooms are pleasantly furnished with light woods and modern furniture with a southwestern air. Most have small sitting areas, terraces, and a vanity apart from the bath. All the rooms have mini-bars, coffeemakers, remote control TVs, and phones in the bath. The Presidential Suite is especially handsome, with large glass doors that open onto a terrace overlooking one of the main pool courtyards. Guests staying there will have no need to use that pool, however, since the suite has its own outdoor pool and Jacuzzi.

The resort has two swimming pools—one with a waterfall, the other with an adjacent hot tub and bar. Tennis is available on four outdoor clay courts and two indoor courts. The health club has two racquetball courts, steam rooms, saunas, and whirlpools. Golf can be arranged nearby.

Lunch and light meals are served in the Palm Pavilion. For dinner, Spazzizi's offers Italian and regional cuisine. Of course, a menu is also available for those who just want to lounge by the pool all day.

Texas

Four Seasons Resort and Club
4150 North MacArthur Boulevard
Irving, Texas 75038
214-717-0700
800-332-3442
Fax: 214-717-2477

General manager: Jim FitzGibbon
Accommodations: 315 rooms
Rates: single or double, $175–$230; suites, $325–$1000

Added: 8.25% tax
Payment: Major credit cards
Children: Free in room with parents
Pets: Small pets only with approval
Smoking: Nonsmoking rooms available
Open: Year-round

Hidden between Dallas and D/FW International Airport is a sparkling community named Las Colinas. A composite of office and residential development, it's an innovative town. The Four Seasons, which opened in 1986, sits on a hill overlooking a Tournament Players Golf course. It was predated by a sophisticated fitness center, now run by Four Seasons. The combined facilities give vacationers a multifaceted resort. It's also a fine conference center, but that doesn't interfere with a leisure traveler's enjoyment.

The roster of activities offers something for everyone. The 18-hole golf course is the only TPC course in northern Texas and provides elevated areas for watching tournaments, such as the GTE Byron Nelson Classic, held each May.

Racquet sports include indoor and outdoor tennis, squash, and racquetball. (Several professional tennis events are held on the stadium court during the year.) The fitness section has Nautilus equipment, treadmills, bicycles, rowing machines, and a gym. There are also outdoor and indoor pools, jogging tracks, and aerobics classes.

The spa is one of the best equipped in the Southwest. Herbal wraps and loofah scrubs, facials, pedicures, saunas, whirlpools, and massages are all included. A trained staff can perform tests geared toward achieving optimal health through exercise and nutrition.

The sports and spa facilities don't come cheap ($92 for 18 holes of golf with cart rental, $30–$34 per hour for tennis, $60 for a Swedish massage), but lots of packages combine lodging with sports and spa services.

Throughout the hotel there's a sense of spaciousness. The public areas and guest rooms overlook lush grounds. The Café on the Green is casually elegant. Daily buffets are bountiful, but the restaurant also offers dishes that are low in calories, sodium, and cholesterol.

The accommodations get high marks for comfort and luxury—overstuffed chairs with ottomans, three phones, a large tub and separate shower, and balconies.

The resort has a professionally run child care center for infants and children up to eight years old. Hotel parking is complimentary.

South Shore Harbour Resort and Conference Center

2500 South Shore Boulevard
League City, Texas 77573
713-334-1000
800-442-5005
Fax: 713-334-1157

General manager: Austin Frame
Accommodations: 250 rooms and suites
Rates: single, $105–$145; double, $115–$145; suites, $300–$1,040
Payment: Major credit cards
Children: Under 14 free in room with parents
Pets: Not permitted
Smoking: Nonsmoking rooms available
Open: Year-round

When South Shore Harbour opened in 1988, many skeptics gave it little chance of surviving in the depressed Texas economy brought on by the mid-1980s oil bust. The doubters have been proven wrong, however, and the resort is not only surviving, it's thriving.

One wouldn't intentionally put League City, Texas, on an itinerary, and yet South Shore Harbour's location is one of its chief assets. On Clear Lake, an inlet from Galveston Bay, the hotel overlooks a yacht marina and a picturesque lighthouse. About halfway between Houston and Galveston and only minutes from NASA, the resort is ideally situated for sightseeing in the area. And its attractive setting and relaxed atmosphere provide a welcome weekend respite for harried Houstonians.

The nearby fitness center, which guests can use for $5 per day, offers state-of-the-art exercise equipment, jogging tracks, tennis courts (one is air-conditioned; $5 extra), racquetball courts, a lap pool, and a gym. The South Shore Harbour Golf Course is also available for guests. Parasailing or deep-sea fishing excursions can be arranged through Clear Lake Charter Boats, right in the hotel lobby.

The guest rooms are tastefully and comfortably furnished in rich colors. Jacuzzi suites, with hot tubs placed to take full advantage of the view, are a popular choice with couples. And while many hotels have presidential suites that are large for the sake of being large, the penthouse suites at South Shore Harbour are truly special. Luxurious but not ostentatious, they have expansive windows that extend the width and height of the two-story suites, bringing the seascape indoors and filling every corner with the rich blues of the ocean and sky.

Dining on seafood in the hotel's Harbour Club while the sun sets over the water is a thoroughly enjoyable experience. Open only to hotel guests and private members, the restaurant feels exclusive, and it is. The waiters are attentive and the meals satisfying. Fresh seafood from the Gulf is the main attraction, but savory desserts are equally tempting. Deep burgundies, burnished woods, brass railings, and leather sofas complete the setting.

Paradise Reef Restaurant, serving all three meals, is less formal. The nautical Hooker's Nook Bar serves beverages and sandwiches on the pool and marina level, and RSVP is the resort's nightclub. Piano music and tropical birds create a soothing environment to sip cocktails by in the hotel's lobby bar.

The tropical pool is surrounded by majestic palms (unfortunately, some of them were damaged by a rare winter freeze) and seems to stretch endlessly. Children will no doubt enjoy swimming under its cascading waterfall, and adults will appreciate the swim-up bar.

Hospitality comes naturally to the staff at South Shore Harbour. Service is never forced; the employees just seem to enjoy their jobs. Room service operates from 6:00 A.M. to midnight, and parking in the hotel lot is free.

Grand Old Mansions

These lovely old homes date from the days when the Southwest was still considered frontier country.

Texas

Browning Plantation
Route 1, Box 8
Chappell Hill, Texas 77426
409-836-6144

Innkeepers: Dick and Mildred Ganchan
Accommodations:
Main house: 4 rooms (shared baths)
Detached building: 2 rooms (private baths)
Rates: single, $80–$110; double, $90–$120
Included: Full breakfast and tax
Payment: Personal check
Children: Over 12 welcome
Pets: Not permitted
Smoking: Not permitted
Open: Year-round

Welcome to Tara in the Texas Hill Country—a grand old mansion set on sprawling grounds, reminiscent of a bygone era. Drive up the gravel road to a world conducive to relaxation: here you can relive the life of southern gentry, sipping cool drinks on the verandah and luxuriating in oversize guest rooms.

Listed on the National Register of Historic Places, the Browning Plantation was built in 1857. Dick and Mildred Ganchan discovered the deteriorated structure in 1980 and decided "somebody had to do something." For the next three years they painstakingly restored it, retaining the historical integrity of the building and transforming it into a magnificent house.

Although furnished with antiques, the Greek Revival home has more comfort than elegance. The guest rooms are enormous. In addition to the expected plantation and tester beds, there are specialty pieces such as a "mammy bench," designed for rocking babies. One doorway still bears marks designating the height of the children who stood against it in 1872.

The third floor is a delight. Throughout the rest of the home the Ganchans remained true to the original design, but in this space, the original attic, they gave their imagination full rein. To supplement the half-baths next to each guest room on the second floor, they created two bathrooms with whimsical decor. For ladies, the theme is Victorian bordello—a chandelier, mirrored wall, fuzzy rug, even a stained glass skylight. The men's bathroom shouts of masculinity—rough cedar walls, a pine dressing table, zebra-skin rug, and antlers doubling as towel racks. From here you can climb to a rooftop observation deck, which offers an excellent view of the surrounding farmland.

A swimming pool in the backyard keeps you from losing touch with the 20th century. Also on the grounds is a restored log cabin, now an antiques and crafts shop (a low-key operation, open only on special occasions or when guests ask).

Breakfast is served in the dining room at an antique table. The fare is bountiful—a full country breakfast. Stained glass doors lead to the modern kitchen, built on the site of the original one.

So popular is the plantation home that another building has been added. Resembling a 19th-century train depot, it's next to a scaled-down model train, the pet project of "a railroad nut" in the Ganchan family.

The Castle Inn
1403 East Washington
Navasota, Texas 77868
409-825-8051

Innkeepers: Tim and Helen Urquhart
Accommodations: 4 bedrooms (all with private bath)
Rates: single, $74; double, $84
Included: Continental breakfast
Added: 13% tax
Payment: Personal check

Children: Over age 13 welcome
Pets: Not permitted
Smoking: Nonsmoking rooms available
Open: Year-round

Step into the Victorian era at the Castle Inn in this quiet East Texas town, an hour and a half northwest of Houston. On two acres overlooking one of the main streets of Navasota, the 1890s mansion is indeed a castle, complete with turret. Every room is exquisitely decorated with American antiques.

You enter a world of elegance through a porch enclosed with 110 panes of beveled glass. Built by German craftsmen, the house has nine and a half bays, resulting in octagonal rooms. Curly pine, now extinct, is used throughout the home. So are carved wood trims and ornate brass hardware. Every room is thoughtfully furnished with articles of beauty that have special meaning to the owners. China dolls are dressed in Victorian baby clothes handed down through the family. Two child-size dolls wear costumes that Helen Urquhart and her brother once wore for a tap-dance performance. The music room, where socially prominent ladies used to gather for their bridge luncheons, is decorated with musical instruments, including a player piano.

Sliding doors fourteen feet tall open into the most beautiful room in the house, the dining room. Its ornate ceiling, hand-painted borders, and tiger oak walls form a work of art. Upon request, the hosts serve elegant dinners—in period clothes, of course. (Dinners are made available when all four bedrooms are reserved by one party; they run about $20 per person.)

The bedrooms are on the second floor. A spool staircase leads past a 20-foot stained glass window (original to the house) to a parlor and adjoining balcony, where Continental breakfast is served. This is also the gathering spot for wine and cheese in the evenings. The beds are a rosewood Louisiana plantation, a half-tester, or a carved high-back bed. Marble-top dressers, accent pieces such as fainting couches, and memorabilia, including quilts handed down through the family, complete the feeling of Victorian elegance. The Bridal Suite is striking, decorated in fuchsia and pink, with an alcove bed and a claw-foot tub.

The Urquharts carry out their theme completely, giving guests a ride in a 1930 Ford coupe with a rumble seat. The house is also used for luncheon tours and private parties.

Hotel St. Germain
2516 Maple Avenue
Dallas, Texas 75201
214-871-2516
Fax: 214-871-0740

Proprietor: Claire L. Heymann
Accommodations: 7 suites
Rates: suites, $200–$600
Included: Breakfast
Added: 13% tax
Payment: Major credit cards; no personal checks
Children: Discouraged
Pets: Not permitted
Smoking: Permitted
Open: Year-round

The St. Germain is in the McKinney Avenue section of Dallas, a shopping, dining, and entertainment area near downtown. The Victorian mansion, built in 1906, has been beautifully converted into a small luxury hotel by owner Claire Heymann. Named for Heymann's French grandmother and the left bank of Paris (Heymann studied at the Sorbonne), the St. Germain opened in late 1991, making it one of the newest additions to the Dallas lodging scene and certainly one of the most unique. With only seven suites, it has an intimate feel, yet offers the same services as larger hotels, such as nightly turndown complete with a chocolate, valet parking, room service, and a round-the-clock concierge.

The suites are tastefully appointed with fine antiques, elegantly draped canopy beds, and fireplaces. Many of the furnishings came from New Orleans, where the owner lived for a number of years. All suites have cable television, Jacuzzi or deep soaking tubs, terrycloth robes, and Roger Gallet toiletries in the baths. Two of the guest suites have their own porches, accented with fanciful wrought-iron railings. Outside there's an inviting New Orleans–style walled courtyard for guests to enjoy.

In the morning, a silver breadbasket arrives at your door filled with brioche, croissants, sticky buns, fruit danish and other tempting pastries, along with hot café au lait. On Friday and Saturday evenings, meals are served in the hotel's dining room, which is graced by a magnificent crystal chandelier. The four-course prix fixe dinner is $65 per person, and entrées range from poached salmon and julienne of truffle, leek, and radicchio in a champagne butter sauce served with a baked dumpling and asparagus tips, to seared sirloin of beef with a dijon garlic crust and topped with a chanterelle sauce. Dinners are open to the public, and since seating is limited, reservations are necessary.

La Maison Malfacon

700 East Rusk Street
Marshall, Texas 75670
903-935-6039

Innkeepers: Jim and Linda Gililland
Accommodations: 4 rooms (shared baths)
Rates: single or double, $35–$70
Included: Continental breakfast
Added: 13.5% tax
Payment: Major credit cards
Children: Additional charge for children over 7
Pets: With approval
Smoking: Only on verandah
Open: Year-round

One of the warmest and most thoughtfully decorated B&Bs in the Southwest is La Maison Malfacon. This historic house reigns with dignity over a quiet street in Marshall, a sleepy East Texas town that was once the fourth largest city in the Lone Star State; today it boasts nearly sixty historical markers.

The first floor of the Greek Revival house was built in about 1866. The second story was added in 1896, resulting in a mix of architectural styles. The house is intriguing—its wide front porch is straight out of a southern novel. J. Paul Getty played on the grand staircase as a boy. Handsome woods, handmade trims, and antique furnishings appear throughout the house. Look for the gentleman's drinking chest, a courtship mirror, and signed pieces of china. Other special finishing touches that make the house special include an open 1920s suitcase with a gentleman's suit from Saks Fifth Avenue, a turn-of-the-century curling iron, and a trunk with family treasures.

The Gilillands are an enthusiastic young couple with a bent for the dramatic, and their sense of fun enlivens this historic inn. They dress in Victorian clothing on special occasions and they own a bicycle built for two, which guests are welcome to ride. Jim's boyhood collection of Lionel trains is on display in the "train room." And for guests who like to swim, there's an outdoor swimming pool.

Breakfast of homemade strawberry, blueberry, or peach muffins arrives at your door each morning in a basket (complete with Linda's own recipe for honey butter) so you can enjoy a comfortable breakfast in bed.

The bedrooms are a visual feast. The Shakespeare Room has an 1840s hand-carved bed and dresser, each topped with a carved bust of the playwright. The Plantation Room has a 200-year-old four-poster bed from a Marshall plantation; the bed is covered with a 19th-century quilt. The Children's Room is decorated with antique children's clothing and toys. There's even a bassinet for visiting babies. Christina's Room is the most elegant, with a 200-year-old canopy bed once owned by royalty.

The Victorian Inn
511 17th Street
Galveston, Texas 77550
409-762-3235

Innkeepers: Janice and Bob Hellbusch
Accommodations: 5 rooms (1 with private bath)
Rates: $80–$150
Included: Breakfast
Added: 13.75% tax
Payment: Major credit cards
Children: Over age 12 welcome
Pets: Not permitted
Smoking: On porches only
Open: Year-round

This stately three-story brick mansion has stood on 17th Street since 1899, serving as a sanctuary from the storms that have hit this coastal city. Today, in the heart of the East End Historical District, it offers travelers an escape from the ordinary. Resident managers welcome guests to the spacious lodging.

The interior of this beautifully designed home illustrates the artistic craftsmanship of the late 1800s—spindled fretwork, floors of inlaid maple, bird's-eye maple wainscoting, a handsome staircase of stained oak, and Belgian tile fireplaces.

Four guest rooms are on the second floor. Mauny's Room is cheerful, with a king-size bed dressed in yellow, white wicker chairs, and a wonderful semicircular porch. Amy's Room, with a king-size bed, has a small adjoining room with a twin bed. All of the rooms share a bath with their neighbor; some have private porches while others share. Access to the porches is by walk-through windows, reflecting the local architectural style. Zachary's Room, a three-room suite, is on the third floor. Modern in decor, it has one large bedroom, another small bedroom with a double bed, a sitting room, and a private bath, but no porch. (If privacy isn't your prime consideration, choose a second-floor room. The porches are a definite advantage.) All the rooms have ceiling fans and are air-conditioned.

Breakfast, served at the dining room table, is hearty Continental. Snacks and beverages are kept on hand at the hospitality bar in the old butler's pantry.

From the inn you can walk to the Strand entertainment and restaurant district. The beach is a short jog or drive away.

Grand Old Resorts

In a region where leisure travel is still relatively new, these resorts have been welcoming guests for the better part of the 20th century.

Arizona

Arizona Biltmore
24th Street and Missouri
Phoenix, Arizona 85016
602-955-6600
800-528-3696
Fax: 602-954-0469

General manager: Bill Lucas
Accommodations: 502 rooms
Rates: single or double, $210–$290; suites start at $600
Added: 10.25% tax
Payment: Major credit cards
Children: Under 18 free in room with parents
Pets: Small pets permitted with deposit
Smoking: Nonsmoking rooms available
Open: Year-round

Built in 1929, the Arizona Biltmore is the grande dame of Phoenix, and it offers much more than a long and distinguished history. Spread over 200 acres, it's filled with activities—two 18-hole championship golf courses, 17 tennis courts (16 lighted), three outdoor swimming pools, a putting green, lawn chess, shuffleboard, a health club, croquet lawns, bicycle paths, and jogging trails. Two of its restaurants, the Orangerie and the Gold Room, have won awards for their cuisine and decor. Best of all, the hotel's staff works hard to please guests, providing a full range of services with a smile and a high degree of professionalism.

Few hotels can claim such a totally distinctive look, both

inside and out. Frank Lloyd Wright was the consulting architect on the project, and his inspiration is clear throughout the hotel. Precast concrete blocks, molded on the site using Arizona sand, are the primary building material. This technique was developed by Wright, and the Biltmore was the first large structure to be constructed in such a manner. Newer buildings have been added on over the years, and each has been designed to resemble the exterior of the original structure.

The rooms are in one of five buildings or in cottages spread over the lush, exquisitely planted grounds. Called traditional, classic, and resort, they range from moderate-size spaces with a mini-bar to extra-large units with a bedroom and sitting room, a mini-bar and refrigerator, a large bath with a separate shower and bath stall, and a private balcony or patio. To say the rooms are colorful is an understatement. Vibrant purple velour upholstery is set off against neon green bedspreads, or your room may be decorated in brilliant fuchsias, oranges, and greens. No matter what the color scheme, it's bound to capture attention, as does the furniture—modern in design but unlike anything you'll see in other resort hotels, due to the Biltmore's unique architectural history. Rooms have views of the golf courses, mountains, or the beautiful gardens. In the gardens is an Olympic-size pool, evocative of an earlier era with its private cabanas.

Dining is important at the Biltmore. The Gold Room (named for its gold-leaf ceiling) has always been the main dining room. The Orangerie is the fine restaurant, where you can expect meals such as pan-seared Chinook salmon with a three-pepper crust and champagne watercress butter ($17.50), roast rack of Colorado lamb with a guava mustard rosemary glaze served with braised Swiss chard and artichokes on Merlot peppercorn sauce ($22.50), and grilled jack on mixed summer greens and plum tomato sorrel vinaigrette ($14.50).

For lighter fare, the Café Sonora features American and Mexican dishes. There's also a snack bar by the pool, two cocktail lounges, and the Aztec Theatre, where plays are performed in a cabaret setting.

The entire hotel seems transported from a slower, more gracious time, and ongoing renovation is further enhancing it. The Arizona Biltmore is now managed by Westin Hotels.

Self-parking at the resort is free. There are a few fine gift shops just beyond the hotel lobby, but if you desire a more extensive shopping excursion, the exclusive shopping center, Biltmore Fashion Park (the hotel came first), is just down the road.

Arizona Inn
2200 East Elm Street
Tucson, Arizona 85719
602-325-1541
800-933-1093
Fax: 602-881-5830

General manager: Patty Doar
Accommodations: 80 rooms
Rates: single, $52–$150; double, $62–$160; suites start at $120
Added: 9.5% tax
Payment: Major credit cards
Children: Additional $10 for children over 10
Pets: Not permitted
Smoking: Permitted
Open: Year-round

A mourning dove watches as two tennis players approach the court along a walk lined with hedges. Near a fountain surrounded by flowers, a young couple sips coffee. Palms and oleander, cypress and citrus trees grace the grounds of this estate. The Arizona Inn is a classic, having acted as grand hostess of the Southwest for six decades. It is now on the National Register of Historic Places. Many of the employees are students from the nearby University of Arizona, and their youth and enthusiasm add spirit to the inn.

From the beginning, the Arizona Inn was designed to have a residential feeling and a sense of privacy. It opened in 1930 as the creation of Mrs. Isabella Greenway, a sophisticated, dynamic community leader. She was Arizona's only congresswoman, serving from 1933 to 1936, and she established a furniture company to employ disabled World War I servicemen. One of the original purposes of the inn was to serve as a market for their furniture, and their craftsmanship can be seen throughout the inn today.

Mrs. Greenway had a hand in every aspect of the inn. During construction, to be sure that her guests could wake up and see the flowers, birds, and trees, she went around the site with a makeshift bed to check that each windowsill was at just the right height; if it wasn't, she'd have the workmen change it. It is that kind of attention to detail that makes this place so special. The inn is still owned by the same family (Patty Doar is Mrs. Greenway's granddaughter), and Mrs. Greenway's commitment to quality and service remains at the heart of its operation.

The pink adobe inn is surrounded by vine-covered walls which screen it from the rest of the world. Inside it is so peaceful that you forget you're just a hop, skip, and a jump from downtown Tucson. Low, residential buildings sprawl over 14 acres of beautifully landscaped grounds connected by winding paths.

The public rooms are grand and gracious. The library, with a vaulted ceiling and polished wood floors, comfortable seating and shelves of books, feels like a lodge. It's the type of place where guests—many of whom return year after year—borrow a book and return it on their next visit. (Notice the large photograph taken of the inn in 1935. You'll see how little it has changed—but the vegetation has gotten taller.) The Audubon Bar, with a white piano and a skylight encircled by a vine, is decorated with 19th-century Audubon prints. One of the dining rooms has hand-colored George Catlin lithographs from Mrs. Greenway's collection.

The guest rooms are charming; each is spacious, well-furnished, and has its own character. The pieces were individually selected, and many were made by the servicemen. Hand-painted windows with delicate patterns, writing desks, overstuffed chairs, and sofas are just a few of the special touches. Guests often become attached to particular rooms. It is said that one guest was so disappointed when his "regular room" was already booked that he asked that all its furniture be moved to the room he was staying in.

The rooms are designated as standard, midrange, and deluxe. Some have fireplaces, many have private patios with comfortable patio furniture, and all have TVs, radios, and air conditioning. The closets are bigger than average—in the 1930s, guests settled in for a season with their trunks, and the closets had to accommodate them.

The inn's swimming pool is a private world, adjoined by glassed-in gardens and a bar beneath vine-covered arbors. The porches alongside the pool can be heated on cooler winter days; ceiling fans circulate the air in warmer weather. The pool itself always seems to be just the right temperature. The nearby Har-Tru clay tennis courts are popular, and guests need only sign up on a chalkboard to reserve court time.

Dining at the inn is a pleasure, especially on the romantic, open-air courtyard. Entrées such as swordfish steak with pesto ($12.95), smoked chicken breast ($9.50), and linguine with sun-dried tomatoes and herbs ($7.95) are deliciously healthful and attractively presented.

Because of the inn's popularity, reservations should be made well in advance. On fall weekends, the inn fills up quickly for the University of Arizona's home football games.

The Wigwam
300 E. Indian School Road
Litchfield Park, Arizona 85340
602-935-3811
800-327-0396
Fax: 602-935-3737

General manager: Cecil Ravenswood
Accommodations: 331 rooms
Rates: single, $230; double, $250; suites start at $380; in the
　　summer, singles start at $80 and suites start at $170
Added: 9.05% tax
Payment: Major credit cards
Children: Under 18 free in room with parents
Pets: Not permitted
Smoking: Nonsmoking rooms available
Open: Year-round

The Wigwam sprawls over 75 acres in Litchfield Park, a small, quiet, palm-lined community 17 miles west of Phoenix. With three championship golf courses and excellent service, it has long been a top choice for golfers. The Gold and the Blue courses were designed by Robert Trent Jones, Sr., the West Course by Robert Lawrence. The Gold Course has been named one of the hundred best in the country.

Dating from 1929, the Wigwam has an interesting history. In 1915 the vice president of Goodyear, Paul Litchfield, developed a revolutionary tire that required fabric woven from staple cotton. This cotton was grown in only two places: the Sea Islands off the Georgia coast and the Nile Valley in Egypt. Both sources were threatened, one by boll weevils and the other by the start of World War I. When Goodyear found that an area in southern Arizona approximated the Nile's climate, he bought thousands of acres and began producing cotton.

Goodyear then developed a community to support his operation. To accommodate business visitors, he built a lodging house; when it became popular, he opened it to the public. Over the years, the Wigwam helped establish the Phoenix area as a winter vacationland.

In late 1986, the resort was sold to SunCor Development, which undertook an extensive renovation project, from the guest rooms to the famed golf courses. The results are stunning: abundant green lawns and thriving gardens bring glorious color to the desert locale. The common areas in the main building are tastefully accented with original art. There are intimate lounges and comfortable sitting areas throughout.

The rooms are in low casas or in the newer two-story buildings spread over the grounds. The extra-large interiors are attractively decorated in southwestern themes. Rooms have wet bars, refrigerators, safes, televisions, VCRs, phones, large closets, and private patios or terraces. Baths have separate vanities, makeup mirrors, scales, and Caswell-Massey toiletries. Most units can sleep up to four people. Some rooms have Murphy beds. Premier rooms have fireplaces and sitting areas.

At mealtime, there are many dining options. The Arizona Kitchen with its open kitchen is the most inventive, with dishes such as rattlesnake fritters and chocolate tacos. (Dinner entrées average about $20.) The Grill on the Greens serves a breakfast buffet, a soup, salad, and deli buffet at midday, and specializes in steaks and seafood for dinner. The Terrace Dining Room is the resort's main restaurant, serving American bistro cuisine in a pleasant atmosphere. Tables on the terrace overlook the pool area, and dinner entrées such as venison, mixed grill, and pot roast average about $15. The Kachina Lounge just down the hall has a copper topped bar, and the Arizona Bar has live entertainment in season.

The main swimming pool is free-form with a waterslide and fountain. There's a volleyball net on one side, and a poolside cabana serves drinks, snacks, and a full lunch every day. The estatelike resort is also known for its tennis (eight Plexi-Pave courts) and its western program. There's a stable on the grounds, and special events include stagecoach and haywagon rides and desert steak broils. An activities director makes sure that everyone has a good time, including children.

In the summer the resort operates the Pow Wow program, a day camp for children aged four through teens. Pow Wow activities include horseback riding, bicycling, roller skating, swimming, and movies.

New Mexico

The Bishop's Lodge
Box 2367
Santa Fe, New Mexico 87504
505-983-6377
800-732-2240
Fax: 505-989-8739

Innkeepers: Jim and Lore Thorpe
Accommodations: 74 rooms

Rates: single, $120–$180; double, $160–$315; suites, $205–$345
Added: 9% tax
Payment: Personal checks or cash; no credit cards
Children: Welcome
Pets: Not permitted
Smoking: Permitted
Open: April to January 2

Downtown Santa Fe is only 5 minutes away, but here at the Bishop's Lodge, which occupies 1,000 acres in the foothills of the Sangre de Cristo Mountains, guests find peace and quiet far from the crowds.

Retreating to these juniper-studded foothills at the head of the Tesuque Valley is not without precedent. In fact, at the heart of the lodge's charm—its gentleness and hospitality—is the memory of the man for whom it is named. Archbishop Lamy of Santa Fe (the model for the main character in Willa Cather's *Death Comes for the Archbishop*) came to this very spot about a century ago for rest and eventually retirement. Over time he planted an orchard, supplementing the fruit trees planted by the Franciscan Fathers during the early 17th century. Remnants of the orchard are still sprinkled over the grounds.

Next to his adobe home the archbishop built a private chapel —a simple structure with vaulted ceilings and painted-glass windows that simulate the stained glass of the cathedrals in his native France. The tiny chapel, now on the National Register of Historic Places, still stands, creating an atmosphere of warmth, peacefulness, and history.

Only a few steps away down a path lined with flowers is the main lobby, where guests can sign up for activities, eat in the central dining room, and enjoy spectacular sunsets from the terrace bar. Life is casual here. While men are asked to wear jackets at dinner and women are requested to "dress accordingly," there's an informal air throughout the resort. Breakfast and lunch are served buffet-style. Cocktails are served in El Charro lounge as well as on the terrace.

The guest rooms are spread out in several one- and two-story buildings, all reflecting their New Mexico heritage. In a wide assortment of sizes and configurations, they are especially spacious, well lit, and well furnished. The decor is ranch-style southwestern, with kiva fireplaces, simple wooden furniture, and earth-tone fabrics with splashes of color. Some rooms have beamed ceilings, some have private balconies or terraces. The bathrooms are larger than average and designed for convenience. Air conditioning, TVs, and telephones are standard features.

The Bishop's Lodge has an impressive roster of recreational choices. There are ample facilities for horseback riding, tennis, volleyball, swimming, and skeet shooting as well as lots of extras: a playground (complete with a tepee), fishing pond for children (stocked with trout), maps with hiking trails, and lists for bird watchers (more than 110 species can be observed on the grounds). Golfers are welcome at any of three private courses in the area.

The lodge also offers an abundance of special activities such as a newcomer's cocktail party held by the Thorpes, exercise classes, fashion shows, storytelling on the front lawn, steak fries, children's cookouts—the list goes on and on. The resort also keeps guests informed of events in the area.

In the summer, there's an excellent program for children aged four to twelve that includes hiking, swimming, pony rides, and arts and crafts. Teens get special attention. There's a dining table especially for them, and events such as swim parties are planned, depending upon the number of young guests.

Horseback riding is important here. Most of the guests ride, whether they are experienced or have never mounted a horse before. With more than 60 horses, the resort offers daily guided rides ($20 per person), plus special breakfast and picnic rides.

Since 1918, when James R. Thorpe developed the Bishop's Lodge as a ranch resort, three generations of the family have owned and run the lodge. Previously, the property had belonged to the newspaper publisher Joseph Pulitzer, who established the Pulitzer Prizes.

The Lodge
P.O. Box 497
1 Corona Place
Cloudcroft, New Mexico 88317
505-682-2566
800-395-6343
Fax: 505-682-2715

Owners: Carole and Jerry Sanders
Accommodations: 47 rooms
Rates: single or double, $65–$95; suites, $95–$165
Added: 9.25% tax
Payment: Major credit cards
Children: Welcome
Pets: Not permitted
Smoking: Permitted
Open: Year-round

Even in July, the air is cool high in the Sacramento Mountains. In the lobby of the Lodge, guests enjoy a crackling fire while at the mountains' base, 15 miles away, folks swelter in the desert heat.

The Lodge, intimate and secluded, is a romantic escape. Here you can play golf or hike during the summer, ski or snuggle by the fire in the winter. The original lodge, built in 1899 by the Alamogordo and Sacramento Mountain Railway, was destroyed by fire in 1909; two years later, this lodge was constructed. Over the years it has undergone numerous renovations, though its Bavarian-style exterior has remained essentially the same.

You should know that the hotel has a friendly and flirtatious ghost named Rebecca. According to the legend, beautiful Rebecca was a chambermaid at the Lodge in the early 1930s. She mysteriously disappeared after her lumberjack lover found her in the arms of another man. Some people swear that they see her ghost from time to time wandering the halls of the old inn.

The legend is so popular that the Lodge's restaurant is named for her, and her portrait hangs at the entrance. (Some say that Rebecca's image in this portrait is missing from their photographs when they're developed.) The restaurant is renowned for its Continental cuisine. With dishes such as charbroiled quail, mahogany chicken with a honey pecan sauce, and shrimp Rebecca (shrimp, shallots, tomatoes, basil pesto, and crushed red peppers served on spinach fettuccine), the menu is a feast in itself. Tableside presentations are a house specialty—the dessert flambés are particularly popular. The breakfast and lunch menus are equally extensive, and the menu itself is printed like a newspaper informing guests of the inn's history as well as seasonal events. Entrées range from $13 to $24 at dinner, from $2.95–$7.95 at breakfast and lunch. Down in the basement is the Red Dog Saloon, with a history of its own (ask about the dollar bills encased in glass). And upstairs is a Victorian bar from Al Capone's home.

One of the Lodge's most distinctive features is its five-story copper tower. Judy Garland wrote her name on the wall here. So did Clark Gable. For a romantic tête-à-tête, reserve the tiny parlor at the base of the tower. (More than one couple has gotten engaged here.) Climb the stairs to the summit and look out over miles of alpine scenery. White Sands National Monument glistens, 40 miles away, and on a clear day you can see much farther—150 miles, it's claimed.

The lobby of the hotel looks like a lodge, with leather couches, bearskins, even a stuffed bear. The guest rooms are much more romantic, decorated in a French country style with antique furniture, matched bed and drapery fabrics, and brass accents. Every room in this personable inn is different in size and shape, and has its own decorating scheme. Common to all are high ceilings, clicking steam radiators, down comforters, and French eyelet linens, TVs, and phones. Family rooms, sleeping up to four, are especially spacious. King rooms tend to be dormer style, with four-poster beds, dormer seating, and shutters with fabric insets.

The Honeymoon Suite features a gold-crowned, mirror-topped bed (you have to see it to believe it) and a Jacuzzi built for two. The Governor's Suite (a real bargain at $165) is the most elegant room at the Lodge. It has a four-poster bed, lace curtains, a plush living room with antique furniture and velvet upholstery, a phone, an old wooden radio that still works, its own entrance hallway, a writing desk in a sunny window alcove, and Oriental rugs. In the bath there are Crabtree and Evelyn toiletries. Supposedly this is Rebecca's favorite room.

The Lodge's 9-hole golf course, at 9,200 feet, is among the highest in the world. Golfers can pause to enjoy the spectacular scenery punctuated with blue spruce and ponderosa pine. The outdoor pool, kept at 80 degrees year-round, and outdoor hot tub are attractive modern features of a hotel that's a throwback to a more graceful era of travel.

A family-oriented hostelry, the Lodge will arrange for baby-sitters upon request. Nearby family activities include skiing at Cloudcroft (25 runs), outdoor fun in Lincoln National Forest, and seasonal festivals.

Rancho Encantado
Route 4, Box 57C
Santa Fe, New Mexico 87501
505-982-3537
800-722-9339
Fax: 505-983-8269

Owners: The Egan Family
Accommodations: 22 rooms, 29 condominiums
Rates:
  Main lodge rooms: $110–$175
  Casitas and cottages: $125–$245
  Condominiums: $100–$300
Added: 10.125% tax
Payment: Major credit cards
Children: Free in room with parents
Pets: Not permitted
Smoking: Permitted
Open: Year-round

When you turn into the driveway at Rancho Encantado, you may wonder whether this is really the place that such celebrities as Jimmy Stewart and Robert Redford choose as a vacation retreat. Don't be deterred by the unassuming sign and unpaved road—in Santa Fe, the best addresses are on dirt roads. Rancho Encantado, in operation since 1968, is no exception.

From the gate, a network of dirt roads winds through fragrant piñon and ruddy arroyos on the 168-acre property. Nestled in the high desert beneath the Santa Fe Ski Basin and Sangre de Cristo Mountains, Rancho Encantado is designed to harmonize with the existing terrain rather than intrude upon it. Although it is only 15 minutes from Santa Fe, 10 minutes from the opera, and 5 minutes from the artists' community of Tesuque, its location feels remote and private.

The main lodge also seems modest compared to similar resorts, but the unpretentiousness of Rancho Encantado is part of its appeal. The lodge's large, dark, southwestern furniture, comfortable sofas, ceramic tile floors, viga ceilings, and small dining room make you feel as though you're visiting someone rather than checking into a hotel. The ranch's "Wall of Fame," featuring photographs of its most famous guests, is in the back sitting room.

The handful of guest rooms in the main lodge are decorated in soft pastel colors and blend marble-topped Victorian tables with simpler southwestern pieces. These rooms tend to be more formal than those in the rest of the resort.

Adobe casitas are the primary accommodation here. Each casita has a refrigerator, kiva fireplace (amply stocked with firewood in colder weather), and a cozy sitting area furnished with traditional southwestern pieces in rich earth tones that complement the landscape. All of the casitas have terraces, but Numbers 25–32 have the best views of the spectacular sunsets over the distant Jemez Mountains.

Twenty-nine luxury condos, with full kitchens, have been built across the road, more than doubling the size of the original resort. Some of them may be rented by guests, based on availability. Rates are determined by the number of bedrooms and guests in your party.

The superb desert vistas and memorable food make dining at the ranch a rewarding experience. Considered one of the best restaurants in the area, the dining room is popular with Santa Feans and guests alike. The menu consists of New Mexican, fresh seafood (a rarity in the Southwest desert), and Continental specialties. A special menu features meals that are low in fat, cholesterol, and sodium, including a delicious Rocky Mountain trout with sun-dried tomatoes, garlic, and basil.

Breakfast has a decidedly New Mexican accent. Dishes are named for local Indian pueblos, such as Santa Clara and Nambe, and include a number of variations of huevos rancheros, some made with the Mexican sausage chorizo.

Sports play an important role at Rancho Encantado. There is a full-time tennis pro, three tennis courts, including one with a basketball net and backboard for pickup games, an outdoor swimming pool and hot tub that are covered and heated in the winter, and a pool table in the cantina. Perhaps the most popular activity is horseback riding, and trail rides leave from the corral twice daily year-round.

Rancho's helpful and friendly staff, many of whom have been here for a number of years, add to the relaxed environment.

Groups

Arizona

Rancho de la Osa
P.O. Box 1
Sasabe, Arizona 85633
602-823-4257
Fax: 602-823-4238

Hosts: The Davis family
Accommodations: 16 rooms
Rates: $90–$105 per person per night, nonriding packages available
Included: All meals and horseback riding
Added: 6.5% sales tax, 15% service charge
Payment: Major credit cards
Children: Up to 3 years, $10; 4–5, $30; 6–13, $70; 14 and older, adult rate
Pets: Not permitted
Smoking: Nonsmoking rooms available
Open: Year-round

About 65 miles southwest of Tucson, near the Mexican border and far from the resorts in the city, there's a ranch that dates from the 1730s. Here you can retreat into an earlier time while enjoying horseback riding, studying nature (especially birds), and taking excursions to nearby sites in Arizona as well as Mexico.

The Davis family has been operating the ranch since 1982. Their program is flexible, and their facilities work well for groups. The adobe cantina was built as a mission in about 1737 by Franciscan monks. While it retains a historic feeling, it's definitely modern on the inside, with pool tables, a big-screen TV with a VCR, and a bar.

The rambling adobe hacienda, or main house, was built in 1860. Today vacationers gather here for hearty ranch meals. The dining room is open to the public for lunch every day and for

Sunday afternoon dinner. Special arrangements for groups include outdoor cookouts under the trees.

The guest rooms are in low adobe block buildings with walls up to three feet thick. Although far from plush, they have lots of southwestern character—hand-painted furniture, Mexican pigskin chairs, and Indian throw rugs. Fires (every room has a fireplace) are lit twice a day. There are electric blankets in the winter and ceiling fans overhead for the warmer months (no air conditioning). The bathrooms, remodeled in the mid-1980s, have showers and tubs.

Horseback rides led by wranglers go out twice a day. Since the ranch raises its own quarter horses, there are always plenty to go around. Rides are leisurely, and riders are grouped according to ability. The swimming pool and spa, shaded with palm trees, are good for relaxing. Of special interest is Buenos Aires National Wildlife Refuge, with more than 200 bird species, a few miles away. Other nearby attractions include Kit Peak Observatory, Tubac, Tucson, and Nogales, Mexico.

New Mexico

La Junta Guest Ranch
Alto, New Mexico 88312
505-336-4361
800-443-8423

Owners: The Finley Family
Accommodations: 27 rooms
Rates: single, $65; double, $75; $200 for large cabins
Added: 7.125% tax
Payment: No credit cards
Children: Welcome
Pets: Permitted
Smoking: Discouraged; nonsmoking rooms available
Open: Year-round

La Junta means "meeting place," which is exactly what this lodging offers—an informal gathering spot for groups of up to 75, whether they want to ski at nearby Ski Apache Resort or enjoy the wooded surroundings at any time of year. The atmosphere is camplike and low key, allowing groups to create their own mood.

Spread over 7 acres of beautiful countryside six miles north of Ruidoso with the smell of pine in the air and occasional mountain vistas, La Junta has a central recreation room and guest rooms in five buildings. Picnic tables and grills are scattered among the trees. Best of all, the managers are willing to help groups meet their specific needs.

The owners are transplanted Louisianians, and happily they have brought a touch of their native state to this part of New Mexico. Each room is named for a Louisiana parish, and the decor reflects the Finleys' penchant for Cajun country. For example, tucked into the basket of goodies awaiting guests—items such as coffee, tea, and ketchup—is a bottle of Trappey's pepper sauce.

Each of the buildings is different, offering a wide variety of accommodations, and each one has a well-equipped kitchen and fireplace. Vermilion and St. Charles can be rented as separate or adjoining units; together they can accommodate twelve. The two units, on top of the recreation building, have a wide upstairs porch and two living room–kitchen combinations in addition to bedrooms.

Orleans and Acadia, the most private of the buildings, have three bedrooms and a deck overlooking the woods. All of the rooms have a rustic flavor, and mismatched fabrics add a sense of fun.

Oklahoma

Lake Texoma Resort
Box 248
Kingston, Oklahoma 73439
405-564-2311
800-654-8240

General manager: Steve Flaming
Accommodations: 99 rooms, 67 cabins
Rates: single or double (cabin), $57–$98; suites, $90
Added: 5% tax
Payment: Major credit cards
Children: Welcome
Pets: Permitted in cabins
Smoking: Permitted
Open: Year-round

Run by the Oklahoma Tourism and Recreation Department, Lake Texoma Resort has a long roster of activities, a casual setting, and bargain rates, making it a good spot for groups and families. Most important, the staff is enthusiastic and proud of their program.

Boating, fishing, horseback riding, golf, tennis, hiking, and biking are all available. The recreation department, housed in a well-equipped facility, offers all kinds of team sports as well as a game room with video games, pool, and table tennis. Its daily activities include water aerobics, ski instruction, arts and crafts, and nature hikes. Family dances or theme parties are held on Saturdays. Most activities have minimal charges or are free. Also in the recreation building is an impressive array of exercise equipment, geared toward fitness instead of muscle building. Special fitness packages are scheduled throughout the year.

For the fishing enthusiast, there's a year-round striper guide, and Striper Camps are offered seasonally. The camps include guides, boats, equipment, lodging, and meals. Two days of fishing for striped bass in Lake Texoma's abundant waters end with a tournament.

The guest rooms in the main lodge have a choice of two twin, one queen-size, one king-size, or one double plus one twin bed. The furnishings are simple. The cabana rooms are the most spacious (king-size bed, queen-size sofa bed, small refrigerator, patio doors opening to pool). Most of the cottages, more modestly furnished than the lodge rooms, have two bedrooms. All have kitchens (bring your own cookware), dining tables, and TVs. For groups, Bayview unit accommodates up to 40.

The lodge's dining room is cheerful, with reasonably priced food.

Texas

Lajitas on the Rio Grande
Star Route 70
Box 400
Terlingua, Texas 79852
915-424-3471
800-527-4078
Fax: 915-424-3277

Managers: The Moores
Accommodations: 81 units
Rates: single, $60; double, $65
Added: 6% tax
Payment: Major credit cards
Children: Welcome
Pets: Small pets permitted

Smoking: Permitted
Open: Year-round

There's no doubt about it: Lajitas is a world apart. First of all, it's not near anything unless you count Big Bend National Park, which isn't near anything either. Alpine is 90 miles north, El Paso is 310 miles to the northwest, and San Antonio is 430 miles to the northeast.

It also belongs to an earlier period, a time when army troops chased Indians and rustlers holed up in desert hideaways. A virtual Williamsburg of the Old West, Lajitas is a great place for families or groups.

The entire town is a development of the Mischer Corporation. It started with a real trading post on the banks of the Rio Grande, and now Lajitas is a tourist attraction as well as a small residential community, complete with condos and a few houses. It boasts a 9-hole golf course, a swimming pool, tennis courts, a livery stable, desert museum, restaurant, saloon, and a handful of shops.

Each lodging reflects a different aspect of the region's history. The Badlands Hotel is straight out of a cowboy movie. The Cavalry Post Motel is built on the site of the cavalry post where General "Black Jack" Pershing housed his troops in the early 1900s. Over at the Officers' Quarters (the exterior is a replica of the officers' quarters in old Fort Davis), guests are housed in style. Then there's a Spanish-style motel, La Cuesta, which reflects the area's proximity to Mexico, just across the river.

Make no mistake: this is desert country. The river, lined with graceful salt cedars, marks the southern perimeter, and rugged mountains are in the distance. The landscape is a composite of prickly pear and ocotillo, yucca and scrub mesquite. Spring and fall are the prime seasons to visit, but the town never closes its doors.

The four accommodations have similar furnishings but different environments. Air conditioning, phones, and TVs are in all units. The upstairs rooms at the Badlands Hotel open onto a long porch overlooking the town. The Officers' Quarters is the most modern, but seems out of step with the overall mood. Some units in the Cavalry Post have fireplaces.

One- and two-bedroom condos are also a good option. Adobe on the outside, they have stone fireplaces, good kitchens, big bedrooms, and larger than average baths. Clustered in a separate section of the town, they resemble a little village.

For small groups or large families, several houses are also available, each with a dramatic setting overlooking the desert terrain. At the other end of the spectrum, there are two bunk-houses right across from the Badlands Hotel. Each has two sleeping sections for seven persons each, adjoining baths, and a central sitting area.

The area is rich in recreational opportunities, including excursions into Big Bend, hiking and backcountry trips, and river rafting. Rockhounds, bird watchers, history buffs, and outdoor enthusiasts can luxuriate in the abundance of choices.

Lazy Hills Guest Ranch
Box G
Henderson Branch Road
Ingram, Texas 78025
512-367-5600
800-880-0632
Fax: 512-367-5667

Hosts: Bob and Carol Steinruck
Accommodations: 26 units
Rates: single, $75; double, $120; weekly rates available
Included: All meals, 6 rides per week
Minimum stay: 3 nights; 1 or 2 nights when space is available for an extra $10 per night per room
Added: 15% gratuity and 6% sales tax
Payment: Major credit cards
Children: Reduced rates for children in same room with parents
Pets: Not permitted
Smoking: Permitted
Open: Year-round

Spread over 750 acres in the pastoral Texas Hill Country, the family-run Lazy Hills Guest Ranch offers friendliness and fun. The pace is slow, with time for strolling and relaxing. Horseback riding fits the mood, and guests can choose one of four hour-long rides a day. (The price of a week's stay includes six rides. For guests staying for a shorter time, rides are $8 per person per hour's guided trail ride.) There's also a large swimming pool, a hot tub, lighted tennis courts, archery, and volleyball as well as exploring along the creek and hiking in the woods.

Often catering to groups, the hosts are happy to arrange activities suited to the age and interests of their guests. The lodging units are clustered, which makes them ideal for groups. The furnishings are simple—more like those at a real ranch than at most guest ranches. Most of the rooms can sleep up to four. Six units have fireplaces.

The remodeled family-style dining room has a friendly feeling. The adjacent sitting room has the only TV on the premises. In a nearby building there's a game room with pool and Ping-Pong tables, shuffleboard, and electronic games.

From mid-November to early January, deer and turkey hunting takes precedence over more typical guest ranch activities. Reduced rates are available from September 15 to May 15 (holidays excepted). No minimum stay is required during the off-season, and B&B plans can be arranged then as well. Groups should inquire about special rates.

Guest Ranches

Guest ranches, with their emphasis on horseback riding, rustic accommodations, and hearty meals, allow you to experience the Wild West today.

Arizona

Circle Z Ranch
Patagonia, Arizona 85624
602-287-2091

Owner: Lucia Nash
Accommodations: Maximum is 45 guests
Rates: single, $690–$955; double, $690–866; cabin with 4 people, $2800–$3000 per week; special rates for long weekends
Included: Horseback riding and all meals
Minimum Stay: 3 nights
Added: 5.5% tax, 15% gratuity recommended
Payment: Personal checks; no credit cards
Children: $463–$640 per week for children aged 5 to 13
Pets: Not permitted
Smoking: Permitted
Open: November 1 through May 15

Forget what you've heard about guest ranches looking rugged and dusty: these adjectives simply don't apply to the Circle Z. There's a sense of gentility about the place that one does not normally associate with a dude ranch.

But a dude ranch the Circle Z certainly is, and, established in 1925, it's the oldest continuously operating one in Arizona. With 70 horses for a maximum of 45 guests, there are plenty to go around, and riding is what most people come here for. Instruction is available for beginners, and each is given plenty of attention due to the limited number of guests. Trail rides go out twice daily for about two hours, and there are picnic rides on Saturdays and day-long rides once a week.

After a day on the trail, guests unwind in the cantina with hors d'oeuvres and B.Y.O.B. cocktails and then sit down to a hearty meal of mesquite cooked steak, lasagna, or barbecued meat. All breads and desserts are homemade. The pleasant dining room, with hand-painted chairs and wooden tables, has a nice view and is perfect for bird-watching. Children eat a half hour earlier than adults in a separate dining room, and they have their own cantina complete with juke box and pool table.

Lodging is in small adobe casitas that surround the central lawn. Simply furnished, the casitas have cheerful hand-painted furniture, ceramic Mexican plates for decoration, and tile baths. There are no phones or TVs in the rooms, encouraging guests to socialize in the main lodge's living room, where one can play cards or sink into a comfortable sofa and enjoy a fire on chilly evenings. (The ranch is at an elevation of 4,000 feet, and it gets much colder at night here than in other parts of southern Arizona.)

Horseback riding is the only planned activity, but the ranch does have an outdoor pool and tennis court. Nogales, Mexico, is not far away, and makes for a fun trip across the border.

Flying E Ranch
Box EEE
2801 W. Wickenburg Way
Wickenburg, Arizona 85358
602-684-2690

Owner/Manager: Vi Wellik
Accommodations: 16 units
Rates: single, $110–$140; double, $175–$200; family house, $220
Included: All meals and ranch activities except for riding
Minimum stay: 2 nights; 4 nights over holidays
Added: 6% tax
Payment: No credit cards
Children: up to 2 years, $25; 3–6, $35; 7–12, $45; $13 and over,
    $60; children apart from parents charged as adults
Pets: Not permitted; kennels are available nearby
Smoking: Permitted
Open: November to May

By the flip of a coin, Vi Wellik and her husband George discovered the Flying E Ranch in 1949, thereby changing their lives. The couple, both flyers, first noticed the ranch on a flight to Texas in their private plane. "It looked like a motel in the middle of the desert," says Vi. Their curiosity was sparked. That night they tossed a coin to decide whether to go back. Not only did they return, but they ended up buying the ranch and have operated it as a guest ranch since 1960.

Guests, many of whom visit Flying E year after year, find friendly folks and a relaxing atmosphere at this small ranch. The clock by the pool sets the tone: instead of hands, it says, "Who cares?" This is the kind of place where you can do what you want when you want.

Horseback riding is a good option. There's an extra fee—$15 per day for one ride, $24 for two rides, or $125 weekly. With more than 20,000 acres of riding terrain, there's lots of room to roam, starting from the ranch's site on a 2,500-foot mesa. The rides, all led by wranglers, are separated into groups according to riders' abilities. When you aren't riding, you can soak in the pool and hot tub, play tennis (one court), basketball, volleyball, shuffleboard, life-size chess (inspired by the owner's recent trip to Europe), exercise in the small workout room, or socialize with other guests. Vi, now a widow, is a history buff who restores old properties, so she can entertain guests with local lore.

Meals are served family-style on red and white checked tablecloths and feature good ol' home cooking. Breakfast cookouts and chuckwagon dinners are highlights. Nonriders are escorted to the serving site via hay wagon. Cocktail hour (B.Y.O.B) is from 6 P.M. to 7 P.M. in the ranch's cozy "saloon."

The guest rooms are in motel units spread out from the main living–dining room. With wood paneling, traditional furnishings (twin or king-size beds), Navajo rugs, and baths with bird and cactus tiles, they're comfortable and well maintained. All the rooms have wet bars and refrigerators; they are electrically heated and cooled, and stocked with electric blankets for extra-nippy nights. TVs with VCRs are available for rent.

Kay El Bar Ranch
Box 2480
Wickenburg, Arizona 85358
602-684-7593

Host: Jane Nash
Accommodations: 10 rooms (all with private bath)
Rates: single, $105; double, $195; suites, $205
Included: All meals and 1 ride per day
Minimum stay: 2 nights
Added: 6% tax
Payment: Major credit cards
Children: Welcome
Pets: Not permitted

Smoking: Nonsmoking rooms available
Open: Mid-October through May 1

One of the oldest guest ranches in Arizona—its first guests checked in back in 1926—Kay El Bar is a National Historic Site. Shaded by magnificent salt cedar and eucalyptus trees, the buildings consist of several hacienda-style adobes.

With only twenty guests at a time, Kay El Bar is low key, laid back, and downright friendly. The breakfast bell, nestled in the trees, rings at about 8:00 A.M. Guests gather in the dining room, where photographs of Hollywood cowboys line the walls, and guests have contests to see who can name the most stars. The morning ride goes out at around ten. Depending on the crowd, it may come back mid-afternoon or stay out all day, ending with a cookout. Those who choose not to ride can lounge by the heated pool, arriving at the cookout site just in time for barbecued chicken or fajitas.

At night, guests gather in the main lodge, a cozy sort of room with a mock bearskin rug in front of a crackling fire in the big stone fireplace, shelves upon shelves of books, and an array of games. Sometimes the hosts show an old Western on the VCR. When the mood is right, somebody may play a tune on the piano. Over to the side there's a stocked bar.

Eight guest rooms are in the main lodge. Their ranch-style furniture dates from the 1920s dude ranch. These rooms have a nostalgic air, with Remington prints, cowboy lampshades, and Indian rugs.

A separate two-bedroom, two-bath cottage with a living room and fireplace can be rented as a whole or as a two-room suite.

Price Canyon Ranch

P.O. Box 1065
Douglas, Arizona 85607
602-558-2383

Owners: Scotty and Alice Anderson
Accommodations: 5 units
Rates: single, $85; double, $160
Included: All meals and horseback riding
Minimum Stay: 2 nights
Added: Tax
Payment: American Express and personal checks
Children: 1–5 years, $10; 6–9, $25; 10–12, $35; 13–15, $45; 16 and
    older considered adults
Pets: Permitted if well-behaved

Smoking: Permitted
Open: Year-round

For such a small place, Price Canyon Ranch offers immense variety. The ranch is between Douglas and Apache on the slopes of the Chiricahua Mountains (elevation 5,600 feet). The bumpy dirt road that leads to the ranch is long, but at the end the hospitable Andersons are ready to introduce you to their way of life. A working ranch, and working is the operative word —this is not the type of ranch where guests "play" at being cowboys— Price Canyon invites visitors to experience real ranch life by pitching in with the chores, from branding and rounding up cattle to repairing fences. In between, Scotty Anderson leads horseback rides across the desert and into the mountains.

Although horseback riding is the only scheduled activity, guests can also go hiking, bird-watching, or cave exploring. For those interested in archaeological study, the ranch sits on a pre-Columbian Indian site. Hunters can arrange guided hunts for deer, bear, and javelina. Adventure-seekers can arrange 1- to 12-day guided pack trips (for 4 to 20 people). The ranch also has a youth riding program in the summer.

Groups can rent a spacious "people barn," with kitchen and bath facilities as well as living, sleeping, and recreation space. Ten camper and trailer sites are also on the premises. The ranch can house three or four families or thirty individuals. Accommodations are in the Andersons' 1870s ranch house, a nearby bunkhouse, and a modern apartment. All are pleasant and comfortable. Explain your needs to the Andersons and they'll match you with the best unit.

Meals are served family-style, featuring home cooking, with fresh vegetables, beef raised on the ranch, and hot apple pie.

You don't have to know how to ride to stay at Price Canyon. Scotty and his hands are experienced teachers. And there are 400 miles of trail to practice on. There's also a small catfish pond and a spring-fed swimming pool on the property.

Rancho de los Caballeros
P.O. Box 1148
Wickenburg, Arizona 85358
602-684-5484
Fax: 602-684-2267

General manager: Dallas C. Gant, Jr.
Accommodations: 74 rooms
Rates: single, $154–$198; double, $258–$355; suites, $455;
   group rates available

Included: All meals
Added: 6% tax
Payment: Personal checks; no credit cards
Children: Welcome
Pets: Not permitted
Smoking: Permitted
Open: Early October to mid-May

In the Wickenburg area, renowned for its guest ranches, Rancho de los Caballeros reigns supreme, adding a touch of class to the Southwest. Its name, Ranch of the Gentlemen on Horseback, pays tribute to the Spanish explorers who introduced horses to the Indian culture. Both a working and a guest ranch, with 20,000 acres of hills and desert terrain, Los Caballeros has been welcoming guests since 1948. The overall style is casual yet tasteful; men are asked to wear sports jackets or western shirts with vests or bolo ties in the evening; women wear sports suits or dresses.

The main lodge sets the tone. Its spacious living room has a vaulted ceiling, fanciful trim and molding, lots of sofas and chairs for lounging, and a large copper-shielded fireplace. Off to one side is the library, overlooking a putting green. Card tables are set in window nooks for amicable contests, and in an adjoining room there's a pool table. Outside, lush green lawns and border gardens are alternated with natural desert landscaping—native grasses, saguaros, and other cacti.

Naturally, horseback riding is a star event at the ranch. With 75 or more horses, two rides are offered each day. Guests pay an extra fee—$26 for morning rides, $18 for afternoon rides. A wrangler comes to your table in the dining room to sign you up.

Los Caballeros Golf Club is on the ranch grounds; its 18-hole championship course is one of the finest in Arizona. There's an extra charge of $37 for 18 holes, and $13 for cart rental. The resort also has trapshooting, 4 tennis courts, a swimming pool, and miles of wide-open spaces. During appropriate seasons, a children's program (ages 5–12) is offered at no extra charge. Activities include riding, hiking, swimming, and games.

Near dinnertime, guests congregate in Los Caballeros Saloon, which is colorful, fun, and friendly. Large windows offer views of the Bradshaw mountains. Meals are served in the adjacent dining room, with ornate Spanish decor. Lunch is served buffet-style; breakfast and dinner entrées are ordered from the menu. Twice a week the ranch throws an all-western evening cookout at South Yucca Flats or Vulture Peak, featuring barbecued ribs and hot apple crisp, followed by campfire entertainment.

The variety of accommodations, spread over the grounds, have recently been redecorated. Sun Terrace rooms, in one wing of the main building and in bungalows, have hand-painted beds, simple curtains and carpeting, and small modern baths with Mexican tile accents. Sunset rooms, which face the mountains and the open desert, are the most secluded. From their patios quail and roadrunners are often seen scampering across the desert terrain. Available in one-, two-, or three-room units, they have fireplaces and Mexican furnishings. Bradshaw Mountain rooms are the most modern. They have one or two large bedrooms, ample closet space, a parlor with lots of comfortable seating, a fireplace, and a kitchenette. You can rent just a bedroom portion of a Bradshaw Mountain unit or you can combine a bedroom with the living-kitchenette segment.

White Stallion Ranch
9251 West Twin Peaks Road
Tucson, Arizona 85743
602-297-0252
800-782-5546
Fax: 602-744-2786

Owners: The True Family
Accommodations: 29 rooms
Rates: single, $119–$130; $102–$120 per person in double; $113–$145 per person in suite
Included: All meals and horseback riding
Added: 6.5% tax and 15% service charge in lieu of tips
Payment: Personal checks; no credit cards
Children: Welcome
Pets: Not permitted
Smoking: Permitted
Open: October through April

White Stallion Ranch spreads over 3,000 acres of beautiful desert and mountain terrain 17 miles northwest of Tucson. Both a working and a guest ranch, it's been owned and run by the True family since 1965. The nicest guest ranch in the Tucson area, it's everything you expect a dude ranch to be.

Year-round, the Trues raise Texas longhorn cattle, but in the winter season they go all out to show guests a slice of the West. Over the years visitors have arrived from fifty or so countries (look for the collection of flags representing the guest list). Many return year after year for what White Stallion has to offer: four rides a day, informal rodeos, nature walks, home cooking, and a warm family atmosphere.

The Trues own about 60 horses, and one of their specialties is matching riders with the right horses. Some rides are designed to be slow and scenic, others fast. Trails lead from flat desert up into the mountains. Children 5 and older are allowed to ride on their own; younger children ride with their parents.

Some guests never ride, preferring to soak up the western atmosphere. There's a Saturday afternoon rodeo, which features roping, bulldogging, and barrel racing, breakfast rides, hayrides and cookouts, and a weekly barbecue, with the whole meal — roast beef, carrots, onions and potatoes — cooked in an outdoor Indian brick oven.

Areas for relaxing include the comfortable and spacious main lodge (TV room, pool room, library, self-serve bar) open around the clock, an outdoor pool surrounded by palms, and an enclosed redwood hot tub (one of the most popular spots on the ranch). There is also tennis (two courts), horseshoes, volleyball, basketball, and shuffleboard; and sometimes guests form their own impromptu softball games. For kids, there's a separate air-conditioned rec room complete with pool table, television, and piano.

One unusual feature is the ranch's wildlife zoo — fallow deer, mouflon bighorns, llamas, pygmy goats, miniature horses, and pheasants. Spread over a wide expanse, the zoo attracts lots of attention from adults as well as children. And special notice goes to Dewey, the Vietnamese potbellied pig that answers to his name when you call him. Nature walks are a weekly feature, led by a wildlife biologist.

Accommodations are comfortable and fairly simple. Three units are in the main lodge; the others are scattered over the grounds. Most have a double and twin bed and can be rented either as a bedroom or suite. Baths are modern with cultured marble. The newest units, called deluxe suites, have fireplaces and whirlpool tubs. Several small units have been especially designed for single people, enabling them to stay at a lower price. All rooms are air-conditioned. There are no phones or TVs in the rooms since guests are supposed to be getting away from it all, but for those who need to keep in touch with the outside world, there is a TV in the main lodge, a pay phone, and the latest copy of both *USA Today* and the *Wall Street Journal.*

Meals, often buffet-style, are served in the main lodge. Chicken, pasta dishes, and quiches are alternated with traditional meat and potatoes to give guests a variety. Catering to groups as well as single people and families, White Stallion can arrange transportation to and from the airport.

Texas

Mayan Dude Ranch
Bandera, Texas 78003
512-796-3312
512-796-3036
Fax: 512-796-8205

Hosts: The Hicks Family
Accommodations: 66 units
Rates: single, $95; double, $105 suites, $190; weekly rates available
Included: All meals and horseback riding
Added: 10% service charge in lieu of tips and 8.1% sales tax
Payment: Major credit cards and personal checks
Children: Up to 12 years, $40; 13–17 years, $50
Pets: Not permitted
Smoking: Nonsmoking rooms available
Open: Year-round

It doesn't take long to settle into a cowboy frame of mind at the Mayan, a sprawling ranch with plenty of space to ramble and an informal tone conducive to relaxing. The Hicks family has been welcoming guests since the early 1950s, and they have it down pat. Along with hearty cowboy grub, they serve up a big helping of hospitality and fun.

It all starts with orange juice and coffee delivered to your door in the morning (probably by one of the Hicks offspring). Then you choose whether to have breakfast on the trail or in the dining room. (We're talking about a real breakfast here — thick bacon, homemade sausage, hash browns, grits, and biscuits.)

Morning trail rides lead into the hills or down by the cool green Medina River. Guests are entitled to two rides a day, led by well-trained guides. Don't worry about knowing how to ride, the Mayan Dude Ranch prides itself on teaching you. When you aren't riding, there's swimming in the large pool, tubing in the river, fishing, hiking, and playing tennis. During the summer, there's a full roster of group activities, including contests, theme nights, and hayrides. If bad weather drives you indoors, the informal saloon is a good gathering spot over a beer or margarita in the evenings. There's a big-screen TV in the round-up room, and a small game room with video games should keep the children happy for a while.

Less is scheduled in the off-season, but activities still include riding, cowboy breakfasts, barbecues, and hayrides. Families, groups, seminars, and conventions make up the guest roster. Foreigners especially enjoy the ranch because it's the closest thing to the "Wild West" they'll ever experience.

Accommodations are in stone cottages or in one of three lodges (6 to 16 rooms). It's hard to go wrong here, and there's lots of variety. Some of the cottages are designed for large families. The exteriors are rustic, but the interiors are spacious and comfortably western, with wagon wheel light fixtures, ceiling fans, and natural wood everywhere. If views are important to you, be sure to mention it, for some rooms have views of the surrounding hill country. The units are sprinkled throughout the woods, creating a sense of space.

One of the most attractive features of this ranch is the outdoor deck next to the dining room. It's the perfect place to relax as you watch the sun set beyond the hills, or perhaps you'll catch a glimpse of a deer or the peacock that roams the ranch.

Reservations, especially for the summer, need to be made well in advance.

Prude Ranch

P.O. Box 1431
Fort Davis, Texas 79734
915-426-3202
800-458-6232
Fax: 915-426-3502

Owners: The Prude Family
Accommodations: 35 motel rooms; cottage rooms and bunkhouses
Rates: single or double, $50–$75; rates higher for triple or quad; group rates available
Added: 10% tax
Payment: Major credit cards

Children: Welcome
Pets: Permitted if on leash
Smoking: Nonsmoking rooms available
Open: Year-round

There's nothing fake about Prude Ranch. It's not a Hollywood-style guest ranch, with city folks pretending to be cowhands. It's the real thing—a working ranch, high on Texas hospitality with reasonable rates. The Prude family has been welcoming guests since 1911, but the ranch itself dates from 1898. Three generations of Prudes operate the ranch today, and the pint-size fourth generation is in training.

The ranch raises its own horses and has 60 or more ready to ride. Guided rides cost $9 per hour. In the Davis Mountains at an elevation of 5,500 feet, the ranch has trails crossing miles of scenic terrain. For other recreation, there's a heated indoor pool (large and attractive), lighted tennis courts, mountain hikes, and miles of open space.

Meals are served in a large western dining room. The fare is hearty, and since the ranch produces some of its own meats (beef, pork, sausage), it's top quality. A typical dinner, served cafeteria-style, includes barbecued chicken and beef, potato salad, beans, homemade bread, and cherry cobbler.

The nicest accommodations are those designated as motel, but they bear little resemblance to the usual image conjured up. With four units to a building, they are true western in flavor—real wooden walls, a solid wood rocker, cowboy prints on the wall. Happily, there's air conditioning and a ceiling fan, but no TV or phone. The porch is the best part, an excellent setting for putting your feet up and doing some serious mountain gazing.

One of the best things about the ranch is that the Prudes aim to please. Special arrangements for groups are easy to make—just ask. Group lodging choices include family rooms (predating the motel units), bunkhouses, campsites, and RV hook-ups.

There's often something special going on at Prude Ranch, such as the Davis Mountains Fitness Camp, or "Snowbird" week, so be sure to check the schedule. Summer camps (for ages 7–16) are the focal point from mid-June through July.

Y.O. Ranch Hilton
2033 Sidney Baker Street
Kerrville, Texas 78028
512-257-4440
800-531-2800 in Texas
Fax: 512-896-8189

General manager: Jerry Harrell
Accommodations: 200 rooms
Rates: single, $75; double, $85; each additional adult $10;
   suites, $150–$230
Added: 12% tax
Payment: Major credit cards
Children: Under 18 free in room with parents
Pets: Under 30 pounds permitted if well-behaved
Smoking: Nonsmoking rooms available
Open: Year-round

In the heart of the Texas Hill Country, the Y.O. Ranch Hilton is
cowboy plush. Stride into the lobby—one of the most distinctive in the Southwest—and you know you're in cattle country.
The chandeliers are fashioned from branding irons, there's a
very lifelike stuffed bear that looks as if it's about to strike, wild
game trophies surround the room, guns and saddles are displayed in glass cases, hand-carved chairs are covered in raw-
hide, and a vaulted wooden ceiling all make you feel as though
you're in a wilderness hunting lodge, not in downtown Kerrville.

Although the motel-style lodging is 30 miles from the famed
Y.O. Ranch, it bears close kinship with it. A working ranch, the
Y.O. has one of the finest herds of Texas Longhorns in the
country, as well as exotic game. Hotel guests can use a direct
phone line to the ranch to sign up for tours. Both the hotel and
the ranch are owned by the Schreiner family, the descendants of
Captain Charles Schreiner, who founded the 50,000-acre ranch.

The guest rooms are comfortable, with Queen Anne furniture, Saltillo tile floors, and well-designed baths. Some have
balconies overlooking the pool (with a giant Y.O. brand on the
bottom). The suites are special here. The American Indian
Suite is decorated with beaded and silver artifacts, arrowheads,
and Indian portraits. The Longhorn has mementos depicting
the history of the breed. Some suites have fireplaces.

Dine at the Sam Houston Room, serving Texas specialties
and exotic game, some of which comes directly from the ranch
(dinner entrées range from $12.95 to $18.95), and be sure to visit
the Elm Waterhole saloon. There's a hot tub next to the pool, a

tennis court on the grounds, and a municipal golf course next door.

Ranch tours are offered Tuesday through Sunday for $25, which includes lunch. Children aged 7 to 12 pay half price; those under 7 are free.

Private game hunts are also offered at the Y.O. Ranch. Stocked with game animals from all parts of the world, it has herds of axis deer; aoudad, mouflon, and Corsican sheep; American elk; and Indian black buck antelope. Year-round hunting for both native and exotic game is available.

Hideaways

A hideaway is a separate lodging, often a charming guest house, that allows you to relax in complete privacy.

Arizona

The Triangle L Ranch
P.O. Box 900
Oracle, Arizona 85623
602-896-2804
606-623-6732

Innkeepers: Tom & Margot Beeston
Accommodations: 4 cottages
Rates: single, $40–$55; double, $55–$75; $15 per day each additional person
Included: Full breakfast
Added: 6% tax
Payment: Major credit cards
Children: Welcome
Pets: Not permitted
Smoking: Outside only
Open: Year-round

Although the entrance to Triangle L Ranch is only a couple of hundred yards from Highway 77 in Oracle, the ranch is set down in a valley all its own. You feel yourself being drawn into an earlier era as soon as the gate closes behind you. A lazy dog sleeps on the dusty dirt road as you approach the main house. Off to one side a windmill stands high above the low-lying buildings, which are spread out over the 80-acre property. In the spring the front garden is alive with color.

The ranch was established in the 1890s by William Ladd, a sheep and cattle rancher. In the 1920s, Triangle L became the first guest ranch in southern Arizona, and cattle remained on the property until the 1960s. In 1978 the Beestons bought the ranch and began restoring the buildings, most of which were built during the late 1800s and early 1900s. The Beestons began welcoming guests in four of the cottages in 1988.

The cottages are simple and cheerful. Rooms decorated with family pieces and original furnishings from the ranch—tin roofs, old refrigerators, stoves that predate the 1940s, hooked rugs, brass and metal beds, and clawfoot tubs—have a nostalgic air. Although the cottages are not air-conditioned, they are well ventilated, and at an elevation of 4,500 feet, a comfortable breeze always seems to be blowing through.

The Hill House is the largest cottage, with three bedrooms, a full kitchen, and nice views from the front porch. The Foreman's House is the most secluded. It has a screened-in porch, kitchen cabinets made from packing crates, and a patio with a gas grill. Yellow tombstone roses drape over the front entrance to the Trowbridge House (named for the man who turned the working ranch into a guest ranch). Inside there's a large stone fireplace and a Victorian bed that belonged to the owner's great grandmother. The Guest House has a darling sleeping porch complete with two twin beds. All of the cottages are freestanding, offering a great sense of privacy.

Full breakfasts, cooked on an old-fashioned wrought-iron stove, are served around a large farmhouse kitchen table in the main house. Eggs come from the ranch's chickens, and visiting children are welcome to help collect the fresh eggs right from the source. For guests wanting a stronger than average cup of coffee, cappuccino or espresso are offered; and breads, pancakes, and waffles are always homemade.

It's not uncommon to see quail and various desert animals crossing the ranch grounds. Margot, an avid bird watcher and animal lover (she is a licensed wildlife rehabilitator), can help identify unfamiliar species for guests. Tom restores stringed instruments, and is happy to give tours of his workshop.

A visit to the ultramodern environmental experiment Biosphere II (just four miles down the road), offers a fascinating contrast to the ranch's old-time flavor. Tucson and its many sights is just a 45-minute drive, and nearby hiking opportunities abound.

New Mexico

Canyon Road Casitas
652 Canyon Road
Santa Fe, New Mexico 87501
505-988-5888
800-279-0755

Innkeeper: Trisha Ambrose
Accommodations: 2 units
Rates: casita, $85–$105; suite, $145–$165
Included: Self-serve Continental breakfast and tax
Payment: Major credit cards
Children: Free under 10
Pets: Not permitted
Smoking: Not permitted
Open: Year-round

Lined with galleries, boutiques, restaurants, and fine homes, Canyon Road is Santa Fe's most exclusive street. Yet hidden down a quiet driveway, Canyon Road Casitas offer a secluded environment for travelers craving privacy and downtown convenience both.

Guests check in at the quilt shop on Canyon Road, run by the same owner, and are given a key to a walled courtyard that is shared by parties in both the casita and the suite. Wisteria, lilacs, and roses surround the pleasant patio, and there's an outdoor dining set and grill ready for a barbecue.

The suite is the larger of the two units. It has its own separate glass-roofed dining room, small kitchenette, kiva fireplace, bedroom, bath, and sitting room. The decor is southwestern, with Indian rugs, tin light fixtures, dried flower arrangements made with New Mexico chiles, Indian pot lamps, and tile in the bath and kitchen. The carved queen-size bed is covered with a handsome patchwork quilt (not surprising considering the owner's other business), and the futon in the sitting room opens into a double bed. The casita is similarly furnished, but is much smaller, and has a wood-burning stove rather than a fireplace (firewood is supplied).

A bottle of wine and a cheese tray await guests upon check-in. Breakfast foods are stored in the kitchenettes, so guests can help themselves — there are no set meal hours here. Overall, the most appealing features of Canyon Road Casitas are privacy, flexibility, attractiveness, and location.

Rancho Jacona
Route 5 (Pojoaque)
Box 250
Santa Fe, New Mexico 87501
505-455-7948

Innkeeper: Sheri Tepper
Accommodations: 5 casitas
Rates: $85–$160
Added: 5.63% tax
Payment: Major credit cards
Children: Welcome
Pets: With prior approval
Smoking: Permitted
Open: Year-round

Rancho Jacona is a world unto itself, located about halfway between Santa Fe and Los Alamos. Guest casitas dot expansive grounds; the Sangre de Christo mountains can be seen in the distance. Rare breeds of farm animals such as the San Clemente goat and Shetland sheep (there are only six herds in the entire United States) are raised here. The Pojoaque riverbed backs the property, and from there it's a quick escape to the high desert mesas.

Accommodations are comfortable and unusually spacious. Rabbit House is the largest casita, with a huge living room, kiva fireplace, cable television, two bedrooms (one with its own fireplace), and a full kitchen complete with a washer, dryer, and ironing board. Piglet House and Parrot House are the only casitas to share a common wall. Billed as two room studios, they are still roomier than your average hotel room. Each has a sitting area, kitchenette, and fireplace. Views of the Rio Grande valley and Jemez Mountains are framed by the bedroom window in Piglet House. Lifelike parrots hang from the ceiling in Parrot House.

Coyote House is a personal favorite, and the most private because it is farthest from the main house and other casitas. The views from Coyote's front porch and living room window are among the best on the property: you can almost see the ski runs at the Santa Fe Ski Basin (with binoculars you probably would). Lace curtains, colorful rag rugs and wooden furniture add a homey touch. Rooster House, a long adobe with a low ceiling, is the oldest casita. Built about 200 years ago to house farmhands, it is cheerfully furnished in yellows and blues. Both Coyote House and Rooster House have two bedrooms, and all of the casitas have kitchens and fireplaces. The casitas are economical for families or couples traveling together because they are so roomy and have food storage and cooking facilities. Also, the rates are based on the size of the casita rather than the number of guests staying in each unit. A full-size crib is available for infants.

Parents should know that there is plenty here to capture the attention of little ones. A pond out front is stocked with koi, a swimming pool is open during the summer months, and each casita has an outdoor grill. One of the goats is a petting goat, and pigs are also raised on the ranch.

Although Rancho Jacona feels remote, it is a convenient jumping off point for sightseeing in northern New Mexico. Santa Fe and Los Alamos are both 20 minutes away (with Bandelier National Monument just 15 minutes from Los Alamos); the beginning of the "high road to Taos" is a 5-minute drive from the ranch; and the Puye Cliff Dwellings are nearby, as are a number of Indian pueblos.

Texas

Austin Cottage and Guest Suites

406 Austin Street
P.O. Box 488
Jefferson, Texas 75657
903-938-3153
800-874-9429

Owner: Cindy Edwards
Accommodations: 2-bedroom guest house; 2 suites in
  separate building
Rates: $94 for 2, $114 for 4 (midweek rates are lower)
Included: Continental breakfast
Added: 13% tax
Payment: Major credit cards
Children: Over 13 welcome; $10 additional per night
Pets: Not permitted
Smoking: Permitted
Open: Year-round

In Jefferson's historic district, just a block from downtown, is a little red cottage where you can hide away in between jaunts to nearby attractions. Austin Cottage is romantic, decorated with quilts and chintz, white wicker furniture, and country crafts, many of which were handed down by the owner's grandmother.

A restored 1920s batten board cottage, it has two bedrooms, a living room, a sun room, and a fully equipped kitchen. There's a TV, board games, and a front porch that invites you to sit and rock. Out back is a brick patio where you can eat breakfast, featuring homemade breads and fresh fruit. A newspaper is delivered to your doorstep on weekends. Rented in its entirety, the cottage is perfect for two couples traveling together.

Two suites in a separate building are also good options. While their construction is new, the suites have a historical feel, for their French doors, windows, and woodwork were salvaged from earlier structures. Each has a private bath, sitting and dining area, small kitchen (refrigerator and microwave oven), bedroom, and bath. Nonie's Niche has a king-size bed; Texie's Favorite has two double antique iron beds.

Gant Guest House

936 Bowie Street
P.O. Box 112
936 Bowie Street
Columbus, Texas 78934
409-732-5135

Owner: Laura Ann Rau
Accommodations: 2 bedrooms (shared bath)
Rates: 1 bedroom, $65; both, $95
Included: Continental breakfast
Added: 10% tax
Payment: Personal checks
Children: Over 12 welcome
Pets: Not permitted
Smoking: Not permitted
Open: Year-round

In Columbus, the site of one of the oldest settlements in Texas, you can stay in a tiny restored German cottage dating from the 1870s. In recent years the house was moved from nearby Alleytown to its present location on a quiet street in this town of 4,500 residents.

An itinerant German painter probably stenciled the walls and ceilings of this home. His work, hidden by years of soot, was uncovered by Laura Ann Rau when she set out to restore the gem of a house. His stenciling is so charming that the Texas Society of the DAR copied the entire room to put in the DAR Museum in Washington, D.C.

Antique furniture, some native to Texas, fills each room. Two small bedrooms with double beds and a hall sitting room with a daybed accommodate up to five people in one party. Don't worry about having to rough it: there's a modern kitchen (cooking is allowed), a small bath with a tub-shower, central air conditioning and heating, and a TV. Breakfast is put in the refrigerator before your arrival, so you can eat when you choose. A few blocks away are antiques and gift shops, conducive to lazy afternoon browsing.

The Rau family also runs a bed-and-breakfast down the street in a lovely Victorian built in 1887. The house has been given a state historic marker due to its intricate porch trim, three marble mantelpieces, and other fine craftsmanship characteristic of the period. The inn does have modern conveniences, however, such as central heating, air conditioning, and a swimming pool. Called Raumonda, it is more of a traditional B&B than a "hideaway," but you may want to inquire about it if the guest house is full.

Historic Hostelries

Each of these hostelries offers comfort and service combined with historic ambience.

Arizona

The Bisbee Grand Hotel
P.O. Box 825
61 Main Street
Bisbee, Arizona 85603
602-432-5900
800-421-1909

Owners: Bill Thomas and Gail Wade
Accommodations: 9 rooms and suites
Rates: $50 without private bath; $65 with private bath; suites,
  $95
Included: Breakfast
Added: 10.5% tax
Payment: Major credit cards
Children: Not permitted
Pets: Not permitted
Smoking: In restricted areas only
Open: Year-round

In a town that has remarkably preserved its origin as a bustling turn-of-the-century mining town, the Bisbee Grand Hotel recaptures the lively, almost bawdy spirit of the day. The hotel, originally built in 1906, burned to the ground in the great fire of 1908. Immediately rebuilt, it stands today as a reminder of an earlier era. In the late 1980s, Bill Thomas and Carol Wade purchased the hotel and turned it into a stylish bed-and-breakfast with a sense of fun.

Guests check in at the saloon on street level. The saloon itself dates back to 1883 and has fixtures once owned by Wyatt Earp, red velvet–cushioned bar stools, and a pressed tin ceiling. Adjacent to it is an elegant ladies' parlor with a large fireplace, sofa, baby grand piano, and a number of easy chairs, which invite guests to socialize in a more refined environment. Beyond the parlor is the theater where the inn's murder mystery weekends take place.

Guest rooms are reached by climbing a staircase carpeted in vibrant maroon. A shimmery stuffed peacock stands at one end of the stairwell, and velvet upholstered chairs add to the central hallway's plush Victorian feel. Each room is decorated with antiques and has its own theme. The Hunter Room is small but appealing. There are prints depicting quail on the walls, and a riding crop rests across the bed. The Gray Room, furnished in gray and burgundy, has a brass bed. The Coral Room is feminine.

The Oriental and Victorian suites, both with two rooms, are the most luxurious. The Oriental lives up to its name: its ornate brass bed is topped with satin pillows embroidered with Asian motifs, and there's an elaborate gold fan above the bed. In the living room, an Oriental screen shields the fireplace, an attractive chest with intricate scenes sits in one corner, and Oriental prints adorn the walls. Fabric wallpaper with Oriental themes and bamboo print curtains add to the mood. The Victorian suite is opulent, furnished with period pieces—most notably the bed, lavishly canopied in fringed red velvet drapes. Both suites have their own bathrooms. The other guest rooms share appealing baths which have lace shower curtains.

Breakfast is served in the guest rooms or on the second-floor balcony overlooking the street below. If you can't live without television, there's a big-screen TV in the saloon. In Bisbee, you can take the City Mine Tour or visit the Mining and Historical Museum. Bisbee has many interesting shops, and the town of Tombstone, not too far away, is worth a visit.

Clarion Carriage House Inn Hotel Vendome

230 S. Cortez Street
Prescott, Arizona 86303
602-776-0900
800-CLARION

General manager: Vickey Andrada
Accommodations: 21 rooms (all with private bath)
Rates: single or double, $45–$70; suites, $80–$110
Added: 8.5% tax
Payment: Major credit cards
Children: Free in room with parents

Pets: Not permitted
Smoking: Nonsmoking rooms available
Open: Year-round

This small wood and brick hotel, built in 1917 and restored in 1983, sits near the center of downtown. It's a simple, pleasant lodging, making no pretense of being elegant. The tiny lobby doubles as an informal bar. Guests can sit at the cherry counter and enjoy wine or coffee and doughnuts.

Behind the front desk is a charming reminder of the hotel's vintage—a two-way signaling system that enables guests to buzz the front desk or vice versa. The system still works; ask for a demonstration.

The guest rooms stretch along wood-paneled central hall-ways accented with brass light fixtures on the first and second floors. All have a tailored, uncluttered look, with solid blue bedspreads, mini-blinds in place of curtains, and either one queen-size or two twin beds. Two-room suites are a good choice for families, with a sofa bed in the parlor. The bathrooms, which have also been nicely renovated, have either a clawfoot tub with a shower or an oversize sunken tub. The lighting is good, with open bulb fixtures reminiscent of theatrical dress-ing rooms. Cable TVs, phones, and ceiling fans in lieu of air conditioning are in every room.

Copper Queen Hotel

P.O. Box Drawer CQ
Bisbee, Arizona 85603
602-432-2216
Fax: 602-432-5287

General manager: Karen Carrera
Accommodations: 42 rooms
Rates: single, $70; double, $80; suites, $90–$100
Added: 10.5% tax
Payment: Major credit cards
Children: $5 additional if more than 2 people in a room
Pets: Seeing-eye dogs only
Smoking: Nonsmoking rooms available
Open: Year-round

Sit on the upstairs porch of the Copper Queen Hotel and look down on the bustling town below. Straight ahead is a mountain —so near you can almost touch it. On both sides is the historic town of Bisbee, stair-stepping up the side of Mule Pass Gulch. It doesn't take much imagination to pretend that you're in a turn-of-the-century mining town.

In 1902, when the Copper Queen was built, Bisbee was the largest copper mining town in the world. Right around the corner was Brewery Gulch, the site of about forty bars where the miners caroused. Today's residents like to point out that Bisbee was never a boom town but was built to last. At one time it had two opera houses in addition to a host of brick buildings, many of which remain.

Refurbished in the mid-1980s, the Copper Queen has lots of character. The saloon looks like a Western come to life. On one wall hangs a painting of a reclining nude with a winged cherub nearby. There's an old-fashioned safe behind the check-in desk. Red patterned wallpaper and old trunks give the hallways an old-fashioned feel.

The guest rooms are upstairs, and each is individual in size and decor. In one of the nicest rooms, burgundy curtains are tied back with lace. The wallpaper is also burgundy, and the bed is covered with a colonial white spread. The bathroom is decorated to complement the room nicely. The Teddy Roosevelt is a three bedroom suite with a sofa in the large bedroom and slanted ceilings in the two smaller rooms. Another room in rich greens, pinks, and creams has two brass beds, an armoire, and a large bath. Baths and modern conveniences such as air conditioning, telephones, and televisions have been added to all the rooms.

Unexpectedly for a historic hotel, the Copper Queen has a swimming pool. There is also a picturesque dining room and a sidewalk café that's great for people-watching. Waitresses wearing long blue skirts serve such dishes as veal Sonoita, chicken Dream (chicken stuffed with cheese and asparagus tips and topped with hollandaise), and scampi Carrera. Dinner entrées are priced from $8.50 to $16.95.

Hassayampa Inn

122 E. Gurley Street
Prescott, Arizona 86302
602-778-9434
800-322-1927 in Arizona
Fax: 602-778-9434, ext. 109

Owners: William and Georgia Teich
Accommodations: 68 rooms
Rates: single or double, $70–$95; suites, $100–$125

Included: Breakfast and evening cocktail
Added: 8.5% tax
Payment: Major credit cards
Children: Over 6, additional $10 per day
Pets: Not permitted
Smoking: Nonsmoking rooms available
Open: Year-round

Hassayampa Inn was truly a grand hotel when it opened in 1927. A product of its age, it was flamboyantly elegant. As a social leader, it was one of the first hotels in Arizona to cater to automobile travelers. The El Paso architect Henry Charles Trost (who also was responsible for the historic Gadsden Hotel in Douglas, Arizona) designed the red brick Hassayampa, combining mission and Italian Renaissance styles.

In 1985 the restored grande dame resumed her rightful place in society. Listed on the National Register of Historic Places, the Hassayampa offers a sense of history coupled with style. The lobby has tile floors, Oriental rugs, oversize easy chairs, a leather sofa, an antique piano, and potted palms, but the focal point is the beamed ceiling, decorated with Spanish and Indian motifs. During the renovation the ceiling was meticulously restored, using photographs of the original.

Ride up the attended birdcage elevator, part of the original building, to the second- and third-floor guest rooms. More than half of the rooms feature Castilian walnut furniture inset with Spanish tiles—the same pieces that decorated the rooms in 1927. Televisions, air conditioning, and heating are modern additions. With color schemes of deep blue and mauve or peach and green, the spacious rooms have high ceilings and are fresh and inviting. Original watercolors of local Prescott scenes adorn the walls. Beds are dressed in comforters, dust ruffles, and pillow shams, with coordinating draperies and lace curtains. Several suites are available, including one with a large whirlpool tub. One suite that's rumored to be haunted by a young woman who was abandoned in the suite on her honeymoon has its own porch overlooking Prescott's main street. (Apparently she's a friendly ghost because members of the housekeeping staff have sworn that she's helped them in cleaning the room.)

The Peacock Room, which has tapestry print booths and etched glass accents, is the hotel's pleasant dining spot. All three meals are served here. For lunch, there is a wide variety of salads and sandwiches as well as a list of hot entrées which includes, of all things, beef liver, an item you don't see on many menus these days. Dinner entrées range from pork schnitzel to

Scapparelli (chicken fillets and sausage sautéed with broccoli topped with white wine sauce and served on fettuccine) and start at $8.95. For light lunches or evening cocktails, try the Hassayampa Bar and Grill. It's decorated with beveled glass, a copper ceiling, and fringed cocktail tables.

San Carlos Hotel
202 North Central Avenue
Phoenix, Arizona 85004
602-253-4121
800-678-8946
Fax: 602-253-4121 Ext. 209

Owners: The Melikian Family
Accommodations: 120 rooms and suites
Rates: single or double, $69–$89; suites, $99–$159
Added: 10.25% tax
Payment: Major credit cards
Children: Under 12 free in room with parents
Pets: Not permitted
Smoking: 2 nonsmoking floors available
Open: Year-round

When the San Carlos Hotel opened in 1928, it was considered one of the most modern hotels in the Southwest, for it had air conditioning and circulating ice water. Built on the site of the city's first elementary school, it was the first high-rise hotel in Phoenix. Now its seven stories seem modest in comparison with the taller skyscrapers surrounding it. The San Carlos has seen its fortune come and go, as has downtown Phoenix, but with the recent revival of the city center, the hotel has once again risen to prominence.

Just one look inside the elegant bistro will assure you of the San Carlos' renewed glory. The maitre d' snaps to attention and leads you to your table in the pleasant dining room. An original oil by Erté hangs at the entrance, while a larger than life art deco flapper (also by Erté) stands watch over the diners at the far end of the bistro. Inventive entrées such as sautéed frogs' legs with celery, carrots, and leeks in a white wine cream sauce and steamed mussels in garlic, shallots and wine topped with a curry cream sauce are an interesting, contemporary contrast to the nostalgic 1920s mood.

The lobby is an intimate, pretty space, with crystal chandeliers and potted palms. The guest rooms are also attractive; some are decorated in mauves and greens with rich wood furnishings while others are decked out in chintz. At the request of

Historic Hotels of America (of which the San Carlos is a member), some of the baths still have original fixtures. (Older washbasins have an extra faucet that draws up the coldest water from the well in the hotel's basement.) All rooms have the expected amenities, but executive king suites have two baths, two large closets, a TV in the living room and in the bedroom, ceiling fans, a refrigerator, and a coffeemaker.

In the past, celebrities such as Clark Gable, Carole Lombard, and Spencer Tracy stayed at the San Carlos. Today, a healthy portion of the guests are business travelers, and the hotel operates a full-service concierge communication center on the second floor. There is a small rooftop swimming pool on the third floor and a beauty salon on the street level. The Herberger Theatre, Museum of Science and Technology, Convention Center, and Symphony Hall are all within walking distance of the hotel. The staff at the San Carlos are friendly and eager to please.

New Mexico

El Rancho Hotel
1000 East 66 Avenue
Gallup, New Mexico 87301
505-863-9311
800-543-6351

Owner: Armand Ortega
Accommodations: 99 rooms in hotel and motel, 3 suites
Rates:
   Hotel:
      single: $36–$48
      double: $42–$54
      triples and quadruples: $58–$60
      2-bedroom suites: $72
   Motel:
      single: $31–$45
      double: $41–$49
      triples and quadruples: $55
      2-bedroom suites: $68
Added: 11.07% tax
Payment: Major credit cards
Children: Under 6 free in room with parents
Pets: On leash and with owner supervision only

Smoking: Nonsmoking rooms available
Open: Year-round

The stone and timbered exterior of El Rancho looks out of place among the fast-food restaurants, gas stations, and modest motels that surround it, but the hotel existed long before anyone knew what fast food was. El Rancho was built in 1937 and is on the National Register of Historic Places. It served as the headquarters for numerous movie stars and production teams while filming in the area during Hollywood's heyday: Ronald Reagan, Gregory Peck, William Holden, and Kirk Douglas are just of few of the luminaries that made pictures here. After a period of decline, the hotel was restored and it reopened in 1988 with a new vigor.

The lobby looks like a hunting lodge—it has a timbered ceiling, a stone and log double staircase, casual sofas, Navajo rugs, stuffed elk and deer heads, and a stone fireplace. On one wall a mural depicts the early history of New Mexico, and a striking amethyst crystal encased in wood stands near the registration desk. The balcony walls upstairs look like a veritable who's who of moviemaking—one could spend hours looking at the photos of famous Hollywood idols. Many have been personally autographed with endearing messages for the hotel.

Guest rooms, western in tone, are decorated in pleasant shades of rose and cream. The rooms have wagon wheel headboards, attractive wood furniture, ceiling fans, clock radios, TVs, phones, sand paintings, and southwestern prints. Suites include a bridal suite and a presidential suite. El Rancho also rents out rooms in an adjacent motel.

El Rancho's restaurant has a Mexican feel, though the theme here is Hollywood as well, and dishes are named after stars. The "Errol Flynn" is a French dip sandwich; the "Mae West" is a stacked ham or beef sandwich; the "Rita Moreno" is an enchilada plate. The 49'er bar is down the hall.

A gift shop adjacent to the lobby sells Indian jewelry, and there is a laundry room on the premises for guest use.

Hotel St. Francis
210 Don Gaspar Avenue
Santa Fe, New Mexico 87501
505-983-5700
800-666-5700
Fax: 505-989-7690

General manager: Michaleen Sawka
Accommodations: 82 rooms
Rates: single, $60–$135; double, $75–$150; $15 each additional person; suites, $175–$300
Added: 10.25% tax
Payment: Major credit cards
Children: Under 12 free in room with parents
Pets: Not permitted
Smoking: Nonsmoking rooms available
Open: Year-round

In a town that dates from 1610, a hotel built in 1924 is a relative newcomer. Yet the St. Francis, which was renovated in 1987, adds charm and flavor to the cultural capital of the Southwest. A wide front porch with white wrought-iron furniture, great for people-watching, opens onto Don Gaspar Avenue, only a block and a half from the Plaza. The hotel's high-ceilinged lobby has the look of elegance, with classic white columns, Queen Anne furniture, Oriental rugs, and saltillo tile floors. In keeping with the mood, afternoon high tea is served in the lobby in front of a roaring fire during the winter months, and on the verandah in warm weather. The hotel's restaurant features a changing menu from a variety of cuisines. In the summer you can dine in the pleasant garden courtyard.

There's a hint of romance and history throughout the St. Francis. The halls leading to the guest rooms are wide and grand, with white walls, deep blue carpets, and sitting areas next to the stairwell. There's an old-fashioned switchboard right next to the modern pay phones.

The guest rooms, although relatively small, are delightfully decorated, featuring white iron and brass beds, period furniture, and matched petit floral fabric bedspreads and curtains in blue and rose tones. The beds have pillow shams and dust ruffles. The bathrooms, also on the small side, are adorned with marble. Other amenities include safes for valuables and small refrigerators.

In order to maintain the hotel's original flavor, the decision was made during renovation not to add a swimming pool, as it would have required altering the building's structure too much. With all Santa Fe has to offer, you probably wouldn't have much time to swim anyway.

Plaza Hotel
230 Old Town Plaza
Las Vegas, New Mexico 87701
505-425-3591
800-626-4886
Fax: 505-425-9659

General manager: William Slick
Accommodations: 38 rooms
Rates: single, $50; double, $55; suites, $90
Added: 9.88% tax
Payment: Major credit cards
Children: Welcome
Pets: With $25 deposit
Smoking: Nonsmoking rooms available
Open: Year-round

In 1879 the railroad came to Las Vegas, making it the first large town in the territory to be reached by rail. Of course, a railroad town needed a hotel, so in 1881 the local businessmen, headed by Don Benigno Romero, formed the Plaza Hotel Company. Their three-story hotel, hailed as "The Belle of the Southwest," opened in 1882.

In its earliest days, notorious outlaws such as Billy the Kid were among the Plaza's patrons. Then in 1913 the hotel brushed shoulders with Hollywood: the popular silent film star Romaine Fielding selected the Plaza as his studio headquarters, renaming it the Hotel Romaine (the lettering can still be seen on one facade of the building). Later, the cowboy actor and director Tom Mix came to town. Scenes for several of his movies were filmed in Las Vegas and included shots of the renamed Plaza Hotel.

An agricultural depression hit the area in the mid-1920s, and the hotel suffered along with the rest of the town. The decline of the onetime "Belle" continued until 1982, when Wid and Katherine Slick joined with it owners Lonnie and Dana Lucero to restore it.

Now on the National Register of Historic Places, the Plaza Hotel is a lodging with charm. Its guest rooms are spacious and airy, with high ceilings and twice as much square footage as the original rooms. Antique furnishings include a superior collection of armoires, some with inlaid patterns, not only convenient for the traveler but also conducive to camouflaging TVs. Touches such as fringed lampshades, botanical prints, frosted glass fixtures, and lace curtains add nostalgia. The baths are simple, with separate dressing areas. Happily, modern comfort has not been overlooked. The rooms are air-conditioned, and of course there are telephones.

Just off the lobby, furnished with antiques but not opulent in style, are Byron T's western saloon and a pleasant dining room. Breakfast in the dining room is very reasonable, starting at $1.95. The lunch menu is basic, consisting mainly of sandwiches, burgers, and salads, while dinner selections range from New Mexican specialties to filet mignon ($6.95–$13.95). Byron T's often features entertainment in the evenings.

Las Vegas has other historic sites, beginning with a walking tour of the Plaza area. There's also the Rough Riders Memorial and City Museum, with Rough Rider memorabilia, Indian artifacts, and city history. Outdoor activities include horseback riding, fishing, hay rides, and pack trips into the Pecos Wilderness. The Indian ruins at Pecos National Monument, about halfway between Las Vegas and Santa Fe, are worthwhile, as is the drive between the two cities.

St. James Hotel
Route 1, Box 2
Cimarron, New Mexico 87714
505-376-2664

Owners: The Sitzbergers
Accommodations: 13 rooms in the hotel (most with private
   bath), 12 rooms in the annex
Rates: single or double in the hotel, $65–$75; annex rooms,
   $35–$40
Added: 9% tax
Payment: Major credit cards
Children: Welcome
Pets: With approval only
Smoking: Permitted
Open: Year-round

In the dusty little town of Cimarron, about an hour's drive southwest of Raton, is a historic hotel with delightfully different rooms and a restaurant guaranteed to please. It all started back in 1873, when the man who had been Abraham Lincoln's personal chef headed west. Henri Lambert, a French immigrant, never found the gold he was seeking, but he bought some land at a stop along the Santa Fe Trail and built a saloon. In 1880 he added a hotel of thick adobe.

Back then, Cimarron was a tough kind of place — a hangout for desperadoes, horse thieves, mountain men, and traders. The hotel, as the center of the town's social life, ended up being the last stop for some of its patrons: twenty-six men were killed within its walls. Bulletholes in the tin ceiling of the former bar (now the restaurant) bear testament to the violence that became legendary. Outlaws like Blackjack Ketchum, Jesse James, and the notorious gunman Clay Allison stayed at the St. James. So did lots of respectable folks. Annie Oakley met with Buffalo Bill Cody here and joined his Wild West show. Zane Grey wrote a novel here. Frederic Remington stayed here while he sketched nearby scenes. Wyatt Earp and Doc Holiday also stayed at the St. James.

In 1985 the charmingly restored St. James opened its doors, saved by the Sitzbergers, who had lovingly nursed it back to health. Ed, a native of Cimarron, grew up behind the hotel. Although the crumbling exterior has seen better days, the inside is beautiful. Furnished throughout with period pieces, the hotel is now a showcase of western history. The lobby immediately sets the tone. There are Victorian velvet sofas, exotic birds, and an elk, moose, or buffalo head on each wall. There's an old safe in one hallway, a roulette table in another, and old photos line the main hallway to the guest rooms.

The Jesse James Room has red brocade wallpaper, red velvet chairs, a brass bed with a red quilt, and a cranberry lamp. The Thumbelina Room, named for Tom Thumb and his wife, who performed in the Wild West show, is especially attractive, with a fabric-draped ceiling and white fireplace. Bat Masterson's room has green velvet wallpaper, a marble top dresser, a mountain lion rug, lace curtains, and a separate sitting room with a daybed. Buffalo Bill's room is the largest. Next door is a tiny poker-playing room — past and present.

Most of the rooms have fireplaces (no longer used), marble washstands, a private bath, and some of the tubs have hand-held showers. There are no TVs or phones in the rooms, but both are available in the lobby and the lounge. Motel-style rooms are available in the annex, but these are not recommended since the point of coming to the St. James is for its history.

It's only fitting for a classic hotel to have a fine restaurant. Crystal chandeliers and cloth napkins lend a touch of elegance, and the food is the best for miles around. Feast on stuffed flounder Florentine, filled with crabmeat and fresh vegetables and topped with velouté sauce. Or pollo Gismonda — breaded chicken breast in a spiced spinach ring, covered with sautéed mushrooms. Broiled swordfish steak, shrimp Diablo, veal Marsala, tournedos of beef, pasta carbonara, plus a dozen or more other entrées give you plenty of choice. Dinner entrées range from $10.95 to $16.95.

Unexpectedly for such a hotel, the St. James has a swimming pool. It was built for the adjacent motel, which now serves as the annex for the hotel. In addition to the main restaurant, there's also a very informal dining room and a bar. Across the street is the Old Mill Museum, filled with history (open from late spring to early fall). A National Historic District, Cimarron has other sites worth a visit. Two miles down the road is the Philmont Scout Ranch, the national campgrounds for the Boy Scouts of America. Fishing, hunting, and skiing are popular area attractions.

With such a past, it's no wonder that the St. James is rumored to have ghosts. But the Sitzbergers are excellent hosts, and the food is fantastic, so have an extra glass of wine and enjoy.

The Taos Inn

125 Paseo de Pueblo Norte
Taos, New Mexico 87571
505-758-2233
800-TAOS-INN
Fax: 505-758-5776

Manager/Owner: Carolyn Haddock
Accommodations: 39 rooms
Rates: double, $80–$195
Added: 10.25% tax
Payment: Major credit cards
Children: Welcome; additional charge if extra beds are needed
Pets: Not permitted
Smoking: Nonsmoking rooms available
Open: Year-round

In keeping with its history, the Taos Inn is a center of activity in this popular tourist town. The Plaza is only a block away, and within a few blocks are dozens of galleries, shops, and restaurants. The hotel's lobby, originally a small plaza with the town's well in the center, is still a gathering spot for locals, artists, and travelers alike.

The hotel is truly special, for it is composed of several houses that once faced the tiny plaza. In 1936 Helen Martin, the widow of popular Doc Martin, the town's only physician for many years, bought the surrounding houses, enclosed the plaza, and converted it all into a hotel. In 1982 the hotel was lovingly restored, resulting in an inn that exudes a sense of history combined with modern comfort. Now on the National and State Registers of Historic Places, it is a noted Taos landmark.

Fewer than half of the guest rooms are in the main building. Only a few steps behind it is the Sandoval House, dating from the 1850s, with six rooms. Because of the age of the building, the rooms here tend to be the smallest—taller patrons need to stoop to get through the front doors. An additional sixteen rooms are in a one-story complex surrounding a courtyard to one side of the Sandoval House. The courtyard rooms, built in the 1930s, are the inn's most spacious.

Each room is different, but all are steeped in southwestern decor, from handloomed Indian bedspreads (made by the Zapotecs especially for the inn) to hand-crafted Taos furniture. Most rooms have kiva fireplaces, crafted by the local adobe artist Carmen Velarde, and are decorated with Indian designs. All the rooms have comfortable seating, TVs, and phones. The bathrooms, of average size, are festively adorned with tiles and have tub-showers. (When the inn opened in 1936, it was the first building in Taos to have indoor plumbing!) Some rooms also have vanities with lavatories. Most rooms have fans; only three have air conditioning.

The small two-story lobby has an informal feeling—conducive to relaxing in southwestern surroundings. In its center is a tile fountain, once the town's well. To one side of the lobby is the Adobe Bar, originally the Tarleton house. Popular with Taos residents and visitors alike, it features New Mexican fare, a great espresso/dessert menu, live entertainment, a wide selection of international beers, and a host of specialty drinks. How about a Cowboy Buddha or a Hairy Dog? In the summer, the outdoor patio is inviting and relaxing.

Next to the lobby on the opposite side is Doc Martin's Restaurant, in a building that was once the good doctor's home and office. (His birthing room is now a cozy dining area.) But history only counts for so much in a dining establishment; the best reason to visit Doc Martin's is for the outstanding cuisine. Specializing in international dishes and emphasizing fresh, indigenous foods, the dinner menu changes daily. Diners can expect such innovative entrées as grilled Pacific red snapper with a citrus glaze or buffalo medallions with a roasted garlic cream and corn demiglace. The extensive wine list is one of the best in the state, and selections from the list are available to take home.

Breakfast is no ordinary meal at Doc Martin's either. Piñon nut waffles, specialty omelettes, blue corn and blueberry hotcakes, and stuffed sopaipillas ($4.50–$7) are a wonderful way to start the day. Offered at lunch are New Mexican or seafood dishes, and some of them, such as the shrimp burritos, combine elements of both ($6–$8).

The inn's Meet the Artist series is a semi-annual event, running from mid-May to mid-June and from mid-October to mid-December. On Tuesdays and Thursdays, Taos artists talk about their work. Studio tours, demonstrations, slide shows, videos, music, or readings are part of the presentation. Contact the inn for upcoming schedules. Participation is free and open to the public, but seating is limited. Reservations are required for some sessions.

A popular lodging for skiers, the inn offers ski packages, and the shuttle bus to Taos Ski Valley stops at the front door. Also on the grounds are a small swimming pool, open during the summer, and a hot tub to help soothe ski-bruised bones is open year-round.

Texas

Gage Hotel
P.O. Box 46
Marathon, Texas 79842
915-386-4205

Innkeepers: Bill and Laurie Stevens
Accommodations: 20 rooms (4 with private bath)
Rates: double (shared bath), $40; with private bath, $55
Added: 6% tax
Payment: Major credit cards
Children: Welcome
Pets: Permitted
Smoking: Not permitted in the dining room
Open: Year-round

Welcome to West Texas—both in location and flavor. In Marathon, one of the major gateways to Big Bend National Park, the Gage is an oasis, for civilization stops at least 100 miles before you reach its doors.

The hotel was built in 1928 by Alfred Gage, a prosperous banker and rancher from San Antonio. Since there were few places to stay when he visited his 500,000-acre ranch near Marathon, he built the hotel to serve as his headquarters. In 1982 the once-grand hotel was restored, and today it offers an atmosphere reminiscent of turn-of-the-century West Texas.

The Gage sits right on the edge of U.S. 90. A rather plain yellow brick building, inside is a treasure of unusual furnishings and artifacts, most with a historical tie to West Texas. There are tools crafted by the Tarahumara Indians (now in northern Mexico, they once lived in West Texas), a table designed for shearing sheep, and tiles representing some of the oldest cattle brands in the county. A Spanish colonial trunk came from Peru; the large breakfront was originally in the Gage Inn in England.

The barroom is delightful. The bar itself was an altar in a Mexican church; the wine rack comes from the post office in a nearby town. And guests are fascinated by the chusa table, a roulette-style game (circa 1890) from Chihuahua, Mexico.

Meals are served in a western dining room decorated with Indian artifacts. The innkeeper-chef serves border cuisine. Feast on red snapper sautéed in ranchero sauce, fajitas and enchiladas, or good ole chicken-fried steak. Entrées range from $6 to $15.

The guest rooms are named for area landmarks. Some are rather plain, but all are appealing, with their primitive western atmosphere. Each has a lavatory, air-conditioning unit, and ceiling fan. In keeping with the Old West flavor, there are no modern conveniences, like phones or TVs.

Several rooms are special. Persimmon Gap has an 1840s four-poster bed plus a day bed; it's decorated with 19th-century santos and a black cross made by the Mennonite colony in Mexico. This room shares a bath with Stillwell's Crossing, with a handsome brass bed and Indian rugs. Jacal de Luna, with a private bath, is more spacious than the rest and has two double beds.

In planning a trip through West Texas, note that the busiest seasons at the Gage are spring and holidays; the slow season is mid-July through October.

Landmark Inn
502 Florence
Castroville, Texas 78009
512-538-2133

Manager: Texas Parks and Wildlife Department
Accommodations: 8 rooms (4 with shared baths)
Rates: single, $35–$40; double, $40–$50; additional adults, $5
Added: 10% tax
Payment: Personal checks; no credit cards
Children: Under age 6, free; ages 6–12 in same room with
    parents, $2 extra per night; over age 12, $5 extra per night
Pets: Not permitted
Smoking: In designated areas only
Open: Year-round

Colonists from Alsace and Lorraine settled Castroville in 1844, bringing with them their language, customs, and architecture. Remnants of all three exist in modern Castroville, a town of about 2,000 residents. One of the best-preserved examples of Alsatian architecture is the Landmark Inn, a charming lodging that is the focal point of the Landmark Inn State Historical Park, run by the Texas Parks and Wildlife Department. Built in 1849 as a home and general store for Cesar Monod, who became the mayor in 1852, the hotel is open for touring. So is a historic stone grist mill and an exhibition depicting life in early Castroville.

The Landmark is a place for history lovers as well as those who like to get off the beaten track. It is said that Robert E. Lee stayed here after it became the Vance Hotel in the 1850s and that a lead-lined water tank on the second floor was melted down to make Confederate bullets during the Civil War. The Parks Department has made every effort to preserve the historical nature of the structure, so don't expect TVs, telephones, or even air conditioning. However, rooms are supplied with fans in the summer and panel heaters in colder weather.

Your first sight of the inn is of a quaint, two-story, curbside building. Save your judgment until you walk around to the back; the tiny white hotel overlooks beautiful grounds and a graceful garden, planted with shrubs and flowers representative of the town's early days. All the rooms in the main building open onto the gardens. The simple guest rooms are furnished with antiques. (Don't worry—authenticity doesn't go as far as the mattresses, which are modern.)

The old bathhouse has been converted into two tiny bedrooms, one above the other. Each has a double bed and private bath. While the one on top (number 8) is often booked by honeymooners, people who tend toward claustrophobia or those who are large (whether tall or plump) should avoid it.

The inn has no restaurant or cooking facilities, but the town has a number of eating establishments, including an Alsatian bakery. The Landmark does have free parking for guests.

The Tremont House

2300 Ship's Mechanic Row
Galveston, Texas 77550
409-763-0300
800-874-2300
Fax: 409-763-1539

General manager: Roy Chen
Accommodations: 216 rooms
Rates: single, $145; double, $160; suites, $350–$550
Added: 13% tax
Payment: Major credit cards
Children: Under 18 free in room with parents
Pets: Not permitted
Smoking: Nonsmoking rooms available
Open: Year-round

The original Tremont House, built in 1839, was for many years the largest and finest hotel in the Republic of Texas. From its balcony, Sam Houston delivered his last public address. The hotel's guest register included presidents, foreign ministers, and entertainers. Rebuilt in 1872 after a fire seven years earlier, the hotel again welcomed the rich and famous. But after the devastating 1900 hurricane, the Tremont, like the city itself, never recovered, and the hotel was demolished in 1928. Today its namesake, in Galveston's Historic Strand District a few blocks from the original hotel site, is in the beautifully restored Leon and H. Blum Building, constructed in 1879. Conceived and owned by the oilman and real estate developer George Mitchell and his wife, Cynthia (they are a prime force behind Galveston's historic preservation movement), the hotel is one of their ten historic restoration projects.

Designed to recreate the atmosphere of the old Tremont, the hotel is intimate yet grand. At the center of its design is a four-story rectangular atrium. About half of the guest rooms overlook the atrium; interior bridges connect the upper halls across it. In the atrium is the Toujouse Bar, featuring a rosewood bar built in 1888, white wicker chairs with flowered cushions, and potted palms. To one side is the Merchant Prince restaurant, named for Leon Blum, who was Galveston's "Merchant Prince," with a million-acre empire stretching across Texas. A jewel of a restaurant, the Merchant Prince has a splendid menu featuring nouvelle American cuisine. With entrées such as grilled shrimp over fettuccine in a chili cream sauce, grilled breast of chicken with shiitake mushrooms and pesto, tenderloin of beef with jalepeño béarnaise, and crabmeat with penne and tomato sauce ($10–$17), the restaurant is well worth a visit wherever you stay.

Interiors at the Tremont are sophisticated and stylish. Decorated in chic black and white, the high-ceilinged guest rooms have white enamel and brass beds, lace curtains, white eyelet bedspreads, black and white rugs on hardwood floors, and baths with hand-painted Italian tile. Even the bath amenities are packaged in black and white. Eleven-foot-high windows open onto ironwork balconies. Although the black and white color scheme is used throughout the hotel, no two guest rooms are exactly alike in terms of shape, size, and furnishings.

Complimentary valet parking, a full-time concierge, terrycloth robes, heated towel racks, oversize towels, imported chocolates at turndown, and 24-hour room service are all part of a Tremont House stay. The Tremont's historic downtown location can be a refreshing alternative to the strip along Galveston's Seawall Boulevard.

There is no swimming pool at the Tremont, but guests can use the recreational facilities at the San Luis, a sister property.

Lakeside

All of these lodgings have access to a lake, offering activities ranging from fishing and swimming to boating.

Oklahoma

Shangri-La Resort
Route 3
Afton, Oklahoma 74331
918-257-4204
800-331-4060
Fax: 918-257-5619

General manager: J. Patrick Bark
Accommodations: 432 rooms
Rates: single or double, $59–$120; suites, $89–$625
Added: 5% tax
Payment: Major credit cards
Children: Free in room with parents
Pets: Not permitted
Smoking: Nonsmoking rooms available
Open: Year-round

Spread over 660 acres on the shores of 59,000-acre Grand Lake O' the Cherokees is a resort with enough recreational features to keep most vacationers happy and so many restaurants that you can try a different one every day.

Pick your favorite sport and it's probably there: golf (36 holes), tennis (8 courts: 4 indoor, 4 outdoor), boating, outdoor and indoor swimming, racquetball, biking, and jogging. The huge recreation center is unusually well equipped, with everything from a health spa to bowling alleys. At the marina you can arrange for water skiing, fishing boats and/or fishing guide service, pontoon boats, cruisers, and scenic cruises. Greens fees, including a cart, range from $50 to $75. Tennis is $7 an hour outdoors, $16 indoors. Ski boats are $45 per hour. Fishing boats are $90 for 4 hours, $150 for 8 hours, including a guide and equipment.

The lodging options are extensive, with rooms in the main lodge, an 11-story tower, and several condo complexes. Personal favorites are the main lodge (close to most of the activities) and Shangri-La Estates (condos tucked beneath the trees near the golf course—definitely the most romantic). The interiors are spacious and modern.

The Garden Café, the Greenery, and the Bay Club Restaurant & Dance Club are Shangri-La's restaurants. The dining areas are imaginative, providing diverse environments that suit different moods. During July and August there is live entertainment in the Greenery. The resort also has a snack bar and lounge, and room service is available.

Texas

Del Lago Resort
600 Del Lago Boulevard
Montgomery, Texas 77356
409-582-6100
800-833-8389
Fax: 409-582-4918

General manager: Hugh Barrett
Accommodations: 310 tower suites, 48 golf cottages
Rates: Start at $95 for singles, $105 for doubles, $175 for suites
Added: 10% tax
Payment: Major credit cards
Children: Under 14 free in room with parents
Pets: Not permitted
Smoking: Nonsmoking rooms available
Open: Year-round

Undeniably, Del Lago is a conference center. In fact, hotel check-in is at the conference building instead of the hotel tower. But Del Lago is also a resort, offering couples and families a lakeside vacation complete with a marina, golf course, tennis courts, and health spa.

On the shores of Lake Conroe, northwest of Houston, the resort has a 300-slip marina as its focal point. Some guests arrive with their own boats, but others can rent sailboats, ski boats, bass boats, or low pontoons. (Ask about reserving a boat when you book your room; weekend rentals should be arranged at least four days ahead.)

The 18-hole championship golf course is one of the resort's most popular features. Opened in 1982, the Jay Rivere–Dave Marr course has lush fairways. Tennis is also important at Del Lago. The 13 hard-surface courts are all lighted, and there's a good pro shop. The spa is outstanding, with a well-equipped exercise room, racquetball courts, sauna, steam, whirlpool, tanning, and massage. All sorts of classes and clinics are geared toward health and fitness, from water exercise to foot massage to nutrition. Guests can use the spa (it's also a private club) for $5 a day; extra fees are charged for some services.

There's always something special going on at Del Lago—fishing tournaments, family bike rides (rental bikes are available), festive theme night buffets. Some events are just for children—beach parties, games on the green, movie nights. Weekend packages feature golf, tennis, or just getting away.

The 20-story hotel tower, right on the lake, has rooms suited for families. The sleeping and sitting areas are separated, and there's a couch and a kitchenette (fine for snacks).

Café Verde serves all three meals; food service is available by the pool on a seasonal basis. Fiddler's Lounge, overlooking the marina, has pool tables and a big-screen TV. On weekends, there's live entertainment at Tiffany's.

Horseshoe Bay Country Club Resort
1 Horseshoe Bay Boulevard
Horseshoe Bay, Texas 78654
512-598-2511
800-252-9363 in Texas
800-531-5105 in U.S.
Fax: 512-598-5338

Executive vice president: Ron Lynn Mitchell
Accommodations: 75 rooms, 50 condos
Rates:
    Mid-March–November: double, $120–$400
    December–mid-March: double, $99–$347
Added: 6% tax
Payment: Major credit cards
Children: Under 12 free in room with parents; over 12 additional $10 per day
Pets: Not permitted
Smoking: Nonsmoking rooms available
Open: Year-round

On the shores of Lake LBJ in the gently rolling Hill Country west of Austin, Horseshoe Bay is a 4,000-acre residential resort community that can boast the best of country life as well as city sophistication. Deer roam freely and the pace of life is slow, but at your fingertips is exceptionally fine dining and a wealth of recreational facilities, including the largest Robert Trent Jones golf complex in the world.

At the heart of the community is Horseshoe Bay Country Club Resort, a private club with extensive facilities for its members and temporary members (the status accorded guests). Enhancing the already beautiful landscape are gardens and fountains, waterfalls, and statues. In all, the resort has an idyllic air—restful and aesthetically pleasing.

Golfers can choose from three courses, all with unusually scenic terrain—a combination of cliffside lake views, cedar- and mesquite-studded countryside, and ravines and streams. The newest course, Applerock, was named Best New Resort Golf Course in the country by *Golf Digest* in 1986. Tee times should be arranged a week in advance.

Boat and ski rentals and fishing guides are all available. It's advisable to reserve a boat before you arrive.

The tennis complex, covering 18 acres and surrounded by Oriental gardens, has 14 Laykold courts; 4 are covered. The resort also has several outstanding swimming pools; a two-tier pool, fed by waterfalls cascading off bedrock granite outcrops, overlooks the golf course. One of the pools has an adjacent spa. Horseback rides take scenic trails across the countryside.

Many of the lodgings, in several low buildings, are directly on the marina. Several styles are available, from one- to three-bedroom units. Refreshingly, the units don't resemble standard condo designs: the space is used innovatively, the interiors are large, the furnishings are modern and well done, and the kitchens and baths have lots of extras.

Dining is a major attraction at Horseshoe Bay. The Captain's Quarters is formal, with a varied menu and an exclusive atmosphere that requires coat and tie for men, evening attire for women. There are also two informal restaurants, romantic in style as well as in their lakeside setting.

Lakeway Inn
101 Lakeway Drive
Austin, Texas 78734
512-261-6600
800-LAKEWAY
Fax: 512-261-7322

General manager: Toby June
Accommodations: 138 units
Rates: single or double, $130–$160; suites, $140–$170,
   weekend packages available
Included: Breakfast
Added: 6% tax
Payment: Major credit cards
Children: Free in room with parents
Pets: Not permitted
Smoking: Permitted
Open: Year-round

On cliffs overlooking Lake Travis about 20 miles west of Austin, Lakeway Inn is at the center of a huge resort and residential community. There are many recreational choices here — two 18-hole championship golf courses, a marina with lots of boats for rent (fishing, sailing, ski, pontoon, and deck boats), 32 tennis courts (the renowned World of Tennis Club), horseback riding on 25 miles of trails, and several swimming pools.

The guest rooms and suites are spread out in low buildings near the main lodge or in two- to four-bedroom villas next to the World of Tennis complex (about a 5-minute drive from the lodge). Single bedrooms or bedrooms joined by parlors (you can rent one to three segments of a unit) are very spacious and modern, with private balconies overlooking the lake. Many have big stone fireplaces. The villas have fully equipped kitchens and fireplaces. Each cluster of villas has its own tennis court, supplementing the complex a few hundred yards away. There's a dining room and lounge at the main lodge and at the World of Tennis. Some sample fees are: greens fees for 18 holes of golf, $44–$50; cart rental, $20 for shared use; tennis at Lakeway Tennis Center, $15 all day, per court, per player; World of Tennis courts, $20 per hour (indoor); fishing boat, $18 per hour; fishing boat with guide, $120 per half day; ski boat, $72 per hour with driver; pontoon boat with a 12-person capacity, $54 per hour; sailboat, $18 per hour; horseback riding, $15 per hour; parasailing, $35 per person per trip.

For children aged 5 to 12, there's a supervised day camp during the summer with sports, nature walks, movies, and arts and crafts. The daily fee, $25, includes lunch, a camp T-shirt, and all camp activities.

National Parks

Two of the Southwest's six national parks have fine accommodations right in the park.

Big Bend National Park

Chisos Mountains Lodge
National Park Concessions
Big Bend National Park, Texas 79834-9801
915-477-2291
Fax: 915-477-2352

General manager: Garner B. Hanson
Accommodations: 72 units
Rates: single, $53–$69; double, $61–$69; $65 for 3 in cottages,
  $8 for each extra person
Added: 6% tax
Payment: Major credit cards
Children: Under 12 free in room with parents
Pets: Permitted
Smoking: Nonsmoking rooms available
Open: Year-round

In the heart of the Chisos Mountains you'll find a motel and several stone cottages. Walk outside to mountains you can almost touch. Eat at the lodge and look out at a magnificent panorama of mountains caressed by clouds. Hiking, river rafting, and horseback riding are the top attractions in this magically beautiful, wild, rugged, and untamed park. Lodging is limited (most visitors camp in the three campgrounds), so make reservations as far ahead as possible. For fall, spring, and major holidays, book at least a year in advance.

The motel units, in a long, low modern building, have two double beds, a bath with tub and shower, and individual air conditioning and heating. Don't expect luxury, but they are comfortable enough. Pay phones are nearby. The one-room cottages are more picturesque, tucked away in the trees. They have one to three double beds, baths, and small porches.

The Chisos Mountains Lodge Dining Room and Coffee Shop serves meals throughout the day. Dinner choices, from $7 to $12, are basic American fare—roast turkey, ham, pork chops, steaks. Whatever you order, it's guaranteed to taste great; the mood is convivial and the setting is hard to beat.

Grand Canyon

Bright Angel Lodge and Cabins
P.O. Box 699
Grand Canyon, Arizona 86023
602-638-2631
Fax: 602-638-9247

General manager: Bill Bohannon
Accommodations: 60 units
Rates: single or double, $53–$101; suites, $201
Added: 5.61% tax
Payment: Major credit cards
Children: Under 12 free in room with parents
Pets: In kennels; not allowed in lodgings
Smoking: Permitted
Open: Year-round

Bright Angel Lodge dates from 1896, when it began as cabins and tents on the very edge of the Grand Canyon's South Rim. The name comes from Bright Angel Creek, which was christened by John Wesley Powell, the first white man to explore the inner gorge of the Grand Canyon.

Today the lodge is a conglomeration of facilities. At the low end of the scale are simple rooms with no baths or half baths. The most expensive unit is the Bucky Suite—an 1890s cabin built by Bucky O'Neil. Right at the canyon's rim, it is a delightful old structure with two rooms, a king-size bed, one double sofa bed, a fireplace, full bath, phone, and two TVs.

The stone and log rim cabins, built in 1935, are the best choice. Views don't come any better than this, and the price is right. These cabins are roomy, and their simple furnishings are more than adequate. With an incredible view through your windows, it's hard to ask for more. Some of the cabins have stone fireplaces. All have a bathroom (shower and tub), phone, and TV. The cabins labeled "historic" have little to recommend them except their location within a few hundred feet of the Grand Canyon.

The standard rooms are in rambling, one-story buildings connected to the main lodge by breezeways. A typical room has two double beds, a dresser, and two chairs, with pine walls and shag carpeting. The bathroom has a clawfoot tub.

In the main lodge, a casual restaurant serves sandwiches and burgers as well as steak and seafood entrées ($6–$11). The lobby is the headquarters for booking bus tours and mule rides.

It is best to make reservations four to six months in advance, although it is sometimes possible to get a room at the last minute. Reservations are accepted as far as "two years minus two days" in advance.

El Tovar Hotel

P.O. Box 699
Grand Canyon, Arizona 86023
602-638-2631
Fax: 602-638-9247

General manager: Bill Bohannon
Accommodations: 65 rooms
Rates: single or double, $101–$151; suites, $166–$251
Added: 5.61% tax
Payment: Major credit cards
Children: Under 12 free in room with parents
Pets: In kennels; not in lodgings
Smoking: Permitted
Open: Year-round

The grandest place to stay at the grandest of all canyons is El Tovar. Built in 1905 on the South Rim, it looks down on the 190-mile-long chasm carved by the Colorado River.

This lodge was named for Don Pedro de Tovar, who in 1540 became the first European to visit the Hopi Indians. It was built using native limestone and logs shipped from Oregon. Although it was renovated in 1990–91, El Tovar still retains its historic character. The rooms are stylishly furnished and most are spacious, with two double, two queen-size, or one king-size bed. The baths are larger than average and have showers and tubs. Some rooms look out over the canyon; four suites are designated as "guaranteed view" accommodations.

The front porch, lined with rockers, is welcoming. The lobby, handsome and dark with its log columns and hunting lodge design, bustles with activity. A cocktail lounge is off to one side. So is the dining room, like a lodge in architecture yet with a more formal air. Stone fireplaces stand tall at each end. The menu features fowl, beef, and seafood entrées ($10–$23).

One of the most pleasant areas in the hotel is the mezzanine lounge, overlooking the lobby. Reserved for guests, it serves Continental breakfast and light meals in a relaxed atmosphere. For the best views of one of the world's grandest natural sites, however, head to the cocktail lounge or dining room.

Adventurous travelers may want to stay at the Phantom Ranch, which is also run by Grand Canyon National Park Lodges. At the bottom of the inner gorge, it can be reached only by foot, mule, or rafting the Colorado River. Reservations can be made through the same phone number as El Tovar.

Grand Canyon Lodge North Rim
602-638-2611
Reservations: TW Recreational Services
P.O. Box 400
Cedar City, Utah 84721
801-586-7686
Fax: 801-586-3157

Accommodations: 200 units
Rates: double, $46–$68
Added: 5.61% tax
Payment: Major credit cards
Children: Welcome
Pets: Not permitted
Smoking: Permitted
Open: Mid-May to late-October

In the spruce and fir forests on the Grand Canyon's North Rim, far from the crowds of the South Rim, there are four types of lodgings near the rim itself. The cabins are built of logs, while the motel is wood frame. The Frontier cabins are the smallest, with one double bed, one single bed, and a bathroom with a shower. The Pioneer cabins have two rooms, each with two twin beds, and a small bath. The Motel rooms have two double beds and a bath with a shower. The Western cabins are the top of the line, with two double beds, a private porch, full bathrooms, and a telephone. All the units are carpeted and have individual heating.

The Grand Canyon Lodge, built of native stone and logs, has one of the best porches in the world, directly overlooking the magnificent canyon. There are no guest rooms here, but the dining room serves all three meals. (Dinner entrées range from $8 to $14; be sure to make reservations.) You can also arrange for a picnic lunch.

By air, the North Rim is 15 miles from the more commonly visited South Rim; on the road, it's about 200 miles. The pace is slower here. There's time to experience the serenity and to drink in the grandeur of the surroundings. You can hike, ride mules, or drive to see more of the canyon's splendor. Mule trips range from 1 to 8 hours. Hiking trails are from half a mile to 10 miles long. The North Kaibab Trail is the only one that leads into the canyon. Hiking to Roaring Springs, 3,041 feet below the rim, and back to the trailhead takes from 6 to 8 hours.

One of a Kind

These accommodations have such a distinctive atmosphere or history that they defy being categorized.

New Mexico

Bear Mountain Guest Ranch
Silver City, New Mexico 88062
505-538-2538

Owner: Myra McCormick
Accommodations: 15 units
Rates: single, $65; double, $114; suites, $126
Included: All meals
Added: 10.5% tax
Payment: Credit cards not accepted
Children: Welcome
Pets: Permitted
Smoking: In guest rooms or outdoors only, not in public areas
Open: Year-round

Nature is the star attraction at Bear Mountain Guest Ranch, which has been run by Myra McCormick since 1959. An expert nature guide, she cordially invites guests to get to know her part of the world. More than 200 species of birds have been spotted in the Bear Mountain area. Mountain chickadees, Mexican jays, canyon towhees, and Gambel's quail are among the frequent visitors.

Myra's specialties are birding, wild plants, archaeology, and ghost towns. Throughout the year special events are held at the ranch, such as archaeological digs and birding expeditions. She also helps guests to plan excursions—spelunking, whitewater rafting, exploring canyons, rock hunting, fishing, and sightseeing.

Guided tours to archaeological sites of the Mimbres Indians, a culture that flourished between A.D. 1000 and 1150, can be arranged. The Mimbres produced sophisticated pottery, "the most unique of any," says Myra, explaining that their work was decorated with black on white geometric designs and human and animal figures.

Bear Mountain Guest Ranch is about four miles outside Silver City. Ringed by distant mountains, it sits on grassy meadowland speckled with junipers. The location is quiet, peaceful, and secluded—even the stars in the night sky seem to shine more brightly at the ranch.

The hacienda-style ranch house was built in the late 1920s as a home and school for emotionally disturbed children. The main room is welcoming, with native stone fireplaces, cupboards filled with rocks and minerals, casual sitting areas, and a vast array of magazines. Off to one side is the sun porch, dubbed by Myra "the bird-watching room."

Guests can choose between rooms in the main house (there are three downstairs and four upstairs) or in cottages nearby. The furnishings are casual and simple, reminiscent of the 1920s and 1930s, with electric blankets on the beds to help take the chill out of the mountain air. The windows are large and seem to be everywhere, letting in the fresh air and the sun. A cottage called the Bear's Den has five bedrooms, each with a private bath, and a large central sitting area. The other two cottages have one bedroom each. Since the cottages have kitchens, guests there may cook for themselves or eat in the ranch's dining room.

Guests are asked to introduce themselves at the dinner table just before each meal, and this usually has the effect of stimulating lively conversation, for the ranch's guests tend to be as interesting as the place itself. Meals are served family-style in the main house. Everything is cooked from scratch using natural foods. Dinner usually consists of homemade bread, a meat dish, a potato dish, a vegetable, salad, and a homemade dessert.

At breakfast there's a hot entrée (generally eggs of some sort), cereal, and freshly-baked muffins, often made from Mrs. McCormick's secret low-calorie recipes. Guests are sent off with bagged lunches to fortify them on their bird-watching or sight-seeing excursions.

The ranch holds special 6-day programs on subjects such as the geology of New Mexico, Indians of the Southwest, and stress management Southwest style. The programs are popular and reasonably priced, so be sure to arrange your stay as far ahead as possible.

Casita Chamisa
850 Chamisal Road NW
Albuquerque, New Mexico 87107
505-897-4644

Owners/Hosts: Kit and Arnold Sargeant
Accommodations: 3 rooms
Rates: single, $60; double, $75–$80; $10 each additional person
Included: Breakfast
Payment: Major credit cards
Children: Welcome
Pets: Permitted with prior approval
Smoking: Outside only
Open: Year-round

Casita Chamisa made local headlines in the late 1980s when an archaeological excavation on the property uncovered some 150,000 pottery shards and 15,000 animal bones left by six different American Indian pueblos that occupied the site for 350 years, from around A.D. 1300. The Sargeants knew their house was on an archaeological site when they purchased it in the 1970s, but they had no idea what the excavation would yield when they decided to add a bedroom and swimming pool. Kit is an archaeologist, and he supervised much of the excavation; he is now working on a book about the project.

Although most of the excavated area has been covered for preservation purposes, a small exposed portion remains in the basement, and Kit will be happy to interpret the site for interested guests. It is just one aspect of this truly special B&B.

Casita Chamisa, with wide floorboards and low ceilings, has all the charm of an adobe farmhouse built in the 1850s. Decorated with artifacts from the Sargeants' travels in Central and South America, the living and dining rooms are intriguing. In warmer months, breakfast is served in the adjoining sun room, whose skylight is shaded by an intricate network of bamboo branches (grown in the yard) that make unusual patterns on the adobe walls below.

Outside, horses neigh from their corral, roosters and chickens roam the property, as do several friendly dogs and cats, and honeybees buzz in their hives (at a safe distance from the house, of course). There are porch swings for lounging, two redwood decks for sunning, fragrant flower gardens and a small orchard to enjoy. Rare for a B&B, Casita Chamisa has a good-size heated indoor swimming pool (with a diving board) and a hot tub. Another unusual treat—robes and sandals are provided.

The accommodations are designed for privacy. The large guest room attached to the main house, directly above the excavation, has its own entrance, patio, and bath. The hall that leads from the guest room to the swimming pool has a small sitting area under a mollusk shell–shaped bay window sculpted by Arnold. A separate guest house has a Mexican tile bath, two bedrooms (one with a queen-size bed, the other with two twins that can be made up to form a king), a sitting room with a cute kiva fireplace, and a small kitchenette. There's a greenhouse off the back bedroom and a lively mural painted on one side of the cottage. Conveniences such as TVs, clock radios, and telephones have not been forgotten.

Even breakfast at Casita Chamisa has its own story. There is always homemade jam and either fresh or baked fruit from the orchard, honey from the bees, and fresh orange juice. But the real highlight is Arnold's sourdough—sourdough blueberry Belgian waffles, sourdough pancake roll-ups, and sourdough bread made with freshly-ground wheat.

Arnold got the sourdough in Pocatello, Idaho, 20 years ago. At that time it was 90 years old and could trace its origins to a Basque sheepherder. When the Sargeants took it with them to Central America, they had to find an icehouse every two days in order to keep the dough alive in such a hot climate. Now Arnold celebrates the dough's birthday on July 1 with a traditional birthday cake and ceremony. Special guests are allowed to take a small portion of the sourdough with them, but they must promise to send a birthday card every July. This all may seem like a lot of fuss over "just a sourdough," but when you taste its truly delicious products, you'll realize how extraordinary it is.

Casita Chamisa, in one of the loveliest and lushest parts of Albuquerque, is a beautiful five-mile drive from historic Old Town. The Sargeants gladly provide guests with information on attractions in the area and can even arrange a massage for you at the end of a long day.

The Stewart House
P.O. Box 2326
Taos, New Mexico 87571
505-776-2931

Innkeepers: Don and Mildred Cheek
Accommodations: 4 rooms
Rates: single or double, $80–$120
Included: Full breakfast
Added: 10.25% tax
Payment: Personal checks
Children: Welcome
Pets: Not permitted
Smoking: Not permitted
Open: Year-round

In a town where adobe buildings are the norm, the Stewart House certainly stands out — its whimsical construction probably would attract attention just about anywhere. Built in the 1960s by artist Charles Stewart with what he called "parts of reclaimed history," the house looks much older than it is. Using primarily wood and stone, and combining Mayan, Moorish, Scandinavian, and Spanish elements, Stewart created a structure that is undeniably unique.

At first you may not know what to make of Stewart House's exterior. (In fact, you may not even be sure that the bridge from the parking lot to the front yard will hold you, but it will). A haphazard stone fireplace is interrupted by nichos filled with Mexican ceramic figures, and red tile is used on the roof and as a decorative accent. To the left of the front entrance is a door with a kachina motif carved by Stewart and topped with a mini-balcony.

Inside, the main room is more "normal," with its high ceilings and large windows looking out onto the Taos valley and the beautiful mountains beyond. Breakfast is served here each morning. The Cheeks, the current owners, run an art gallery in town, and the artwork on the walls is for sale.

The adjoining front guest bedroom has a wood-burning stove and a log cabin feel. The other guest rooms are in separate buildings behind the main house. Do not be frightened by their rustic looks — they are furnished with a sense of fun. The Artist's room has a bathtub that once belonged to the painter R. C.

Gorman. The Casita West suite is nicknamed "the bordello" by the owners because its brass bed is covered in burgundy satin. The door at the entrance was once used as an Old West movie prop. The clawfoot tub in the bath is shrouded in lace, and each "claw" is painted differently—polka dots on one, sharp nails on another, and a poinsettia on yet another. This suite has the best views of all the guest rooms.

There's an outdoor hot tub for guests to enjoy, and the inn is conveniently located between Taos and the Taos Ski Valley.

Outdoor Pursuits

These accommodations gear their programs to outdoor and sports enthusiasts, often specializing in golf, tennis, hunting, or fishing.

Arizona

John Gardiner's Tennis Ranch on Camelback
5700 East McDonald Drive
Scottsdale, Arizona 85253
602-948-2100
800-245-2051
Fax: 602-483-7314

General manager: Eleni Koliambas
Accommodations: 100 units; casitas and 4- and 5-bedroom casas (some with their own court)
Rates: $195–$325 single or double, $480–$540 for 2-bedroom casitas (up to 4 people), weekend packages from $550 per person double occupancy, 1-week packages from $1,425 per person double occupancy
Included: Breakfast, lunch, and court time
Added: 9.05% tax and 15% service charge
Payment: Major credit cards
Children: During junior clinics only
Pets: Not permitted
Smoking: Permitted (few guests smoke)
Open: October through mid-May

If you like tennis combined with luxury, John Gardiner's Tennis Ranch is the place for you. The resort's 50-plus acres are beautifully landscaped: citrus trees, bougainvillea, and oleander seem to be in bloom everywhere you turn. Scottsdale with its glitzy resorts is a stone's throw away, but here on Camelback Mountain, the rest of the world seems distant.

Tennis is king at this private club resort, which holds such tournaments as the annual invitational U.S. Senators' Cup. Take your choice of 24 championship courts. In keeping with tradition, players almost always wear white on the court. (The ranch's official dress code states "predominately white.") Weekly clinics offer 21 hours of instruction, 6 hours of optional tournaments, complimentary court time, and two half-hour massages—which you may need after all that tennis. (Weekend "tiebreaker" packages are also available.) More than thirty pros provide instruction at a ratio of one pro to every four guests. Workouts include computerized ball machines and videotape replay. In between sessions on the court, guests can relax in three swimming pools, saunas, and whirlpools or have a massage.

Lodging is in casitas or casas off of palm-shaded paths with names like "Forty Love Lane" and "High Lob Avenue." Casitas come in three sections, with a living room in the middle and a bedroom on each side. You can rent any part or the entire unit. Some have sun rooms and private balconies with views of Camelback or the valley below. Since all of the units are privately owned, each is individually decorated, but southwestern themes predominate. All are luxuriously comfortable with spacious living rooms, fireplaces, and kitchenettes that come fully equipped with tableware, coffeemakers, cutlery, ice makers, full-size refrigerators, toasters, and blenders. Each section of the casitas has a phone and TV, and some units even have VCRs and washer-dryers. And while the casitas feel like private homes, special touches such as daily housekeeping, fresh fruit upon arrival, and freshly-squeezed orange juice and the newspaper on your doorstep each morning let you know that you're at a fine resort.

For the ultimate in tennis luxury, opt for a casa. Casa Rosewall (the home of Ken Rosewall) has a rooftop court and private pool. The spacious Gardiner house has its own pool and tennis court as well. Additional bedrooms with separate entrances that open onto the pool can be rented by small groups or families requiring more than the casa's one main bedroom.

Meals are served buffet-style in the clubhouse, which by day wears a sporty look and at night is more formal. (Guests are asked to wear evening attire.) You can eat indoors or outdoors, overlooking the valley.

Enchantment Resort

525 Boynton Canyon Road
Sedona, Arizona 86336
602-282-2900
800-826-4180

General manager: Dr. Brightbart
Accommodations: 120 units
Rates: single or double, $155–$210; suites, $220–$560; $35
    additional per person per day for more than 2 guests in
    room or suite
Included: Buffet breakfast, tax and gratuities
Payment: Major credit cards
Children: Welcome
Pets: Not permitted
Smoking: Permitted
Open: Year-round

Enchantment Resort is a luxurious getaway in a breathtaking
setting, surrounded by the Coconino National Forest and the
glowing rock formations of Boynton Canyon. About 10 minutes
from the center of town, Enchantment is right in the heart of
Sedona's famed Red Rock country, letting you experience its
magic firsthand. A trail leading to Indian canyon dwellings
(now in ruin) starts right at the edge of the resort. If you don't
want to hike, there's a telescope in the main lounge that will
bring the ruddy landscape into closer view. After dark, the
telescope is moved upstairs to an outdoor deck for stargazing.
In the evenings, deer snack on the lush green grass of Enchantment's pitch-and-putt golf course.

When you're not out exploring the area's glorious terrain,
there is plenty to keep you busy at the resort. Twelve tennis
courts and four swimming pools are spread throughout the
grounds, giving the resort an uncrowded feel. This also makes
them convenient to each casita. Court time is free for guests, but
for those who want more intensive tennis programs, instruc-
tional packages are available. There's a full-service spa and fitness center with steam rooms, saunas, and whirlpools. Also on
the property are three croquet courses; and if the pitch-and-putt
won't satisfy your golf craving, a round of 18 holes can be reserved at a nearby course. A helicopter ride to the Indian ruins
from the resort's own helicopter pad can also be arranged.

Guests stay in casitas that are so roomy they feel like private
homes. Built of adobe to blend in with the landscape, they are
decorated tastefully in a southwestern style. Black Indian pot-

tery and Taos drums add personality. Two bedroom casitas have a large central living room with a kiva fireplace, a deck with a built-in barbecue, and a kitchenette. Two casitas have their own pool—one with a poolside Jacuzzi—and a number have garages.

Guests who don't feel like whipping something up in their kitchenette can eat in the fine dining room at the resort's clubhouse, which has outstanding views, or order from room service. The restaurant cuisine is primarily southwestern, and spa meals are available for those watching their calories. On Friday and Saturday nights there is musical entertainment, and the southwestern buffet on Saturdays is a popular event. On Sundays a champagne brunch is offered.

A security gate at the entrance to the resort ensures that it remains a secluded hideaway for guests only. A concierge is on duty in the clubhouse from 8:00 A.M. to 6:00 P.M., and there are laundry facilities on the property.

Tubac Golf Resort
1 Otero Road
P.O. Box 1297
Tubac, Arizona 85646
602-398-2211
800-848-7893

Owner: Al Kaufman
Accommodations: 16 casitas and 16 posadas
Rates: $74–$98 for posada rooms, $89–$124 for casitas without kitchenettes, $102–$137 for casitas with kitchenettes, special extended stay and golf packages available
Added: 6.05% tax
Payment: Major credit cards
Children: Over 12, $15 per day
Pets: Permitted
Smoking: Permitted
Open: Year-round

Built on the 400-acre site of the Otero Ranch (established in 1789), the Tubac Golf Resort is about a mile outside of the artsy town of Tubac. While not as posh as some of Tucson's large resorts, the Tubac Golf Resort offers comfortable lodging and 18 holes of golf in a tranquil setting. People come to the resort to relax, not to be seen.

Beautiful views of the Santa Rita Mountains enhance any round of golf at the resort, and the course, dotted with cottonwoods and mesquites, is well maintained. There's a convenient pro shop, and after a day on the greens, the lobby lounge overlooking the course is a genial spot for drinks and complimentary chips and salsa. Montura's restaurant, in a building next door that was once the ranch's stables, serves all three meals. Dark wooden booths, stone floors, copper light fixtures, Indian rugs, and a stone fireplace add atmosphere. Steak, seafood, and Mexican entrées range from $9.50–$18 at dinnertime.

Lodging is in red tile–roofed buildings sprinkled around green lawns and a central swimming pool. Casitas are the largest units with a separate living and bedroom, a fireplace (firewood is supplied), and a kitchenette (one unit has a full kitchen). The posadas are smaller and have more traditional hotel room configurations. Decor in both is Mexican and southwestern, and all rooms have Mexican tile baths with separate vanities.

In addition to golf and swimming, there is one tennis court on the resort, as well as facilities for volleyball and horseshoes. Tubac has many shops and galleries worth investigating, and arts and crafts festivals are held in the town on a regular basis. Tubac Presidio State Historic Park and Tumacacori National Monument are nearby, and Nogales, Mexico is about a half an hour's drive.

New Mexico

The Lodge at Chama Land and Cattle Company
Chama, New Mexico 87520
505-756-2133
505-756-2519

General manager: Frank Sims
Accommodations: 12 rooms
Rates: $2,500–$8,600 for an all-inclusive hunt (rate depends on type of game), $375 (deluxe suites higher) per day including meals, guide, transportation, horseback riding, and fishing (special lodging only rates and arrangements can be made for nonhunting/fishing companions)
Added: 5.375% tax
Payment: Personal checks; no credit cards
Children: Under 12, $100 per night, over 12, $200 per night
Pets: Not permitted
Smoking: Permitted
Open: Year-round; hunting seasons September to January

Chama Land and Cattle Company, in the San Juan Mountains of northern New Mexico, is a working ranch with more than 32,000 acres. The ranch spreads over beautiful terrain ranging from oak foothills and meadows of aspen and spruce to alpine country of up to 10,000 feet.

On its land, hidden from public view, is an exclusive, luxurious lodge catering to hunters and anglers as well as business groups. Repeat visitors account for three fourths of its clientele.

Elk hunting is at the heart of the lodge's operation. The ranch has one of the largest elk herds on private land in the country. Ninety percent of its hunters take 6 x 6 bull elk or better; the rest take 5 x 5s. Each hunter has a private guide, and travel is by four-wheel-drive vehicle, horseback, or on foot. Hunts last about three or four days. Other game hunted include mule deer and black bear.

Guests fish in mountain lakes stocked with rainbow, German brown, brook, and native cutthroat trout. Comments in the guest register tell the story. "Better fishing than in Alaska," wrote one.

The stone lodge is a sprawling ranch house on a hill overlooking the Chama Valley. (There's a security gate at the entrance, so be sure you're expected.) The main room, appropriately named the Trophy Room, is truly handsome, with a 22-foot stone fireplace in the center and original western art. Stuffed elk, deer, and bear—all native to the area—as well as wildlife from other parts of the world set the tone. The owner, Grady Vaughn, is a collector and has assembled an impressive display.

The guest rooms line the adjoining hall. Large and luxurious, each has its own theme, with wildlife as the focal point. Leather and wood, Indian pottery and woven work, make the rooms distinctive. The huge junior suites have kiva fireplaces and rugs made by the famous Ortega weavers in Chimayo.

The hot tub room, next to a sauna, is truly luxurious. Guests take meals in the Trophy Room. All of the food is made from scratch served with a flair. An open bar is included in the rate.

During the winter, the lodge is a great place for mountain vacationing, especially if you like cross-country skiing, sleigh rides, and observing wildlife.

Quail Ridge Inn and Tennis Ranch

P.O. Box 707
Taos, New Mexico 87571
505-776-2211
800-624-4448
Fax: 505-776-2949

General manager: Peter French
Accommodations: 110 units
Rates: single, $75–$95; double, $75–$120; suites for 4–6, $150–$300
Added: 11.25% tax
Payment: Major credit cards
Children: Under 18 free in room with parents
Pets: Not permitted
Smoking: Permitted
Open: Year-round

Adobe casitas hug the ground at the foot of the Sangre de Cristo Mountains, blending unpretentiously into the landscape. The town of Taos is four miles to the south; Taos Ski Valley is twelve miles north. Quail Ridge Inn offers the essence of Taos, from its southwestern architecture to its recognition of local art.

A year-round resort, the inn is always brimming with activity. Tennis is one of its strongest attractions (if you can take your eyes off the view long enough to play), with eight Laykold courts (two under a bubble), a tennis pro, clinic instruction, and tournaments. There is no outdoor court fee for guests; indoor courts cost $15 an hour.

Quail Ridge's landscaped 20-meter pool and deck, added in 1987, is one of the most attractive in New Mexico. There's also a large hot tub, children's pool, and fitness center.

When snow blankets the nearby mountains, Quail Ridge becomes a ski lodge, and shuttle buses run to Taos Ski Valley. At this inn, skiers can easily combine a sports vacation with trips into Taos. Nonskiers can also find plenty to do in town while the rest of the group is on the slopes.

The simple accommodations, furnished in a southwestern style, include hotel rooms (queen-size bed, queen-size sleeper sofa), studios (Murphy bed, sitting area, full kitchen, patio or balcony), one-bedroom suites (hotel room plus studio), and two-bedroom suites (two hotel rooms plus studio). Every room has a kiva fireplace as well as a TV and telephone. Individually owned, the units are well decorated. The kitchens are fully equipped, with countertop appliances and cookware as well as a full-size refrigerator and stove, dishwasher, and garbage disposal.

Carl's French Quarter is the inn's restaurant, with such specialties as trout almandine, shrimp Créole, and veal Marsala. Prices range from $12 to $19.

One of the true delights of this inn is sitting on an adobe patio, gazing at the distant mountains by day or the star-sprinkled sky by night.

Unser's Oso Ranch and Lodge

P.O. Box 808
Chama, New Mexico 87520
505-756-2954
800-882-5190

Managers: Bruce and Martha Peck
Accommodations: 6 rooms
Rates: single or double lodging only; $45–$65; including breakfast, $65–$85; including all three meals, $100–$150; extra adults are charged half of listed rates
Added: 9% tax
Payment: Major credit cards
Children: Additional charge if meals are taken
Pets: Not permitted
Smoking: Permitted
Open: Year-round

On the banks of the Chama River, about two miles south of Chama, is a lodge geared to outdoor enthusiasts year-round. Guests fish in the river or lake during the spring, summer, and fall, and there's ice fishing in winter. During the summer there's horseback riding and hiking; in the winter, snowmobiling and cross-country skiing. Hunting for elk, deer, and bear gets the emphasis in the fall. Friendly managers and Oso Ranch's intimate size make it an inviting place to visit during any season.

Built as a private lodge, Oso Ranch is now owned by the famous racecar drivers Al Unser, Sr. and Jr. (they live nearby), and covers 800 acres of rolling country dotted with juniper, pine, and spruce. The guest rooms are in a log building that doubles as a dining room and social center.

The main lodge room is log cabin rustic, decorated with hunting and fishing trophies, Indian and western art, and a large stone fireplace. Guests can relax by the antique woodstove and enjoy the wide-screen TV, pool table, and a library of western history. Meals are served here family-style. The fare is good country food—soups, stews, biscuits, grilled meats. Breakfasts are hearty.

One hall leads to the guest rooms, with a choice of twin, queen-or king-size bed. The door of each room is a work of art — a suede and leather creation depicting an animal indigenous to the area. Not only are the rooms comfortable, but they are thoughtfully decorated, and the work of local artists hangs on the walls. Each room has its own theme; for instance, the one with a rainbow trout on the door has such accents as a rod, creel, and tackle box mounted on the wall and a display of fishing flies. Some rooms have ceiling fans; all have TVs.

Without a doubt, fishing is the most popular activity at Oso Ranch. Anglers have a choice of the Chama, Little Navajo, and Brazos rivers and private streams for rainbow, brook, or brown trout and Kokanee salmon. The ranch also has a private lake stocked with rainbow trout.

Oso Ranch becomes a hunting lodge in the appropriate seasons. Elk, mule deer, mountain lion, and black bear are the predominant game. Oso Ranch (oso is Spanish for "bear") offers two types of hunts: fully outfitted and lodge. The fully outfitted version includes a guide, transportation while hunting, game care, lodging, meals, and hunting permits. (New Mexico license and hunting fees are extra.) An outfitter takes hunters via four-wheel-drive vehicle or horseback. Lodge hunts include private land hunting permits, transportation while hunting, and assistance in retrieving game when needed, but no guide service. Lodging and meals are also included in the price. (Contact the lodge directly for current package rates.) The ranch will arrange for taxidermy, meat storage, and freezing upon request.

Horseback riding, pack trips, hayrides, and cookouts can be arranged by Oso Ranch. The Cumbres and Toltec Scenic Railroad, with departures from Chama, is a popular day trip. The train runs daily from June to mid-October.

Vermejo Park Ranch
P.O. Drawer E
Raton, New Mexico 87740
505-445-3097
505-445-3474

General manager: John Conner
Accommodations: 45 rooms
Rates: $265 per person per day, $1,500–$7,500 for up to 5-day hunt
Included: Meals and fishing privileges with daily rate, meals, guides, and transportation with 5-day hunts
Added: 5.5% tax

Payment: Personal checks; no credit cards
Children: Permitted
Pets: Not permitted
Smoking: Nonsmoking rooms available
Open: Overnight accommodations: June 1 through Labor
Day; during hunting season, accommodations for pre-
reserved hunt guests only

Vermejo Park Ranch is one of the largest blocks of privately
owned land in the country. Its 588,000 acres in the Sangre de
Cristo Mountains date from an 1840s land grant encompassing
2 million acres. The ranch, owned since 1973 by the Penzoil
Company, is now an outdoor recreation resort and a working
cattle ranch. As a hunting and fishing destination, it offers
extensive private grounds far removed from the masses.

The nucleus of the resort is about 40 miles from Raton,
reached partially over a private road. In the early 1900s a
wealthy businessman from Chicago owned the ranch, and he
built a mansion for himself and several houses for guests.
Today's guests stay in seven of the houses (the mansion, exquisitely furnished with antiques, is only used on special occasions)
or in wonderfully rustic Costillo Lodge, 28 miles from the
headquarters. Accommodating up to twelve guests, it is usually
reserved for groups.

In 1911, elk were reestablished at Vermejo Park after having
been killed off in the entire area in the early 1890s. Today
Vermejo claims to have New Mexico's largest elk herd. Its hunters generally have an overall 85 percent success rate, and more
than 70 percent of all bulls taken score 6 × 6 or larger. Heavily
populated with wildlife, the ranch also offers hunts for mule
deer, antelope, bear, mountain lion, buffalo, and Merrium turkey. All the hunts include a private guide, four-wheel-drive vehicle, hunting license, and game skinning and quartering.

Anglers can fish in ten lakes and 25 miles of creeks. Cutthroat, brook, rainbow, and brown trout, along with Coho

salmon, are the featured catches. Fly-fishing schools are scheduled several times during the season. There's a limit of 12 fish per day. Other activities include horseback riding, hiking, and skeet shooting.

The lodging here is truly different from anywhere else in the Southwest. The setting is magnificent. You're in a small village surrounded by miles and miles of open wilderness. The guest houses are indeed houses, with a variety of floor plans, and are set apart from each other, as in a village. The furnishings are modern but not particularly luxurious or atmospheric. The bedrooms have either double or twin beds.

Meals are served in the new $2.5 million log cabin lodge with a rustic, southwestern interior. The cuisine leans toward meat and potatoes, and guests are allowed to choose an entrée from the menu that is printed daily. While lunch is served in the dining room, most guests ask for box lunches. Those staying at Costillo Lodge have their own dining room.

Casa Grande, the former owner's mansion, is truly grand, with hand-carved ceilings, interior marble columns, Oriental rugs, and a 1904 Steinway. Its remote location makes you feel as if you've stumbled upon an undiscovered castle. Be sure to ask for a tour.

Texas

The Farris 1912
201 North McCarty Avenue
Eagle Lake, Texas 77434
409-234-2546
Fax: 409-234-2598

Proprietors: William and Helyn Farris
Accommodations: 24 rooms (6 with private bath)
Rates:
   November–February: $110–$120 per person based on
      double occupancy; $150–$175 per person based on single
      occupancy including all meals
   Other months: $65–$85 single or double including
      Continental breakfast
Added: 10% tax
Payment: Major credit cards
Children: Over 12 welcome; families traveling with children
   under 12 must stay in the guest house
Pets: Not permitted

Smoking: In guest house only
Open: Guest house, year-round; main lodge is closed in
   summer unless groups rent the entire building

The Farris 1912 wears two faces. From November through February the historic hotel, known as "Eagle Lake's birthplace," caters to hunters drawn to the area by excellent duck and goose hunting. During the rest of the year it welcomes sightseers—particularly during March and April, when the colorful Texas wildflowers are at their peak.

Guests have access to the owners' nearby lakeside property for observing wildlife. The Attwater Prairie Chicken Refuge, a 3,400-acre sanctuary dedicated to the near-extinct birds, is six miles from the Farris.

The area is so popular for bird hunting that the hotel attracts international guests in the winter, for this is no ordinary hunting lodge. Casual elegance is the theme, and the public areas are richly decorated with antique furniture, lace curtains, silver candelabra, mirrors, and floral carpets. A sign by the back door advises: "Hunters, Unload Guns! No Muddy Boots in Hotel, Please." In a small separate building is a facility for cleaning guns as well as refrigerated storage.

All meals are provided during hunting season. As on a cruise ship, food is omnipresent, with an "eat all you want" philosophy. Continental breakfast is served the rest of the year, except during wildflower season, when lunch is offered daily. For groups and private parties, supplemental food service can be arranged. No gratuities are permitted at any time for lodging or food services.

Accommodations are in the main hotel and in the 1920s guest house next door. The hotel rooms, cheerfully but simply furnished, have double or twin beds, and two have private baths. The VIP Room has an antique spool bed as well as one twin bed. All the rooms open onto a sprawling mezzanine, a popular gathering spot with couches, easy chairs, and game tables. The suites in the guest house have private entrances, a bath with a shower, a parlor, wet bar, refrigerator, and TV.

Rancho Viejo Resort
P.O. Box 3918
Rancho Viejo, Texas 78520
210-350-4000
800-531-7400
Fax: 210-350-9681

General manager: Timothy Trapp
Accommodations: 100 units

Rates: single, $88; double, $113; suites, $133; villas, $206–$309
Added: 6% tax
Payment: Major credit cards
Children: Under 14 free in room with parents
Pets: Not permitted
Smoking: Permitted
Open: Year-round

About 10 miles north of Brownsville is Rancho Viejo, both an incorporated town and a 1,400-acre resort. The resort consists of two 18-hole championship golf courses, guest villas, private homes, and grounds dotted with palms.

Once the site of a citrus orchard, the resort has retained some of its history. Casa Grande, the original hacienda, is now a fine supper club where roving troubadours entertain.

Golf is the headliner at Rancho Viejo. El Diablo and El Angel courses draw visitors all year, especially in the winter, when sun-starved Midwesterners head south. The courses are open only to members, resort guests, and golfers who belong to reciprocating clubs. The greens fee is $30; cart rental is $24. (Golf packages are available.) Once you check into Rancho Viejo, you can put your wallet aside. Guests sign for services, even at the two restaurants, which, like the golf courses, are not open to the public.

There's also a great swimming pool with a huge waterfall and swim-up bar and two tennis courts. Mexico is about a 20-minute drive; the beaches of South Padre are about 30 minutes away. Brownsville has an excellent zoo dedicated to rare and endangered species, and the Confederate Air Force Museum in Harlingen has a collection of American World War II combat aircraft.

Residential-style lodging is spread across the resort's grounds. Plan to drive to the dining rooms and recreational facilities; courtesy vans will also pick you up on request. Bicycles are a good way to get around the resort; they can be rented for $12 per day or $50 per week.

Villas, in two-and three-bedroom styles, have modern furnishings, fully equipped kitchens, and washers and dryers. Executive suites are two-story condo-style units.

Romantic Getaways

These run the gamut from resort hotels to B&Bs to historic homes, yet all have one thing in common—a romantic ambience.

Arizona

Stouffer Cottonwoods Resort
6160 North Scottsdale Road
Scottsdale, Arizona 85253
602-991-1414
800-HOTELS-1
Fax: 602-951-3350

General manager: Claudia Danks
Accommodations: 171 rooms
Rates: single, $85–$195; double, $95–$205; suites, $115–$265
Added: 9.05% tax
Payment: Major credit cards
Children: Not permitted
Pets: Under 25 pounds permitted with a $50 refundable deposit
Smoking: Nonsmoking rooms available
Open: Year-round

Scottsdale Road is lined with glamour—a mix of golden resorts, boutiques, and restaurants. In the midst of it all, the Stouffer Cottonwoods provides a tranquil hideaway, close to the glitter yet removed, offering the best of both worlds.

There's a residential, clublike feeling about the place. One-story villa suites are scattered over its 25 acres of grounds, with flower-lined paths draped with cottonwoods. The pace is unhurried here. Tucked away among the villas and courtyards is a large swimming pool that invites you to lounge. The sunken tennis courts, along grassy banks, have an intimate feeling. A jogging track with par exercise stations circles the grounds, leading past natural desert landscapes. There's a putting green and croquet course on the property, and you can play golf at any of five nearby golf courses. Bicycles can be rented at the resort's gift shop.

Scottsdale's cosmopolitan atmosphere is a few steps away— literally. The Borgata Shopping Village, which was designed after an Italian hill town, has boutiques, galleries, and restaurants just across the parking lot.

The villas have been designed for privacy, and each has a secluded patio. Decorated with a southwestern scheme, they have beamed ceilings and touches of regional art. The Flagstaff villas are the smallest, though somewhat larger than the average hotel room. They are furnished with one king-size or two double beds, a refrigerator, safe, and a vanity. The Tucson villas have a living room with a wet bar, large bedroom, and a private spa on the patio. The Phoenix villas are top-of-the-line, with a large living room and fireplace, a kitchen, a huge bath, a bedroom with a king-size bed, and an enclosed courtyard with a hot tub—truly a romantic setting.

The Moriah Restaurant is comfortably elegant and serves outstanding southwestern dishes. Tumbleweeds, the poolside bar and grill, is open daily. Other dining choices can be found in the shopping complex.

New Mexico

Casa de las Chimeneas
Box 5303
405 Cordoba Road
Taos, New Mexico 87571
505-758-4777

Innkeeper: Susan Vernon
Accommodations: 2 rooms, 1 suite
Rates: single, $93; double, $103; suite, $148
Added: 9.375% tax
Included: Breakfast and afternoon hors d'oeuvres
Children: Welcome, $15 additional if cot is needed
Pets: Not permitted
Smoking: Permitted only outside
Open: Year-round

Casa de las Chimeneas, set apart from its humbler surroundings by a light adobe wall that encompasses the property, is a lush oasis. About a half a mile from the Taos plaza, the inn is a world unto itself. Birds can be heard happily chirping in the majestic cottonwoods above. During the warmer months, gardens that border the house and fill the backyard come to life. There are daisies, iris, tulips, daffodils, geraniums, roses, petunias, snapdragons and more—creating a kaleidoscopic bouquet of color everywhere you look. Mexican fountains bubble with water, and the whole effect is both invigorating and pastoral at the same time.

Innkeeper Susan Vernon has taken the same care in decorating the guest rooms and common areas of the bed-and-breakfast as she did in creating her magnificent gardens. An orange tree grows right up through the center of the main entrance hallway. The adjoining living room, where guests are welcome to lounge, is comfortably elegant in a southwestern style. Gourmet breakfasts may include huevos rancheros, cheese crêpes with blueberries, eggs Benedict, green chile tortilla, or french toast made with orange date-nut bread topped with bananas and cinnamon maple syrup. Artfully presented hors d'oeuvres are served in the afternoon in the dining room on a long pine table—these might be caviar cream pie or baked potatoes with cheese and cracked red pepper (often garnished with edible flowers and herbs from the garden). Cold drinks are always available to guests in the dining room's wet bar.

Although the inn has only three guest rooms, each is tastefully appointed. The Library suite is the largest, with two rooms—one could outlast any winter storm (although in New Mexico the opportunity would not likely arise) holed up in its library with all it has to offer. Floor-to-ceiling bookshelves are filled with magazines and books, and there's a game table with a giant backgammon board and jigsaw puzzles. A large TV with cable access is hidden in an armoire. Best of all, there's a fireplace to relax in front of on chilly nights. The romantic bedroom has a queen-size brass bed, eyelet lace pillow covers, and a hand-stitched patchwork quilt. The bathroom is sweet with strawberries hand-painted on the Talavera tile (each bath has its own motif—strawberries, pineapples, and so on). The owner calls the walk-in closet in the Library suite the "Imelda Marcos," for it has numerous shelves that look as if they were specially designed to hold hundreds of pairs of shoes. The other two guest rooms, named Blue and Willow, are equally appealing, and each has a kiva fireplace. All of the rooms have their own thermostatic controls, top-of-the-line linens, high quality mattresses, sheep's wool mattress pads, natural soaps, and extra towels.

Susan, who had her own wedding at the inn, knows how important the right bed-and-breakfast is on one's honeymoon. She welcomes newlyweds with a bottle of champagne adorned with flowers. Guests celebrating birthdays, anniversaries, or other notable events also receive special treatment. For everyday indulgences, there's a hot tub in the backyard garden that's ideal for unwinding in after a long day of sightseeing or skiing.

Hacienda del Sol
Box 177
109 Mabel Dodge Lane
Taos, New Mexico 87571
505-758-0287

Innkeepers: John and Marcine Landon
Accommodations: 7 rooms
Rates: single, $45–$90; double, $55–$115; suites, $125–$155
Included: Breakfast
Added: 10.25% tax
Payment: Cash or check
Children: Additional $20 per night; $10 per night for a crib
Pets: Not permitted
Smoking: Not permitted
Open: Year-round

Years ago, when the art patron Mabel Dodge Luhan was searching for a home for herself and her Indian husband, Tony, one of her choices was the adobe house now known as Hacienda del Sol. D. H. Lawrence, Georgia O'Keeffe, Willa Cather, Thomas Wolfe, and Aldous Huxley all came to call. Today the 180-year-old house has a feeling of history, enhanced by the efforts of the Landons. They enjoy introducing visitors to Taos, suggesting sights, and talking about the area's history.

Don't despair when they give you directions. Yes, Hacienda del Sol is directly behind Lotta Burger, about 1 mile north of downtown. When you turn off Highway 64 onto the little dirt road leading to the front door, you may have second thoughts. But once you step inside the courtyard, you never think again about the commercial development nearby. On an acre lot, graced with ancient cottonwoods and ponderosa pines, the Hacienda adjoins Indian reservation land of more than 95,000 acres, providing an uninterrupted view all the way to Taos's Magic Mountain.

Inside, ancient vigas, kiva fireplaces, oak and brick floors, and handmade furniture please the eye. Throughout there's a homey look. Hacienda del Sol is a place where guests come and go with regularity and relax in the kitchen over a cup of coffee. Most of the artwork in the house is for sale, and many of the paintings are by Carol Pelton, a former owner, and local Native American artists.

La Escondida is the smallest guest room, distinctive with its viga and plank ceiling, skylight, stained glass window, and antique double bed. One of its doorways opens onto the front courtyard. The bath is across the hall. La Sala del Don, Tony's Room, is a large room with a kiva fireplace and a queen-size Spanish bed. Windows open onto peaceful gardens with hundred-year-old apple trees. La Sala del Sol, which opens onto the patio, is decorated in peach tones with aspen-pole beds and a willow branch chair.

The most popular guest room is Los Amantes—the Lovers Room. Not only is it romantically appointed, but it's next to the best part of all—a spa room with a black marble hot tub on a mahogany platform in the center. There's even a skylight above the tub. The bedroom includes a fireplace and a Mexican wooden bed with metallic accents, and French doors open onto the back courtyard.

If the Lovers Room is already booked, there are two casitas apart from the main house that also afford lots of privacy. For families or couples traveling together, they can be connected to form a suite. The casitas both have front porches with fabulous mountain views. Nearby, there's a large outdoor hot tub with a redwood sundeck that all guests can use by signing up for a specific time. The sign-up sheet ensures that each guest won't be interrupted, and once again—the mountain views are unrivaled.

Breakfast usually consists of fresh fruit, baked treats, fresh juice, and the inn's own blend of coffee; it is served outdoors in the warmer months or in front of the fire in the winter. Afternoon snacks are served in the living room or on the patio when weather permits.

Sarabande Bed and Breakfast
5637 Rio Grande Blvd. NW
Albuquerque, New Mexico 87107
505-345-4923

Innkeepers: Margaret Magnussen and Betty Vickers
Accommodations: 2 rooms

Rates: single, $65; double, $75–$90
Included: Full breakfast and afternoon refreshments
Added: 5.75% tax
Payment: Major credit cards
Children: Not permitted
Pets: Not permitted
Smoking: Not permitted
Open: Year-round

Sarabande is a charming bed-and-breakfast in Albuquerque's affluent North Valley. Run by two nurses who wanted to try their hand at a new occupation in their retirement, the inn is firm evidence that they made the right choice.

Two guest rooms share the main portion of the house (Betty and Margaret live in a separate wing), affording guests lots of living space and privacy. The large living/dining room has a shepherd's fireplace and an elegant dining table accented with a fine silver tea service and candlesticks. The real conversation piece, however, is a massive wood and glass refrigerator in the adjoining kitchen that dates back to 1923. It still works, and holds three times what today's standard refrigerator does. Guests are welcome to help themselves to refreshments stored in it.

The Rose room has a four-poster bed topped with a rose coverlet. There is a ceiling fan, TV, viga ceilings, and an interesting frosted glass door with a dragonfly pattern. And the best part is a raised platform with a deep soaking tub that you step down into. There's also a vanity, a washbasin with brass fixtures, and a separate shower across the room. A door at the far end of the room opens onto a fountain patio with a climbing rose bush—hence the room's name.

The Iris room across the hall is smaller but equally inviting. Furnished in mauves and grays, it has two twin beds that may be made into a king. A striking stained glass window with an iris motif gives the room its name. The room opens onto the front fountain and garden courtyard that has a built-in barbecue for guests to enjoy. Thoughtful touches in both the guest rooms include fresh flowers, electric towel warmers, and plush terry robes.

On one side of the house there's a wonderful Japanese garden complete with shady ramadas and a lily pond. Out back there's a 50-foot lap pool and adjoining hot tub—a real treat, especially when you consider that with only two guest rooms you're likely to have them all to yourself.

Full breakfasts are served in the dining room each morning. German pancakes with apples, eggs, coffee, and freshly-squeezed orange juice is a typical meal, but the hosts always try to accommodate any special dietary needs. In the afternoon, guests can unwind with a glass of wine and a selection of cheeses.

Texas

Inn on the Creek
Center Circle
P.O. Box 261
Salado, Texas 76571
817-947-5554

Innkeepers: Suzi and Lynn Epps
Accommodations: 7 rooms plus guest cottage (all with private bath)
Rates: double, $65–$115
Included: Full breakfast
Added: 6% tax
Payment: Major credit cards
Children: Welcome
Pets: Not permitted
Smoking: Not permmitted
Open: Year-round

On the banks of shady Salado Creek there's a stately Victorian home with a back porch just made for creek-watching. Inside, the Epps family are delightful hosts, making you welcome with bountiful breakfasts or even elegant dinners. (Dinners have become so popular with both guests and the public that the Eppses have recently added a 19th-century home to serve as a dining facility for up to fifty people.) At night, there's a chocolate on your pillow.

Suzi Epps is a registered architect, so when the couple decided to move an 1880s home from a nearby community, she was able to oversee the project. For over a year they restored the old house, doubling its size in the process. The fine wooden trims of the original home were retained and new trims milled to duplicate them. This is a picture-perfect home, with exquisite decor where everything matches.

The guest rooms are all decorated with handsome antiques, and each room has a TV and phone. A personal favorite is the Tyler Room, a swirl of peach with a white iron bed and wicker furniture. The best room in the house is the McKie Room, on the third floor. It has a brass king-size bed with a canopy, and there's a mirrored armoire, Queen Anne chairs, and an idyllic reading alcove overlooking the creek. Extras befitting its grandeur come with the room—chilled champagne and breakfast in bed.

The Eppses bubble with creativity, offering such special events as murder mystery or gourmet weekends. If you wish, they will help you plan your stay in the historic Salado area.

McKay House
306 East Delta
Jefferson, Texas 75657
903-665-7322 Jefferson
214-348-1929 in Dallas

Innkeepers: Tom and Peggy Taylor
Accommodations: 7 rooms
Rates: $75–$135
Included: Full breakfast
Added: 13% tax
Payment: Major credit cards
Children: With approval
Pets: Not permitted
Smoking: Outside only
Open: Year-round

This pristine 1850s Greek Revival cottage stands proudly in the heart of historic Jefferson, a town little changed since the steamboat era brought it prosperity and notoriety. Across the street is the House of the Seasons, a grand old mansion that is one of the most popular attractions in town. Thirty structures bearing Texas Historic Markers are within a five-block radius, and there are more than a hundred historic homes in all of Jefferson. The McKay House itself, built in 1851, is both a historic Texas building and is listed on the National Register of Historic Places.

Here on East Delta Street, life moves slowly, so slowly that it doesn't take long to get caught up in the tranquillity. The Taylors are adept at creating the illusion of living in an earlier era. They greet guests with lemonade and tea cakes on the front porch, where you can rock in white wicker chairs or enjoy the porch swing. At bedtime, ladies find Victorian nightgowns in the armoire and men, long sleep shirts. A Gentleman's Breakfast consisting of hearty country fare is served in period costume in the conservatory overlooking the garden.

In the main house are the three original guest suites, each of which has a 14-foot ceiling, a fireplace, a private bath, and distinctive antique furnishings. The McKay Room, decorated in blue, has a law library and rare papers in honor of Captain Hector McKay, an attorney and the owner of the house more than a century ago. The Quilt Room and the Spinning Room are aptly named and warmly appointed. Recently, the Taylors opened two large guest suites upstairs. Each has a separate sitting area in a restored Victorian gable and opens onto a balcony overlooking the garden.

Two other guest rooms are in a late 1890s Victorian cottage called Sunday House. It reflects a simpler lifestyle than the grand McKay House, but the decor is just as appealing and imaginative. The Keeping Room is a favorite with repeat guests because of its large fireplace, feather bed, and clawfoot tub.

Room with a View

These lodgings all boast beautiful settings as well as fine accommodations.

Arizona

The SunCatcher
105 North Avenida Javalina
Tucson, Arizona 85748
602-885-0883
800-835-8012

Innkeeper: Dave Williams
Accommodations: 4 rooms
Rates: single or double, $110–$130; each additional person $25
Included: Full breakfast and afternoon hors d'oeuvres
Added: 6.5% tax
Payment: Major credit cards
Children: Not permitted
Pets: Not permitted
Smoking: Not permitted
Open: Year-round

When you pull into the driveway at the SunCatcher, on the outskirts of Tucson, you will instantly understand why innkeeper Dave Williams, a veteran world traveler, chose this spot to settle on. Magnificent mountains and desert flora surround you. You half expect a lizard or coyote to run across your path at any moment, and you can in fact hear the call of coyotes in the distance when darkness falls.

The rather modest looks of the 1960s house do not prepare you for the beauty and elegance that await inside. A slanted clearstory sheds lots of light on a combination living room, dining room, kitchen and bar area. Exquisite Oriental rugs, bought on an excursion to the Far East, adorn the floor. At one end of the room there is a sunken sitting area encircling a fireplace; nearby there's a mesquite bar. Large picture windows frame the majestic mountains and desert landscape, and the best spot to enjoy the view from is the graceful dining table that extends the length of one wall.

With the exception of the Oriental, the guest rooms do not have exterior views, but in these impeccable rooms, the view is within their own four walls. Each is modeled after a world-class hotel — the Oriental after the Oriental in Bangkok, the Four Seasons after the Four Seasons Hotel in Chicago, the Connaught after the Connaught Hotel in London, and the Regent after the Regent Hotel in Hong Kong. Dave has visited these hotels in his travels, and all are known for their style and service. The Connaught room is decidedly British in tone with classic mahogany and Chippendale-style pieces. The Four Seasons, decorated in greens and beiges, has a canopy bed, a mahogany drop lid writing desk, and a stained glass window in the bath.

The Regent's decor blends the best of modern and Oriental styles for a sophisticated look. The headboard above the bed is illuminated; a stunning hand-painted fan from China is on display, as is a Tibetan prayer rug; and a cloisonné plate rests on a desk with inlaid leather, accompanied by a yew-backed writing chair. The Oriental-looking television table was actually purchased by the owner in Nogales, Mexico. The bath has a large sit-in shower, and the room itself opens onto the swimming pool and patio.

The Oriental is the most luxurious guest room, with matching inlaid Oriental furnishings including a graceful writing desk. But it's the Oriental's bath that's the most sumptuous of all. With marble floors, brass fixtures, a bidet, a large oval Jacuzzi, and a separate shower, you could spend hours pampering yourself and never leave the bath. Other amenities such as a hair dryer, makeup mirror, scales, Crabtree and Evelyn toiletries, extra towels, and large bath sheets for the pool are standard in all of the rooms. Also standard are a TV, VCR (there's a video library for guests to borrow from), telephone, extra pillows and blankets, reading chairs, and nightly turndown complete with a chilled bottle of mineral water. As further evidence of the care taken with each room, waste baskets are lined with rice paper and sprinkled with potpourri from the SunCatcher's own rose garden, and fresh flowers from the garden along with a welcoming note from the inn's gracious host await each guest in their room upon check-in. This is an inn where comfort and service are truly first rate.

Breakfasts, which alternate between sweet and savory, are served in the dining room. Perhaps it's an egg strata one day, stuffed french toast the next, and southwestern eggs the following day. Or if you prefer a cold breakfast, there will be bagels, muffins, cereal, and fruit. No matter what you have you won't go away hungry, and Dave always tries to prepare meals according to his guests' tastes. There is a different flavor of fresh brewed coffee each morning, and in the afternoon hors d'oeuvres are served on the bar or by the pool.

Active guests will enjoy the heated swimming pool, hot tub, and tennis court. The trailhead at Saguaro National Monument is only a quarter mile from the inn. For some, lounging by the pool and soaking up the sun and relaxed ambience are vacation enough.

New Mexico

Best Western Swiss Chalet Inn
1451 Mechem Drive
Ruidoso, New Mexico 88345
505-258-3333
800-477-9477

General manager: Gavin Mier
Accommodations: 82 rooms
Rates: single or double, $54–$74; $8 each additional person
Added: 10.82% tax
Payment: Major credit cards
Children: Under 12 free in room with parents
Pets: Small ones permitted with deposit
Smoking: Nonsmoking rooms available
Open: Year-round

Although the Swiss Chalet is just off of Highway 48 in Ruidoso, it has the remarkable feel of an inn in the Swiss Alps. Set on a hill, the inn has a white exterior accented with bright blue trim—it has an alpine look, as does the light pine-paneled lobby. Ahna-Michelle's, the hotel's German-style restaurant with checked tablecloths and cuckoo clocks, seems to stretch right out into the trees. It has floor-to-ceiling views of Sierra Blanca peak. A German buffet is offered on Friday nights, and entrées such as Weiner Schnitzel, a German sausage platter, and Die Drei Ecken (an omelette with German sausage, swiss cheese, potato pancakes and applesauce), add to the Bavarian ambience.

Rooms on the back side of the building have views of Sierra Blanca—a striking peak that's snow-capped for about two thirds of the year. Rooms are spacious and tastefully decorated in soft roses and blues. The rich wood furnishings are good reproductions of fine antiques. Guest rooms at the front of the hotel are off a glassed-in hallway, and although they don't have views, they are cheerful with painted headboards and dressers. Family and king suites have sleeper sofas.

The Honeymoon suite is the best in the house—it has a canopied four-poster king bed, extra pillows and dust ruffles, pretty floral prints, a comfortable sitting area, and a Jacuzzi bath.

For leisure, there is a small swimming pool in a glassed-in atrium designed to capture mountain vistas. A hot tub and sauna are nearby. The Swiss Chalet is one of the closets inns to Ski Apache, and Ruidoso Downs is only eight miles away.

Salsa del Salto

P.O. Box 453
El Prado, New Mexico 87529
505-776-2422

Innkeepers: Mary Hockett and Dadou Mayer
Accommodations: 6 rooms
Rates: single or double, $95–$160; $10 each additional person
Included: Breakfast
Added: 9.25% tax
Payment: Major credit cards
Children: Welcome
Pets: Not permitted
Smoking: On patio only
Open: Year-round

Not long after passing through the funky town of Arroyo Seco you will see the sign for Salsa del Salto. Set at the end of a private road in the Taos valley, the inn has expansive views that radiate in all directions. But the inn's location (about halfway between the town of Taos and the Taos Ski Valley) and incredible vistas are only two of the reasons to visit Salsa del Salto. There's a swimming pool, hot tub, and tennis court that allow guests to enjoy resort amenities without having to share them with the crowds one finds at a typical resort.

The inn itself is a new two-story adobe. Guest rooms open onto a quiet central courtyard, and are comfortably furnished in southwestern style. The Master's suite is a favorite of honeymooners, and has panoramic views and its own fireplace. The Truchas has views of the Truchas peaks, and La Familia has two connecting rooms. All rooms have private baths and king-size beds covered in cozy down comforters.

Gourmet breakfasts are served next to a stone fireplace and old-fashioned cast iron stove. Fresh croissants and homemade jams and jellies are specialties. Chips and salsa are served in the afternoon.

For skiers, who make up a large part of the inn's winter clientele, there's a ski rack in the main entrance hall where they can feel at home leaving their equipment. Throughout the inn, the recognition of one's need for rest and recreation sets it apart from more average bed-and-breakfasts.

Ski Lodges

New Mexico is the ski center of the Southwest, and its slopes are among the best in the country. All of these lodgings are within one mile of the slopes.

New Mexico

Austing Haus Hotel
Box 8
Taos Ski Valley, New Mexico 87525
505-776-2649
Fax: 505-776-8751

Innkeeper: Paul Austing
Accommodations: 26 rooms
Rates: $45–$115 in the summer, $88–$170 during ski season
Included: Continental breakfast
Added: 9.25% tax
Payment: Major credit cards; no personal checks
Children: Under 5 free in room with parents
Pets: Permitted
Smoking: Permitted
Open: Year-round

As you drive towards the Taos ski basin, you can't miss the Austing Haus Hotel—it has a white and black timber and glass exterior adorned with fanciful flowers. The cheerful building suggests the Bavarian Alps rather than northern New Mexico, but the two locales may not be as different as their distance would indicate since their terrain is so similar. The Austing Haus has the flavor of European ski chalet inside as well, especially in the restaurant.

The lodge's dining room is light and airy, with large picture windows, plants, stained glass panels, and country quilts on the walls. Queen Anne–style chairs pull up to light-toned wood tables. The meals here are widely considered to be the best in the ski valley. Entrées such as shrimp scampi, wienerschnitzel, medallions of beef Bordelaise, and veal Grecque range from $12 to $20. Paul Austing is the chef, serving his specialties of roasted duck with black Bing cherry sauce and rack of lamb. The menu at the Glass Dining Room proclaims, "If there is something you like that is not on the menu, by just asking it will be prepared for you." Your potential dining choices are almost limitless. (Unfortunately, the restaurant is open only during the winter.)

In 1984, Paul Austing and Chuck Jeanette proudly completed the 14-room lodge, a timber-framed construction with more than 3,000 interlocking joints and 1,600 oak pegs. Built of Douglas fir and ponderosa pine, it's lovingly referred to as "one giant piece of furniture." Beams are exposed both inside and out. The guest rooms, on two levels, are especially spacious, with queen-size beds and furniture made by Austing. Glass-walled hallways extend the length of the building, bringing you close to the wooded terrain.

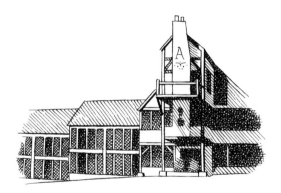

This is not the place to party late into the night since skiers tend to rise early to get the best snow. Hence quiet hours start at 10:30 P.M. and last until 7:00 A.M. Skiers will also appreciate the equipment storage lockers just off the lobby. The loft hot tub room, a charming nook with views of the snow-covered mountains, is a popular spot for relaxing after a day on the slopes.

All in all, a stay at Austing Haus is like a visit to a friend's home. Less expensive than most of the accommodations at the ski valley, and only a mile from the slopes, the inn offers excellent service in a pleasant environment. Paul Austing also operates the Columbine Inn next door, so if the hotel is full, he may be able to accommodate you at the Columbine. During the off-season, Austing Haus meets the needs of groups, pricing services according to their requirements. For example, groups can cut costs by acting as their own cleanup crew, both in the dining room and in the lodging areas.

The Legends Hotel
P.O. Drawer B
Angel Fire, New Mexico 87710
800-633-7463
Fax: 505-377-6401, ext. 617

General manager: Gary Plante
Accommodations: 157 rooms
Rates: $70–$150 during ski season, $50–$85 other times
Added: 10% tax
Payment: Major credit cards
Children: Welcome
Pets: Not permitted
Smoking: Permitted
Open: Year-round

In the Moreno Valley of the Rocky Mountains, 26 miles east of Taos, Angel Fire is a sprawling year-round resort village. Ski season gets top billing, with a 2,180-foot vertical drop and 55 downhill ski trails. A sophisticated snowmaking system covers 60 percent of the terrain, making this resort a good bet whatever the yearly snowfall.

When the ski slopes close in early April, Angel Fire begins its transformation for the spring, summer, and fall. Its championship 18-hole golf course has rolling greens backed by mountains. Tennis, horseback riding, and boating are all popular. Fishing is in a private, stocked lake (no license is needed). Big- and small-game hunting can be arranged through Resort Sports, in the resort village. Chamber music concerts and community theater productions highlight the summer season.

Spread over 12,000 acres, Angel Fire has both condos and single-family residences. The Legends Hotel — the only hotel at the resort — opened in late 1987. Originally the Plaza, the new hotel is a complete renovation, although its site, an Indian burial ground, has caused some to speculate that it's haunted. Right at the base of the ski slopes, the Legends has a contemporary design. A five-story atrium encloses a small swimming pool and hot tub. The Mill serves breakfast and lunch; Springer's is the elegant dining room. Annie O's, named for Annie Oakley, is the place to relax over drinks.

Although the guest rooms lack personality, they are unusually spacious, which is an advantage for skiers with lots of gear.

All have two queen-size beds. The studios, which can be rented separately or in combination with standard rooms, have cooking facilities (four-burner stove, oven, refrigerator) and a Murphy bed. The studios accommodate two people. Suites, which are a combination of a studio and hotel room, can sleep six. Presidential rooms are extra large and have private patios with mountain views.

St. Bernard Condominiums

P.O. Box 676
Taos Ski Valley, New Mexico 87525
505-776-8506

Resident manager: Kathy Humphries
Accommodations: 13 2-bedroom condos
Rates: $2,100–$2,600 per week for up to 6 people; packages available
Added: Tax and gratuity
Payment: Major credit cards
Children: Welcome
Pets: Not permitted
Smoking: In some units
Open: Thanksgiving to mid-April

The most luxurious lodgings in Taos Ski Valley are the St. Bernard Condominiums. About a 5-minute walk from the slopes, they are convenient to the ski area but are much quieter and less crowded than other accommodations in the village. In a long, three-story building, they overlook the valley.

The two-bedroom, two-bath units, accommodating up to six, are individually owned and decorated. They are roomy, and kitchens come fully equipped with microwaves, garbage disposals, and dishwashers. All units have phones, TVs, VCRs, and patios facing the ski slopes. (If you want to check out the skiing conditions on the mountain, all you have to do is step out on your patio.) And you don't have to shovel out your car when it snows—there is covered parking next to each unit.

After skiing, guests can use the hot tub and workout room at Hotel St. Bernard, at the base of the slopes. There's also a ski room in the hotel for the exclusive use of condo guests where skiing equipment can be left; skis don't have to be carried back and forth to the slopes each day. The hotel's restaurant, headed by a French chef, serves dinner.

Ski packages—a week's lodging, dinners at the hotel, ski lessons, and unlimited use of the ski lifts—are convenient and should be arranged in advance.

Spas

These spas are dedicated to revitalizing the body, mind, and spirit.

Arizona

Canyon Ranch Spa
8600 East Rockcliff
Tucson, Arizona 85715
602-749-9000
800-726-3335
Fax: 602-749-0662

Owner: Mel Zuckerman
Accommodations: 153 rooms
Rates: Start at $300 per night; 4-, 7-, and 10-day packages
  available; rates lower in summer
Included: Meals, airport transportation, medical screening,
  local calls, and spa programs
Added: 18% service charge; 6.5% tax
Payment: Major credit cards
Children: Over 14 welcome
Pets: Not permitted
Smoking: Nonsmoking rooms available
Open: Year-round

Canyon Ranch is a place where people go not to relax but to change their lives—for recreation in the literal meaning of the word. Geared to the health of the body and mind, it's a coed fitness resort and spa with an amazing array of facilities, classes, and services, all selected by the participant instead of the staff. People go to Canyon Ranch with different goals—to lose weight, to reduce stress, to become more fit, or to stop smoking. Through a combined program of exercise and nutrition, many find what they want. Unlike some spas, this one attracts as many men as women, all seeking rejuvenation through a healthier lifestyle.

In the Sonoran Desert on the edge of Tucson, the spa offers exercise options that take advantage of the area's beauty, such as hikes to nearby waterfalls and bike rides through Sabino Canyon. The entire complex is connected with paths flanked by desert landscaping.

The spa building itself pulsates with energy. The locker rooms overflow with amenities and are decorated with energy-evoking yellow, red, and orange. More than 30 classes are taught here, from water aerobics to yoga. Personal services are all-encompassing, including massage, herbal wraps, life change counseling, nutrition counseling, astrology, and biofeedback. Facilities include a weight room, gymnasiums, and racquetball courts. Three swimming pools and six lighted tennis courts are also on the grounds.

At mealtime, guests dine in soothingly beautiful surroundings on such delicacies as lamb chops Dijon, paella, and blueberry cheesecake. Menus come with a calorie count and guests choose what they eat. Whole grains, fresh fruits and vegetables, and the absence of refined flour and sugar, along with small portions, are at the heart of the cuisine. Meals are low in salt and have no additives or preservatives, and no caffeine or alcoholic beverages are served. To help guests continue healthy eating habits when they leave, there's a demonstration kitchen to teach food preparation the Canyon Ranch way.

Accommodations are in small buildings scattered over the resort's 28 acres. The standard rooms are fairly small, while executive kings have a sitting area, and casitas have a living room and kitchen in addition to the bedroom. The furnishings are modern and plush.

New Mexico

Vista Clara Spa
Box 11
Galisteo, New Mexico 87540
505-988-8865
800-247-0301
Fax: 505-988-8865

Owners: Chris and Carmen Partridge
Accommodations: 10 rooms
Rates: 3-day spa package $1,350, 1-week package $2,695

Included: All meals and spa facilities and programs
Added: 9% tax
Payment: Major credit cards; no personal checks
Children: No children under 14; 14 and over charged as adults
Pets: Not permitted
Smoking: Outside only
Open: Year-round

By the time you reach this out-of-the-way retreat, having driven the spectacular 22 miles from Santa Fe or the six miles from the Amtrak station in Lamy, past some of the most beautiful desert landscape around, you'll have already started to relax. Once on the property, you unwind even more as the attentive staff and high desert air and surroundings begin to work their charms on you. As you register in a hacienda that was once the last stage-coach stop before Santa Fe, you can smell the aroma of elegant food being prepared in the next room.

Vista Clara Spa was opened in mid-1990 by two New Yorkers, Chris and Carmen Partridge. They bought the property to use as a second home but soon realized that they wanted to spend all of their time here. They then developed the spa as a way to share their beautiful haven with others.

Although the property covers 80 acres, most of the buildings form a fairly compact compound. In addition to the main ha-cienda, there's an old cantina made from mud and logs that now houses a gift shop where spa treatment products are sold, a small but well-equipped gym, the building where guests stay, a new spa facility, and the Partridges' own home. One of the most interesting structures is the circular aerobics building, whose design is based on an Indian ceremonial kiva. Inside it has a sprung oak floor and copies of sacred Indian paintings on the walls. Similar Indian motifs are repeated throughout the spa, including the walls of the treatment rooms, making them a cut above the standard hospital-like rooms found in many spas.

The guest rooms are appealing and well crafted. They smell wonderfully of freshly cut wood and flowers; indeed, you'll find fresh flowers in your room, a basket of fruit, handsome willow branch closet doors, exquisite ornamental tin mirrors, and Per-sian rugs on the hardwood floors. The bathrooms are spacious and splendidly finished with tile and wooden cabinets, offering lots of storage. Each room has a private patio and a clock-radio. No televisions are provided, as guests are meant to be on re-treat. Amenities such as robes, sweatsuits, T-shirts, shorts, and room massage tables are all standard. Since most guests come to Vista Clara by themselves, the rooms have only one or two double beds. The upstairs rooms cost more because of their magnificent mountain views.

As relaxing as Vista Clara is, spa guests are expected to follow a fairly rigorous exercise program. Each participant is interviewed upon arrival by the spa director so that a fitness program can be specifically tailored to him or her. A typical day might include a 6:15 A.M. hike, breakfast, a morning stretch in the spa's "courtyard of the deities," an aerobics class, a body treatment, lunch, a gym training session, an outdoor activity, a massage (either in your room or at the spa), and end with a low-calorie, low-cholesterol, low-sodium meal in the dining room.

While the spa has many modern facilities, including a fair-size outdoor swimming pool (which can be covered in winter for year-round use), a secluded outdoor hot tub with gorgeous views, a steam room, sauna, cold plunge, and European showers, time-honored treatments are also available. In addition to clay body masks and herbal wraps, guests can try therapeutic Indian sweats and holistic fitness treatments. Most of these treatments are available to guests not in the program for an additional fee, and overnight guests are always welcome to use the gym, pool and hot tub free of charge.

Best of all is Vista Clara's size. With space limited to fourteen guests and a ratio of three staff members per guest, the facilities are never crowded, and service is definitely personal. A staff member will pick you up at the airport or arrange horseback riding for you at a nearby stable. (At press time, plans were under way to build stables at Vista Clara, so horseback riding may be a regular part of the program during your stay.) You can have your hair cut and styled right on the property, play volleyball with the other guests, or escape to a desert mesa on your own. If you are searching for a real retreat, you'll probably find it at Vista Clara.

Texas

Lake Austin Resort
1705 Quinlan Park Road
Austin, Texas 78732
512-266-2444
800-847-5637
Fax: 512-266-1572

Executive director: Deborah Evans
Accommodations: 40 units
Rates: $500–$640 for a 4-day fitness program, $875–$1,120
    for a 1-week program, 10 and 14-day programs also available
Included: All meals
Minimum stay: 4 nights
Added: 6% tax and a $22 per day service charge
Payment: Major credit cards
Children: Allowed during family weeks only
Pets: Not permitted
Smoking: Nonsmoking rooms available
Open: Year-round

On the shores of Lake Austin just outside Texas's capital, there's a spa dedicated to fitness education and conditioning. Its atmosphere is unpretentious and friendly; its program is comprehensive, including exercise, nutrition, wellness classes, and beauty services. In a peaceful setting and with personal attention, participants work to achieve their goals, especially weight loss and a more healthful lifestyle, with the help of a physical fitness staff, a dietitian, and an exercise physiologist.

Guests can choose from twenty daily workouts, including Hill Country walks, low to high power aerobics, and an 18-station Swiss Parcourse. Classes on such subjects as relaxation, skin care, and nutrition are integral to the program. For relaxation as well as exercise, there's both an outdoor and indoor pool, a jogging track, paddleboats, and shuffleboard. All exercise facilities are available around the clock.

The guest rooms, in a low building facing the lake, have two double beds, TVs, and phones. The dining room is pleasant and casual. Guests are served a thousand-calorie-per-day menu. The emphasis is on wholesome food, featuring fresh vegetables and herbs grown at the resort. For those wishing to continue their healthful eating habits at home, the resort sells its own cookbook, with more than 450 low-fat recipes.

Pampering services, available at an extra charge, include skin analysis and facials, massages, manicures, and hair and skin treatments. Special spa packages are offered throughout the year.

The Phoenix Fitness Resort
111 North Post Oak Lane
Houston, Texas 77024
713-685-6836
800-548-4701 in Texas
800-548-4700 in U.S.
Fax: 713-680-1657

Executive director: Sally Kerr-Lamkin
Accommodations: 5 rooms in-house, 297 at hotel
Rates: $1350–$1550 for 6 nights
Included: All meals and spa program
Added: 15% tax on hotel rooms
Payment: Major credit cards
Children: Not appropriate
Pets: Not permitted
Smoking: Not permitted
Open: Year-round, except for New Year's and Christmas
weeks

The Phoenix is a top-rated luxury spa dedicated to one's overall health and well-being. Founded in 1980, it addresses physical fitness, nutrition, and the emotions. "Guests come for a new beginning," says a Phoenix representative. "Many want to get their lives in order." Weight loss may or may not be one of their goals.

The spa is in the Houstonian, a multifaceted facility comprising a hotel and conference center, health and fitness club, and a center for preventive medicine. Despite its urban location, the Houstonian is a wooded retreat, with winding paths and a wealth of fitness and recreational facilities. The program is primarily for women over 18, though occasional coed weeks are held.

Spa participants, limited to fifteen, have a choice of two programs. Both include fitness (stretching, toning, low-impact aerobics, advanced weight equipment, water exercise, brisk walks); nutrition (1,000-calorie-per-day menu, low in fat, sodium, and refined sugar); personal testing (body composition; strength, flexibility, and cardiovascular testing; personal fitness consultation); lectures (lifestyle management, fashion, healthy cooking, nutrition, eating disorders); and a beauty program (massages, facials, manicure and pedicure, hair styling).

The more expensive Ultimate Week has a broader beauty program than the Fitness Week Plus. Beauty services are at the Christine Valmy salon, in the fitness club. When guests aren't involved in scheduled workouts, they can use the Houstonian Health and Fitness Club's racquetball and tennis courts, lap pool, outdoor and indoor tracks, whirlpools, saunas, and Swedish showers.

The Ambassador House, once a private home, is a nucleus for the Phoenix. Spa participants eat together in its private dining room, relax at its pool, and gather in the living room for lectures or socializing. Accommodations are on a separate floor of one hotel wing, accessible only to Phoenix guests. Aerobics classes are in a studio used by the Phoenix exclusively.

The staff members include a nutritionist, chef, psychologist, physiologist, and image consultant as well as a physical fitness team.

The atmosphere is casual at the Phoenix: no need to dress for dinner here. The schedule, while regimented, is flexible and can be modified for each person. Guests are encouraged to participate in the full program, but primarily, the staff "want everyone to get out of the program what they came for," says a spokeswoman.

Town Inns

Like small city hotels, town inns have a special character and charm as well as a desirable location.

Arizona

Los Abrigados
160 Portal Lane
Sedona, Arizona 86336
602-282-1777
800-822-2525 in Arizona
800-521-3131 in U.S.
Fax: 602-285-0982

General manager: Paul Poer
Accommodations: 183 rooms
Rates: double, $125–$185; suite, $150–$235; $1000 for the entire old stone house
Added: 10.5% tax
Payment: Major credit cards
Children: Under 16 free in room with parents
Pets: Not permitted
Smoking: Permitted
Open: Year-round

Los Abrigados is in the center of town, yet it is easy to miss because it's tucked behind Tlaquepaque, Sedona's popular shopping village. Tlaquepaque is modeled after an actual arts and crafts village in Mexico, and Los Abrigados has a Mexican look as well. A massive terra cotta and tile fountain stands at the entrance to the hotel; lodgings are spread among red tile–roofed buildings that are peppered with small fountain courtyards.

Guest rooms are decorated in rich plum tones complemented by soothing greens and pinks. Furnishings are contemporary and attractive, if not distinctive. Some rooms have separate sitting areas, others have private patio spas. For a splurge you can rent out the entire Old Stone House, which was built more than sixty years ago.

Los Abrigados has an excellent spa with a weight room, aerobics room, and fully equipped locker rooms that have hot tubs and steam rooms. Pampering services such as massage, body wraps, and tanning beds are available. There is a $10 fee per day for spa use, and special services are extra. The inn also has a pleasant outdoor pool and poolside bar, as well as several tennis courts.

At mealtime, the hotel's Canyon Rose restaurant presents interesting fare that can best be described as nouvelle southwestern. For dinner, entrées such as seared ahi tuna dusted with southwestern seasonings and veal chops topped with a mango salsa sauce and served with potato Napoleon range from $17 to $24. For lunch, dishes such as beer-battered halibut in a tarragon tartar sauce add zest to more traditional noontime offerings. The restaurant's Sunday brunch is a festive affair.

Los Abrigados is ideally situated for exploring Sedona and its environs.

New Mexico

Inn on the Alameda
303 East Alameda
Santa Fe, New Mexico 87501
505-984-2121
800-289-2122
Fax: 505-986-8325

General manager: Gil Martinez
Accommodations: 42 rooms
Rates: single, $145; double, $155; suite, $250
Included: Continental breakfast
Added: 10.125% tax
Payment: Major credit cards
Children: Free in room with parents
Pets: Permitted with $50 deposit
Smoking: Nonsmoking rooms available
Open: Year-round

A small, conveniently located hotel offering personal service —that's the Inn on the Alameda. Only two blocks from the Plaza, this pueblo-style adobe lodging is a quiet retreat, secluded from the hubbub, yet within easy walking distance of many attractions.

The inn opened in 1986, and in a short time it has become one of the most popular in Santa Fe. Its buildings range from eighty to two years old, yet throughout there's a fresh look. It's as though you're entering someone's home when you enter the inn.

The guest rooms are spacious and airy, reflecting their southwestern locale but with a modern flair. Much of the furniture is handmade, such as aspen-pole beds, flagstone tables, and mirrors framed in hammered tin. Wood is an important accent, from pine ceilings to latilla chairs. Most of the rooms have a private patio or balcony, and all have air conditioning, cable TV, terrycloth robes, and phones. The rooms have either one king- or two queen-size beds, some angled for a distinctive look. Six casitas have private entrances, wet bars, and sitting areas in front of cozy fireplaces. The bathrooms are above average for the area, with theatrical bulb lighting and full-length mirrors.

Breakfast is served buffet-style next to the library (or it can be brought to your room from 7:00 to 11:00 A.M. for a $2.50 service charge). Typical fare is coffee cake, croissants, blueberry muffins, raisin rolls, bagels, fresh fruit, fresh juice, and coffee. At night the breakfast room becomes a gathering spot where drinks are served at the latilla bar. Out in the courtyard, an enclosed blue tile whirlpool is shaded by apricot trees — truly a romantic nook.

But the best thing about Inn on the Alameda is its service. The general manager visits with guests at breakfast, and the desk clerks are sincere when they ask how they can help you.

Hotel parking is free.

La Posada de Santa Fe

330 East Palace Avenue
Santa Fe, New Mexico 87501
505-986-0000
800-727-5276
Fax: 505-982-6850

General manager: Michael Swanson
Accommodations: 119 rooms
Rates: single or double, $110–$295; suites, $185–$395
Added: 10.125% tax
Payment: Major credit cards
Children: $10 extra per night for chidren over age 12
Pets: Not permitted
Smoking: 35 nonsmoking rooms available
Open: Year-round

Only two blocks from the bustling Plaza, La Posada is a world unto itself. Its rooms, spread out over six acres surrounding a pleasant central courtyard, offer respite from the nearby summer crowds, and each opens on to its own patio. You never feel as if you're at a city hotel.

The Staab House, named for the well-to-do merchant who built it in 1882, is the focal point of the hotel. There the main dining room specializes in New Mexican cuisine and abundant Sunday brunches. The house also has an impressive oak bar for cocktails, a guest library with burgundy leather couches that's perfect for curling up with a book, an elegant private dining room for small groups, and a number of Victorian guest rooms.

The rest of the rooms are in adobe buildings that were built from the 1930s to 1987. Decorated in Santa Fe style, the rooms are all different. Those at the lower end of the price scale can be small and dark, while the deluxe suites are spacious and beautifully furnished with ornamental tinwork, handmade furniture, flagstone floors, skylights, colorful Mexican ceramic tile bathrooms, viga ceilings, and kiva fireplaces, all made by local artisans. Eight rooms have refrigerators, and most have fireplaces. Since the accommodations vary so much, be specific about what you want when making a reservation.

During the summer, guests can enjoy the outdoor swimming pool and a leisurely meal on the sunny garden patio. In the winter, guests enjoy the Santa Fe Ski Basin, 18 miles from the hotel. Of course, Santa Fe's renowned art galleries are open year-round.

Service at the hotel can be less than courteous at times, but if you like to be able to walk to the city's sights, La Posada is a good choice.

Texas

Townsquare Inn
21 South Bell
Bellville, Texas 77418
409-865-9021

Innkeeper: Deborah Nolen
Accommodations: 9 rooms (most with shared baths)
Rates: single, $45; double, $55; suite, $75
Added: 6% tax
Included: Continental breakfast
Payment: Major credit cards
Children: Welcome
Pets: Not permitted
Smoking: Permitted
Open: Year-round

In the town of Bellville (pop. 2,500), Townsquare Inn is at the center of activity. Part of a group of businesses run by the same owners, it's on the second floor of a building that also houses the Tea Rose restaurant, Tap Room Pub, and Timeless Interiors design shop. Several antiques shops (one of Bellville's claims to fame) are within a few blocks. And, as promised by its name, the inn is indeed on the town square, overlooking the county courthouse.

Deborah Nolen, an interior designer, has converted the second-story space into a lodging of beauty. Chintz, stained glass, and greenery play a large part in the decorating scheme. Comfort is the keynote, from spacious living quarters to such conveniences as digital clock radios. More flexible than most accommodations of this genre, Townsquare has two three-bedroom suites, two adjoining rooms, and a grand suite. Guests in the three-bedroom suites, ideal for small groups, share a parlor with a TV and game table and a bathroom with a clawfoot tub and shower. (One, two, or three bedrooms can be reserved.)

The Court (with a queen-size bed) and the Chambers (twin beds) adjoin and can be used separately or jointly. The baths are across the hall—one for men and one for women. The Bell Suite is worth its $65 price tag. Not only is it spacious, with a parlor and private bath, but its decor is decidedly romantic. The king-size bed is canopied in lace. The elegant bathroom has a clawfoot tub, a toilet with a pull chain, and a dressing table.

Continental breakfast is placed in the kitchenette at the end of the hall long before most guests awaken. But beware—the aroma of country cooking at the Tea Rose may entice you to skip the muffins and head downstairs.

Yacht Club Hotel and Restaurant
700 Yturria Street
Port Isabel, Texas 78578
512-943-1301
Fax: 512-943-1301

Owners: Ron and Lynn Speier
Accommodations: 24 rooms
Rates: single, $35–$45; double, $42–$52; suites, $49–$99 for 2; $10 each additional person
Included: Continental breakfast
Added: 10% tax
Payment: Major credit cards; no personal checks
Children: Under 12 free in room with parents
Pets: Not permitted
Smoking: Permitted
Open: Year-round

Across the bridge on South Padre Island, gleaming new condo towers are the norm. But in the fishing village of Port Isabel, the Yacht Club Hotel puts you in touch with history. The atmosphere is vintage 1920s, the guest rooms are comfortable, and the seafood restaurant is one of the best in the area. The Spanish stucco structure was built in 1926 as an exclusive private club for the most prominent families in the Rio Grande Valley. Then, in 1934, it opened as a fine hotel. But over the years it declined, eventually closing in 1969.

Today the hotel is completely refurbished. New interiors, modern plumbing, and blessed air conditioning have all been added. The overall effect is of a Spanish hacienda. In the back there's a secluded swimming pool bordered by hibiscus. The main dining room, an addition to the original structure, is bright and airy yet in keeping with the Spanish theme.

The guest rooms are small but pleasant, decorated in rich green and white with matching bedspreads and drapes. The baths are completely modern. Telephones, though no TVs, are in each room. The suites are a good choice, with separate bed and sitting rooms. The staff is friendly, setting the tone for guests to socialize.

Wherever you stay, there's hardly a better place to enjoy shrimp, trout, and red snapper than at the Yacht Club Restaurant. Port Isabel calls itself "the Shrimp Capital of the World," and the hotel maintains a high dining standard.

The Southwest

Geography and Climate

The American Southwest is huge. Texas is the second-largest state in the country, New Mexico the fifth largest, and Arizona the sixth. Oklahoma is the Southwest's only "average" size state; with 69,000 square miles, it comes in as the nineteenth largest.

In all, the four states account for nearly 566,000 square miles of land, almost the equivalent of Spain, Portugal, France, and Italy combined. From the western border of Arizona to the eastern border of Texas it is about 1,200 miles by air. From northern Oklahoma to the tip of Texas it is about 800 miles.

The weather in the Southwest varies tremendously. Southern Arizona has mild winters and hot summers, making it popular in the winter and reducing summer rates in some area as much as 50 percent. But even in the summer, the mountains north of Phoenix are pleasantly cool, serving as a retreat for both visitors and natives.

In general, the peak tourist season in the other three states is the summer. Much of New Mexico is mountainous, from Chama and Raton in the north to Cloudcroft and Ruidoso in the south. In New Mexico, the Great Plains meet the Rockies, providing a dramatic contrast. Elevations range from 2,800 to 13,000 feet. In the winter, the mountains turn into winter playgrounds, attracting skiers with long runs and incredibly beautiful terrain.

Oklahoma, whose highest point is not quite 3,000 feet, is characterized by forested rolling hills, sprawling lakes, and widespread plains. Texas's landscapes vary widely. There are vast open spaces in West Texas punctuated by magnificent mountains, huge cattle ranches in the Panhandle and the South, pine woods in East Texas, gently rolling Hill Country, and hundreds of miles of Gulf Coast beaches.

Moving from the east to the west, the rainfall in the Southwest decreases, resulting in semitropical to desert climates. The variety of plant and animal life is remarkable. From the desert, with its low creosote bush and its giant saguaro, the landscape rolls to high mountains with Douglas fir, blue spruce, and quaking aspens. The whooping crane and roadrunner, black bear and ringtailed cat, mountain lion and armadillo, all live in the Southwest.

Not only is the land varied, but so is the style of life. You can drive from a city of three million to a ghost town tucked into the high mountains and on the way pass miles and miles of uninhabited, uncluttered land. Here is the magic of the Southwest, inviting your soul to soar as you revel in the untouched balanced by the civilized.

The Character of the Southwest

Spanish explorers traveled over much of the Southwest, beginning in the mid-1500s. Until the middle of the 19th century, much of this land belonged to Mexico. Then, settlers began streaming in from other parts of the world—not just from the United States but from Europe and the Orient as well. Texas alone claims twenty-six ethnic groups as part of its heritage. The Spanish, and later the Mexicans, left an indelible imprint on the Southwest. In some areas, especially in central New Mexico and Oklahoma, so did the native Indians.

Today, Southwest style refers to the intermingling of the Indian, Spanish, and Anglo cultures. In some regions it is unmistakable. Santa Fe and Taos show it best, with their adobe architecture and Indian and Mexican crafts, such as pottery and weaving. So distinctive is the look that modern artists have been inspired to make their own southwestern statement, resulting in daring sculpture, woodcarving, and art.

In other parts of the Southwest, the Spanish influence, while still present, is more subtle. But you can sense it whether you're ordering enchiladas in Dallas or staying in a casita in Phoenix. Some parts of the Southwest have a very close kinship to Mexico. Two thirds of El Paso's population is Hispanic. The Mexican border with Texas, from Brownsville to Laredo to Del Rio, is almost a country all its own, a beautiful blend of the two cultures. San Antonio celebrates its Spanish heritage every day in its architecture, cuisine, and celebrations.

Oklahoma, with more than seventy Indian tribes, is strongly linked to those who first called the land their home. In the summer, it holds the world's largest Native American celebration, Red Earth.

The Southwest is more than Spanish architecture, Mexican food, and Indian crafts. The cowboy and the Old West are still here—alive and well. Fort Worth and Tucson are good places to experience it. So are the guest ranches in Arizona and Texas. And sprinkled throughout are pockets of other cultures, adding grace and charm to the whole. The German settlements in New Braunfels and Fredericksburg are especially notable. So is Castroville, with its Alsatian history.

Wherever you travel in the Southwest, you'll find it's unlike any other region in the country. Its special cultural mix, exquisite landscape, and excellent cuisine are worth sampling again and again.

Itineraries

These itineraries outline our favorite things to see and do in or near some of the towns where an establishment in the book is located. All the towns that appear in **boldface** *have an establishment described in the book.*

East Texas

The East Texas landscape is rife with pine forests, lakes, and meadowlands. Caddo Lake, mysterious with its moss-draped trees and maze of bayous, offers excellent fishing. The Big Thicket National Preserve is luxuriant with centuries-old trees, brilliant wildflowers, and flora found nowhere else in Texas.

The Alabama-Coushatta Indian Reservation, the oldest in Texas, is in the preserve. There is a Living Indian Village, open to visitors, and mini-tours of the Big Thicket originate here.

East Texas is a good place to touch base with the history of Texas. In the 1800s, steamboats from New Orleans plied Caddo Lake, and more than two hundred a year docked in **Jefferson**, which became the largest city in the region. Today visiting Jefferson, with a population of less than 3,000, is like taking a journey back to a slower era. Antebellum homes open for touring, antiques shops, and Old South restaurants line its streets. Riverboat excursions go to Caddo Lake or on moonlight serenade cruises. Jefferson is worth getting to know. Spend at least one night there and soak up its charm.

Nearby **Marshall**, population 25,000, has many historic houses of its own. Most are open only during special weekends, but a driving tour will put you in touch with the spirit. Several are now B&B lodgings. Marshall can serve as a base for enjoying other East Texas attractions, especially the Texas State Railroad. With twenty-five restored antique coaches, the train runs for 25 miles through the heart of East Texas, connecting Rusk and Palestine.

Farther south, **Nacogdoches**, with a population of 28,000, is one of the most historic towns in Texas. The places to visit include Old Stone Fort, built in 1779 as a Spanish trading post, and Millard's Crossing, with restored 19th-century buildings.

To the northwest, **Tyler** is a bustling business center of 70,000 residents. Its best-known visitor attraction is the municipal rose garden, with more than 38,000 rosebushes in 500 varieties. The peak season runs from April through October, and the annual Rose Festival is in October. Historic homes are in the Azalea District and in Charnwood. Tyler State Park, north of the city, is excellent for fishing, boating, and hiking.

Houston Area

Exuberant **Houston** has numerous historic sites, sophisticated new architecture, glamorous malls, romantic turn-of-the-century shopping villages, and ethnic and elegant restaurants to its credit.

A leader in the arts, Houston has a complete performing arts repertoire and an exciting variety of museums. Architecturally grand Wortham Center, opened in 1987, is the home of the Houston Grand Opera and the Houston Ballet. The Alley Theater has a resident professional theater company presenting plays on two stages. Jones Hall is the home of the Houston Symphony Orchestra.

The Menil Collection museum, opened in 1987, has a rich display of art from primitive to ultra-modern. The Museum of Fine Arts has works from around the world, including a large collection of Remington westerns. The nearby outdoor sculpture garden has more than thirty works by such artists as Matisse, Calder, and Ellsworth Kelly. Bayou Bend is a museum within a museum. The house itself, on spacious grounds, was the home of a prominent Houston philanthropist; inside is a fine collection of American art and furnishings.

Other attractions include the Museum of Natural Science and Planetarium, the Houston Zoo, Sam Houston Park (restored houses in a park beside the city's skyscrapers), and San Jacinto Battleground and Monument, commemorating the site where Texas won its independence.

Sports fans will enjoy seeing the Houston Astros and Oilers play in the Astrodome. A feat of modern engineering, tours are given of the dome when there are no games. Astroworld/Waterworld, just down the road, is great for family entertainment. So is Fame City, a stylish indoor entertainment mall. The Children's Museum has participatory exhibitions, such as a video recording studio, computer center, and Texas frontier town. The Great Southwest Equestrian Center has thousands of acres of riding space as well as a large arena where horse shows are held on most weekends.

Johnson Space Center, south of Houston, is one of the most popular attractions in Texas. Self-guided tours take you through exhibitions in seven buildings of the NASA complex, ending with a visit to Mission Control.

Galveston

Proud of its heritage, Galveston has a strong commitment to preservation, and reconstructions range from a sailing ship to a historic railroad museum. Citywide, more than 500 structures bear Texas Historical Commission Medallions. The East End Historical District is lined with wonderful Victorian homes. The castlelike Bishop's Palace, built in 1877, is considered one of the nation's 100 most outstanding buildings by the American Institute of Architects. The renovated 1894 Grand Opera House, once played by Sarah Bernhardt and Anna Pavlova, welcomes modern performances.

In downtown Galveston, the Strand National Historic Landmark District takes you back to the turn of the century with its gas streetlights and shops straight out of a Victorian novel. You can put a coin in the nickelodeon, watch taffy being pulled at the candy store, and shop for antiques and handmade gifts.

The Railroad Museum (more than a collection of railroad cars) has displays that also take you to an earlier era. A few blocks away is Galveston's own tall ship, *Elissa*, a square-rigged merchant sailing ship that you can explore. Sea-Arama Marineworld, Seawolf Park (with a World War II submarine to tour), and *The Colonel* paddlewheeler (offering daytime and evening cruises) add variety to a rich menu of visitor attractions.

Well designed for tourists, Galveston has a sightseeing train, trolley rides, horse-drawn carriages, and audio walking tours. Pick your favorite.

Of course, you'll also find all of the expected beach activities. Anglers can choose from pier, surf, deep-sea, and bay fishing.

A city that celebrates year-round, Galveston has numerous festivals. The most popular are Mardi Gras, Dickens on the

Strand (early December), the Historic Homes Tour (May), and the Jazz Festival (November). Reservations should be made far in advance.

Bluebonnets to Prairie Chickens

Whatever the season, this part of Texas has idyllic pastoral landscapes, historical interest, and country charm. It's the sort of countryside with a village every 15 miles, each one inviting you to stop awhile.

A good place to start is Washington-on-the-Brazos State Historical Park, where the Texas Declaration of Independence was signed in 1836. From 1842 to 1846, Washington served as the capital of the Republic of Texas. The Star of the Republic Museum commemorates this portion of the Lone Star State's history.

Historic **Navasota**, a town of 6,000, is nearby. In addition to touring its own sites, you can visit a winery near Bryan. To the south is **Chappell Hill**, once called "the Athens of Texas." The home of two colleges in the mid-1800s, it was a real intellectual center. Today there are fewer than 400 people in the community, but homes from its grand era remain. More than 25 structures have historical markers.

Bellville is bigger than Chappell Hill. It even has a town square. Antiques shops abound in Bellville. So does rural charm. Down the road in **Columbus**, population 4,000, there are historic homes, interesting shops, and a restored opera house. Called the City of Live Oaks, it's nostalgic and romantic.

Weimar, about 15 miles west of Columbus, is a country town with a look of the West. Antiques shopping and kolache eating are the best reasons to visit.

About prairie chickens. **Eagle Lake** is only 17 miles south of Columbus, yet it has an entirely different look. Gone are the massive live oaks; instead, you gaze upon miles of grassland where rice farming is the main industry. Duck and goose hunting is the most popular sport. Nearby is the Attwater Prairie Chicken Refuge, a sprawling expanse dedicated to saving the declining prairie chicken population. One of Eagle Lake's most prominent landmarks is the Farris 1912 hotel, which caters to hunters during season, from November through January.

Other interesting towns include Winedale with its music festivals, Round Top with a reconstructed historic village, and Egypt with a restored plantation.

Austin Area

The capital of Texas is renowned for its beauty. The pink granite capitol stands tall at one end of downtown. Nearby is the University of Texas, with more than 45,000 students. At the other end of the central business district is Town Lake, a gem with a beautifully landscaped shoreline. In midtown is Old Pecan Street/Sixth Street, Austin's version of Bourbon Street, lined with restaurants, clubs, and shops.

Attractions in **Austin** include the LBJ Presidential Library and Museum, the O. Henry Home, and the Elizabeth Ney Museum, the studio of Texas's first eminent sculptress. The Laguna Gloria Art Museum displays 20th-century pieces in a Mediterranean villa on the shores of Lake Austin.

Children will enjoy Barton Springs, in Zilker Park. The spring-fed natural swimming pool is nearly as long as a football field. The nearby Rose Gardens and Oriental Gardens are well worth a stop.

Lake Travis, west of the city, is one of seven Highland Lakes, popular for fishing and boating. To the northwest, outside Johnson City, the LBJ Ranch is popular for touring.

About 40 miles north of Austin is the village of **Salado**, a stagecoach stop on the Old Chisholm Trail. Life moves slowly in Salado. There are a handful of historic sites and a pleasant assortment of country shops—all to be enjoyed at a leisurely pace.

Southeast of Austin is Bastrop, another slow-paced town with a bent toward history. The oldest weekly newspaper in Texas is published here. More than 130 sites are listed on the National Register of Historic Places. Bastrop State Park, with boating and hiking, is one mile from town.

When you're ready to relax and absorb the essence of the Hill Country, head back to Austin to the Oasis Cantina, where dining terraces are tucked into a cliffside overlooking Lake Travis. The Mexican fare is wonderful, and the mood is festive. But the best part comes at sunset. A bell rings to announce its advent. Oohs and ahs come from diners scattered among the terraces. Just as the bright red ball slips below the horizon, the audience applauds. You may never be at the Oasis again, but wherever you are, sunset will take you back.

The communities in the Hill Country have their own character. **Fredericksburg** retains its German heritage. Historic buildings reflect the life of the early settlers, and restaurants serve locally made sausages and pastries. The former Steamboat Hotel houses the Museum of the Pacific War, a tribute to its native son, Fleet Admiral Chester Nimitz.

New Braunfels, also a German settlement, gives visitors a taste of Texas history combined with outdoor fun. Tour the Museum of Texas Handmade Furniture and the Sophienburg Museum (a great introduction to local history). Slide down the Tube Chute at Prince Solms Park. Visit the winery at Gruene and stay to dance in the oldest dance hall in Texas. Spend an afternoon at Schlitterbahn, a water amusement park with the Cliffhanger Tube Chute, Schlittercoaster, and water slides. Wurstfest, in November, is the main event.

On the eastern edge of the Hill Country, the town of **San Marcos** is at the headwaters of the crystal clear San Marcos River. Tubing, canoeing, and kayaking are popular here. At Aquarena Springs, you glide along in a glass-bottom boat. To the west, **Kerrville**, on the banks of the Guadalupe, is a center for arts and crafts, music festivals, and summer youth camps. Its sights include the Cowboy Artists of America Museum and the Hill Country Museum. The Kerrville area is a great base for a family vacation, with lots of opportunities for outdoor fun.

The tinytown of **Bandera**, on the jade-green Medina River, is surrounded by a number of Texas's guest ranches. The countryside, with beautiful rocky limestone cliffs, spring-fed streams, and stately trees, is also popular for hunting.

Dallas/Fort Worth

Dallas, a center for finance, fashion marketing, and technology, brims with cultural, shopping, and entertainment choices. The Dallas Museum of Art, focusing on 19th- and 20th-century American and European painting and sculpture, was the first facility in the downtown arts district. In the West End Historic District is West End Marketplace—a lively complex of shops, restaurants, and nightclubs. Other sites include Old City Park and its twenty-five historic buildings, Fair Park and its multiple museums, the John F. Kennedy Memorial, and Southfork Ranch.

Fort Worth proudly wears the title of Cowtown, and its cowboy heritage is on display in the Stockyards Historical District. Western shops, restaurants, and saloons line the streets in an area that was once a major stop on the Chisholm Trail.

But there's another side to Fort Worth. Renowned for its art collections, the city has an outstanding museum district. The Kimbell Art Museum houses many European masterpieces. The Amon Carter Museum features the work of Frederic Remington and Charles Russell as well as other American artists, including Georgia O'Keeffe and Winslow Homer. The Fort Worth Art Museum focuses on 20th-century works. The Museum of Science and History, the largest such museum in the Southwest, has an Omni Theater presenting simulated adventures such as hang gliding and scuba diving. And there's more —the tranquil and beautiful Japanese Gardens, Log Cabin Village, Sundance Square (a restored Victorian shopping district), and the Water Garden, downtown.

Arlington is a family entertainment center, with Six Flags Over Texas, Wet 'n Wild, and Texas Rangers baseball. International Wildlife Park and Traders Village ("the Disneyland of Flea Markets") are nearby.

Irving's Texas Stadium is the home of the Dallas Cowboys. Visitors can tour the nearby Valley Ranch to see the Cowboys' training area and the cheerleaders' dance studio. In Las Colinas, Mandalay Canal Walk is a small version of San Antonio's Riverwalk. Shops line the banks of the canal, and water taxis take visitors to different sights. "The Mustangs of Las Colinas" is one of the largest bronze sculptures ever created. Also in Las Colinas is the Dallas Communications Complex, a thriving film studio. Its National Museum of Communications has vintage recordings and broadcasts for viewing and listening.

Granbury Country: Opera to Dinosaurs

In the bustling Dallas/Fort Worth area, life moves at a brisk pace. When you yearn for something simpler, head to **Granbury**. The square at the center of this Victorian town is the place to begin. Hood County Courthouse, on the square, was restored in 1969, sparking interest in similar projects. Now antiques stores, craft shops, and country restaurants surround the square.

The Granbury Opera House, built in 1886, has outstanding productions, drawing audiences from throughout the metroplex. Old Hood County Jail, a western jail built in 1885, is open for tours.

Near Granbury is Dinosaur Valley State Park, where you can step inside dinosaur tracks (there's also a visitors center), and Fossil Rim Wildlife Ranch, with more than 800 exotic animals spread over cedar-covered hills.

On the outskirts of **San Antonio** are four Spanish missions, established by Franciscan friars early in the 18th century. At the heart of the city is HemisFair Plaza, the site of the 1968 Texas World's Fair. Its Institute of Texas Cultures highlights the twenty-six ethnic and cultural groups that shaped the state.

El Mercado, a Mexican marketplace with shops and restaurants, is a great place to savor the city's Mexican flavor. La Villita Historic District is a charming walled village next to the Riverwalk. The site of a Spanish settlement two centuries ago, it now has galleries, cafés, and shops in restored buildings.

The McNay Art Museum, housed in a former private mansion, has a collection of impressionist and post-impressionist works. One gallery in the Museum of Art is devoted to Mexican folk art. The Witte Museum focuses on natural history.

Attractions especially for children include Sea World, the 250-acre oceanarium that's kin to Sea World of California and Florida, Brackenridge Park, San Antonio Zoo (with one of the largest bird collections in the country), Hertzberg Circus Museum, and Plaza Theater of Wax, with a spooky Theater of Horrors.

Find time for the performing arts in San Antonio. The beautifully restored Majestic Theater is a work of art in itself. Performances are especially enjoyable in the open-air Arneson River Theater, overlooking the Paseo del Rio.

San Antonio is also a city of festivals, many celebrating its Spanish and Mexican heritage. Ask at the tourism office for a festival calendar.

Only 14 miles west of San Antonio is a town with an entirely different history, **Castroville,** an Alsatian community settled in 1844. The immigrants built their homes of native limestone and cypress, and about 100 of them remain, some inhabited by descendants of the original settlers. The Alsatian culture permeates the community, not just in architecture but in customs. Castroville is a charming, slow-paced town—a good place to go hunt for antiques, with time out to sample the bakeries.

Corpus Christi Area

Texas's largest city on the Gulf of Mexico, **Corpus Christi** sparkles with activity. With a large, landscaped marina at its front door, it also serves as the northern gateway to Padre Island, most of which is a national seashore.

Corpus Christi Bay—dotted with sailboats, yachts, and excursion boats—is the city's focal point. Because of the winds on the bay and the area's warm water, Corpus Christi is often the site of major windsurfing championship races. You can rent sailboards, Jet Skis, and aqua cycles yourself at People Street T-Head. The nearby Water Street Market has several excellent seafood restaurants. Water taxis can give you a tour of the harbor or take you from Shoreline Boulevard to Corpus Christi Beach.

Corpus Christi has several good museums. The Art Museum of South Texas has changing exhibitions of fine art. Corpus Christi Museum is especially good for children, with hands-on exhibitions, a wonderful Barnum and Bailey room, and nature displays. The Texas Aquarium's exhibitions on marine life should appeal to the entire family.

With its beautiful beaches and abundant sealife, the nearby national seashore on Padre Island should not be missed. It is not uncommon to see porpoises and sea turtles while you swim.

Across Corpus Christi bay on Mustang Island is **Port Aransas,** a famous fishing destination. Anglers can take day-long trips into the Gulf for sailfish and marlin or fish for trout, redfish, and drum from the jetties and pier.

Corpus Christi is a good hub from which to explore nearby attractions. Aransas Wildlife Refuge, the winter home of the whooping crane, is 60 miles north. Slow-paced Rockport, 30 miles northeast, has an outstanding historic house, Fulton Mansion. Known as an artists' community, Rockport has art studios and galleries open to the public. King Ranch, the world's largest working ranch, is 40 miles southwest (visitors welcome from 9 A.M. to 4 P.M.).

The Tex-Mex Express train links Corpus Christi to Laredo. You can take a one-day round trip or stay overnight in Laredo. (See La Posada in Laredo.)

South Padre Island

The town of South Padre, incorporated in 1973, is geared to tourism, its shore lined with gleaming high-rises. North of town, the road continues for seven miles, paralleling a wildly beautiful undeveloped stretch of beach.

The beach is the star attraction at South Padre. The sand is white, the water is turquoise, and the climate is semitropical, making it a year-round destination. Vacationing here means sunning, swimming, surfing, strolling, collecting shells, and building sand castles—fun in the sun at a leisurely pace. Fishing is also a favored pursuit, with excellent bay and surf fishing as well as deep-sea excursions.

Back on the mainland, **Port Isabel** is a fishing village with a feeling of history. Its lighthouse is a state historic site.

Laguna Atascosa National Wildlife Refuge, 20 miles northwest, is excellent for bird-watching. Matamoros, Mexico, only 25 miles south of South Padre, is a popular day trip, offering a glimpse of Mexico and shopping for Mexican crafts.

Brownsville, Texas's southernmost city, is connected to Matamoros, Mexico, by a toll bridge. In Brownsville itself there's the Gladys Porter Zoo, a 31-acre preserve with rare and endangered animals in natural surroundings.

McAllen is eight miles from Reynosa, Mexico. The McAllen International Museum has exhibitions of Mexican folk art as well as local history. West of McAllen is the historic town of Rio Grande City, which retains some of its early architecture. Following the river north leads to Falcon Dam and International Reservoir, owned jointly by the U.S. and Mexico. Huge Falcon Lake is famed for fishing, especially for black bass and catfish.

North of the semitropical valley is Laredo, across the border from Nuevo Laredo. More like Mexico than any other major city in Texas, it has a colorful history dating from the 1700s. Seven flags have flown over Laredo: those of Spain, France, Mexico, Texas, the Confederacy, the United States, and the short-lived Republic of the Rio Grande, with Laredo as its capital.

Far West Texas

A land of rugged beauty, West Texas is craggy mountains and a wide-open desert sprinkled with remnants of the past such as frontier forts and Indian trails. So beautiful is the region that it has two national and several state parks.

Big Bend National Park is a dramatic blend of the Chihuahuan Desert and the Chisos Mountains. Long before you get to **Big Bend,** you leave civilization behind. According to legend, *chisos* was an Apache word meaning "ghost," and indeed, there is a mystical feeling in these mountains. Driving through the park whets your appetite to see more. Hiking, backpacking, horseback riding, and whitewater rafting are excellent ways to envelop yourself in the grandeur.

The views from the South Rim are unbeatable. Here you are indeed on a rim: the vertical drop is 2,500 feet. Before you stretches a panorama so wide and so deep that no camera lens can capture it. Old Mexico is straight ahead. Before you is an untouched wilderness. Surely no one else has ever been here.

West of the park is tiny **Lajitas,** a slip of a town in the midst of the starkly beautiful terrain. Once there was a military fort where the western-style town now stands.

The road between Lajitas and Presidio is an experience in itself. With grades as steep as 15 percent, the road roller-coasters over mountains, through canyons (you can almost touch the sheer walls), and across fields strewn with giant red boulders. Surely a sculptor shaped those mountains; surely an artist painted them in brilliant reds and white. All the while the Rio Grande runs below, sometimes with vigor, sometimes serene and slow. There's little sign of civilization here. You share the road with only a few others.

About 80 miles to the north are the gentler Davis Mountains, which offered a refuge for the pioneers who settled the West. Fort Davis National Historic Site puts you in touch with this part of history.

Guadalupe Mountains National Park, which opened in 1972, contains four of Texas's highest peaks. El Capitan, a sheer, 1,000-foot cliff, is distinctive against the desert landscape. For day-trippers, McKittrick Canyon and its beautifully varied vegetation are well worth visiting. A trail leads through the floor of the sheer-walled canyon. Guadalupe is primarily a backpacker's park, laced with miles and miles of trails. (The best place to stay here is in a backpacker's tent, high in the mountains, cuddled up with someone you love.)

Other sites to visit in Far West Texas are Monohans Sandhills State Park (4,000 acres of wind-sculpted sand dunes), Hueco Tanks State Historical Park (860 acres of caves and towering rock formations surrounded by desert), the Caverns of Sonora (a delicate beauty), and McDonald Observatory near **Fort Davis** (visitors center open daily). At the observatory, the giant telescope can be used only on the last Wednesday of each month; write ahead to make arrangements.

Just across the Rio Grande is Juarez, Mexico, the largest city on the border. Residents and visitors move easily between the two cities, intermingling their cultures. Two thirds of **El Paso's** residents are Hispanic, and throughout the city there's a South of the Border flavor.

The city sprawls over 240 square miles. Old Spanish missions, unusual museums, a western ranch with hayrides, and bargain shopping make El Paso a good place for family vacations. In the city is the Tigua Indian Reservation, the home of one of the oldest identifiable ethnic groups in Texas and one of the oldest Indian communities in North America. A tribe that nearly disappeared in the 20th century, the Tiguas reunited in recent years and set about to preserve their culture. At their living pueblo you can see native dances, craft demonstrations, and historical displays. The restaurant is especially popular, serving spicy Indian dishes and bread baked in beehive ovens.

Other attractions include Indian Cliffs Ranch (outdoor western exhibitions and a steak restaurant), Fort Bliss (U.S. Army Air Defense Center for rocket research and combat training, a variety of museums open to the public), the El Paso Museum of Art, and several Indian missions. Sunland Park, for horse racing, is 5 minutes from downtown.

Half of the fun of visiting El Paso is going across the border. Attractions in Juarez include shopping, dog racing, and bullfighting.

Heading into New Mexico, about 45 miles northwest of El Paso at the foot of the Organ Mountains, is **Las Cruces** — a city of 45,000 whose economy is based on agriculture, industry, and education (it's the home of New Mexico State University). Right next door is tiny **Mesilla,** one of the most historic towns in the Southwest. Founded in 1598 and once a major stop on the Butterfield Trail Overland route, it is known as the site of the signing of the Gadsden Purchase. White Sands National Monument is between Las Cruces and Alamogordo.

Silver City is about 100 miles northwest of Las Cruces (you turn north at Deming, famous for the annual Deming Duck Race). The countryside changes from desert shrubs to forests. Silver City, on the southern edge of the Gila Wilderness, is the headquarters for Gila National Forest. The Gila Cliff Dwellings National Monument is about 35 miles north of town.

In 1870 Silver City was an overnight boom town, for indeed silver had been discovered. In more recent years its economy has been based on ranching and copper mining.

In the intervening years cosmopolitan **Oklahoma City,** Oklahoma's capital, has come a long way. At its heart is a rich heritage. Indian culture is prominent, though today's Indians tend to wear business attire. In June 1987 a new annual event made its first appearance: Red Earth is a gathering of Indian tribes to celebrate their traditions, featuring an arts and crafts festival and competitions in such events as Pow Wow dancing.

The Kirkpatrick Center Museum Complex is a treasure house. Indeed, it is a complex, with the Omniplex Science Museum, the Air Space Museum, the Center of the Indian, the International Photography Hall of Fame, and a planetarium. Other attractions in the city include the National Cowboy Hall of Fame and Western Heritage Center, the Oklahoma Museum of Art, and the National Softball Hall of Fame.

About 30 miles north is **Guthrie,** Oklahoma's territorial capital and the first state capital. A town of 10,000 residents, Guthrie values its history. About 100 red brick buildings from the late 1880s still stand, the largest collection of commercial Victorian buildings in the U.S. In addition to picturesque shops and country-style restaurants, the spectacular Scottish Rite Temple is a top visitor attraction.

Tulsa Area

The Gilcrease Museum, built on the estate of the oilman Thomas Gilcrease, is a poignant portrayal of the American frontier — the Indian, the cowboy, the pioneer. With more than 8,000 paintings, thousands of artifacts from various Indian cultures, and a collection of rare books and manuscripts describing life in the New World, the Gilcrease is considered to be the most outstanding museum of its type in the world. Frederic Remington, Charles Russell, George Catlin, Olaf Seltzer, Winslow Homer, and Albert Bierstadt are some of the artists represented here.

The Philbrook Museum of Art, in the Italianate villa of the famed oil baron Waite Phillips, features Italian Renaissance painting and sculpture as well as an art collection from around the world.

Opera, ballet, symphony, and theater all have a full repertoire in **Tulsa.** The Performing Arts Center is a few steps from the Westin Hotel, Williams Center.

Other attractions include Oral Roberts University and the Fenster Gallery of Jewish Art. Families can enjoy Tulsa Zoological Park and Big Splash Water Park.

But whatever else you do, make time for Rodgers and Hammerstein's *Oklahoma!,* presented in an outdoor theater on the outskirts of Tulsa. Named in 1985 by the American Bus Association as one of the Top 100 Events in North America, this musical extravaganza is thoroughly delightful, full of energy and zest. You'll leave the theater singing.

In Claremore, about a 30-minute drive to the northeast, is the Will Rogers Memorial Museum. Galleries in the sprawling hilltop museum display memorabilia of the cowboy philosopher, and videotapes of his life are shown several times a day.

Oklahoma's Outdoors

Oklahoma, the home of more than seventy Indian tribes and settled by hardy pioneers, maintains strong ties to the land. A state of lakes, plains, and rolling hills, some of its best attractions are outdoor adventures.

Oklahoma's Tourism and Recreation Department does an excellent job of operating resorts, each with its own personality and set of attributes. Lake Texoma Resort in south-central Oklahoma is on a 93,000-acre lake; fishing for striped bass is a major draw. Roman Nose Resort, in red shale hills 70 miles northwest of Oklahoma City, has hiking trails and a natural rock swimming pool.

In the northeast corner of the state is Grand Lake O' the Cherokees, a 59,000-acre lake with 1,300 miles of shoreline. The fishing is excellent, with largemouth and white bass, catfish, and sunfish as the favored catches. **Afton** is the center of resort activity.

Lake Eufaula, south of Tulsa and east of Oklahoma City, is the grandest lake of all. Its nickname is the Gentle Giant. Covering 102,000 acres, the lake is surrounded by hickory, elm, maple, and pecan trees. Fishing, boating, and hiking are all popular.

Overall, Oklahoma has 560 parks, lakes, resorts, and campgrounds. Outdoor sports range from golf to tennis, canoeing to hunting, horseback riding to rockhounding.

Albuquerque

Throughout, there's evidence of the three cultures that have shaped **Albuquerque**: American Indian, Spanish, and Anglo-American. Attractions include the Indian Pueblo Cultural Center, depicting the history of the state's nineteen Indian pueblos, the Albuquerque Museum, with the largest collection of Spanish colonial artifacts in the U.S., the Maxwell Museum of Anthropology, with southwestern crafts, and the Albuquerque Museum of Natural History.

Sandia Crest, at an elevation of 10,678 feet, is a year-round attraction just north of downtown. A paved road leads to the top, which offers a panoramic view of the city. Sandia Peak, popular for winter skiing and summer sightseeing, is accessible by tramway, chair lift, and a 1½-mile trail from Sandia Crest. The tramway, the world's longest with a 2.7-mile ride, glides over deep canyons and lush wooded terrain. A restaurant is at the summit of Sandia Peak.

Maps for driving tours are available from the Albuquerque Convention and Visitors Bureau. Choices include a trip through the Sandia Mountains, a Native American culture tour (Petroglyph State Park, Coronado State Monument, Isleta—a living pueblo), science and technology (Museum of Natural History with hands-on exhibitions, National Atomic Museum), nature (Rio Grande Zoo, Rio Grande Nature Center State Park), and shopping in districts ranging from historic to cosmopolitan.

In October, hot-air balloons dot the skies during the spectacular Albuquerque International Balloon Fiesta, the largest such festival in the world. The state fair, held every September, is especially enjoyable with its Spanish and Indian villages, nightly rodeos, and thoroughbred horse racing. Throughout the year colorful Indian dances and festivals are held.

For diehard baseball fans, Albuquerque is the home of the Dukes, a triple-A team in the Los Angeles Dodgers' farm system. Intimate Dukes Stadium is a great place to see a game at close range. Many Dukes players have gone on to be major-league all-stars.

If you're driving to Santa Fe from Albuquerque, take the Turquoise Trail through the old mining towns of Madrid, Cerrillos, and Gold. Many of Madrid's dilapidated miner's shacks are being renovated by artists and opened as studios and galleries. Cerrillos still has the look of the Wild West and is frequently used as a movie backdrop for Westerns.

About an hour west of Albuquerque, Acoma Pueblo—called Sky City because it's built on top of a mesa—is also of interest.

Santa Fe Area

The history, architecture, and culture of **Santa Fe** all combine to make it truly the City Different. Founded in 1610, it served as the capital of the Spanish Kingdom of New Mexico and the Mexican province of Nuevo Mejico. It has been the state capital ever since New Mexico gained statehood, in 1912.

Some of the oldest buildings in the United States are in Santa Fe, and the Spanish-Pueblo adobe architecture unifies the city, giving it a distinct identity and beauty.

Art galleries and special shops, museums, and historic sites offer a vast assortment of things to do and places to see. The Plaza, now as when it was laid out by the Spanish, is the center of activity. Art workshops and galleries stretch along Canyon Road.

Top sightseeing choices include the Palace of the Governors, St. Francis Cathedral, the Mission of San Miguel of Santa Fe, the Wheelwright Museum of the American Indian, the Fine Arts Museum, and the Museum of Indian Arts and Culture. Children will enjoy the outstanding Museum of International Folk Art and the Santa Fe Children's Museum. South of town is Rancho de las Golondrinas, a charming replica of a colonial village, with exhibitions of such crafts as candle making and blacksmithing.

The Santa Fe Opera is one of the top companies in the world. A few miles north of town, the open-air theater is dramatic in itself, overlooking the mountains. The season runs from early July though August. The Santa Fe Desert Chorale and Chamber Music Festival also have regular performances during the summer.

The biggest event of the summer is in August—Santa Fe's annual Indian Market. For one weekend in late August the Plaza is covered by stalls of the finest Indian arts and crafts around, attracting more than 100,000 visitors. Some of the art is so fine that dealers queue up at the booths of renowned artists the night before the market opens in order to have the first pick of the lot the next morning. (Hotel rooms should be booked a year in advance.) The Spanish Market takes place in late July, and Fiesta, kicked off by the burning of Zozobra (Old Man Gloom), takes place the weekend after Labor Day.

Perhaps the best time to visit Santa Fe is during the holiday season, when the entire city is dressed up in luminous farolitos. Santa Fe is one of the few remaining places where traditional Christmas ceremonies still take place, partly due to its Spanish heritage. With a soft snow falling, the pungent smell of piñon luminarias (bonfires), and carolers' songs drifting through the air, the season is truly magical.

Santa Fe is one of the most popular tourist centers in itself, but within an hour's drive are many other attractions. Nearby Indian pueblos include Nambe, **Pojoaque,** Picuris, San Juan, San Ildefonso, Santa Clara, **Taos,** and **Tesuque.** The Shidoni

Foundry and sculpture garden is also at Tesuque. (The foundry can be toured on Saturdays; the garden is open daily.)

Bandelier National Monument, the site of an ancient Indian culture that made its home in cliff dwellings, is 46 miles northwest of Santa Fe. Bandelier is also a nice spot for picnicking and hiking. The drive from Santa Fe, with hairpin turns and breathtaking vistas, is exhilarating. Ruins of an old Indian pueblo are preserved at Pecos National Monument, 27 miles east of Santa Fe.

Los Alamos National Laboratory, the home of the atomic bomb, is 35 miles northwest, and the quiet country town of **Galisteo** is 23 miles south. The High Road to Taos leads to the craft villages of **Chimayo,** renowned for its weavers and sacred Santuario, Cordova, with its woodcarvers, and Truchas, another weaving center in an alpine setting.

Outdoor enthusiasts have a broad range of choices in the area, especially whitewater rafting on the Rio Grande and fishing, hiking, and horseback riding in the Santa Fe National Forest. The Santa Fe Basin ski area, 16 miles northeast of the city, has 3 chair lifts and 38 trails—20 percent beginner, 36 percent intermediate, and 44 percent advanced. The facilities are geared to day use only, with no overnight accommodations.

Whatever else you do in the Santa Fe area, be sure to sample the regional cuisine. Some of the best-known restaurants are the Pink Adobe, Guadalupe Cafe, the Shed (lunch only; for great green chile dishes try its sister restaurant, La Choza), Coyote Café, and Tomasita's. Of course, the best food you eat may be in the little café you discover on your own.

Taos

Taos is New Mexico in microcosm. It's an art colony and a living pueblo, with outdoor adventures, museums of the Southwest, regional cuisine, and personable lodging.

The town is in a high valley at the foot of the Sangre de Cristo Mountains. To the west is a far-reaching desert plain dramatically cut by a gorge. To the north are the mountains.

Taos is not large; it has about 3,600 residents (though the number is growing), and reflects a combination of Indian, Spanish, and Anglo influences. The Plaza is the focus of activity, and there are many art galleries (more than eighty in the area), boutiques, and restaurants to lure you.

Pueblo de Taos, on the Tewa tribe's 95,000 acres, is three miles northeast. Approximately 1,800 Indians live in the terraced adobe buildings, the oldest continuously inhabited structures in the U.S. By choice, the Indians' life is simple, with no electricity or running water. (Fees are charged for entering the pueblo; cameras incur additional charges.)

Numerous sites in Taos recall its history and describe its character. The Kit Carson Home, occupied by the Indian scout from 1843 to 1868, is filled with memorabilia from his era. The D. H. Lawrence Ranch is 15 miles north of town. San Francisco de Assis Church, built over a 35-year period beginning in 1710, is an excellent example of Spanish churches. The Millicent Rogers Museum displays North American and Hispanic art and artifacts.

Much of Taos County is within the Carson National Forest, a scenic playground. Each season brings its own special flavor. The fall's golden aspen leaves give way to winter, when snows cover the nearby mountains and attract skiers. Staying in Taos is a good option, enabling skiers to vary their terrain with day trips to Taos Ski Valley, Angel Fire, Sipapu, and Red River. Springtime is for fishing and hiking. Summer is popular for all sorts of recreation, including whitewater rafting on the Rio Grande. The Taos Box is an exhilarating 17-mile run through Rio Grande Gorge. Raft trips begin at Arroyo Hondo, north of Taos.

Taos has it own small balloon fiesta at the end of October and an annual fall wool festival. Nearby Dixon has an artist's studio in November (well worth the trip to see the artist's eclectic homes alone).

Taos Area Skiing

Although there are beginner slopes, Taos is best known for its expert runs, and new skiers are often intimidated. The top elevation is 11,819 feet; the vertical drop is 2,612 feet. One triple and 6 double chair lifts take skiers to the 71 runs: 51 percent are expert, 25 percent intermediate, and 24 percent beginner.

Taos's ski school, with nearly 100 full-time instructors, prides itself on small classes and personal attention. Children can start classes at age 3. The Kinderkaifig Program, for ages 3 to 6, is a combination of ski lessons and indoor activity.

A shuttle service connects Taos Ski Valley with the town, and special shuttles go to area attractions.

Ski season runs from Thanksgiving until early April. Lodging packages—some with meals, lift tickets, and ski lessons—are available in the ski valley and lodges in town. You can make reservations at any area lodges by calling 800-992-SNOW (U.S.) or 505-776-2233 (New Mexico). Note: If you're staying in a condo on the slopes, buy groceries before ascending the mountain.

Angel Fire, 26 miles east of Taos, is a sprawling village covering more than 12,000 acres in the Moreno Valley. With houses, condominiums, and recreational facilities, it's a year-round playground. Despite an 18-hole golf course, 6 tennis courts, a 37-acre fishing lake, and horseback riding, Angel Fire's top priority is its ski program. With 55 trails—78% of which are beginner and intermediate—it's a good place for families.

The top elevation is 10,680 feet; the vertical drop is 2,180 feet. The longest run, Headin' Home, is a 3½-mile beginner run. Six lifts go up the mountain, and lift lines are usually short. Sixty percent of Angel Fire's mountain is covered by a snowmaking system. The season runs from mid-November through early April.

In addition, Angel Fire also has cross-country skiing, complete with equipment rental and instruction. Snowmobiling is also popular. For the vacationer, there's snowmobile rental and instruction; for the racing enthusiast, there are monthly competitions.

Winter resort activities include hayrides, campfire cookouts, teen activities, sightseeing tours, and swimming in a heated pool. Little Angels Day Care provides supervision for children from 6 weeks to 11 years, with indoor activities and fun in the snow. Numerous ski packages are available, some for families and others for adults.

Northeast New Mexico: Fish to Catch and Stories to Tell

About 40 miles southwest of the pass, near the town of **Cimarron,** Maxwell built a home that looked like a fortress. (Today it's part of Philmont Scout Ranch.) Later he built a mansion, and Cimarron sprang up around it.

Over the years the town developed a well-deserved reputation for being wild and woolly. Outlaws such as Billy the Kid, Clay Allison, and Black Jack Ketchum frequently came to call. Today's Cimarron is a quiet little ghost of a town. Maxwell's grist mill is now a museum, filled with four floors of history. The old stone jail, the original plaza, and other mid-19th-century buildings tell the town's story.

The countryside, especially north and west of Cimarron, is

rich in wildlife, and the waters teem with fish. Eagle Nest, at 8,200 feet, is known for its trout fishing.

South of Cimarron, about 60 miles as the crow flies, is **Las Vegas,** another stop on the Santa Fe Trail. (Two branches of the trail entered New Mexico; the branch passing through Las Vegas was called the Cimarron Cutoff.) By the 1880s it had become a leading commercial center of the West.

Today's Las Vegas has 14,000 residents. Proud of its history, the town has preserved a downtown historical district and residential sections with beautiful Victorian homes. Fishing and hunting are popular here.

Chama

Just south of the Colorado border, in the Rocky Mountains at about 8,000 feet, **Chama** is a popular center for outdoor recreation. A land of ponderosa pine forests, rolling grasslands, lakes, and rivers, it's an excellent setting for fishing, hunting, and hiking. During the winter, cross-country skiing, snowmobiling, and ice fishing are favorite activities.

The top attraction is the Cumbres and Toltec Scenic Railroad, which runs between Chama, New Mexico, and Antonito, Colorado. The historic narrow-gauge steam train winds through 64 miles of mountain country, running daily from mid-June to mid-October. Make reservations as far ahead as possible, and bring warm clothing!

From Chama, the train stops at the midway point, Osier, Colorado (not a town, really; just a water tank and a building). You can either ride the train round-trip to Osier; ride the train one way to Antonito and return by van; or ride the train to Antonito, stay overnight, and return by train the next day.

About halfway between Chama and Santa Fe is the town of Abiquiu. Once you see the colorful rock formations that surround the lake at Abiquiu dam, you'll understand why the painter Georgia O'Keeffe was so inspired by the landscape and made it her home. There is a small museum of desert animals at the visitors center, right on the main highway on the Chama side of the dam.

South Central New Mexico: Horse Racing to Golf in the Sky

Lincoln National Forest spreads across the Capitan and Sierra Blanca Mountains to the north and the Sacramento Mountains to the south. Forests of fir, juniper, and pine, laden with snow in the winter, provide a cool retreat in the summer.

Ruidoso is both a winter and summer playground. Ski Apache, with 38 trails and 8 chair lifts, is 16 miles northwest of town. (There are no accommodations at the slopes.) During the rest of the year the area is popular for hiking, camping, and fishing; nearby Bonito and Nogal lakes are the favored fishing spots. Ruidoso Downs, featuring quarterhorse and thorough-bred racing from May through September, draws thousands of visitors.

Tiny **Cloudcroft,** at an elevation of 8,600 feet, is a year-round destination. In winter there's skiing at Ski Cloudcroft—25 trails and 1 chair lift. Snowmaking covers 60 percent of the ski area. Cross-country skiing, snowmobiling, and ice skating are other winter sports.

In the summer there is golfing on one of the highest courses in the world. There's also horseback riding, hiking, and visiting nearby attractions, especially Sacramento Peak Observatory.

Carlsbad Caverns National Park is 76 miles southeast of Ruidoso.

Phoenix and the Valley of the Sun

In the rolling Sonoran Desert, **Phoenix** is a magnet for vaca-tioners. Its resorts are among the best in the world, with 85 golf courses and more than 1,000 tennis courts in the area; you can also go horseback riding, soar, sail, balloon, ride a riverboat, fish, hike, and pan for gold. Sophisticated shopping and dining and a broad range of cultural activities are also appealing.

The Valley of the Sun refers to the twenty-plus communities around Phoenix. **Scottsdale** is the resort center, with many choices spread along Scottsdale Road and East Scottsdale Drive. **Carefree** is to the north, **Litchfield Park** far to the west.

Greater Phoenix offers many diverse places to visit. The Desert Botanical Garden has an enormous collection of cacti, desert flowers, and unusual plants. The Arizona Living His-tory Museum is a complex of buildings depicting the region's history, from a miner's camp to a Victorian mansion. The Heard Museum shows Indian life in the Southwest, with such displays as kachina dolls, Navajo weaving, and Zuni jewelry. The Fleischer Museum, devoted to American Impressionist painting, opened in 1990. The desert home of Frank Lloyd Wright, Taliesin West, now a school of architecture, is open to visitors. And at the Cosanti Foundation you can see the plans for futuristic cities designed by the urban planner Paolo Soleri.

Other attractions include Frontier Town in Cave Creek, Soleri's futuristic town, Arcosanti, in Cordes Junction (about an hour north of Phoenix), Fountain Hills World's Highest Fountain, Heritage Square in Phoenix, the Phoenix Art Museum, and Arabian horse ranches. There are also many art galleries in the Scottsdale area.

Phoenix is a popular hub for exploring other parts of Arizona. Day trips include Apache Trail, which winds through the desert and mountains to the town of Globe, Mongollon Rim, with a face of multicolored rock (Zane Grey country), the Casa Grande Indian ruins, Montezuma Castle and Well, Prescott, and Sedona. The Grand Canyon is a 5-hour drive.

Winter is the prime time in this area. (Summer rates at resorts are reduced as much as 50 percent.) The Phoenix and Valley of the Sun Convention and Visitors Bureau operates a toll-free number enabling you to make reservations at more than 100 resorts and hotels in the area as well as at Grand Canyon National Park lodges (800-528-0483 in the U.S., 800-221-5596 in Arizona).

Prescott to Sedona

About 35 miles north of Phoenix you leave the flat desert and begin to climb. By the time you reach **Prescott,** the elevation is over 5,000 feet. Surrounded by mountains, the former capital of the Arizona Territory is a quiet town of 20,000 residents.

Prescott hasn't always been quiet. Truth is, before the turn of the century it was a rip-roaring town. In 1863, gold was discovered in the central Arizona highlands, and a year later, Prescott was born. Its Whiskey Row became the whooping-up place for gold rushers.

At the Sharlot Hall Museum you can walk into the town's early days. A collection of historic buildings, it chronicles Prescott's history. (Sharlot Hall, a poet, historian, and preservationist, was one of the first women elected to the Arizona Women's Hall of Fame.) A folk arts fair is held at the museum complex in the spring, featuring such crafts as spinning, weaving, woodcarving, and blacksmithing.

The Smoki Museum displays artifacts of the ancient southwestern Indian. The Smoki People, organized in 1921, are white men and women dedicated to preserving the Indian way of life. The group has become famous for its production of Indian ceremonies and the Smoki Snake Dance.

Scenic drives abound in the Prescott area. One of the most finest is over Mingus Mountain to Jerome. The pages of Arizona Highways come alive as the road twists and turns, then opens onto incredibly beautiful views.

Jerome, a near–ghost town reborn, literally clings to the mountainside. It has its own museum and interesting shops. Then it's on to magical **Sedona** in Red Rock Country, a spectacle of red spires and buttes, pinnacles and mesas. The center of tourism is at the junction of U.S. 89A and Highway 179. Within a few blocks is Tlaquepaque, a tiny village of arts and crafts shops reminiscent of the area in Guadalajara for which it is named.

North of town winds Oak Creek Canyon, thickly wooded and wonderfully scenic. To the south is the Village of Oak Creek. Here the land is equally beautiful but entirely different, with prominent bare red rocks. West of town is mysterious Boynton Canyon, with spectacular red monoliths and wind-sculpted formations.

There's much to do in Sedona. Jeep tours take you deep into Red Rock Country. Hiking, horseback riding, and fishing are also good options. Renowned as an art center, Sedona has lots of galleries and shops.

You can take an interesting side trip to Montezuma Castle National Monument, where prehistoric cliff dwellings are set in a great limestone cliff.

Flagstaff to Grand Canyon

Ten miles to the northeast of Flagstaff is Sunset Crater National Monument. Continuing on U.S. 89 for 27 miles will take you to Wupatki National Monument, the site of prehistoric Indian ruins. East of Flagstaff on I-40, only 7 miles from town, is Walnut Canyon National Monument. Wooded trails lead down into the canyon to Indian cliff dwellings tucked beneath limestone ledges. The visitors center is excellent, with hands-on exhibitions.

Meteor Crater, 3 miles in circumference, is 46 miles east of Flagstaff. To the southeast are Mary, Mormon, and Ashurst lakes, popular for fishing and boating. Oak Creek Canyon is 12 miles south of Flagstaff on U.S. 89A. To the north is Fairfield Snow Bowl, with winter skiing and summer sky rides. The Museum of Northern Arizona and Lowell Observatory are also a short distance north of town.

The grandest sight of all, **Grand Canyon,** is 80 miles north.

Driving along the rim, hiking down trails, riding muleback, and flying over the canyon in a helicopter—all give you different perspectives on the spectacular chasm. The South Rim is the center of tourist activity, with a full range of services. The North Rim, only 15 miles by air but about 200 miles by road, also has accommodations in a wooded, serene setting. With fewer tourists, the mood is more tranquil to the north.

The Petrified Forest and Painted Desert are several hours east of Flagstaff. Even farther, on the Arizona-Utah border, the eerie shapes of Monument Valley look like long forgotten ruins of once glorious temples from a distance. Canyon de Chelly is farther east, near the New Mexico border; while it can't compare to the splendor of the Grand Canyon, it has a tranquil beauty all its own. Escorted pack trips and jeep tours take you to the base of the canyon (on Indian land, so individuals cannot enter unescorted), where you'll find a lush green river valley, Indians living in hogans (traditional circular homes), and the remains of their ancestral cliff dwellers in the red canyon walls.

Wickenburg

Folklore has it that back in the early 1860s, Henry Wickenburg vented his anger at his ornery ole mule by striking it with a rock. But Henry struck more than he bargained for—a lot more. When the rock hit ground, it split open to reveal a streak of gold.

Indeed, there was gold in them thar hills, and the Vulture Mine proved to be one of Arizona's richest. Life was fanned to a frenzy in the gold rush days. You can still see the "jail tree" in downtown **Wickenburg,** used by lawmen to chain up the bad guys. (That was before the town could afford an honest-to-goodness jail.)

The Desert Caballeros Western Museum on Frontier Street depicts the town's early way of life. But the best way to get in tune with the Old West here is to stay one of the guest ranches described in this book.

Tucson

Plan to spend a long time in **Tucson.** There are sights to see, canyons to explore, mountains to hike in, horses to ride, golf courses to play on, and outstanding restaurants to dine in. Tucson itself deserves as much time as you can stay. Then there are day trips to many more places.

In Tucson, you can't help but be fascinated by the saguaro cactus, which grows only in the Sonoran Desert. Many are as tall as 30 or 40 feet, some even taller. With multiple arms growing in every direction, each cactus is different. It's easy to understand why the Indians believed that the cacti dance. As soon as a human being looks at them, they stop—freezing their arms in all sorts of contortions.

Although Arizona is the youngest state in the continental U.S., Tucson is the oldest continually inhabited settlement in the country. When Father Eusebio Francisco Kino, a Jesuit missionary from Spain, first visited the area in 1687, he found the land inhabited by Pima and Sobairpuri Indians.

One of the most famous places in the area is Mission San Xavier del Bac. The mission founded by Father Kino was several miles from the present site. When Apaches destroyed it in the late 18th century, Franciscan fathers built the present one. A mix of Moorish, Byzantine, and Mexican architecture, the cool white structure is known as the White Dove of the Desert. Open for visitors, it is still an active mission.

Some of Tucson's highlights are:

Arizona-Sonora Desert Museum A combination zoo, aquarium, botanical garden, and natural history preserve spread over 12 acres; one of the top zoos in the country.

Old Tucson A replica of Tucson in the 1880s; built as a movie set in 1940 and still used for movie productions; also a western theme park with shootouts and street brawls, stagecoach rides, and Wild West entertainment.

Old Town Artisans An adobe village with more than 300 artists exhibiting their work.

University of Arizona The university has a planetarium, Southwest Indian art, history and art museums, and the Center for Creative Photography.

Historical displays and sites include:

The Arizona Historical Society Near the University of Arizona. John C. Fremont House and Fort Lowell.

Saguaro National Monument Two sections of park preserving the giant cacti: the Rincón Mountain section is east of town, the Tucson Mountain section to the west. There is a visitors center at Rincón Mountain and hiking and nature trails in both areas.

Colossal Cave Called the largest dry cavern in the world (no one has ever discovered its end); famous as a robber's hideaway. Spectacular colors.

Mount Lemmon The highest peak in the Catalina Mountains (9,157 feet). The drive up from the desert goes through six climatic zones—the equivalent of traveling from Mexico to Canada. In the summer there's picnicking, fishing in a trout-stocked lake, and riding the chair lift. In the winter there is skiing on the slopes of the southernmost ski area in the continental U.S.

Sabino Canyon There are streams, waterfalls, hiking trails, and great spots for picnicking. No vehicles are allowed, but there is access by tram.

Kitt Peak National Observatory Here is the largest collection of ground-based optical telescopes in the world, along with exhibitions, films, and guided tours.

Southeast Arizona

This is the land of Cochise and Geronimo, of gun slingers and gold rushers, of pioneer families and the U.S. Cavalry. It's the Old West, kept alive by landscapes and attractions well worth discovering. High-desert valleys and gentle green canyons dot the countryside, with the Dragoon Mountains in the center.

Bisbee, an old copper mining town tucked away in the Mule Mountains, is one of the most interesting towns in all of the Southwest. Turn-of-the-century buildings line incredibly steep streets on mountain faces. The copper mine closed in the mid-1970s, but Bisbee certainly didn't die. Instead it began attracting artists, city folk fleeing the metropolitan life, and tourists. Today it's a delightful expedition into another era.

Tours of the Queen Mine are led by old miners, all with stories to tell. By the end, you'll feel like a miner yourself, with a hard hat, slicker, and lamp. Other sights to help you soak up the flavor of the area are Brewery Gulch (once a row of saloons and brothels, now converted into shops), the Mining and Historical Museum, and the Lavender Pit Mine (named for a mine manager, not its color).

West of Bisbee is Douglas, a town with historic buildings, including the early 1900s Gadsden Hotel. Be sure to step inside and see its stained glass murals and marble staircase. Douglas got its start as the site of annual roundups for area ranches. The Mexican village of Agua Prieta is just across the bridge.

Throughout the countryside are places to explore: Chiricahua National Monument, with natural rock sculptures and the remnants of early ranches (hiking trails); Old Fort Bowie, established to protect travelers going through Apache Pass; Cochise Stronghold, a granite fortress where Cochise sought refuge from the U.S. Cavalry; Tombstone, with Boot Hill Cemetery and the OK Corral; and the ghost towns of **Pearce,** Gleeson, and Courtland.

Glossary

Adobe: sun-dried brick made of mud and straw

Adobe-style building: structure in which the walls are built of adobe bricks and covered with mud plaster; roof built by suspending large beams (vigas) from walls, with latillas arranged on top, covered by straw and then soil

Banco: a curved seating area built into the walls of adobe buildings

Carne adovada: pork cooked in red-hot chili

Casita: Spanish for "small house"; used as the equivalent of villa

Fonda: inn or restaurant

Farolitos: votive candles placed in paper bags weighted with sand; used to decorate buildings in New Mexico and Arizona during the holiday season

Hacienda: an estate, especially one used for ranching; the main house on the estate

Huevos Rancheros: fried eggs covered with spicy red sauce, served on tortillas

Kiva: a large ceremonial chamber, wholly or partially underground, used by the Pueblos

Kiva fireplace: molded fireplace, usually in a corner; also called "adobe fireplace" or "beehive fireplace." (The term is commonly used but considered a misnomer.)

Latilla: small wooden poles laid side by side over the main support beams (vigas) to form a ceiling

Luminarias: small bonfires, usually lit at Christmastime for chilled carolers to gather around and warm themselves

Metate: stone with bowl-shaped depression, used for grinding corn

Nicho: and arched recess in an adobe wall for displaying figurines, china, religious icons, plants, or other knickknacks

Posada: lodge or inn

Pueblo: multiple dwelling, typically built of adobe; an Indian village; also, a member of a group of Indian peoples living in pueblo villages. (First called pueblos by Spanish explorers, these dwellings as built by native Americans are many-roomed structures of two to seven stories, arranged so that the roof of one building is the front yard of the one above. Modern pueblo architecture mirrors this historic style.)

Relleno: a green chili pepper stuffed with cheese, dipped in batter, then fried

Retablo: a religious image painted on a wooden panel

Rincón: Spanish for "corner" or "nook"

Saguaro: giant cactus that grows in the Sonoran Desert in southern Arizona and the state of Sonora, Mexico; tall green columns with as many as fifty branches, attaining heights of up to 60 feet

Santos: Spanish for "saints"; refers to carved wooden religious figures

Sopaipilla: puffy fried bread, thought to have originated in what is now New Mexico

Territorial-style: style of adobe construction: typically a one-story flat-roofed adobe, symmetrical in design with a central hall, modified Greek Revival trimwork, often painted white; in New Mexico, dating from the mid-19th century

Viga: large exposed logs that form the support for a ceiling

Recommended Guidebooks

These books are excellent sources of information for sightseeing and restaurant suggestions. This chapter was excerpted from Going Places: The Guide to Travel Guides, *by Greg Hayes and Joan Wright, Harvard Common Press, 1988.*

The Southwest

Ancient Cities of the Southwest: A Practical Guide to the Major Prehistoric Ruins of Arizona, New Mexico, Utah, and Colorado. *Buddy Mays, Chronicle Books, 1990, 132 pages, paper, $9.95.*

This beautifully done book offers thoughtful descriptions of each ruin in the local and national monuments, tribal parks, primitive areas, and the national parks of four western states. Included are notes on location, access, and, where applicable, a rather dated summary of the hours, facilities, and interpretive services available. An excellent overview.

Bicycle Touring in the Western United States. *Karen and Gary Hawkins, Pantheon, 1982, 366 pages, paper, $11.95.*

This enjoyable book contains more than a hundred pages on equipment, preparation, planning, the hazards of the road, and camping out. The Hawkinses introduce you to the ABCs of touring, then plot some great tours through the western states, including Arizona and New Mexico in the Southwest. Each tour is fully described, down to the nearest grocery store. It would be nice to see an update, but most of the information is still valid.

Fielding's Spanish Trails in the Southwest. *Lynn and Lawrence Foster, William Morrow, 1986, 352 pages, paper, $12.95.*

One of three guides from Fielding that structure themselves around three famous trails of the western United States. This book should prove of considerable interest to history buffs, as it is laced with descriptions and quotations from those who helped to create these famous trails. Along with the historical pieces is a good deal of information on what to see, where to go, walking tours, hotels, restaurants, and the like.

Great Hot Springs of the West. Bill Kaysing, Capra Press, 1990, 208 pages, paper, $14.95.

This comprehensive guide to hot springs in Arizona, California, Colorado, Idaho, Montana, Nevada, New Mexico, Oregon, Utah, Washington, and Wyoming offers locations, descriptions, whether you need a bathing suit, price and phone numbers when possible, and an appendix with good detail maps. Two hundred hot springs are described; nearly 1,700 appear on the maps. The rest are all free-flowing and yours for the finding!

The Great Towns of the West. David Vokac, West Press, 1985, 464 pages, paper, $14.95.

This is a guide to out-of-the-way vacation spots, each one a "great town" in its area. Vokac defines a great town as "an independent, unspoiled community rich in human-scale charms and scenic splendor." For each town that meets his criteria he provides a good overview, including detailed notes on history, weather, etc., as well as some possibilities for lodging of every sort, restaurants, camping, shopping, nightlife, sightseeing, special events, and just general enjoyment. A great idea book, it includes towns in Arizona and New Mexico.

Hiking the Southwest: Arizona, New Mexico and West Texas. Dave Ganci, Sierra Club Books, 1983, 384 pages, paper, $12.95.

One of a series of pocket-size guides for the hiker and the walker, it describes many trails of every length and contains a good, well-organized planning and preparation section. Each hike is carefully detailed, with references to topographical maps and summaries of important points. Good notes on natural history topics are also included. Note that there may be the occasional trail that has been altered since the guide was written, since it is not updated with any frequency.

Hot Springs and Hot Pools of the Southwest. Jayson Loam and Gary Sohler, Wilderness Press, 1991 (2nd ed.), 160 pages, paper, $14.95.

A good resource to available hot tubs and spas in motels and inns as well as good descriptions of improved and unimproved hot pools throughout Arizona, California, Nevada, and New Mexico. Good maps and interesting photos supplement this quality guide.

Indian Villages of the Southwest: A Practical Guide to the Pueblo Indian Villages of New Mexico and Arizona. *Buddy Mays, Chronicle Books, 1990, 105 pages, paper, $9.95.*

A well-prepared guide to 18 picturesque small Indian pueblos, all but one of which is in New Mexico. A bit of history and thought-provoking discussion is combined with practical information on access, when non-Indians can visit, any admission fees or permission needed to enter, what types of photography are allowed, any interpretive services available, special ceremonies, and an overview of arts and crafts produced by the pueblo. An excellent resource.

Journey to the High Southwest: A Traveler's Guide. *Robert Casey, Globe Pequot Press, 1988 (3rd ed.), 476 pages, paper, $18.95.*

This classic guide to the Four Corners region and the Santa Fe area has gotten even better. Let Casey take you on an exciting tour of the natural wonders, archaeological ruins, Indian reservations, parks, and historic sites of this magnificent region. This edition includes tour information to the Flagstaff, Arizona, and Albuquerque, New Mexico, areas, the new Anasazi Heritage Center near Dolores, Colorado, and an expanded shopping guide for southwestern Indian arts and crafts. Guides simply don't get much better than this.

Landmarks of the West: A Guide to Historic Sites. *Kent Ruth, University of Nebraska Press, 1986, 309 pages, paper, $19.95.*

Popular since it first appeared in 1963, this guide is now updated. Beautifully designed and well written, with a fascinating collection of new and old photographs and drawings, it is a thoroughly classy, completely intriguing guide to dozens of historic sites throughout the West—all the states west of the Mississippi. For history buffs, this is must reading.

Senior Guide: Day-Hiking in the Southwestern National Parks and Monuments. *James Campbell, WestPark Books, 1986, 220 pages, paper, $11.95.*

If you are a novice or fairly inexperienced hiker, senior citizen or not, Campbell has a lot of experience to share with you. Nearly half of the book discusses planning, equipment, and clothing needs, hiking hardware that is worth the weight, safe hiking strategies, and more. Campbell, an ecologist and former park ranger, shares his selection of the best day-hike trails throughout the national parks and monuments of the Southwest. He grades each hike, gives you the elevations you will experience, the distances, the best seasons to go, plants and animals to look for, and other special considerations (such as the availability of water!). A superb little book. Campbell is also working on volumes on the Pacific Northwest, Rocky Mountains, and the Intermountain West. He fills a real need—and does it magnificently!

The Sierra Club Guide to the Natural Areas of New Mexico, Arizona, and Nevada. *John and Jane Perry, Sierra Club Books, 1986, 448 pages, paper, $10.95.*

The Natural Areas guides, of which this is a part, include the national parks of the region but go far beyond to address the lesser-known public domain lands (Bureau of Land Management and U.S. forests), wildlife refuges, and other wilderness areas. For each area there is a wealth of detail on its location, physical attributes, the wildlife of the area, the flora, recreational opportunities, and the resources and facilities available. This well-organized, thorough guide presents a multitude of outdoor vacation possibilities, whether you have only a few days or a week to spend. The nationally accepted signs for camping, hiking, hunting, fishing, boating, walking, horseback riding, etc., are used to give you quick visual clues to the appropriateness of a given area to your needs. A wonderful guide for those who love the outdoors.

Traveling Texas Borders: A Guide to the Best of Both Sides. *Ann Ruff, Gulf Publishing, 1983, 120 pages, $9.95.*

Interesting things to do along the Texas-Oklahoma and Texas–New Mexico borders.

Twenty-two Days in the American Southwest: The Itinerary Planner. *Richard Harris, John Muir Publications, 1990, 176 pages, paper, $9.95.*

Part of a series in which the intent is to let you lead your own tour (it's assumed that you have your own vehicle) by giving you clear, well-planned itineraries for classic three-week vacations. There are also side trips that can expand your trip even further. Or you can jump into the plan at any point if you are rushed. While occasional days offer no more than "R and R," these trips are designed for energetic souls. There is a budget orientation to the guide, with good picks for lodging and restaurants.

The whole idea is for you to let the experts lead the way, but not pay someone to actually be there. It's a great idea for those who want some help in planning a vacation.

Arizona

Arizona Hideaways. *Thelma Heatwole, Golden West Publishers, 1986, 128 pages, paper, $4.50.*

Choose your destination from this good collection of romantic small Arizona towns in which to spend a tranquil day or two.

Arizona off the Beaten Path! *Thelma Heatwole, Golden West Publishers, 1982, 144 pages, paper, $5.00.*

A veteran reporter for the Arizona Republic takes you to her favorite out-of-the-way corners. The descriptions of her adventures will tweak your interest, and simple maps will pin down the location (though you will probably want some additional maps).

Arizona Trails: 100 Hikes in Canyon and Sierra. *David Mazel, Wilderness Press, 1989 (3rd ed.), 320 pages, paper, $14.95.*

This is one of the many hiking guides from Wilderness Press. It is well done, thorough, and easy to use. The trail descriptions are particularly excellent, and all the specifics of distances, directions, elevation change, etc., are noted. Includes a full-size, separate topographical map. The "topogs" produced by Wilderness Press are particularly good because the routes described in the book are more clearly plotted than the average USGS map, usually in a bright color. An excellent book we heartily recommend.

Arizona Traveler's Handbook. *Bill Weir, Moon Publications, 1990 (3rd ed.), 505 pages, paper, $13.95.*

This is a very popular title in one of those rare series whose excellence never varies. The orientation is on the young (or young at heart) and adventurous (and usually without a car), but every traveler can glean tremendous value from this superb handbook. Each guide offers an incredible amount of background on the people, arts and crafts, events, and natural history of the area. If you read and study this section before you go, you will be a very well educated traveler. Sightseeing notes are offered in copious detail, and there are always good maps of important areas. Food and lodging recommendations are not neglected, with numerous choices, usually well described, that generally range from budget to moderate. Updated every two years.

Explore Arizona! *Rick Harris, Golden West Publishers, 1986, 128 pages, paper, $5.*

A good collection of ideas for the explorer—ghost towns, old forts, cliff dwellings, caves, hot springs, ruins, pottery, and lots more. Each idea is accompanied by a useful location map and special notes (which will often remind you to look at, enjoy, and leave the artifacts alone for the next person to see as well).

The Hiker's Guide to Arizona. *Stewart Aitchison and Bruce Grubbs, Falcon Press, 1991, 336 pages, paper, $9.95.*

One of the Falcon Press series, an excellent collection of hiking guides with a wide array of hikes of varied length. Reproductions of topographical maps are used, and each hike is well discussed, rated, its special attractions summarized, and other USGS maps recommended.

Hiking the Grand Canyon. *John Annerino, Sierra Club Books, 1986, 320 pages, paper, $12.95.*

One of the small-format Sierra Club Hiking Totebook series. See the write-up under Hiking the Southwest, above.

On Foot in the Grand Canyon: Hiking the Trails of the South Rim. *Sharon Spangler, Pruett Publishing, 1989 (2nd ed.), 194 pages, paper, $11.95.*

This is an interpretive guide, a hiker sharing her adventures with you. But there are enough practical facts here to help you plan your own hike as well, including appendixes that will give you the word on water available, topographical maps you will need, basic geology, and some day-hike suggestions. Enjoyable and stimulating reading!

One Hundred Best Restaurants in Arizona. *John and Joan Bogert, A.D.M. Inc., 1991 (14th ed.), 208 pages, paper, $4.95.*

Actually, 172 places are now described in this popular guide. The emphasis is on inexpensive yet excellent dining, and the prices range from downright cheap to moderate. This guide is written the way we like it: anonymous dining done several times over (at least) without any perks. Chances are the authors experienced the same kind of evening you will. Couple this with a bright, informative text, and you have a first-class book.

Wonderful—and all the practical data is here too, including access for the disabled. Updated annually.

Outdoors in Arizona: A Guide to Camping. *Bob Hirsch, Arizona Highways, 1986, 128 pages, paper, $12.95.*
Here are plenty of camping ideas replete with beautiful color photos, location maps, and charts of important facts. A useful compendium.

Outdoors in Arizona: A Guide to Hiking and Backpacking. *John Annerino, Arizona Highways, 1987, 136 pages, paper, $12.95.*
Forty-eight suggested hikes, many with topographical map reproductions, from the author of the Sierra Club's Hiking the Grand Canyon. Good ideas—and beautiful photos to help you decide where to go.

Roadside Geology of Arizona. *Halka Chronic, Mountain Press, 1983, 320 pages, paper, $12.95.*
A fascinating book on geology "for the rest of us," and right along the highway too! Part of the excellent Roadside Geology Guide series (see Roadside Geology of New Mexico under New Mexico, below).

Shifra Stein's Day Trips from Phoenix, Tucson, and Flagstaff: Getaways Less Than 2 Hours Away. *Pam Hait, Globe Pequot, 1990 (2nd ed.), 192 pages, paper, $9.95.*
This book suggests a great variety of possible trips into the regions immediately next to Phoenix, Tucson, and Flagstaff. The suggested journeys include a clear map, numerous things to do, places to eat, and good ideas for just wandering about, enjoying the sights and sounds of the area.

Ski Touring Arizona: Plateaus of Snow. *Dufald Bremner, Northland Press, 1987, 194 pages, paper, $11.95.*
Snow in Arizona? You bet! And some excellent skiing too. Offered here are over 40 ski tours for beginners and experts. Each is rated, distances noted, a good map provided, directions to the starting point given, other maps you may want to have cited, and each trip discussed clearly. There are also notes on necessary equipment, winter hazard warnings, even suggestions for that most pleasurable of skiing ideas—moonlight touring. A very well prepared guidebook.

This Is Tucson: Guidebook to the Old Pueblo. *Peggy Lockard, Pepper Publishing, 1988 (3rd ed.), 320 pages, paper, $9.95.*

The award for the best guidebook in the state goes to this fine piece. Well written, full of useful information and exceptionally good maps, it covers history, cultural activities, walking and driving tours of the historic districts, sightseeing, hiking, picnicking, seasonal events, tours of the surrounding areas, shopping, restaurants, and more. Every city should have such a superb guide available.

Travel Arizona: Full Color Tours of the Grand Canyon State. *Joseph Stocker, Arizona Highways, 1990, 128 pages, paper, $9.95.*

Sixteen interesting one- to three-day tours are offered for those touring by car. The text is informative, and the beautiful color pictures in this large-format book are typical of those that made Arizona Highways magazine famous. There is also a small section of suggested day hikes.

New Mexico

Children's Guide to Santa Fe. *Anne Hillerman, Sunstone Press, 1984, 48 pages, paper, $4.95.*

Lots of good ideas for things to do with the kids. In spite of the publication date, most of this information should still be reasonably current, but do check where appropriate.

Escortguide: The People's Connection to New Mexico. *Joan Adams, Escortguide, 1986 (3rd ed.), 256 pages, paper, $7.95.*

Here is a different sort of book: a directory of all sorts of services, professional guides, bicycling and horseback excursions, unusual sightseeing ideas, lesser-known inns, ranches, and haciendas, and a whole lot more. Some of this information is designed more for New Mexico residents, but a great deal will be useful to the traveler. An excellent resource.

Hikers and Climbers Guide to the Sandias. *Mike Hill, University of New Mexico Press, 1983 (2nd ed.), 246 pages, paper, $10.95.*

A first-class guide to the beautiful Sandias, east of Albuquerque. There are good sections on weather, plant life, geology, and important notes on hiking and climbing in these rugged mountains. The many trails described vary from very short, easy walk/hikes to strenuous back-breakers. A separate, fold-out topographical map is included.

How to See La Villa Real de Santa Fe: Walking Tour of Historic S.F. *Lou Ann Jordan, Sunstone Press, 1986, 32 pages, paper, $4.95.*

An interesting, large-format walking tour booklet done entirely by hand, with illustrations and text about the historic sites.

Insider's Guide to Santa Fe. *Bill Jamison, Harvard Common Press, 1991 (rev. ed.), 150 pages, paper, $8.95.*

This superb, well-researched book covers every need of the traveler to this spectacular city in three parts. Part One describes Santa Fe's heritage—the pueblos, the early Spanish settlers, the coming of the American armies in the early 19th century, and the art colony that has since evolved. Part Two explores the living museum that is Santa Fe—the Plaza, the museums, the fiestas, the mountain trails, and more. Part Three is a great rundown of the best places to stay, eat, and shop. Definitely the best guide to Santa Fe we know.

New Mexico: A New Guide to the Colorful State. *Lance Chilton et al., University of New Mexico Press, 1985, 647 pages, paper, $22.50.*

Six excellent authors have created this massive, large-format book as a tribute to the famous 1940 WPA publication of the same name. Here are finely crafted essays on everything from history and politics to arts and literature. The bulk of the book is eighteen well-conceived driving tours to every corner of the state. The maps are clear, and the amount of interesting and useful information is truly remarkable. There is also a helpful section of special events in a month-by-month format. One of the great sightseeing guides, destined to be a classic.

New Mexico's Best Ghost Towns: A Practical Guide. *Phillip Varney, University of New Mexico Press, 1987, 204 pages, paper, $14.95.*

An excellent large-format guide to the many ghost towns of New Mexico. Varney has put together a great selection of photographs and a fine narrative that is sure to tweak your interest. Included are good directions, some location maps, topographical maps for each area, and comments on how important such maps are to your safe exploration of these ghosts of history.

Roadside Geology of New Mexico. *Halka Chronic, Mountain Press, 1987, 255 pages, paper, $9.95.*

This book in the great Roadside Geology series is specifically directed at what you will see from your car window—or what you can see if you pull over at the right time and take a look. It is written for the average person—no need to know all those multisyllabic words. Organized by highway, the book is totally fascinating, and we recommend it highly.

The Santa Fe Guide. *Waite Thompson and Richard Gottlieb, Sunstone Press, 1991 (6th ed.), 64 pages, paper, $6.95.*

If you put a premium on size, this tiny guidebook will give you a solid overview of history, culture, things to see and do, weather information, and transportation. There is also a list of suggested restaurants, though it notes only the type of food without further comment.

Santa Fe on Foot: Walking, Running and Bicycling Routes in the City Different. *Elaine Pinkerton, Ocean Tree Books, 1989 (rev. ed.), 120 pages, paper, $7.95.*

A wonderful book on interesting routes to walk, run, or bicycle. The fine text will not only provide you with route information and plenty of background historical material but a pleasurable reading experience as well.

Santa Fe Then and Now. *Sheila Morand, Sunstone Press, 1984, 96 pages, paper, $14.95.*

This interesting book shows you how the sights you are seeing now looked 100 years ago. Morand has placed old and new photos side by side and found each place on a street map to let you take a firsthand look.

Six One-Day Walks in the Pecos Wilderness. *Carl Overhage, Sunstone Press, 1984 (rev. ed.), 60 pages, paper, $4.95.*

This booklet carefully describes six strenuous hikes from 11 to 21 miles for the experienced hiker. Each has a fold-out map and elevation chart. Appropriate topographical maps are recommended, and instructions on how to reach each area are included. Some great ideas, if you are ready to really step on out.

Summer People, Winter People: A Guide to Pueblos in the Santa Fe Area. *Sandra Edelman, Sunstone Press, 1986 (rev. ed.), 32 pages, paper, $4.95.*

A helpful brochure with overviews of the various pueblos near Santa Fe. Included are the dates of special fiestas, dances, and ceremonies.

Tours for All Seasons: 50 Car Tours of New Mexico. *Howard Bryan, Heritage Associates, 1986, 128 pages, paper, $4.95.*

A veteran reporter who writes a weekly column on New Mexico lore for the Albuquerque Tribune, Bryan shares his best automobile tours with you. The dozens of possibilities are grouped by the season in which they most appropriate, and there's a section of trips to do anytime. Simple orientation road maps are included, though you will certainly want to have better ones at hand. There are many good ideas to consider in this compact book.

Oklahoma

Guide to Oklahoma Museums. *David Hunt, University of Oklahoma Press, 1981, 256 pages, paper, $10.95.*

A comprehensive guide to the museums of Oklahoma as well as important historic sites and zoological parks. In all, nearly 150 places are described, including some of the most unusual museums—oil and doll museums and three national halls of fame: softball, wrestling, and cowboy. A fine but aging directory. Be sure to confirm any dated material.

Texas

The Alamo and Other Texas Missions to Remember. *Nancy Foster, Gulf Publishing, 1984, 96 pages, paper, $9.95.*

This large-format book will let you in on a good deal of the history, architecture, and the tours available at various missions in the state. You will also learn about the special events that are held each year. In addition, there are clear locator maps and nicely chosen photographs. A helpful guide to Texas's fascinating history.

Amazing Texas Monuments and Museums: From the Enchanting to the Bizarre. *Ann Ruff, Gulf Publishing, 1984, 104 pages, paper, $9.95.*

Where else can you find a guide to monuments erected to the strawberry, pecan, roadrunner, mosquito, and jackrabbit? Where else can you find museums featuring 10,000 birds' eggs or Lee Harvey Oswald's can opener? This is the one, with lots of tombstones too. A lot of sightseeing fun.

Backroads of Texas. *Ed Syers, Gulf Publishing, 1988 (2nd ed.), 176 pages, paper, $12.95.*

You will find Syers's 62 tours of the backcountry well planned, well written, and just plain fun. It's time to explore the ghost towns, boom towns, farm towns, cow towns, and all those places of interest in between. Comprehensive, compact, and definitely first class.

Beachcomber's Guide to Gulf Coast Marine Life. *Nick Fotheringham and S. L. Brunemeister, Gulf Publishing, 1989, 144 pages, paper, $12.95.*

Let this popular naturalist's guide increase your enjoyment of the fascinating Gulf Coast. Instead of puzzling over the shell you just picked up, you will be able to learn something about it, perhaps even identify it precisely.

The Best of Texas Festivals: Your Guide to Rootin' Tootin' Downhome Texas Good Times! *Ann Ruff, Gulf Publishing, 1986, 100 pages, paper, $9.95.*

Here is just the ticket—a single resource in a monthly format, giving you all the inside scoop on sixty Texas festivals: a citrus fiesta, a peach jamboree, the fiddlers' festival, and the hushpuppy Olympics. Here is all you need to know plus addresses and phone numbers if you want to know more.

Eyes of Texas Travel Guide: Dallas/East Texas. *Ray Miller, Cordovan Press, 1988 (2nd ed.), 224 pages, paper, $10.95.*
Eyes of Texas Travel Guide: Fort Worth/Brazos Valley. *Ray Miller, Cordovan Press, 1991, 224 pages, paper, $10.95.*
Eyes of Texas Travel Guide: Hill Country/Permian Basin. *Ray Miller, Cordovan Press, 1980, 214 pages, paper, $13.95.*
Eyes of Texas Travel Guide: Panhandle/Plains. Ray Miller, Cordovan Press, 1982, 204 pages, paper, $13.95.

This well-known series combines Miller's penchant for history with the facts and figures of modern Texas. Packed with photographs, these regional guides make excellent supplements to more standard travel guides.

Flashmaps: Instant Guide to Dallas/Fort Worth. *Fodor's Travel Guides, 1987, 72 pages, paper, $4.95.*

A small, practical guide that slips easily into a purse or pocket, it offers information on hotels, restaurants, theaters, transportation, libraries—whatever—via "flashmaps," single-subject maps that locate each place precisely. The style is functional, with no thought of being comprehensive, but within its limited format, this guide is quite useful. And it's updated annually.

Fort Worth and Tarrant County: A Historical Guide. *Ruby Schmidt, Texas Christian University Press, 1984, 102 pages, paper, $5.95.*

A very well done assemblage of the history behind a vast array of buildings, homes, churches, cemeteries, schools, etc., in the Fort Worth area. Arranged alphabetically, those in Fort Worth proper are accompanied by several hand-drawn maps. Nonetheless, you will want another map of the surrounding area to help you find other important sites. Most sites have a historical marker to help you locate them; however, the notes in this book go well beyond those on the marker itself. An index allows you to see all the references to one type of historical site.

Frontier Forts of Texas. *Charles Robinson, Gulf Publishing, 1986, 86 pages, paper, $9.95.*

This large-format guide delivers the practical facts you will need along with fascinating accounts of those adventurous events of yesteryear. The stories cover the more than two dozen forts that have survived as well as those that were destroyed. Includes information on visitor facilities and local events at each of the forts.

Great Hometown Restaurants of Texas. *Mary Beverly, Gulf Publishing, 1984, 150 pages, paper, $9.95.*

This large-format guide is a lot of fun, with great write-ups on all sorts of intriguing spots where home style cooking is the rule. It includes all the practical data, too, so you won't get lost along the way, but be aware of its age.

A Guide to Bicycling in Texas: Tours, Tips, and More. *George Sevra, Gulf Publishing, 1985, 96 pages, paper, $9.95.*

A great collection of tours—one-day, intercity, as well as longer routes panning the entire state—that will prove to you, once and for all, that Texas is not just "flat and empty." There are also helpful lists of bicycle shops, sources of maps (though some good-size detail maps are included in this large-format book), and Chambers of Commerce in towns you will pass through and where you may want to stop and explore a little more.

A Guide to Historic Texas Inns and Hotels. Ann Ruff, Gulf Publishing, 1985 (2nd ed.), 132 pages, paper, $9.95.

A popular guide from a popular writer, this large-format book offers excellent descriptions of the best of the historic lodging spots. The practical facts are listed separately in the margin for easy access, and each selection is accompanied by a line drawing or photograph. Very well done.

A Guide to Texas Rivers and Streams. Gene Kirkley, Gulf Publishing, 1983, 120 pages, paper, $12.95.

A large-format guide to whitewater canoeing and kayaking, float trips, fishing, and just plain fun along Texas's many waterways.

Hiking and Backpacking Trails of Texas. Mickey Little, Gulf Publishing, 1989 (3rd ed.), 176 pages, paper, $14.95.

Here is another fine book that proves Texas to be something more than flat and empty. There is some beautiful country out there, and Little has done a quality job in pointing the way. The state is divided into four regions in this large-format book. In each region trails are clearly located, adequate trail notes and distances included, and maps, sometimes topographical ones, are provided as well. Among your choices are a number of short day hikes.

Historic Homes of Texas: Across the Thresholds of Yesterday. Ann Ruff and Henri Farmer, Gulf Publishing, 1987, 130 pages, paper, $18.95.

Take a look at the homes built by the cattle and oil barons and the genteel women who came west in times gone by. Each is recognized by the Texas Historical Commission, many are on the National Register of Historic Places, and all are open to the public. Included is all the information you will need to find and enjoy each site. Also included are details for tours of other homes not normally open to the public.

A Marmac Guide to Houston and Galveston. Dale Young, Pelican Publishing, 1988, 270 pages, paper, $8.95.

One of the Marmac Guides, a series that offers very solid,

well-organized views of major cities. You will learn the ropes of
each city and some of its history and tradition. There are many
hotels and restaurants; each is presented by geographic area,
then alphabetically (hotels) or by type of cuisine. The prices run
the gamut, but moderate is the most common. The restaurant
section is particularly well done. Additional sections cover
shopping, sightseeing, museums, sports, nightlife, theater, excursions, walking tours, and transportation. The format will
serve you well. Updated every two years.

Places to Go with Children in Dallas and Fort Worth. *Joan
Jackson and Glenna Whitley, Chronicle Books, 1987, 144 pages,
paper, $7.95.*

Ideas, ideas, ideas. More than 350 possibilities in every category you can think of: art, culture, sports, science, nature,
parks, history—on and on. There are ideas here for every age
group, including the grownups. Each resource is briefly described and all the particulars presented. Amusements parks,
science stores, a culture center, and special restaurants where
kids are most welcome. You'll never run out of good ideas with
this great resource.

Ray Miller's Texas Forts: A History and Guide. *Ray Miller,
Gulf Publishing, 1985, 240 pages, paper, $13.95.*

Miller presents a lively history of the many forts, including
the Alamo, that sprung up during the 19th century and were
important during the Mexican War, the Indian wars, and the
Civil War. Includes many interesting photographs.

Ray Miller's Texas Parks: A History and Guide. *Ray Miller,
Gulf Publishing, 1984, 248 pages, paper, $13.95.*

You will find good practical information on the numerous
parks in the state system, but you'll also get a large measure of
the history behind what you see. Some specifics about each
park may be dated—call ahead to see—but this is an excellent
resource nonetheless.

Shifra Stein's Day Trips from Houston. *Carol Barrington,
Globe Pequot Press, 1991 (4rth ed.), 176 pages, paper, $9.95.*

Part of the well-done Shifra Stein's Day Trip Guide series. See
Shifra Stein's Day Trips from Phoenix, Tucson, and Flagstaff
under Arizona, above.

Six Central Texas Auto Tours. *Myra McIllvain, Eakin Press,
1980, 220 pages, paper, $9.95.*

These driving tours, filled with historical notes and anec-
dotes, are all in Central Texas, around Austin. Some of the roads
have changed since this book was published, but most of the
copious detail should still stand you in good stead.

***Texas — Family Style: Parent's Guide to Hassle-free, Fun Travel
with the Kids.*** *Ruth Wolverton, Gulf Publishing, 1988 (2nd ed.),
104 pages, paper, $10.95.*

This large-format guide has lots of good ideas for what to do
with the entire family.

***Texas Golf: The Comprehensive Guide to Golf Courses and Re-
sorts of the Lone Star State.*** *Frank Hermes, Taylor Publishing,
1987, 192 pages, paper, $7.95.*

As the title suggests, this is your best compendium of golfing
information in Texas.

Texas Restaurant Guide. *Pat Pugh, Pelican Publishing, 1987,
243 pages, paper, $4.95*

Pugh offers information and opinion on more than 450 restaurants in the big cities and cow towns alike. Both budget and
pricey selections are included, along with all the necessary
data.

Traveling Texas Borders: A Guide to the Best of Both Sides. *Ann
Ruff, Gulf Publishing, 1983, 120 pages, paper, $9.95.*

A good description of the many things to do and see along
Texas's vast border. Included are activities in Arkansas, Louisiana, Mexico, New Mexico, and Oklahoma. This large-format
guide has plenty of interesting suggestions.

Twenty-Two Days in Texas. *Richard Harris, John Muir Publications, 1990, 176 pages, $9.95.*

Part of the 22 Days series, this pocket-size guide will help you
discover the best of Texas through suggested daily itineraries,
rated sightseeing highlights, and dining and lodging recommendations. If you don't have time to take the entire three-week
trip, weekend and day trips can easily be extracted from this
well-organized book, which covers both metropolitan and
rural areas. Maps and driving directions are also included.

Why Stop? A Guide to Texas Historical Roadside Markers.
Claude and Betty Dooley, Gulf Publishing, 1985 (2nd ed.), 560
pages, paper, $14.95.

There are more than 2,600 roadside markers in Texas with
historical notes on all sorts of subjects. With this guide, you can
read the markers without stopping the car. Even if you stop, this
will prove a handy resource to keep on the back seat.

Appendixes

Budget

Children Welcome

Cooking Facilities

Gant Guest House 232
Hotel Menger 122
Inn of the Hills River Resort 158
Lajitas on the Rio Grande 210
Lakeway Inn 256
Port Royal by the Sea 12
San Luis 13
Seascape 142
Stoneleigh 97
The Ritz Carlton 112
Wise Manor 66

Dining Room Open to Public

State	Place/Page
AZ	Arizona Biltmore 195

Arizona Inn 197
Boulders 171
Bright Angel Lodge and Cabins 259
Copper Queen Hotel 236
El Tovar Hotel 260
Enchantment Resort 271
Garland's Oak Creek Lodge 162
Grand Canyon Lodge North Rim 261
Hassayampa Inn 237
Hyatt Regency Scottsdale at Gainey Ranch 172
Junipine Resort Condo Hotel 138
L'Auberge de Sedona 163
Loews Ventana Canyon Resort 174
Los Abrigados 307
Marriott's Camelback Inn 145
Pointe at Tapatio Cliffs 176
Rancho de la Osa 207
Rancho de los Caballeros 218
Red Lion's La Posada 147
Registry Resort 178
Ritz-Carlton 118
San Carlos Hotel 239
Scottsdale Princess 179
Sheraton El Conquistador Resort and Country
Club 148
Stouffer Cottonwoods Resort 282
Tubac Golf Resort 272
Tucson National Golf and Conference Resort 180

Handicapped Access

Stouffer Dallas Hotel 98
Tremont House 251
Westin Galleria and Westin Oaks 113
Westin Hotel Galleria Dallas 99
Westin Paso del Norte 102
Wise Manor 66
Worthington Hotel 106
Wyndham Austin Hotel at Southpark 83
Y.O. Ranch Hilton 225

Murder Mystery Weekends

State Place/Page
AZ   Bisbee Grand Hotel 234
     Hassayampa Inn 237
     Marriott's Camelback Inn 145
     Red Lion's La Posada 147
     Tucson National Golf and Conference Resort 180
NM   Lundeen's Inn of the Arts Bed and Breakfast
     Monjeau Shadows 44
     St. James Hotel 244
TX   Adolphus 85
     Crystal River Inn 51
     Inn on the Creek 288
     La Colombe d'Or 168
     Omni Melrose Hotel 96
     Plaza San Antonio 125
     Townsquare Inn 311
     Wise Manor 66

Pets Allowed

State Place/Page
AZ   Arizona Biltmore 195
     Bisbee Inn 144
     Boulders 171
     Lynx Creek Farm 24
     Marriott's Camelback Inn 145
     Phoenician 175
     Price Canyon Ranch 217
     Red Lion's La Posada 147
     Sheraton El Conquistador Resort and Country
     Club 148

Smoking Not Allowed

Sports/Archery

Sports/Badminton

Sports/Beach

Sports/Fishing

Sports/Golf

Sports/Hiking

Sports/Hunting

Sports/Indoor Pool

Sports/Jogging Track

Sports/Outdoor Pool

Sports/Rafting

Sports/Racquetball

Sports/Riding

Sports/Sailing

Sports/Shuffleboard

Wyndham Paradise Valley Resort 183
TX   Inn of the Hills River Resort 158
        Lake Austin Resort 303
        Wyndham Austin Hotel at Southpark 83

Sports/Skating

State   Place/Page
TX   Westin Hotel Galleria Dallas 99

Sports/Skiing

State   Place/Page
AZ   Birch Tree Inn 16
NM   Austing Haus Hotel 296
        Best Western Swiss Chalet Inn 293
        Legends Hotel 298
        Quail Ridge Inn and Tennis Ranch 274
        Salsa del Salto 294

Sports/Squash

State   Place/Page
AZ   Scottsdale Princess 179
OK   Waterford Hotel 117
TX   Four Seasons Resort and Club 184
        Loews Anatole Hotel 92

Sports/Swimming Hole

State   Place/Page
AZ   Garland's Oak Creek Lodge 162
        Junipine Resort Condo Hotel 138
OK   Lake Texoma Resort 209
        Roman Nose Resort 156
        Shangri-La Resort 253
TX   Chain-O-Lakes 70
        Del Lago Resort 254
        Indian Lodge 157
        Inn on the River 55
        Lakeway Inn 256
        Landhaus Bed and Breakfast 56

Sports/Tennis

Sports/Trapshooting and Skeet Shooting

Sports/Volleyball

Index

Best Places Report

We appreciate any information you can supply about the quality of the lodging. Detailed information about the building, furniture, service, food, and setting is most important. Describe as many rooms as you can, including living rooms, dining rooms, other common rooms, and of course bedrooms. A note about activities and nearby signts would be helpful. Tell us what category you think the place belongs in and why. Finally, how did you hear about the place, and how long have you been going there?

We will be happy to send you a free copy of the next edition of the book if we use your suggestion.

To: Chris Paddock
      Best Places to Stay in the Southwest
      The Harvard Common Press
      535 Albany Street
      Boston, Massachusetts 02118

Name of hotel _____

Telephone _____

Address _____

_____ Zip _____

_____

Description _____

_____

_____

_____

_____

_____

_____

Your Name _____

Telephone _____

Address _____

_____ Zip _____

_____

Best Places Report

We appreciate any information you can supply about the quality of the lodging. Detailed information about the building, furniture, service, food, and setting is most important. Describe as many rooms as you can, including living rooms, dining rooms, other common rooms, and of course bedrooms. A note about activities and nearby signts would be helpful. Tell us what category you think the place belongs in and why. Finally, how did you hear about the place, and how long have you been going there?

We will be happy to send you a free copy of the next edition of the book if we use your suggestion.

To: Chris Paddock
     Best Places to Stay in the Southwest
     The Harvard Common Press
     535 Albany Street
     Boston, Massachusetts 02118

Name of hotel _____

Telephone _____

Address _____

_____ Zip _____

_____

Description _____

_____

_____

_____

_____

_____

_____

Your Name _____

Telephone _____

Address _____

_____ Zip _____

_____

Best Places Report

We appreciate any information you can supply about the quality of the lodging. Detailed information about the building, furniture, service, food, and setting is most important. Describe as many rooms as you can, including living rooms, dining rooms, other common rooms, and of course bedrooms. A note about activities and nearby signts would be helpful. Tell us what category you think the place belongs in and why. Finally, how did you hear about the place, and how long have you been going there?

We will be happy to send you a free copy of the next edition of the book if we use your suggestion.

To: Chris Paddock
     Best Places to Stay in the Southwest
     The Harvard Common Press
     535 Albany Street
     Boston, Massachusetts 02118

Name of hotel _____

Telephone _____

Address _____

_____ Zip _____

_____

Description _____

_____

_____

_____

_____

_____

_____

Your Name _____

Telephone _____

Address _____

_____ Zip _____

_____

Best Places Report

We appreciate any information you can supply about the quality of the lodging. Detailed information about the building, furniture, service, food, and setting is most important. Describe as many rooms as you can, including living rooms, dining rooms, other common rooms, and of course bedrooms. A note about activities and nearby signts would be helpful. Tell us what category you think the place belongs in and why. Finally, how did you hear about the place, and how long have you been going there?

We will be happy to send you a free copy of the next edition of the book if we use your suggestion.

To: Chris Paddock
     Best Places to Stay in the Southwest
     The Harvard Common Press
     535 Albany Street
     Boston, Massachusetts 02118

Name of hotel _____

Telephone _____

Address _____

_____ Zip _____

_____

Description _____

_____

_____

_____

_____

_____

_____

Your Name _____

Telephone _____

Address _____

_____ Zip _____

_____

Best Places Report

We appreciate any information you can supply about the quality of the lodging. Detailed information about the building, furniture, service, food, and setting is most important. Describe as many rooms as you can, including living rooms, dining rooms, other common rooms, and of course bedrooms. A note about activities and nearby signts would be helpful. Tell us what category you think the place belongs in and why. Finally, how did you hear about the place, and how long have you been going there?

We will be happy to send you a free copy of the next edition of the book if we use your suggestion.

To: Chris Paddock
     Best Places to Stay in the Southwest
     The Harvard Common Press
     535 Albany Street
     Boston, Massachusetts 02118

Name of hotel ——————————————————————————

Telephone ————————————————————————————

Address ——————————————————————————————

——————————————— Zip ————————————————

——————————————————————————————————————

Description ——————————————————————————

——————————————————————————————————————

——————————————————————————————————————

——————————————————————————————————————

——————————————————————————————————————

——————————————————————————————————————

——————————————————————————————————————

Your Name ——————————————————————————————

Telephone ————————————————————————————

Address ——————————————————————————————

——————————————— Zip ————————————————

——————————————————————————————————————

Best Places Report

We appreciate any information you can supply about the quality of the lodging. Detailed information about the building, furniture, service, food, and setting is most important. Describe as many rooms as you can, including living rooms, dining rooms, other common rooms, and of course bedrooms. A note about activities and nearby sights would be helpful. Tell us what category you think the place belongs in and why. Finally, how did you hear about the place, and how long have you been going there?

We will be happy to send you a free copy of the next edition of the book if we use your suggestion.

To: Chris Paddock
Best Places to Stay in the Southwest
The Harvard Common Press
535 Albany Street
Boston, Massachusetts 02118

Name of hotel _____

Telephone _____

Address _____

_____ Zip _____

_____

Description _____

_____

_____

_____

_____

_____

_____

Your Name _____

Telephone _____

Address _____

_____ Zip _____

_____

Best Places Report

We appreciate any information you can supply about the quality of the lodging. Detailed information about the building, furniture, service, food, and setting is most important. Describe as many rooms as you can, including living rooms, dining rooms, other common rooms, and of course bedrooms. A note about activities and nearby signts would be helpful. Tell us what category you think the place belongs in and why. Finally, how did you hear about the place, and how long have you been going there?

We will be happy to send you a free copy of the next edition of the book if we use your suggestion.

To: Chris Paddock
     Best Places to Stay in the Southwest
     The Harvard Common Press
     535 Albany Street
     Boston, Massachusetts 02118

Name of hotel _____

Telephone _____

Address _____

_____ Zip _____

_____

Description _____

_____

_____

_____

_____

_____

_____

Your Name _____

Telephone _____

Address _____

_____ Zip _____

_____

Best Places Report

We appreciate any information you can supply about the quality of the lodging. Detailed information about the building, furniture, service, food, and setting is most important. Describe as many rooms as you can, including living rooms, dining rooms, other common rooms, and of course bedrooms. A note about activities and nearby signts would be helpful. Tell us what category you think the place belongs in and why. Finally, how did you hear about the place, and how long have you been going there?

We will be happy to send you a free copy of the next edition of the book if we use your suggestion.

To: Chris Paddock
     Best Places to Stay in the Southwest
     The Harvard Common Press
     535 Albany Street
     Boston, Massachusetts 02118

Name of hotel _____

Telephone _____

Address _____

_____ Zip _____

_____

Description _____

_____

_____

_____

_____

_____

_____

Your Name _____

Telephone _____

Address _____

_____ Zip _____

_____

Best Places Report

We appreciate any information you can supply about the quality of the lodging. Detailed information about the building, furniture, service, food, and setting is most important. Describe as many rooms as you can, including living rooms, dining rooms, other common rooms, and of course bedrooms. A note about activities and nearby signts would be helpful. Tell us what category you think the place belongs in and why. Finally, how did you hear about the place, and how long have you been going there?

We will be happy to send you a free copy of the next edition of the book if we use your suggestion.

To: Chris Paddock
     Best Places to Stay in the Southwest
     The Harvard Common Press
     535 Albany Street
     Boston, Massachusetts 02118

Name of hotel _____

Telephone _____

Address _____

_____ Zip _____

_____

Description _____

_____

_____

_____

_____

_____

_____

Your Name _____

Telephone _____

Address _____

_____ Zip _____

_____

Best Places Report

We appreciate any information you can supply about the quality of the lodging. Detailed information about the building, furniture, service, food, and setting is most important. Describe as many rooms as you can, including living rooms, dining rooms, other common rooms, and of course bedrooms. A note about activities and nearby signts would be helpful. Tell us what category you think the place belongs in and why. Finally, how did you hear about the place, and how long have you been going there?

We will be happy to send you a free copy of the next edition of the book if we use your suggestion.

To: Chris Paddock
Best Places to Stay in the Southwest
The Harvard Common Press
535 Albany Street
Boston, Massachusetts 02118

Name of hotel _____

Telephone _____

Address _____

_____ Zip _____

_____

Description _____

_____

_____

_____

_____

_____

_____

Your Name _____

Telephone _____

Address _____

_____ Zip _____

_____

Best Places Report

We appreciate any information you can supply about the quality of the lodging. Detailed information about the building, furniture, service, food, and setting is most important. Describe as many rooms as you can, including living rooms, dining rooms, other common rooms, and of course bedrooms. A note about activities and nearby signts would be helpful. Tell us what category you think the place belongs in and why. Finally, how did you hear about the place, and how long have you been going there?

We will be happy to send you a free copy of the next edition of the book if we use your suggestion.

To: Chris Paddock
      Best Places to Stay in the Southwest
      The Harvard Common Press
      535 Albany Street
      Boston, Massachusetts 02118

Name of hotel ————————————————————

Telephone ——————————————————————

Address ————————————————————————

———————————————— Zip ————————————

————————————————————————————————

Description ————————————————————————

————————————————————————————————

————————————————————————————————

————————————————————————————————

————————————————————————————————

————————————————————————————————

————————————————————————————————

Your Name ——————————————————————

Telephone ——————————————————————

Address ————————————————————————

———————————————— Zip ————————————

————————————————————————————————